World Youth Day 2002

The Official Souvenir Album

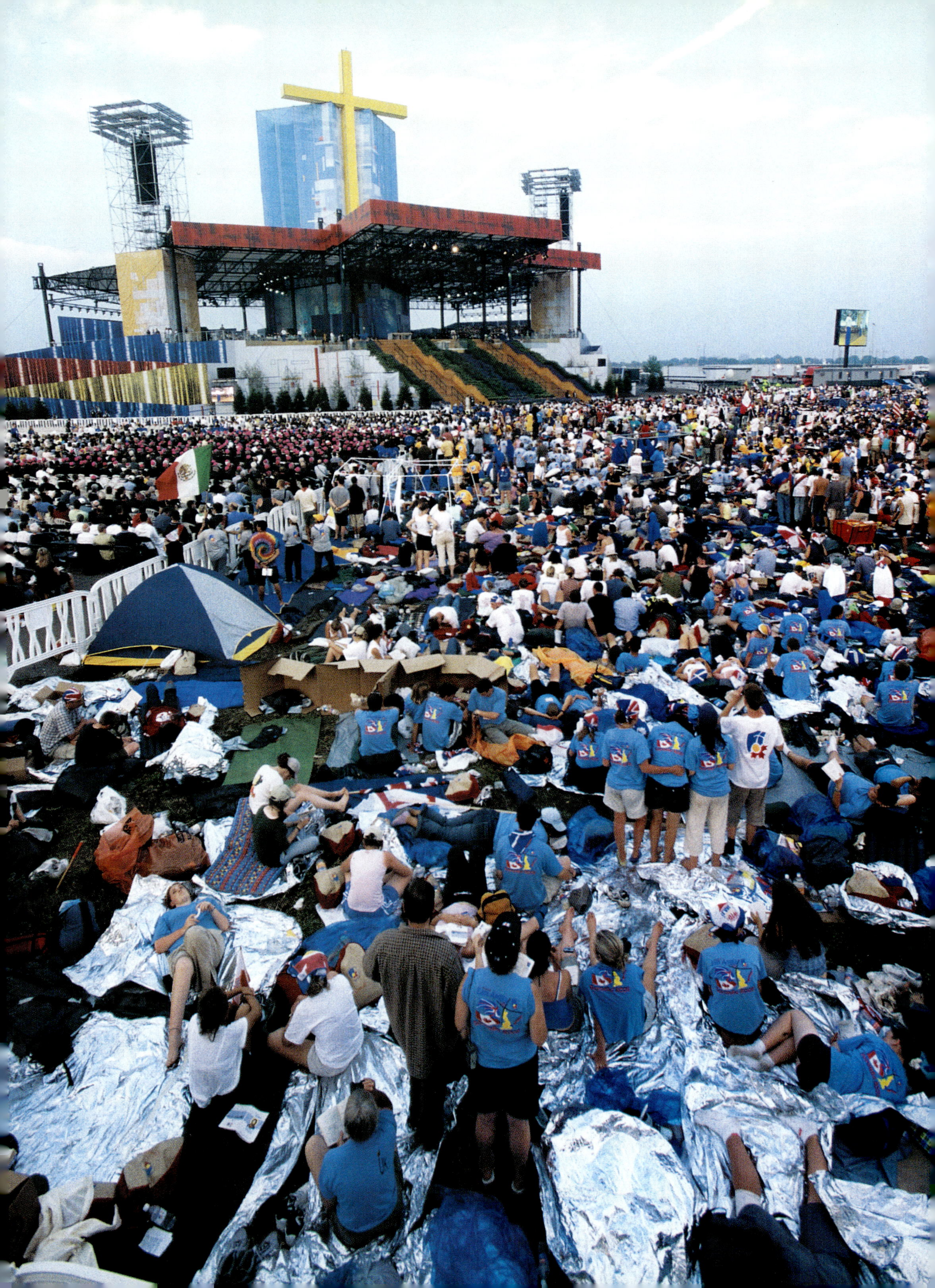

World Youth Day 2002

The Official Souvenir Album

by the Editors of Novalis

Official WYD 2002 Photographer
Bill Wittman

Photographers
Catherine Bauknight, Ian Crysler,
Dick Hemingway, André Leduc, Rebecca Stevenson,
Michael Swan, Maria Delia Zamora

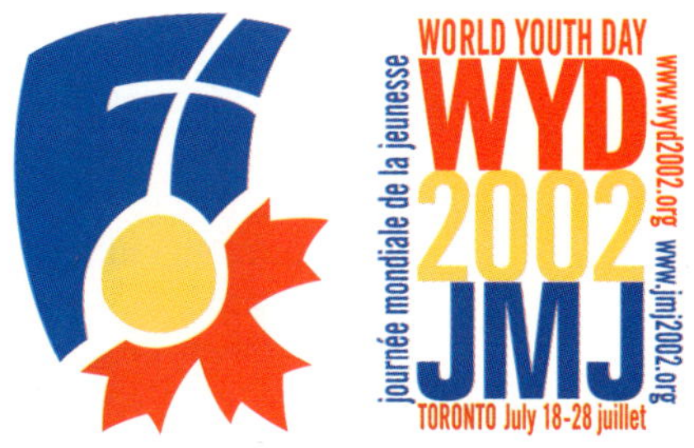

Toronto, Canada

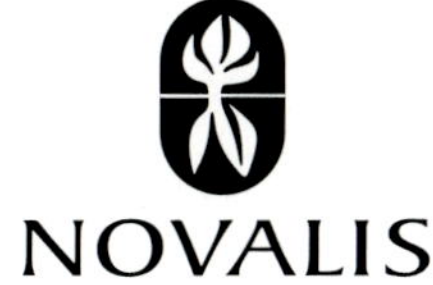

NOVALIS

© 2002 Novalis, Saint Paul University, Ottawa, Canada

Publisher & Editor-in-Chief/Éditeur et rédacteur en chef :
    Michael O'Hearn
Associate Editors/Rédacteurs en chef associés :
    Kevin Burns, Jean-François Bouchard
Project Manager/Chargée de projet :
    Grace Deutsch – Ismant Associates Inc.

Writers/Rédaction des textes :
    Kevin Burns, Jean-François Bouchard, Art Babych
Translation/Traduction :
    Michael O'Hearn, Christine Arnaud, Jacinthe Lacombe,
    Louise Pambrun, Margaret P. Bonikowska
Copy Editors/Révision des textes :
    Anne Holloway, Lise Lachance, Jacinthe Lacombe, Louise
    Pambrun, Margaret P. Bonikowska

Official WYD 2002 Photographer/Photographe officiel de la JMJ 2002 :
    Bill Wittman
Photographers/Photographes attitrés :
    Catherine Bauknight, Ian Crysler, Dick Hemingway, André
    Leduc, Rebecca Stevenson, Michael Swan, Maria Delia Zamora

Photo Editor/Édition photos : Jane Affleck

Front cover photos/Photos de la couverture :
    Bill Wittman – *Official WYD 2002 Photographer/Photographe
    officiel de la JMJ 2002*
Back cover photos/Photos de la couverture arrière :
    Catherine Bauknight, André Leduc, Dick Hemingway,
    Maria Delia Zamora

Design and cover/Conception graphique et couverture :
    Fortunato Aglialoro – Fortunato Design Inc.
Layout/Mise en page :
    Fortunato Aglialoro, Janie Skeete – Skeedoodle Design

Production Manager (Pre-press)/Direction de la production (pré-presse) :
    Anne Chevalier
Production Manager (Press)/Direction de la production (presse) :
    Robert Blanchard
Colour separation and pre-press/ Séparation de couleur et pré-presse :
Book Art Inc., Toronto

*Director of Marketing (English Books)/Direction commerciale
    (Livres anglais) :* Brian MacLean
*Director of Marketing (French Books)/Direction commerciale
    (Livres français) :* Jean Couture

Journée mondiale de la jeunesse 2002 : L'album souvenir official

Une édition en français de cet ouvrage est disponible chez :
NOVALIS
4475 rue Frontenac
Montréal, Québec, Canada
H2H 1T1
Téléphone : 1-800-NOVALIS / 514-278-3025
Télécopieur : 514-278-3030
Courriel : sac@novalis-inc.com

Światowy Dzień Młodzieży 2002
Oficjalny album pamiątkowy
The Polish edition of this book is available from :
GAZETA
215 Roncesvalles Ave.
Toronto, Ontario, Canada M6R 2L6
Phone: 416-531-3230
Fax: 416-531-3245
Email: gazeta@echo-on.net

Special Sales
Novalis books are available at special discounts when
purchased in bulk for premiums and sales promotions as well
as for fund-raising and educational use. Special editions or
book excerpts can also be created to specification. For details,
contact the Director of Marketing at this address:

NOVALIS
49 Front Street East, 2nd Floor
Toronto, Ontario, Canada M5E 1B3
Phone: 1-800-387-7164 or 416-363-3303
Fax: 1-800-204-4140 or 416-363-9409
Email: cservice@novalis.ca

ISBN: 2-89507-239-6

National Library of Canada Cataloguing in Publication

World Youth Day, 2002 : the official souvenir album.

Also published in French under title: Journée mondiale de la
jeunesse, 2002, and in Polish under title: Swiatowy dzien
mlodziezy, 2002.
ISBN 2-89507-239-6

1. World Youth Day (17th : 2002 : Toronto, Ont.). 2. World
Youth Day (17th : 2002 : Toronto, Ont.)–Pictorial works.

BX2347.8.Y7W67 2002 282'.0835   C2002-904110-4

Printed in Canada

Novalis acknowledges the financial support of the Government
of Canada through the Book Publishing Industry Development
Program (BPIDP) for its publishing activities.

10 9 8 7 6 5 4 3 2 1   10 09 08 07 06 05 04 03 02

Table of Contents

Foreword

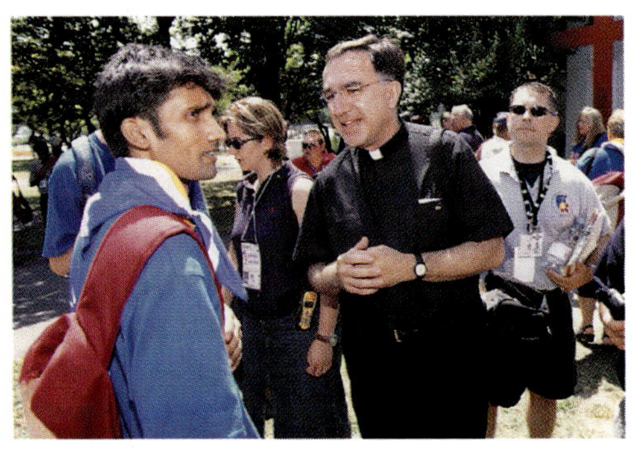

If there is one dominant image in my mind and heart as I think of World Youth Day 2002, it is as though Canada and Toronto had become a huge canvas in God's studio, and that the Creator himself painted bold brushstrokes of extraordinary goodness, kindness, hope, and joy across our country and our city. The event was truly magnificent through its long months of preparation, and from its start on July 18 throughout the country to its culminating moments in Toronto.

Upon his arrival among us on Tuesday, July 23, 2002, Pope John Paul II set the tone for what would take place throughout the week. "Young people are coming together," he told us, "to commit themselves, in the strength of their faith in Jesus Christ, to the great cause of peace and human solidarity."

The vivid images captured in this souvenir album are nothing less than an ode to the infectious joy that touches everyone when youthful exuberance and trust in God embrace. They will help us to bask a while longer in the brilliance of that light which surrounded Canada for those unforgettable days of July, 2002. They will strengthen the bonds between all pilgrims and the One who is the origin and destiny of every pilgrimage: Jesus the living Lord.

Thank you Novalis, for creating this official souvenir album, a pictorial witness of World Youth Day 2002. May it help us savour and remember what happened on those warm summer days of July, when an elderly, infirm Pope walked among us and, through his primary audience of young adults, invited the rest of the world to become young again. May the images serve as a witness to the love between a holy grandfather and his young friends, and to the joyful power of this mutual love that has the capacity to change the world. Thank you for capturing so beautifully in these pages the spirit, the salt and the light of this remarkable event.

Fr. Thomas Rosica, C.S.B.
National Director and Chief Executive Officer
World Youth Day 2002

John Paul II Greets Canada

Dear People of Canada:

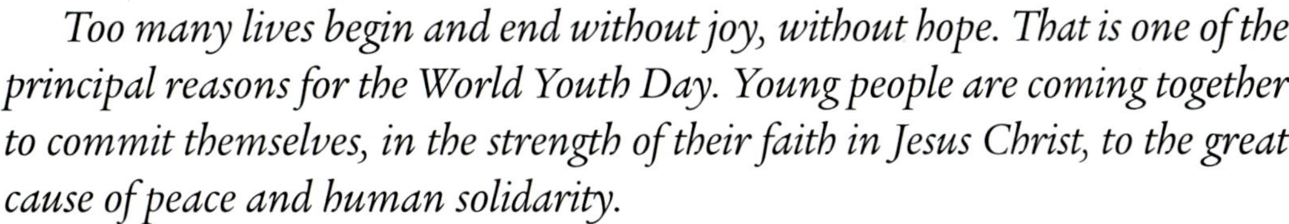

I have vivid memories of my first apostolic visit in 1984, and of my brief visit in 1987 to the First Nations in the land of Denendeh. This time I must be content to stay only in Toronto. From here I greet all Canadians. You are in my thankful prayers to God, who has so abundantly blessed your vast and beautiful country.

Young people from all parts of the world are gathering for the World Youth Day. With their gifts of intelligence and heart they represent the future of the world. But they also bear the marks of a humanity that too often does not know peace, or justice.

Too many lives begin and end without joy, without hope. That is one of the principal reasons for the World Youth Day. Young people are coming together to commit themselves, in the strength of their faith in Jesus Christ, to the great cause of peace and human solidarity.

Thank you, Toronto; thank you, Canada, for welcoming them with open arms!

In the French version of your national anthem O Canada, you sing: "Car ton bras sait porter l'épée, il sait porter la croix ..." Canadians are heirs to an extraordinarily rich humanism, enriched even more by the blend of many different cultural elements. But the core of your heritage is the spiritual and transcendent vision of life based on Christian revelation, which gave vital impetus to your development as a free, democratic and caring society, recognized throughout the world as a champion of human rights and human dignity.

In a world of great social and ethical strains, and confusion about the very purpose of life, Canadians have an incomparable treasure to contribute—on condition that they preserve what is deep and good and valid in their own heritage. I pray that the World Youth Day will offer all Canadians an opportunity to remember the values that are essential to good living and to human happiness.

Dear Friends, may the motto of the World Youth Day echo throughout the land, reminding all Christians to be "salt of the earth and light of the world."

God bless you all. God bless Canada

John Paul II
Upon his arrival in Canada, July 23, 2002

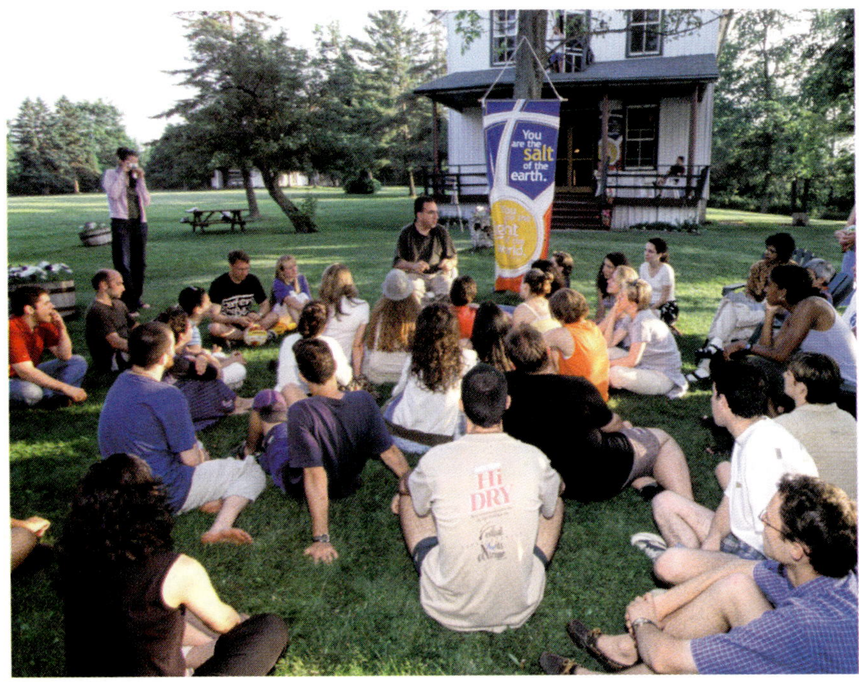

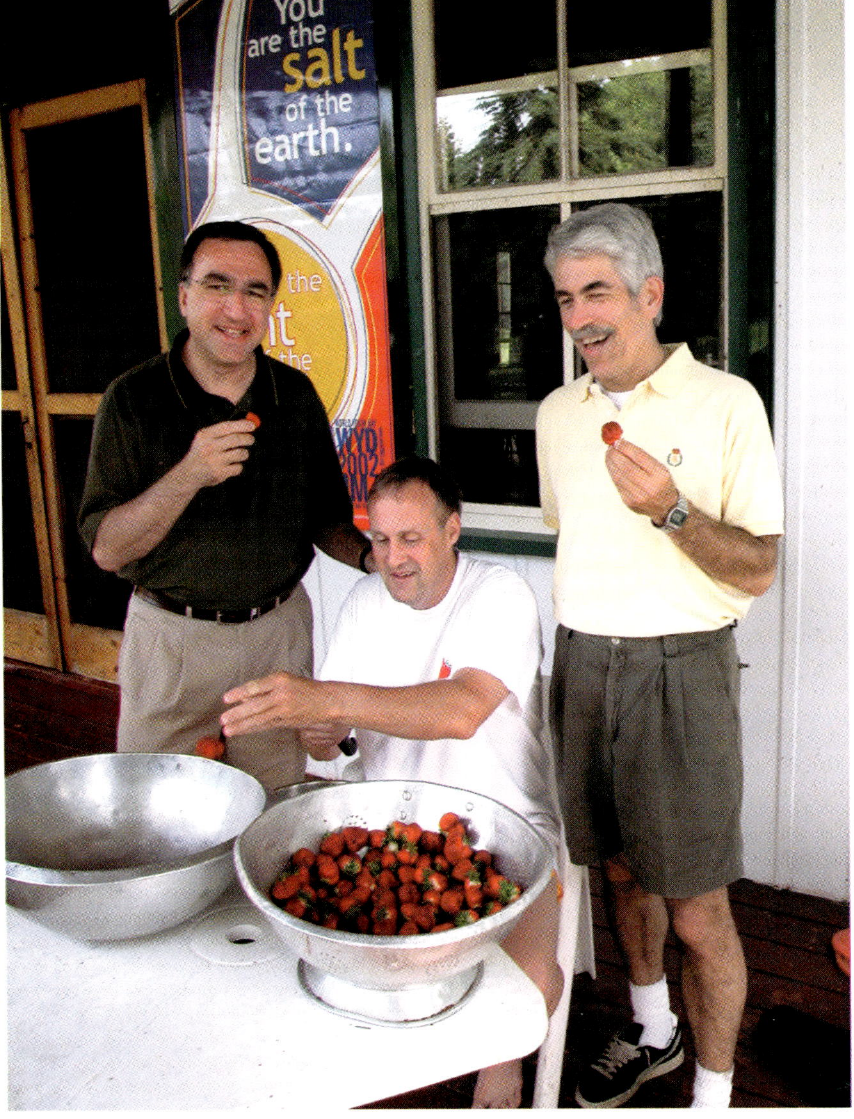

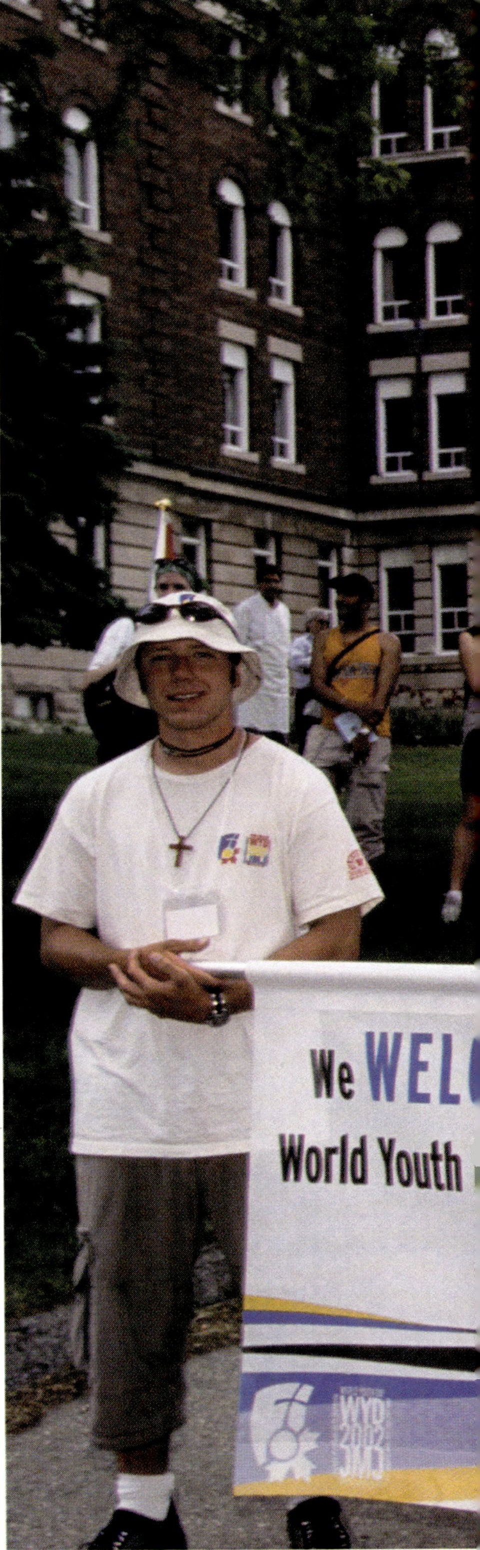

Getting Ready for World Youth Day

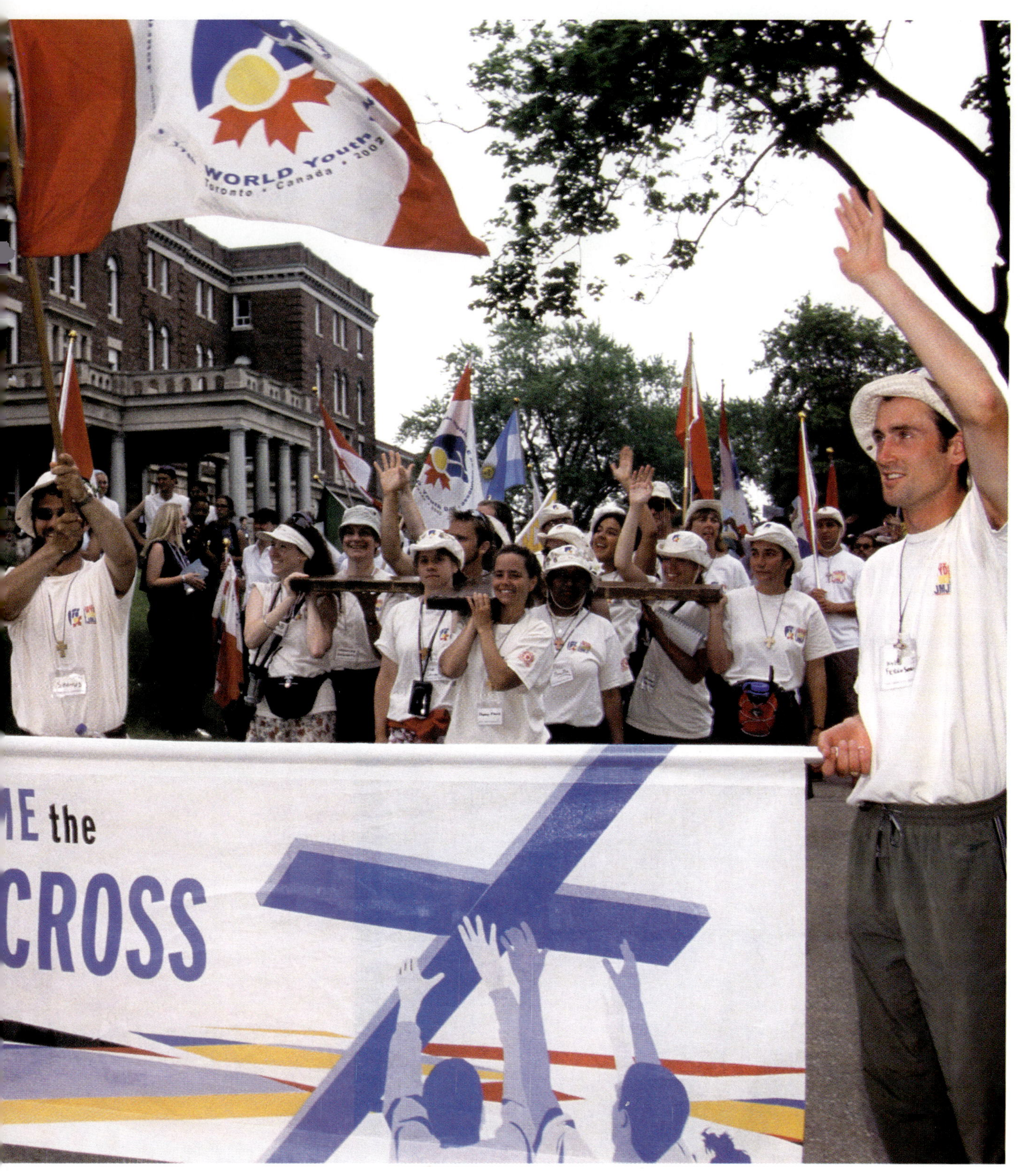

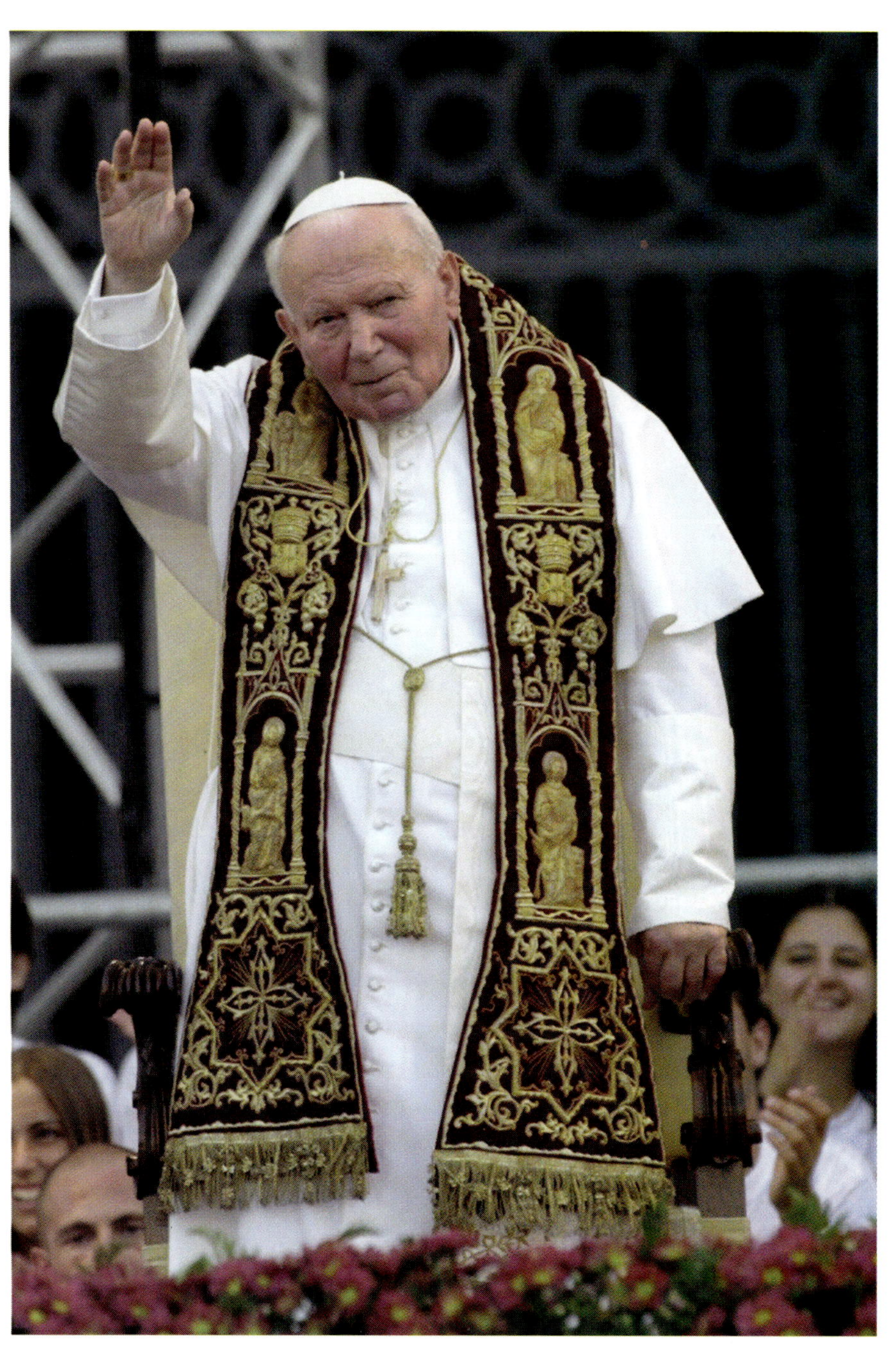

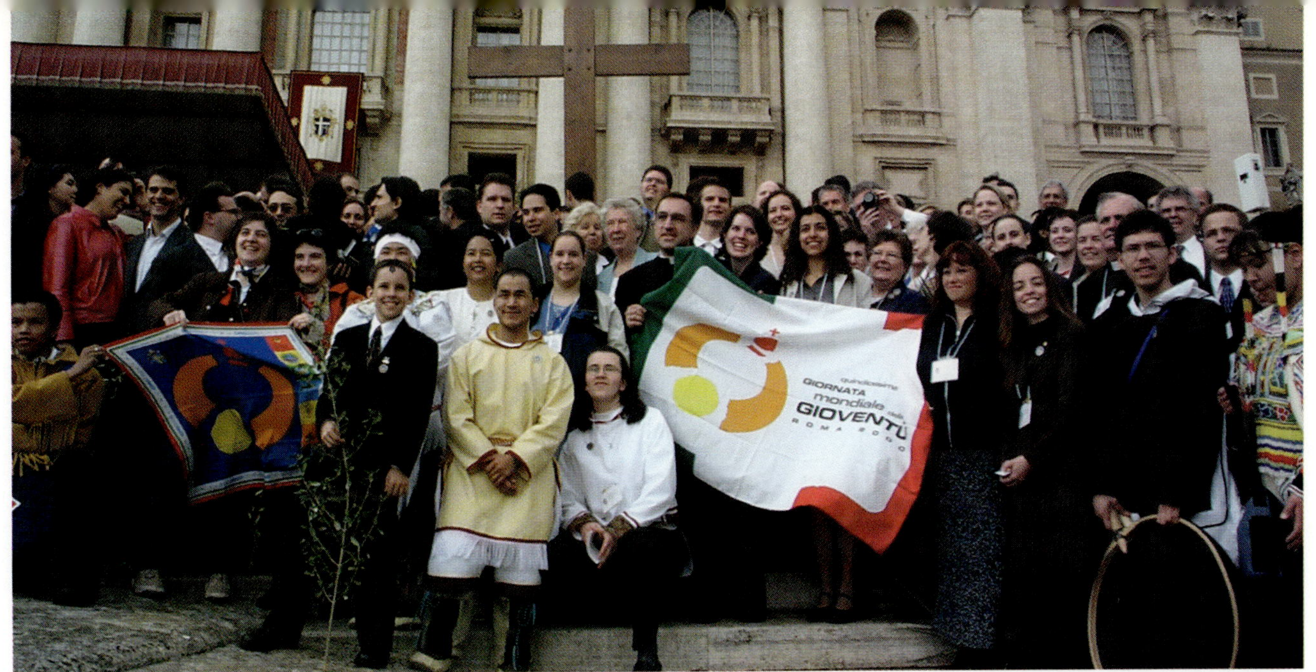

By now, World Youth Day has become an important part of your life and of the life of the Church. I invite you therefore to get ready for the seventeenth celebration of this great international event, to be held in Toronto, Canada. It will be another chance to meet Christ, to bear witness to his presence in today's society, and to become builders of the "civilization of love and truth."

John Paul II

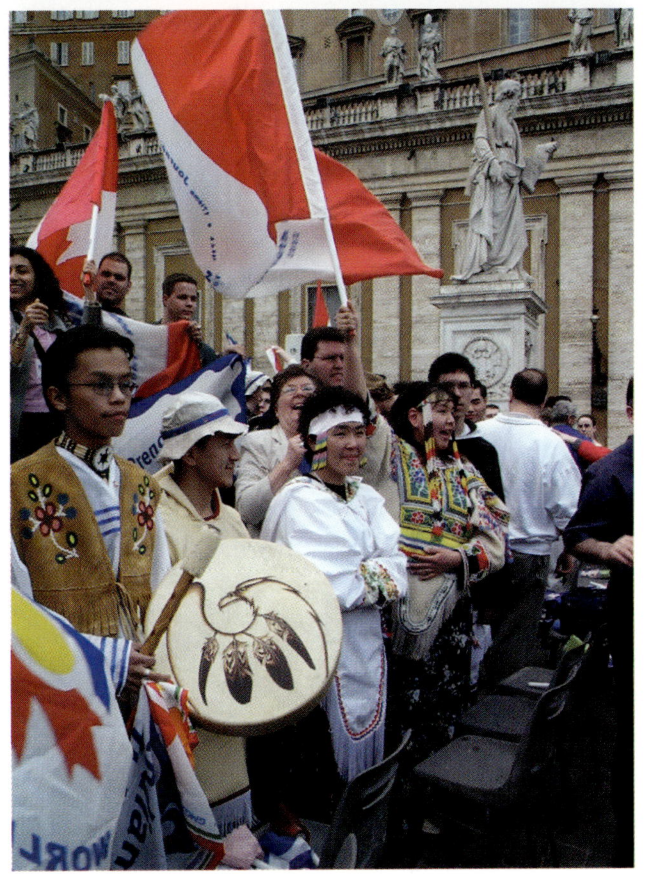

Your generation is being challenged in a special way to keep safe the deposit of faith.

John Paul II

Be not afraid!

In the searing August heat of Rome in the Jubilee Year 2000, the largest Canadian delegation ever to attend a World Youth Day celebration waited breathlessly as Pope John Paul II announced which country would host the next such international gathering in 2002.

The group of some 4,000 young Catholics and several of their bishops erupted into thunderous applause at the news that the seventeenth World Youth Day would be held in Toronto.

The announcement by the Holy Father ended three years of planning and preparation by the Canadian Conference of Catholic Bishops and set in motion a massive Canada-wide action plan to prepare for the largest international assembly in the nation's history.

Founded by Pope John Paul II in 1985, World Youth Day provides an opportunity for young Catholics around the world to join in a celebration and exploration of their faith.

Father Thomas Rosica, C.S.B., the former head of the Newman Centre at the University of Toronto, was appointed in 1999 as the national director for WYD 2002. He said the biggest challenge was to assemble a team that represented Catholics from across the country.

The cost of hosting WYD 2002 in Toronto—an event that would attract hundreds of thousands of young people from more than 170 countries—was estimated at CAN$80 million. Registration fees would pay for more than half of the expenses. Sponsorship donations from individuals, corporations and foundations, government loans and grants, revenue from the sale of merchandise, and two national parish collections were expected to take care of the remainder. (It was reported in August 2002 that there would in fact be a shortfall of some CAN$30 million and a Canada-wide appeal was launched.)

Travel costs and registration fees to get to WYD 2002, including the Days in the Diocese component of the event, were the responsibility of the pilgrims themselves. Fundraising activities were held in parishes across Canada and included bottle drives, car washes, ticket raffles, pancake breakfasts, concerts and fashion shows.

Nothing focused more public attention on the event than the pan-Canadian travels of the World Youth Day Cross. Received from the pope on Palm Sunday, 2001, the four-metre-high WYD Cross symbolizes not only the sacrifice of Christ but also His victory over suffering and death. It travelled from coast to coast to coast with stops in each of the 72 Catholic dioceses in Canada; visited 350 cities, towns and villages; and was transported by air, road, boat, snowmobile, foot and even dogsled. WYD youth also took the cross on a poignant pilgrimage to "ground zero" in New York, where the towers of the World Trade Center stood before the September 11, 2001 terrorist attack. (The cross that came to Canada is not the original World Youth Day Cross, which has become too fragile after years of travel and is now kept in Rome. Nevertheless, it is one of the most travelled crosses in the world.)

Also inviting young Catholics to take part in WYD 2002 were several Canadian celebrities, among them fiddling sensation Natalie

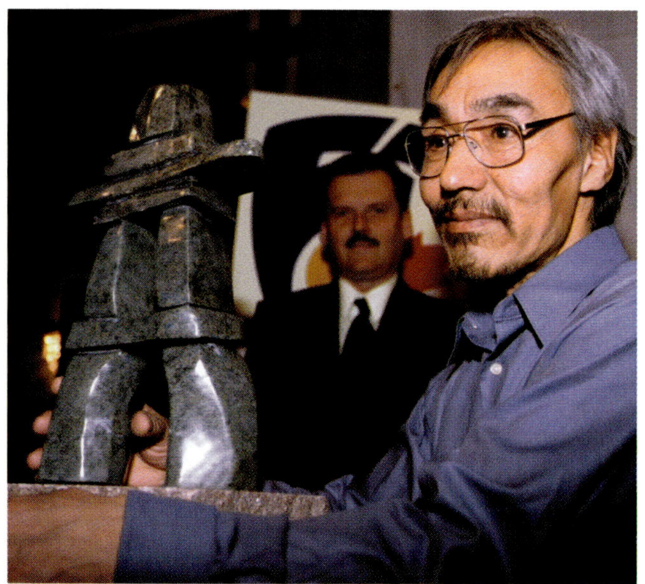

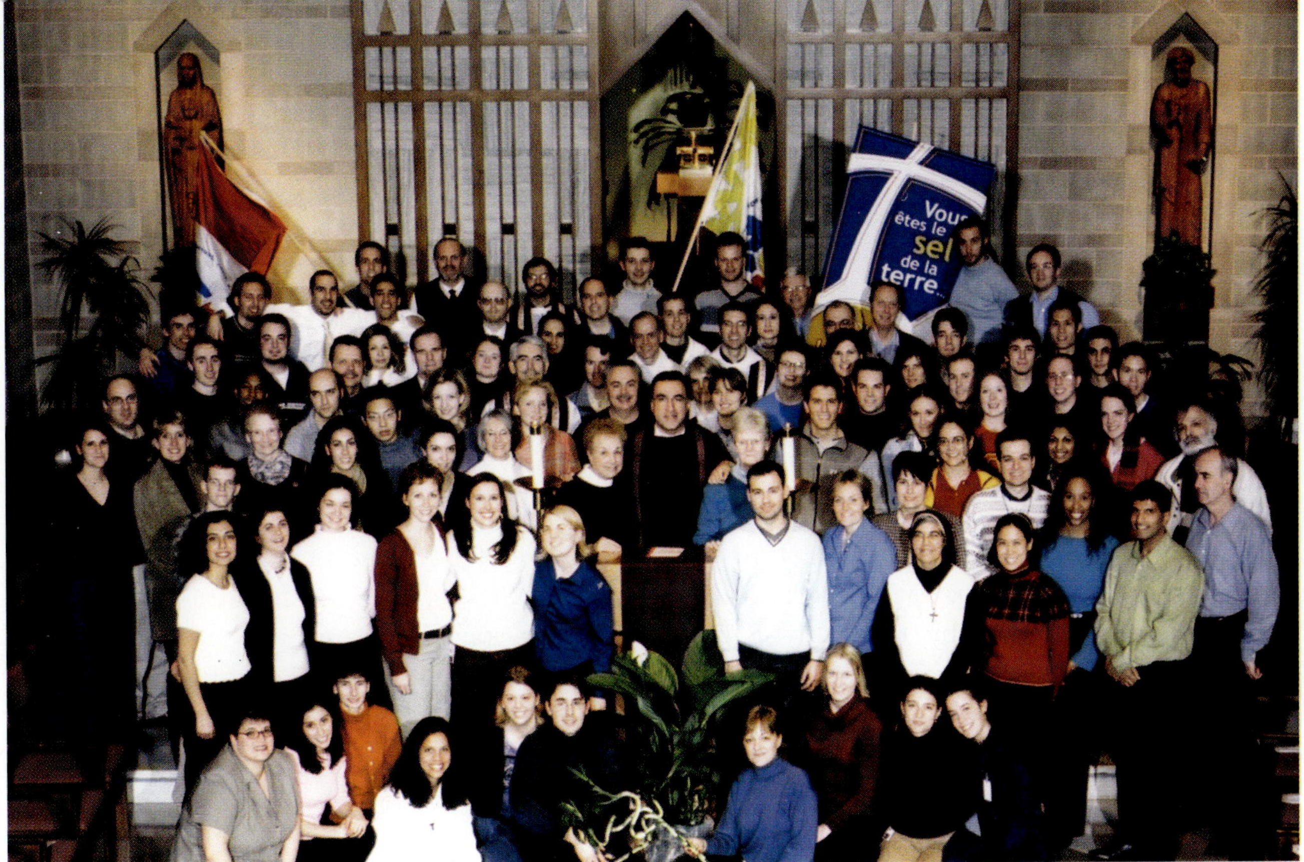

MacMaster and Justin Trudeau, son of the late prime minister, Pierre Trudeau.

Preparing for the massive influx of pilgrims posed special logistical challenges, including the design and construction of a giant stage for the welcoming ceremonies at Exhibition Place and an even larger stage for the papal mass at Downsview Lands in northwest Toronto. WYD facilities at Downsview required a stage that could accommodate 1,300 people, the installation of 21 large video screens and 1,000 speakers, and 7,500 portable toilets.

Commissioned by the City of Toronto, Kellypalik Qimirpik, a Canadian Inuit sculptor, created an inukshuk for World Youth Day. This traditional Inuit sculpture, assembled from rocks and arranged to resemble a human form, serves as a signpost for travellers in the Arctic.

Local parishes were involved in promoting and preparing for World Youth Day. Almost 130 of them opened up their churches for catechetical teaching conducted for the pilgrims by hundreds of bishops, archbishops and cardinals from around the world in the days before WYD celebrations in Toronto.

Leading the international preparations for WYD was Cardinal James Francis Stafford, president of the Pontifical Council for the Laity, the arm of the Vatican responsible for WYD. The pilgrimage to Toronto "will teach young North Americans that the enclosed, isolated, fearful self is not part of human identity," said the former archbishop of Denver at a forum in Toronto in preparation for WYD 2002.

Three thousand musicians and other performers from 35 countries rehearsed more than 300 performances for the WYD Youth Festival on the grounds of Exhibition Place. The official World Youth Day Choir, made up of 500 singers ages 16 to 35, began weekly rehearsals in September 2001 in preparation for their performance at WYD ceremonies.

Quebec composer Father Robert Lebel wrote the WYD song "Light of the World," which was sung at all the major events. He took as his inspiration the WYD theme "You are the salt of the earth ... You are the light of the world," (Matthew 5:13-14) and, in the words of Father Rosica, succeeded in creating a song "that brings together the entire country."

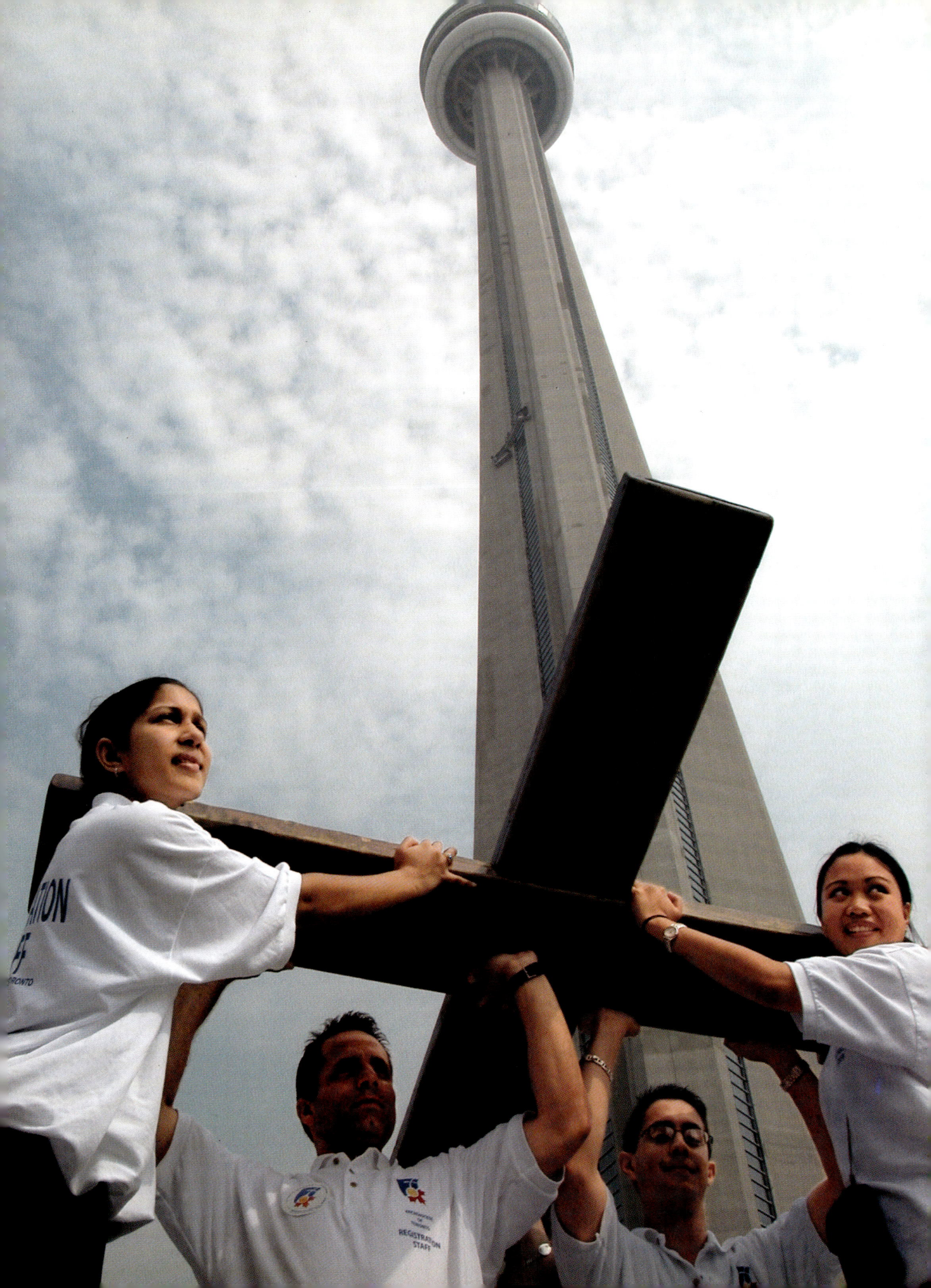

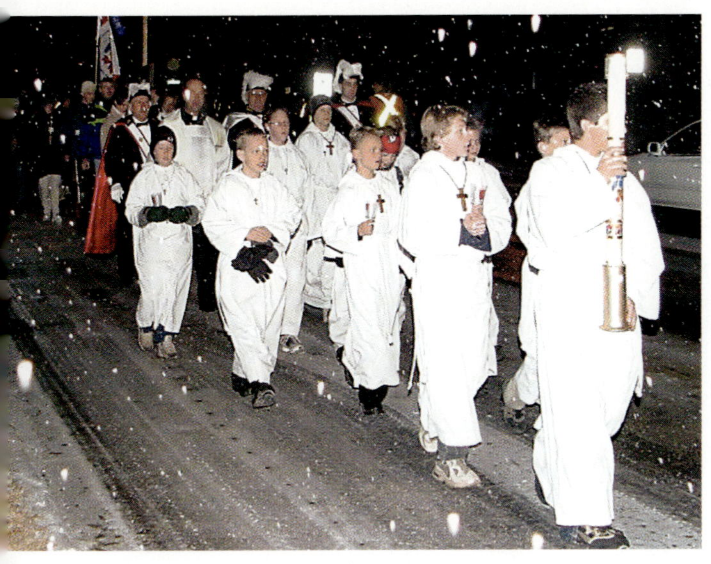

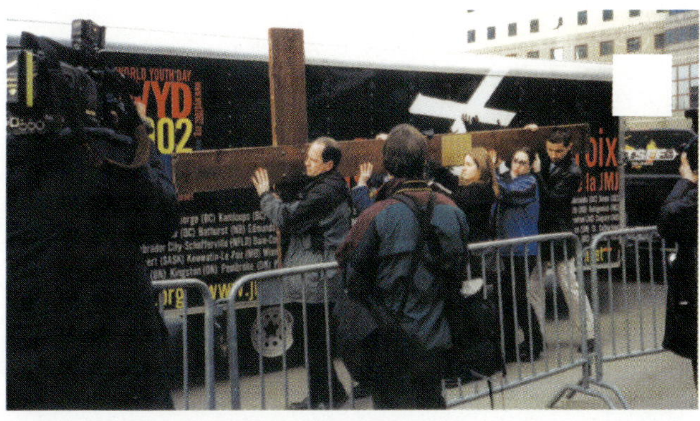

The WYD Cross will travel from diocese to diocese, reminding us of Christ's life, death and resurrection. Its passage will inspire us to become more fully committed to the meaning of WYD 2002 and the welcome that we will give to young people from all continents who will converge in Canada in response to the Holy Father's invitation.

BISHOP GERALD WIESNER, O.M.I.
then president of the Canadian
Conference of Catholic Bishops

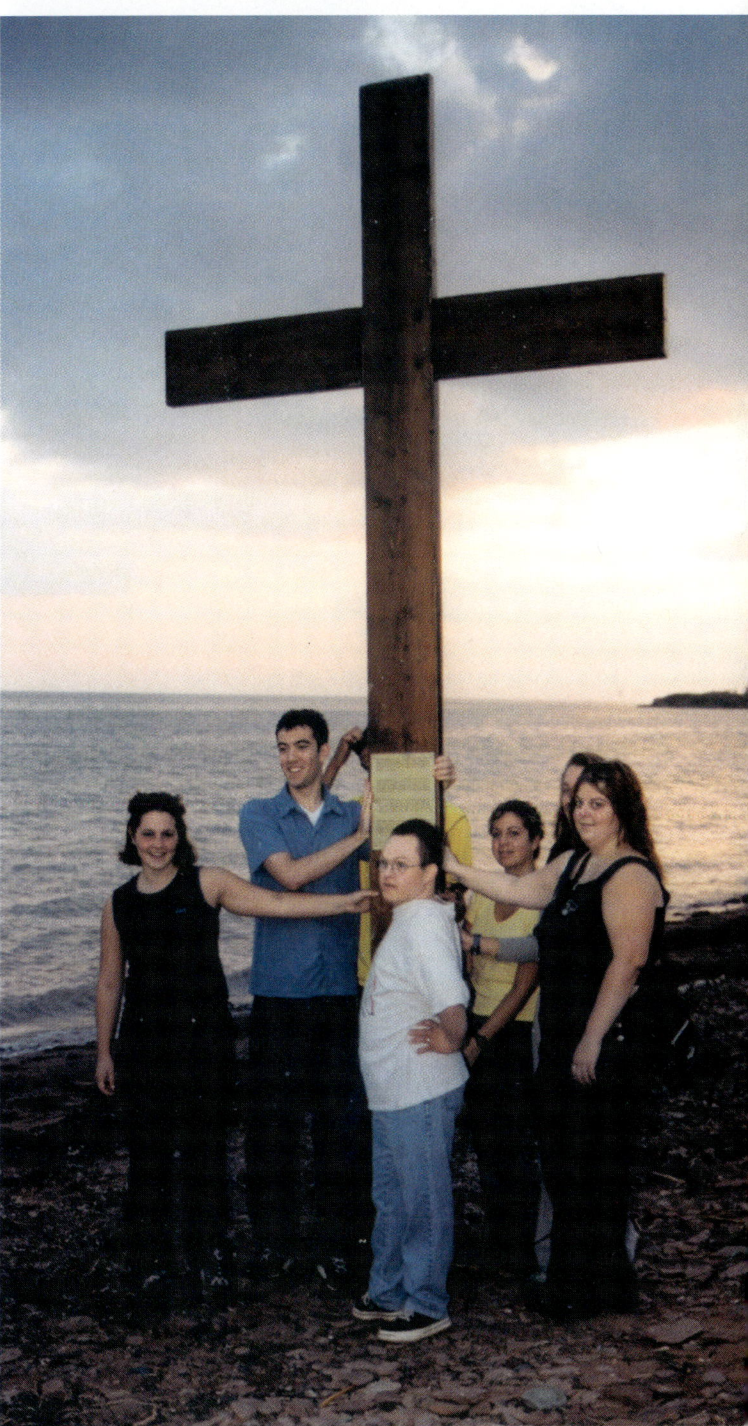

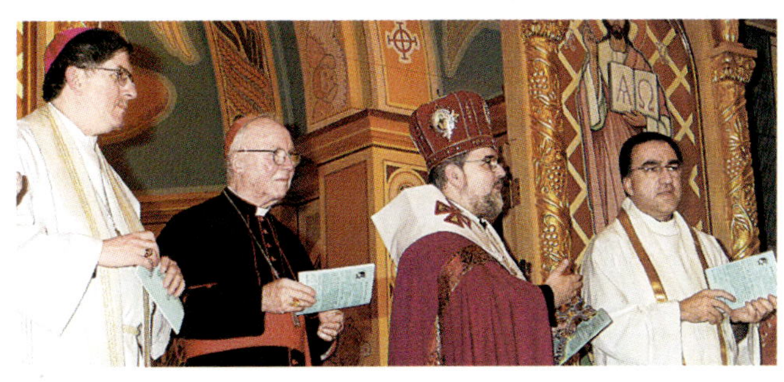

*The young people of Canada, together with their bishops
and the civil authorities, are already preparing
to welcome you with great warmth and hospitality.
For this I thank them with all my heart.
May this first World Youth Day
of the new millennium bring everyone
a message of faith, hope and love!*

JOHN PAUL II

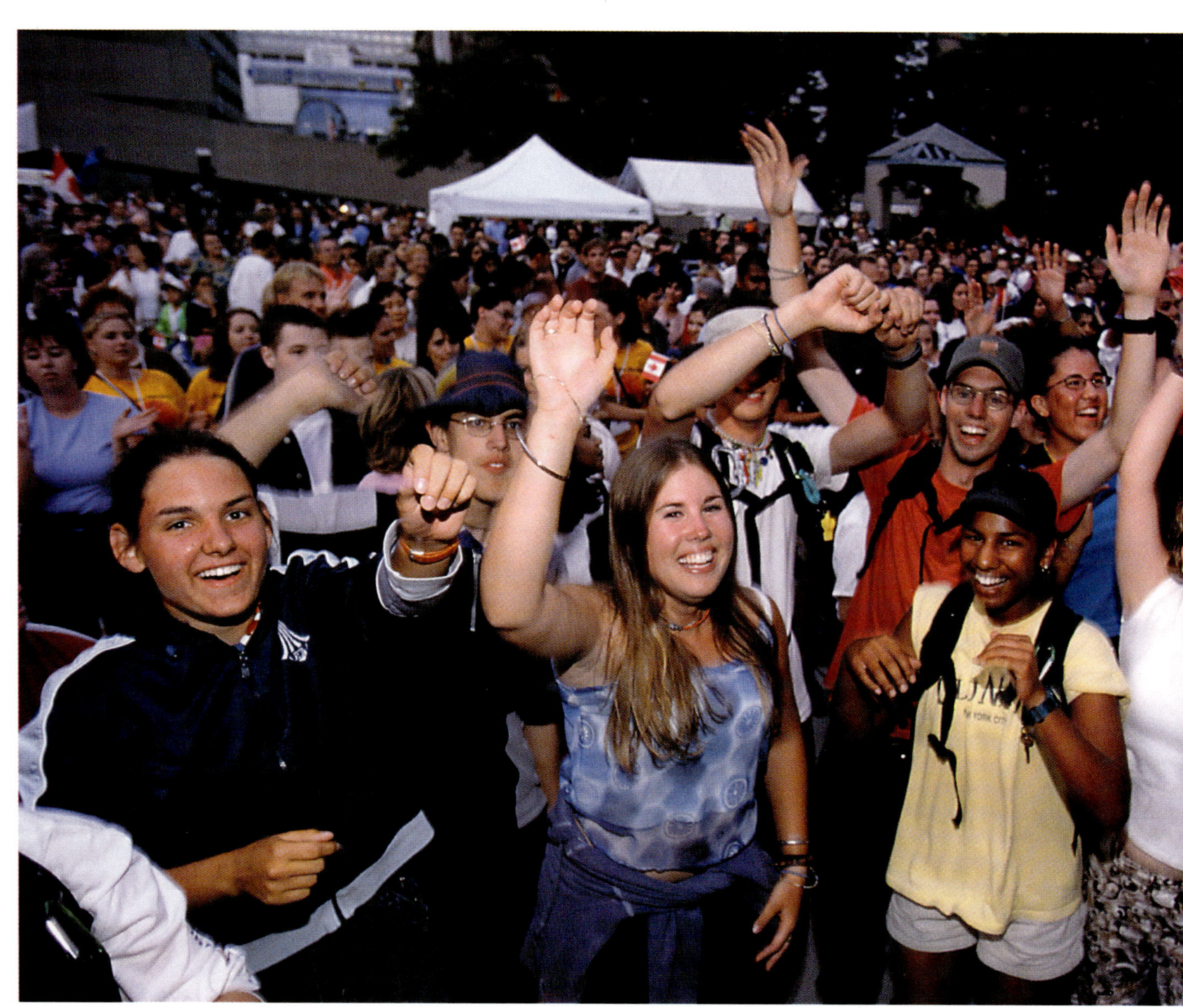

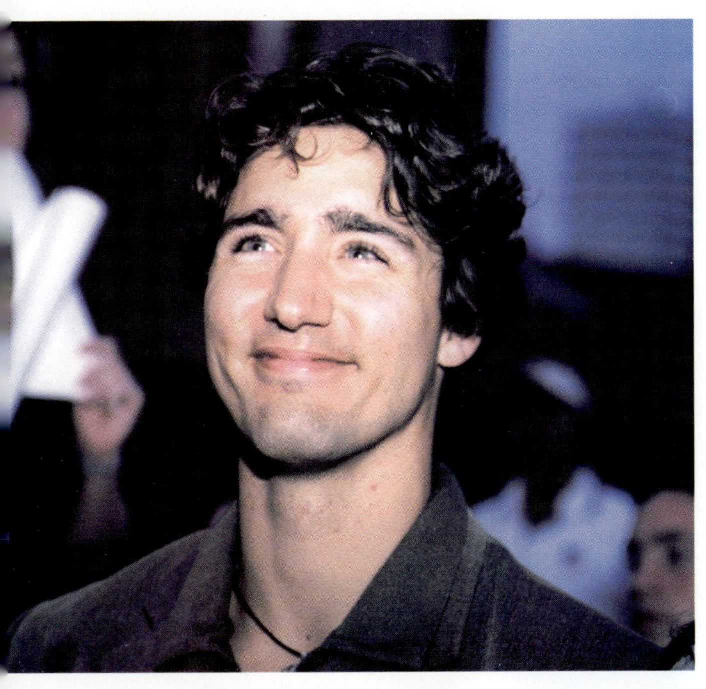

An awesome and exciting task lies before us over the next two years as we prepare for July 2002. May God bless all of us in and through this endeavour.

MOST REVEREND
ANTHONY G. MEAGHER,
Auxiliary Bishop of Toronto
and President of the
World Youth Day 2002 Council

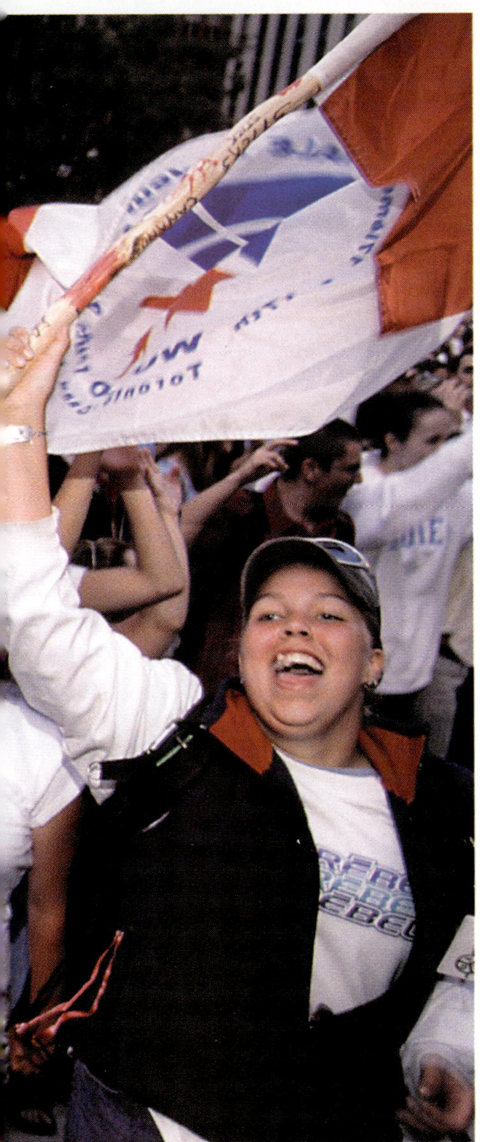

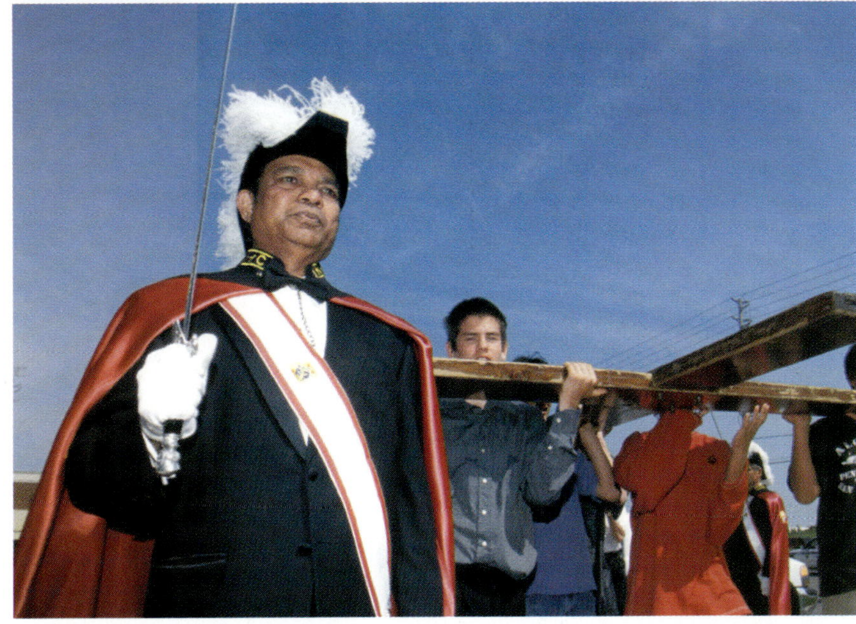

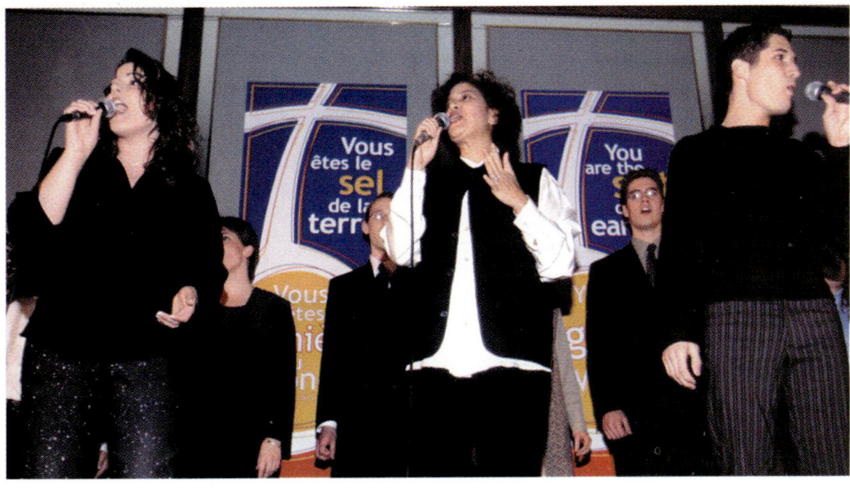

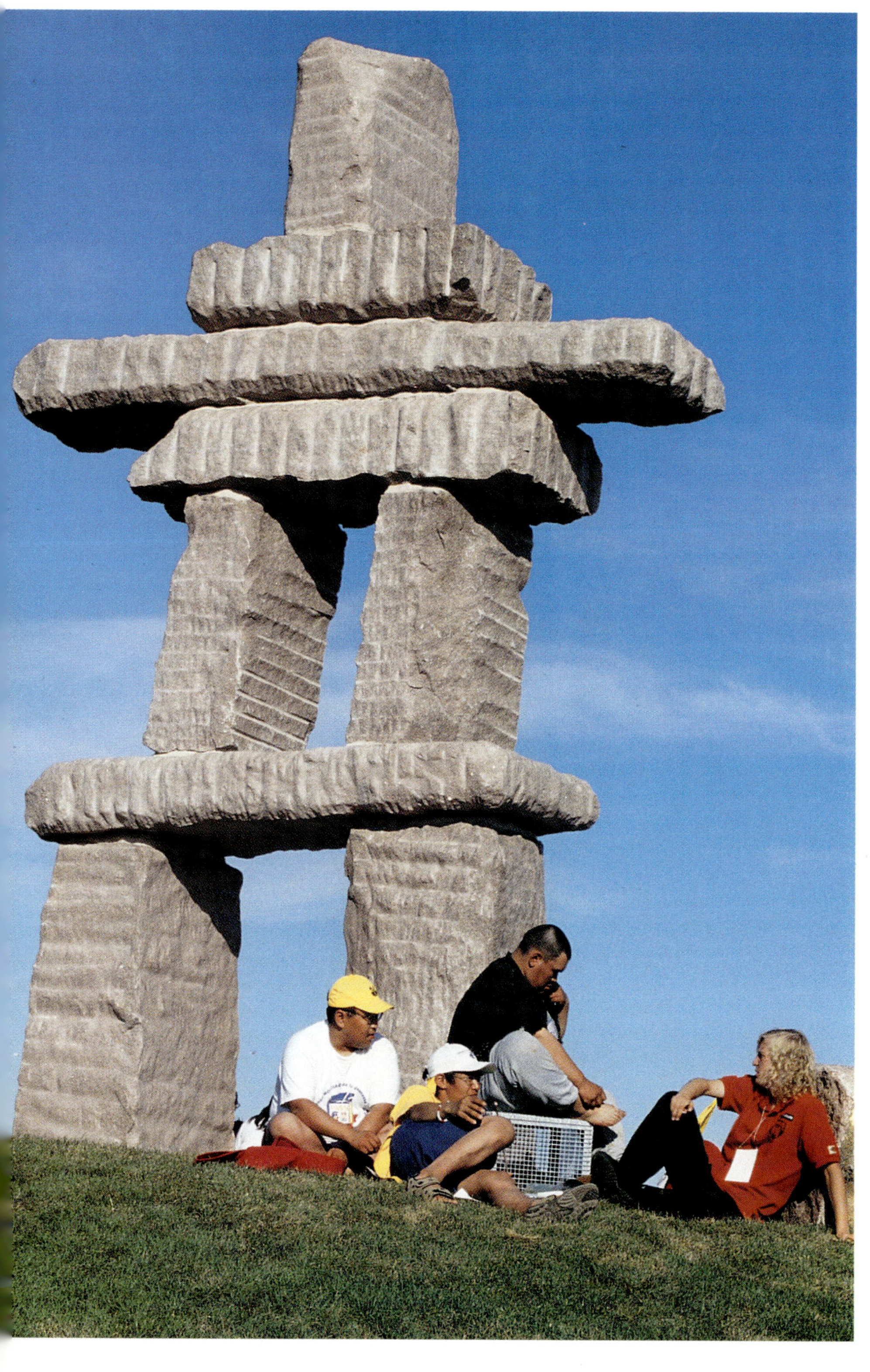

Woorld Youth Day has been a true navigational guide for millions of young people throughout the world. The Toronto inukshuk invites each one of us to become beacons of light and hope, striving for justice and peace in this world. This Toronto inukshuk legacy is a reminder of the immense, wonderful gathering of young people and His Holiness Pope John Paul II, held in Toronto during World Youth Day, July 23-28, 2002.

Mayor Mel Lastman and Toronto City Council

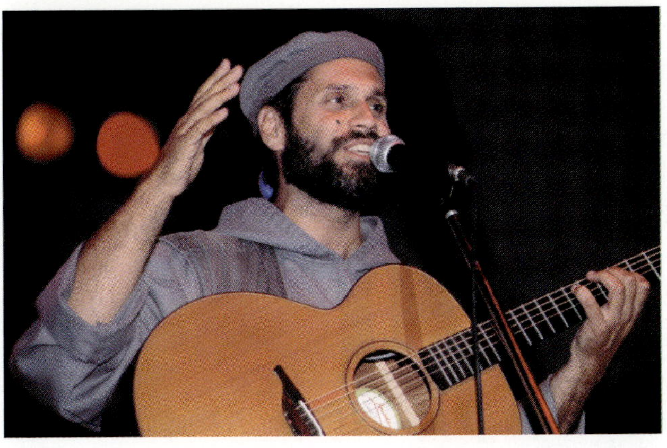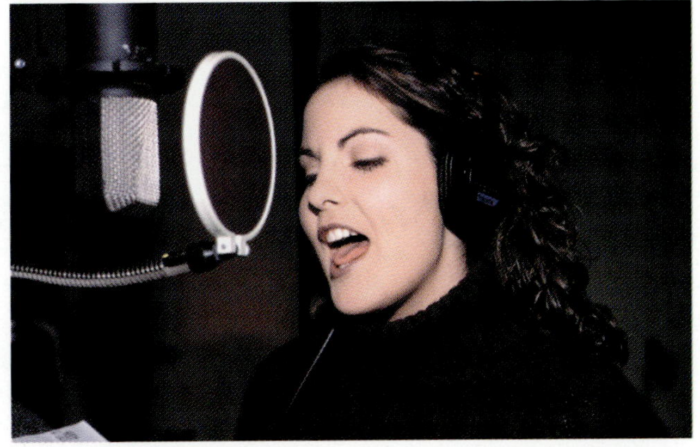

The burden of hope

With the announcement in 2000 that Toronto would host the 17th international World Youth Day, Canada became a beehive of frenzied planning and organizing. And the work didn't end until the closing mass on 28 July, 2002.

There were the usual things to worry about. Foreign visitors fretted about whether or not they'd be able to make the trip. How much would it cost? Would their visas arrive on time? Canadians lost sleep over their ability to welcome so many visitors in their dioceses across the country and in the host city of Toronto. How would they accommodate and feed them all? Where would the money come from to cover the huge expenses?

Certain anxieties proved more difficult to deal with. After the events of September 11, 2001, would people be afraid to fly? Also, would the Church in the United States be able to mobilize its young people who were reeling from the betrayal of trust arising out of the heinous actions of a few clergy? Not least of the organiz-ers' worries was the health of the most enthusiastic pilgrim of all: 82 years old and living with a number of debilitating illnesses, would John Paul II be able to make the long trip?

To the very last moment the organizers were extremely uneasy, but never without hope. The first day was moderately successful, as an estimated crowd of 250,000 attended the opening mass. With each passing day the number of registrations rose. In fact, they rose so quickly the computer finally crashed!

Pilgrims from around the globe took part in the various events. Immense crowds arrived and so, of course, did the Holy Father.

In the final analysis, organizing World Youth Day required tonnes of paper, thousands of kilos of food, light years of insomnia, and lots of Aspirin. But the major requirement was an unshakable faith that could move mountains—the kind of faith that allowed John Paul II to be with his young friends in person, just as he'd promised.

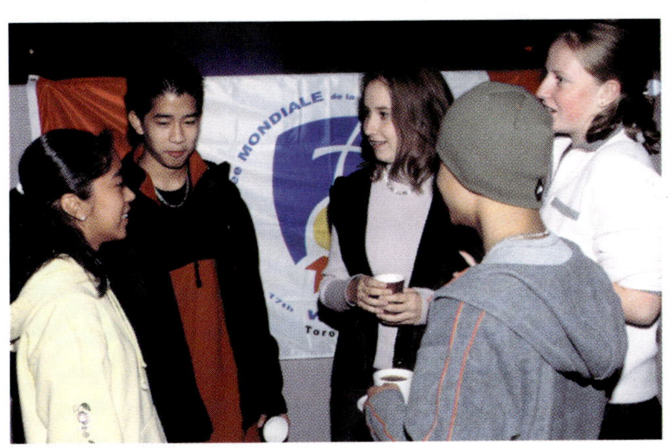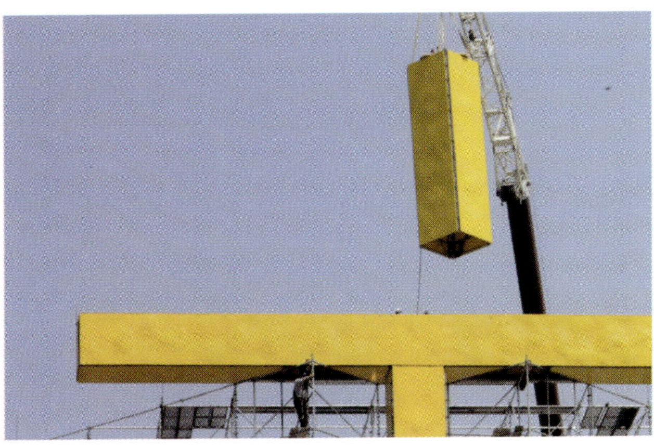

Welcoming the World

Youth from around the world will arrive in cities across our country, be welcomed by the Catholic youth of that city or region and stay with them for three or four days, sharing their culture, ideals, hopes, dreams, prayers and, especially, the meaning and importance of loving Jesus.

MOST REVEREND ANTHONY G. MEAGHER

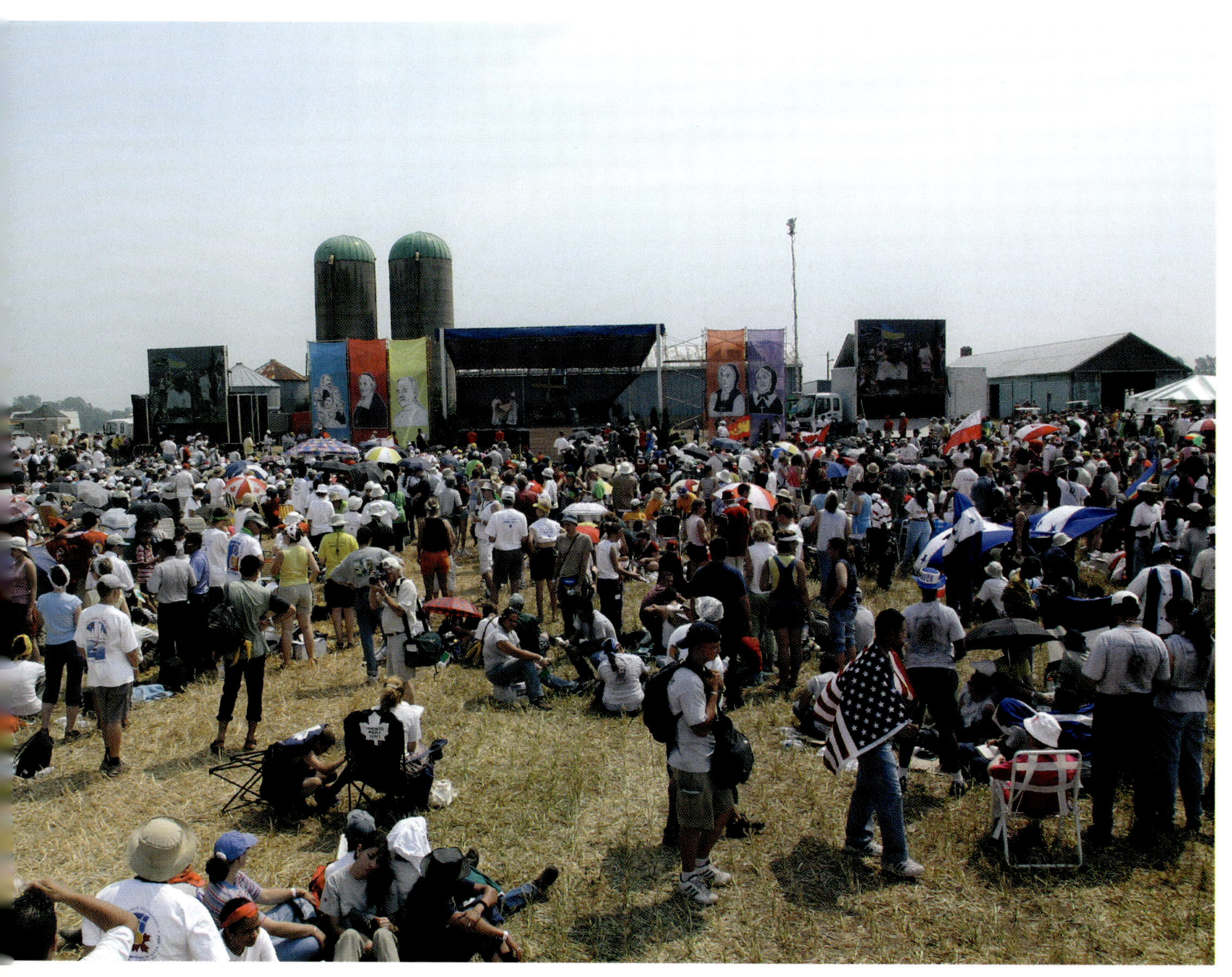

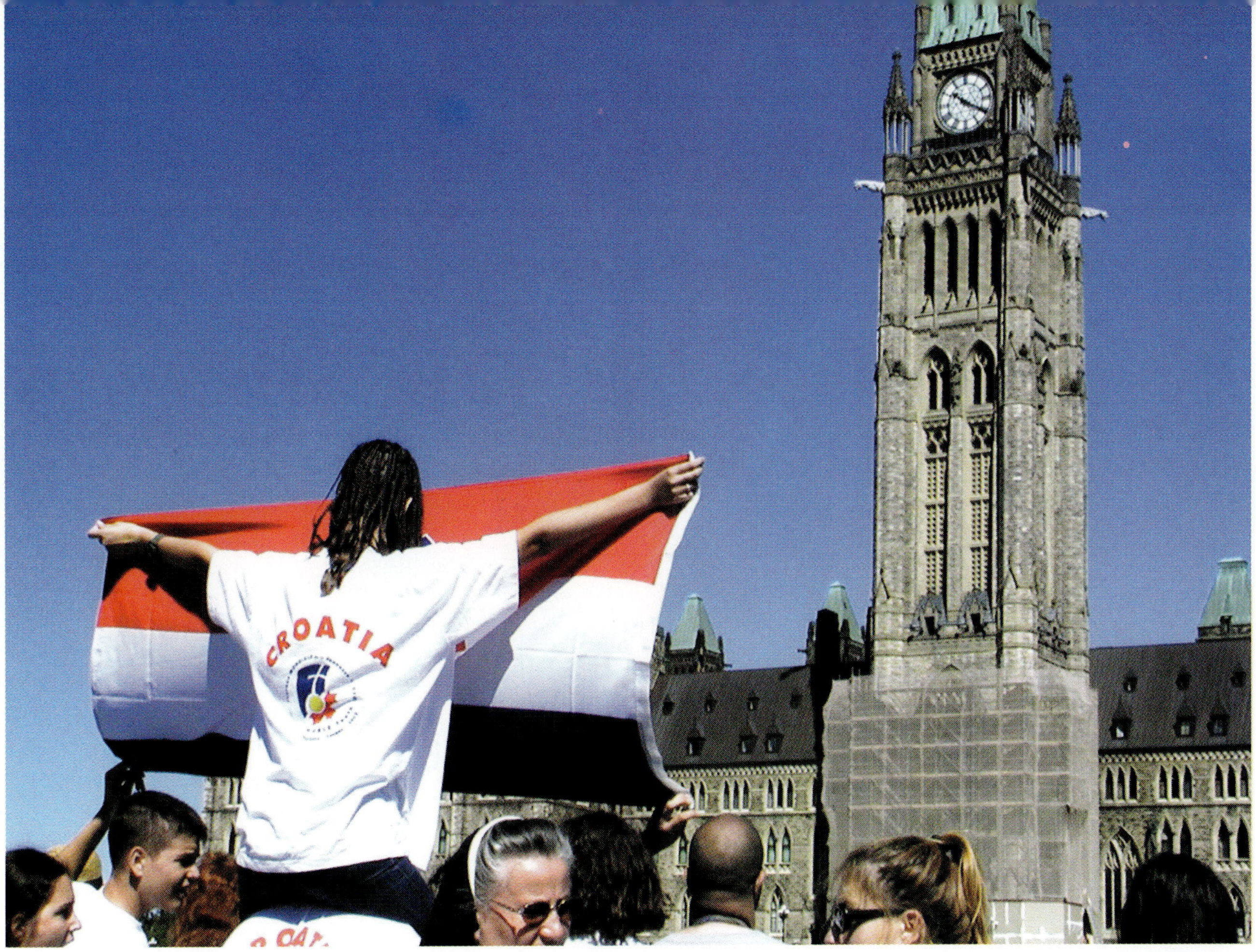

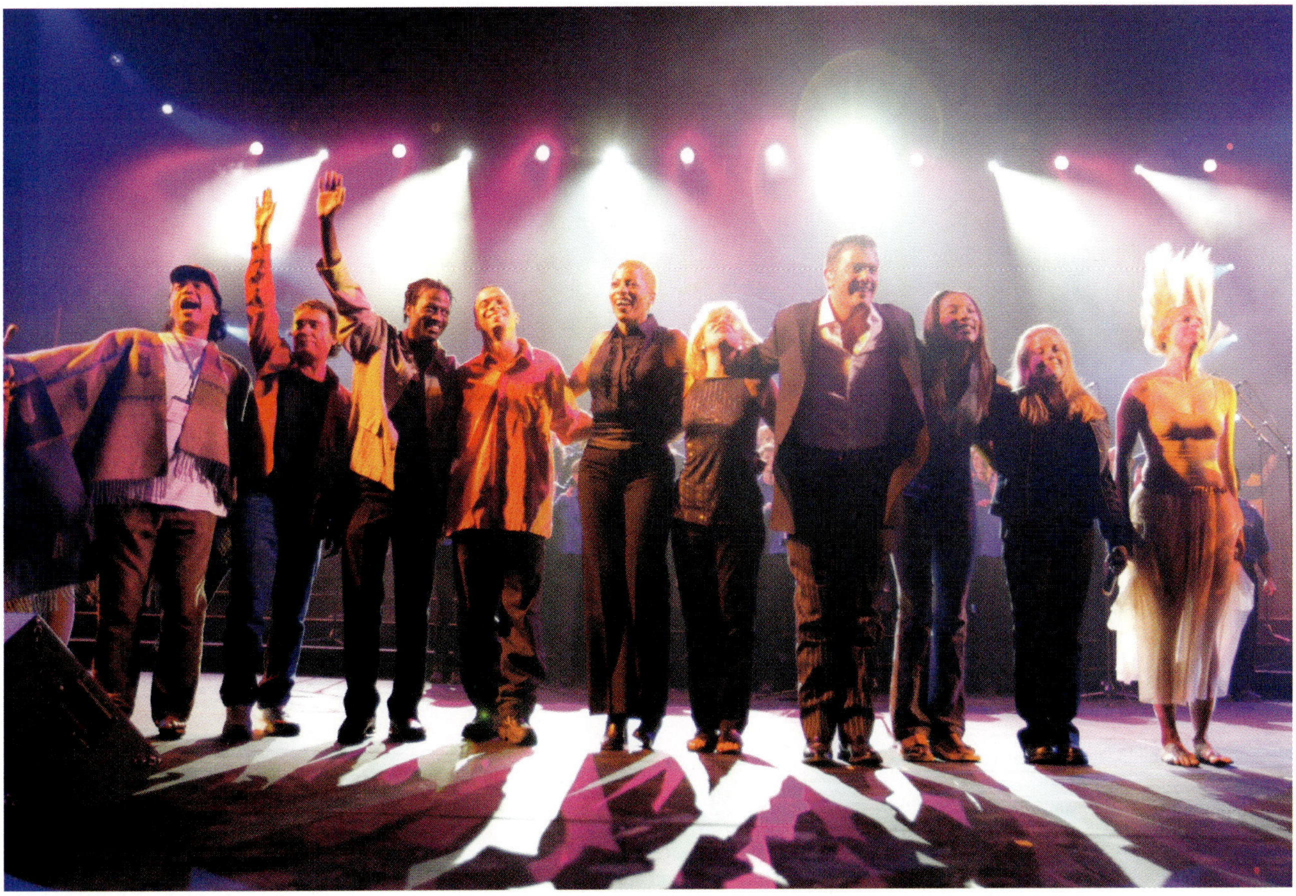

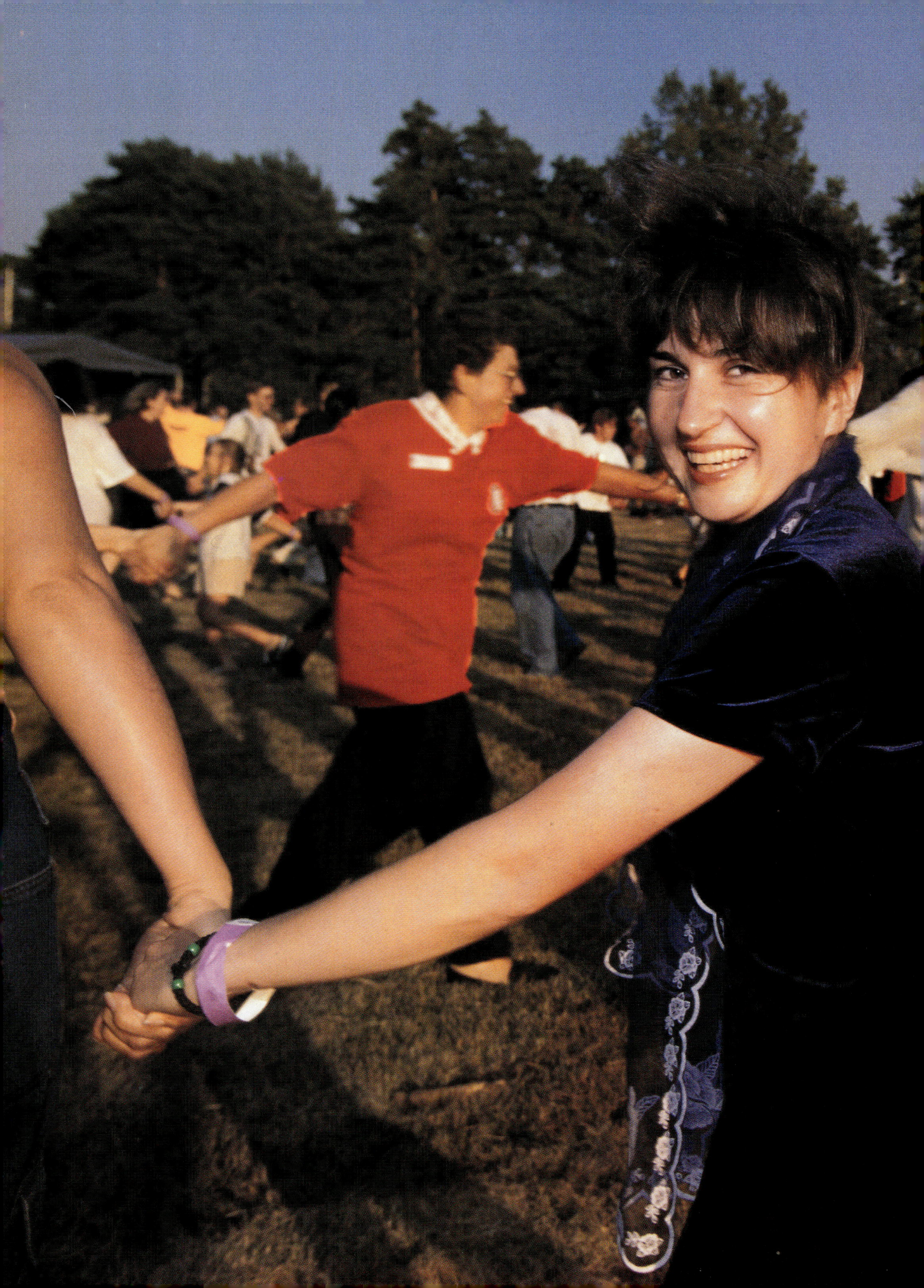

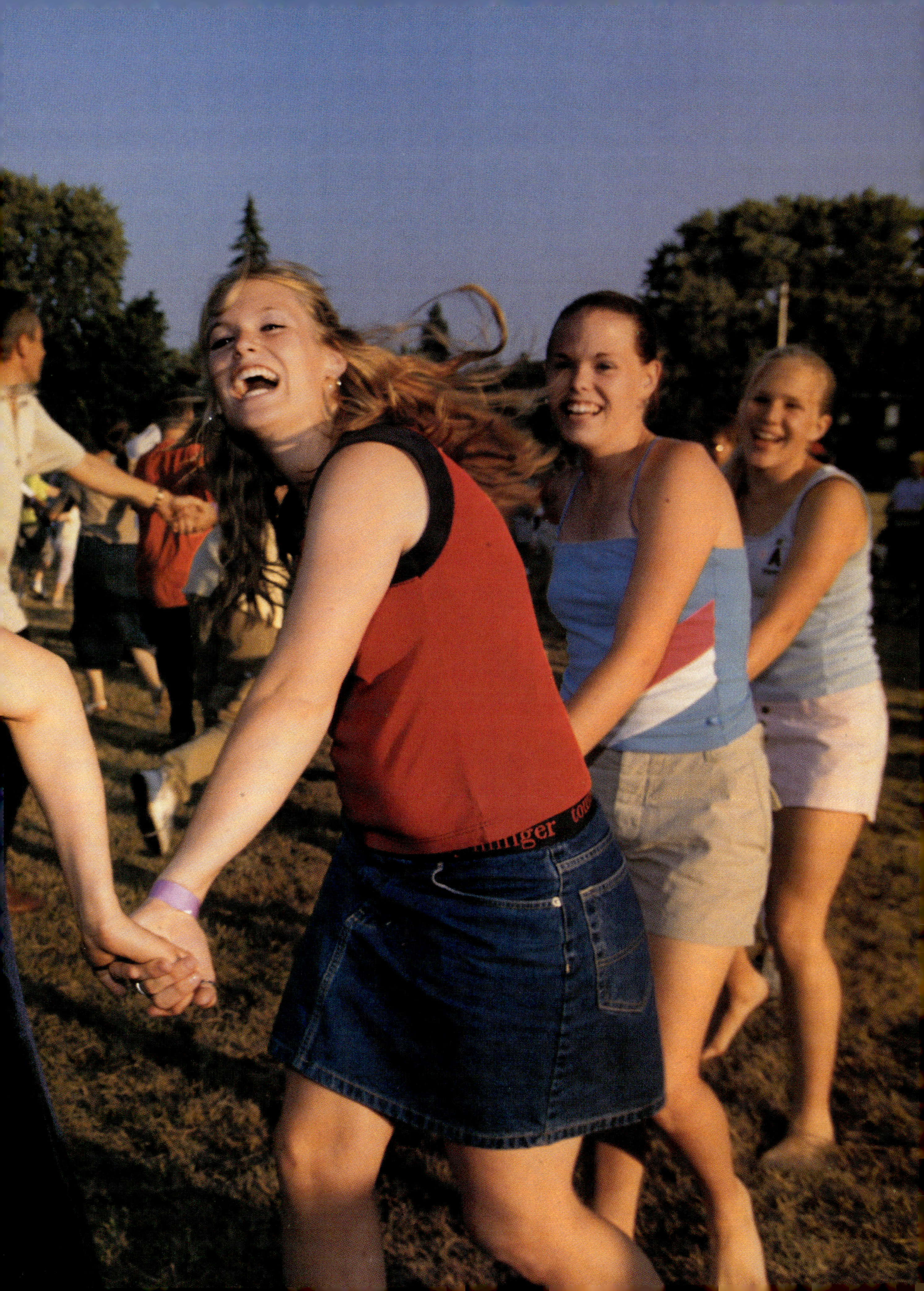

With great warmth and hospitality

The WYD Days in the Diocese (July 18 to 21) offered international visitors a taste of life in Canada before they gathered in Toronto for the concluding celebrations of World Youth Day 2002.

Pilgrims were welcomed with open arms in each of the 51 participating dioceses from coast to coast and were billeted in parish halls, schools and family homes. Their presence gave Canadian youth and their families a unique opportunity to share cultures and to form a truly international community of believers. Pilgrims took part in a wide variety of Canadian social events and joined with their hosts at prayer and at mass. They broke bread together, sharing their deepest thoughts about what it means to be a Christian in today's secularized world.

Deep friendships developed between the hosts and their visitors over the four days they spent together in communities in every region of Canada, including Ottawa, the nation's capital, where pilgrims gathered on Parliament Hill. The dioceses of London, Ontario and Montreal received the most international visitors—about 11,000 each. Some pilgrims from overseas joined members of their own families who had emigrated to Canada years earlier, and for them WYD became a faith-based family gathering.

After Days in the Diocese, it was on to Toronto, where the municipal council and the residents of Canada's largest city welcomed

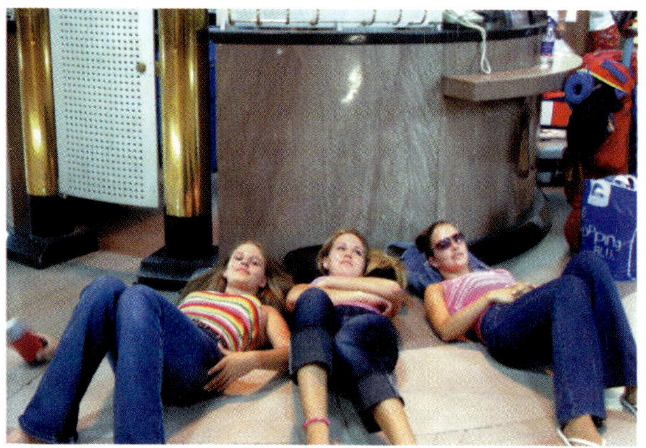

hosts and foreign visitors alike. About 118,000 of the more than 200,000 registered participants stayed in 395 school gymnasiums, another 40,000 were billeted in homes. Some 12,000 were housed in 150 hotels, while the rest were accommodated in various retreat centres, community centres, armouries or other facilities in the Toronto area.

Pilgrims from over 170 nations flooded the downtown core. Easily recognizable by their blue World Youth Day bandanas, and by the flags and banners they carried with them everywhere, the young people took in the city's many sights. They also wore the simple wooden cross that was included in their red and beige pilgrim backpacks, which were produced by inmates in Canada's federal prisons as part of an employment training program. A group of low-income youth from Colombia had crafted the crosses, and the income from the project was used to further their studies and to help their families.

After settling into their temporary quarters, pilgrims made their way by subway, bus, train and foot to Exhibition Place, on the shores of Lake Ontario, for the official welcoming ceremonies for Pope John Paul II. They cheered wildly as large screens set up near the main stage showed his arrival in the city. They gasped, screamed and praised God as the frail, 82-year-old pontiff appeared remarkably well following several days of rest at an island retreat on Lake Simcoe, north of Toronto.

The pope's arrival in Canada a few days before his first public appearance at World Youth Day set the tone for many surprises that would follow. He appeared at the door of the Alitalia airliner, waved to the crowd and, to the surprise of the official welcoming party and the international media, descended the 27 steps to the tarmac without the aid of the hydraulic lift that many had expected him to use.

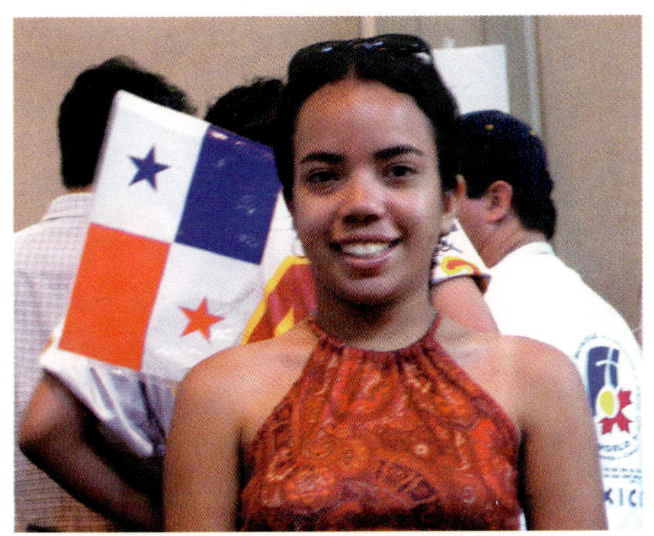 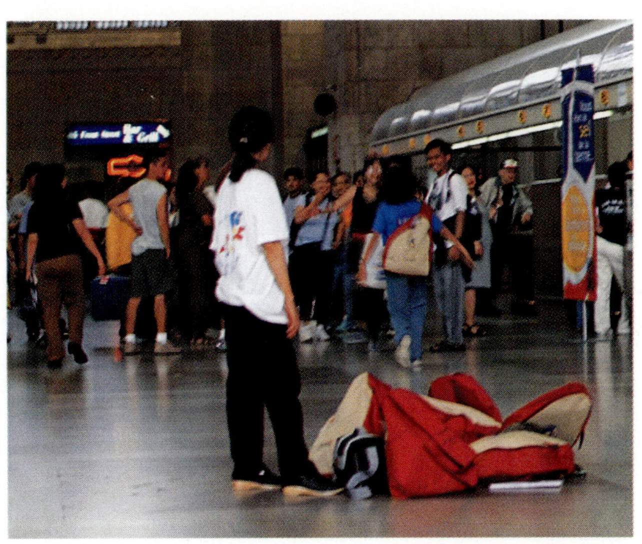

*B*ut today Jesus' voice resounds in the midst of our gathering. His is a voice of life, of hope, of forgiveness, a voice of justice and of peace. Let us listen to this voice!

JOHN PAUL II

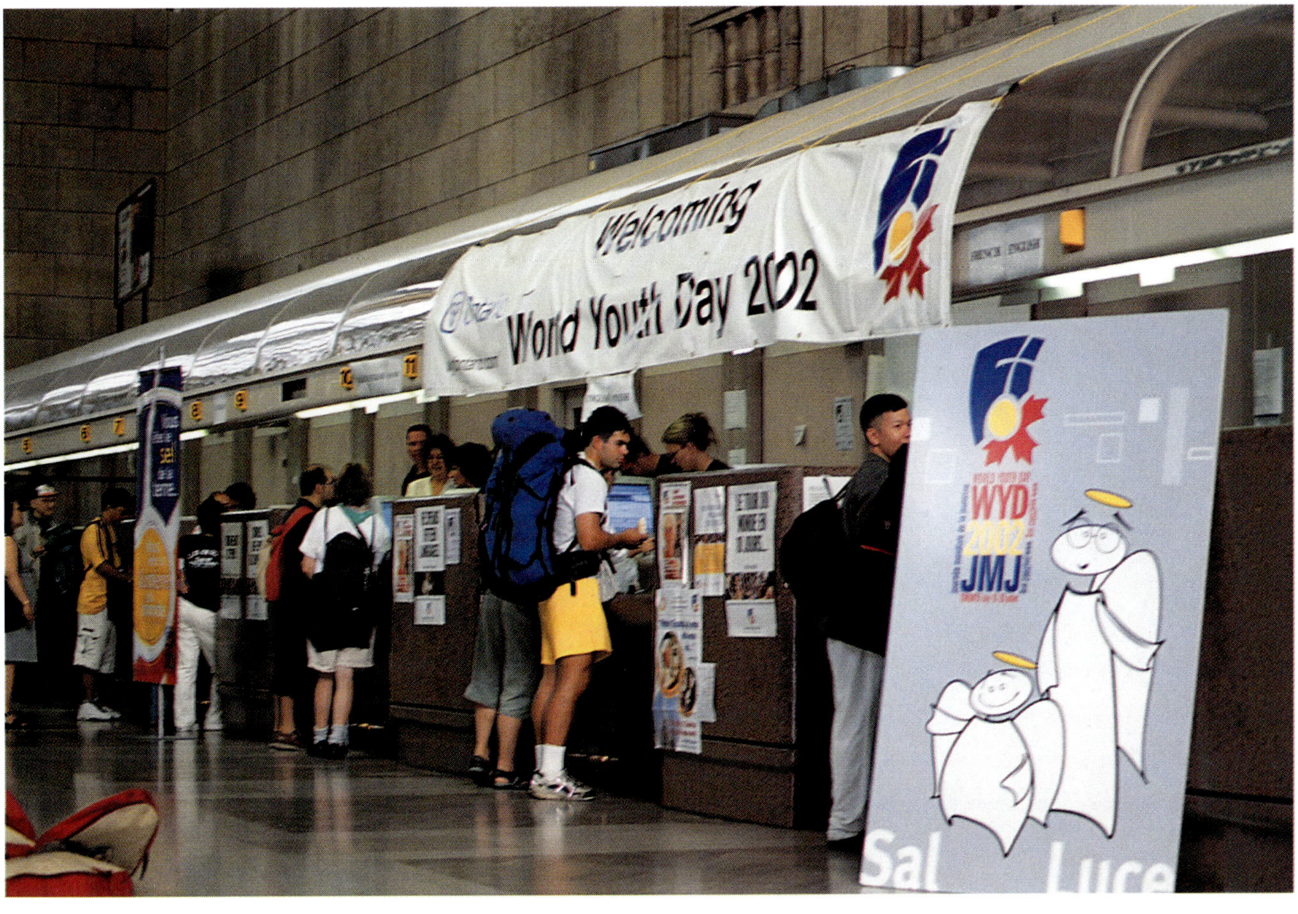

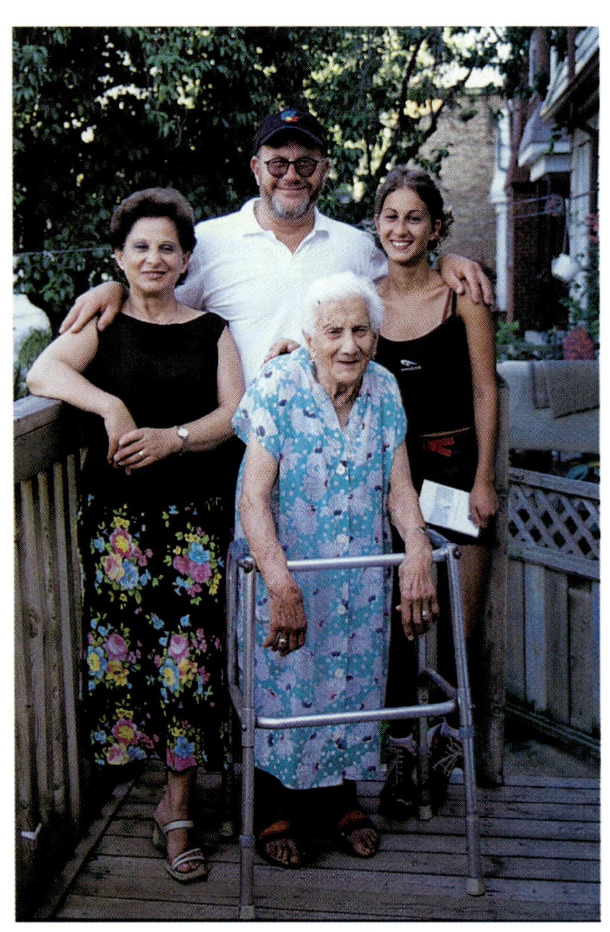

*Communication! Love!
Be a healthy influence on society
to help break down the barriers
that have been raised between
generations! No barriers!
Communion between
generations, between parents
and sons and daughters.
Communion!*

JOHN PAUL II
World Youth Day 1995—Manila

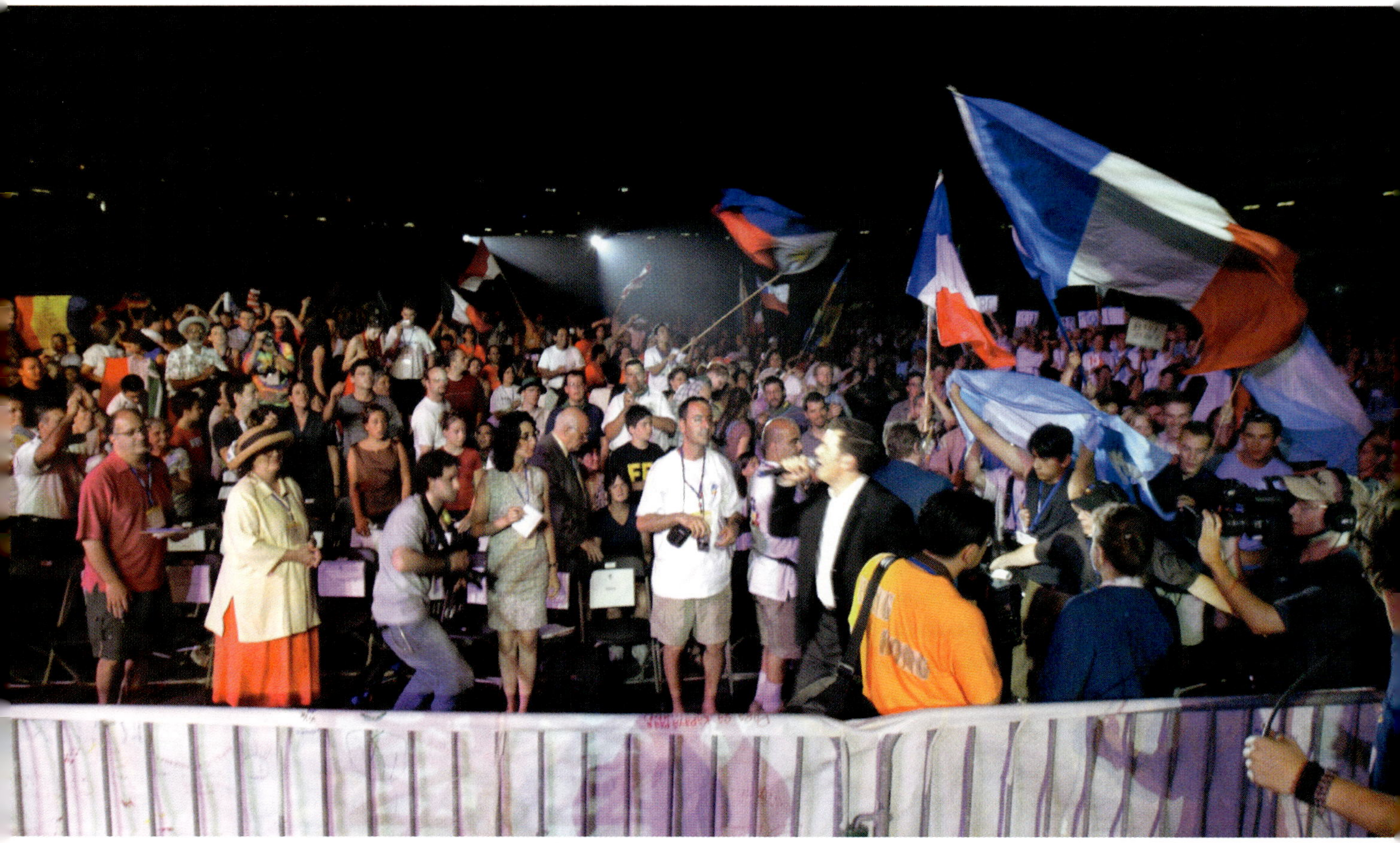

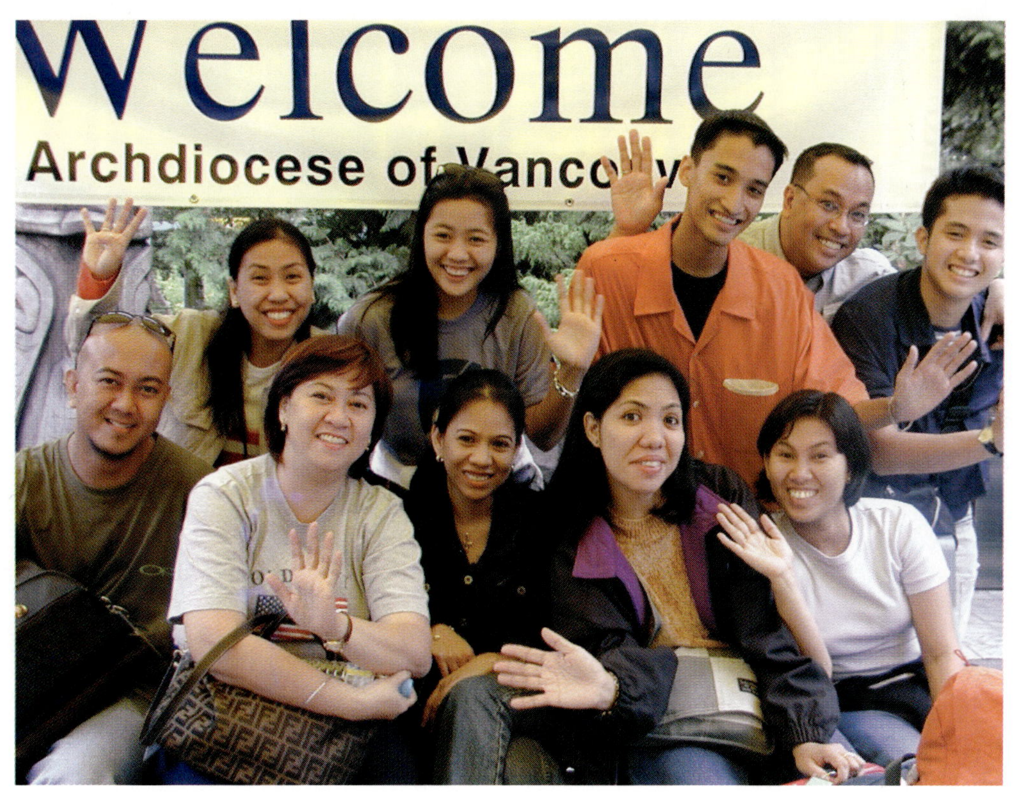

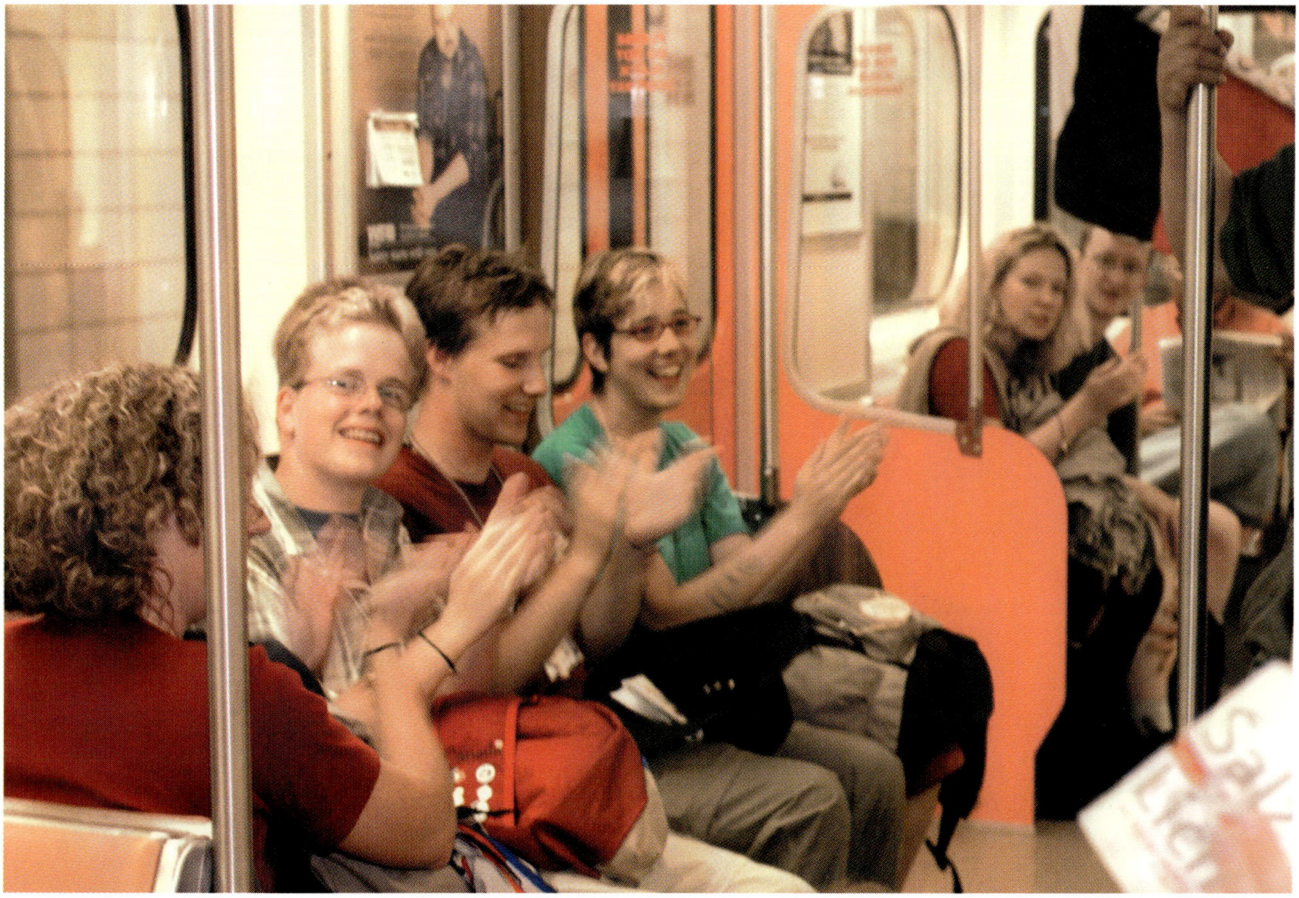

Just like everyone else

It's the end of the first day in Toronto. The streetcar is packed to overflowing. A hundred people, maybe more, all crammed together. Canadians, Belgians, Americans, Mexicans. As they strike up their national anthem or sing their favourite songs—each group louder than the next—the music is punctuated by jokes and great bursts of laughter.

A teenaged girl is seated by the half-open window. Her name could be Anne or Kate or Pat; we'll call her Jessie. She's with a group of young Manitobans, and does she have a set of lungs! Jessie can raise the roof with that voice of hers. She calls out excitedly through the streetcar window to the pilgrims walking along the sidewalk: "Where are you from? What country?" Jessie reacts instantly to any response from the smiling pedestrians with a booming "Hurray for Canada! Hurray for the pope! Hurray for World Youth Day!" She whistles at two handsome guys and exclaims sadly, for all to hear, "They're cute! Too bad they're not from here!" More laughter all around. She plays this little game at least a dozen times. Tourists, bystanders, residents, pilgrims—Jessie's enthusiasm spares no one, not even a clutch of people leaving a funeral home, who are moved to smiles at her infectious exuberance.

There are thousands and thousands of enthusiastic, happy Jessies in Toronto this week for the gigantic religious event known as World Youth Day. And they have absolutely no hangups about gathering together to celebrate their faith and their Catholic identity. Are these young people typical of others their age? After watching Jessie and her companions, it's obvious that they're much like young people the world over: same youth culture, same interests, same needs and wants.

But there is one profound difference: they've discovered Christ's path and they are following it —every day, wherever they are, all the way to Toronto.

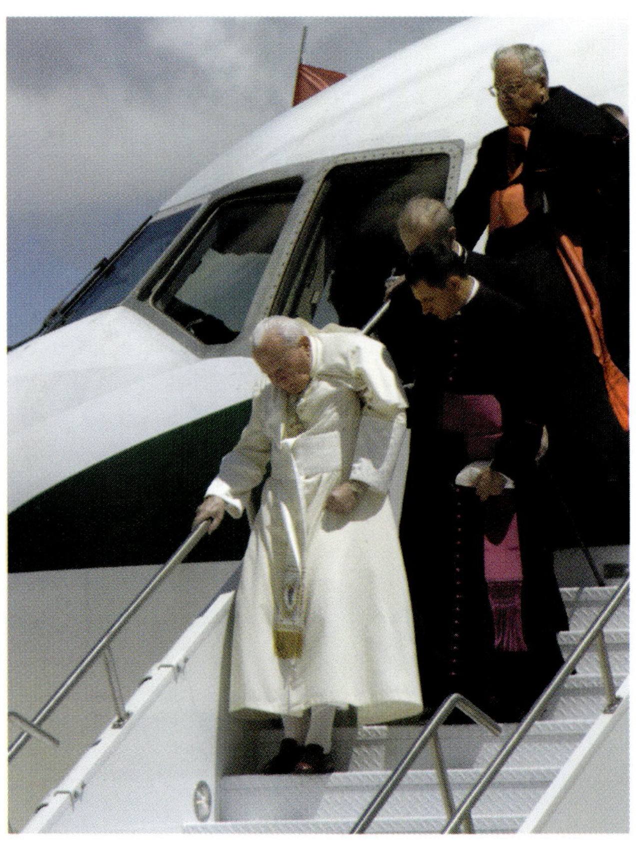

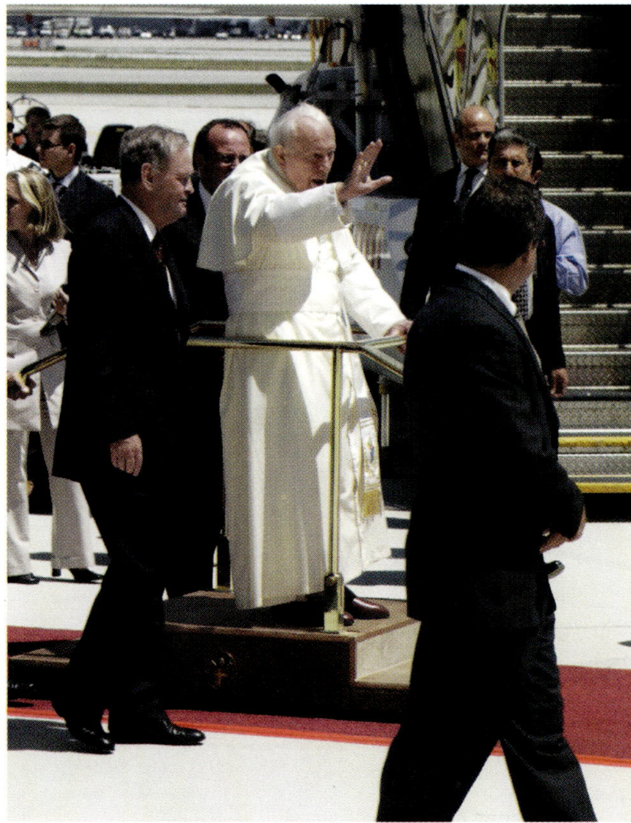

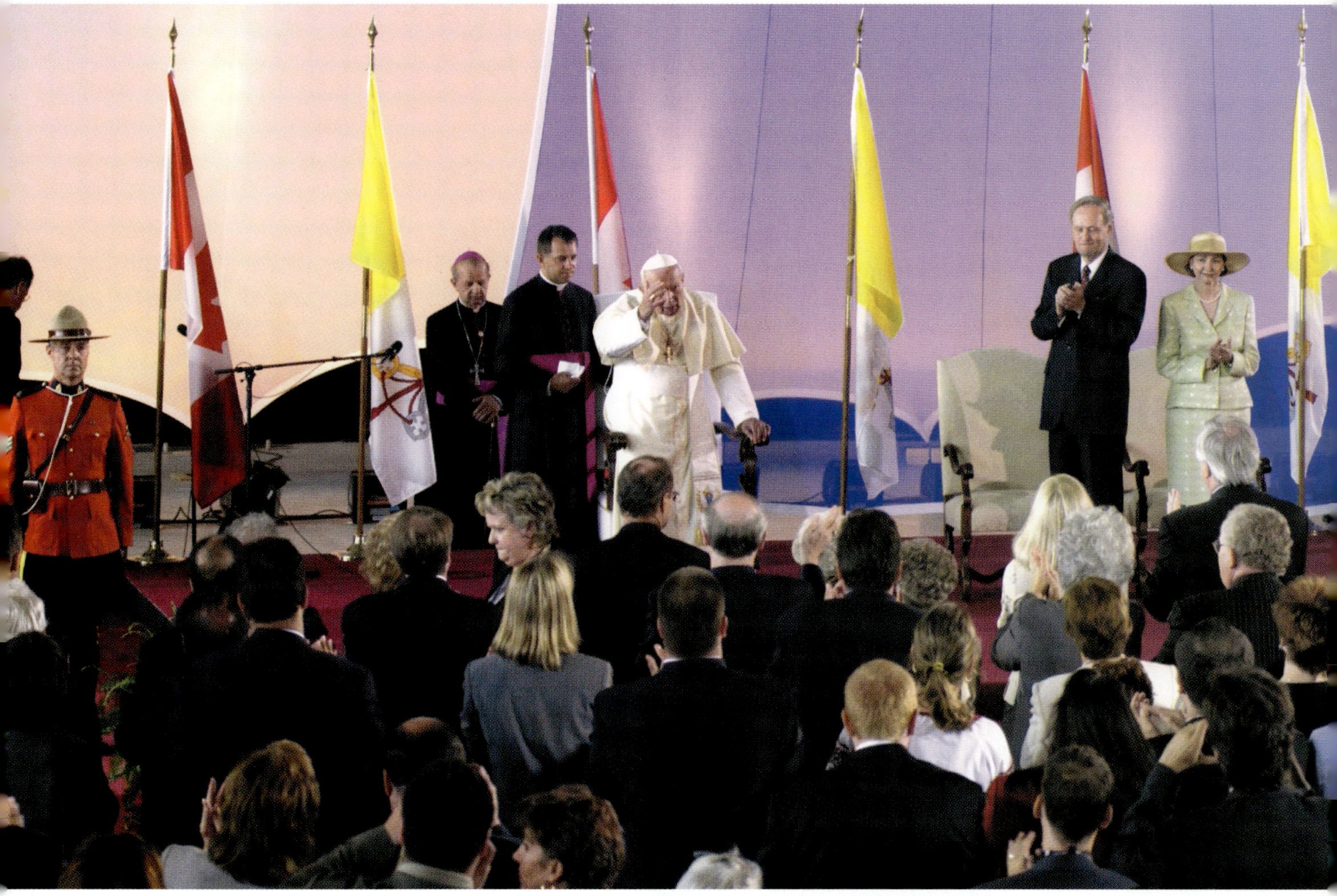

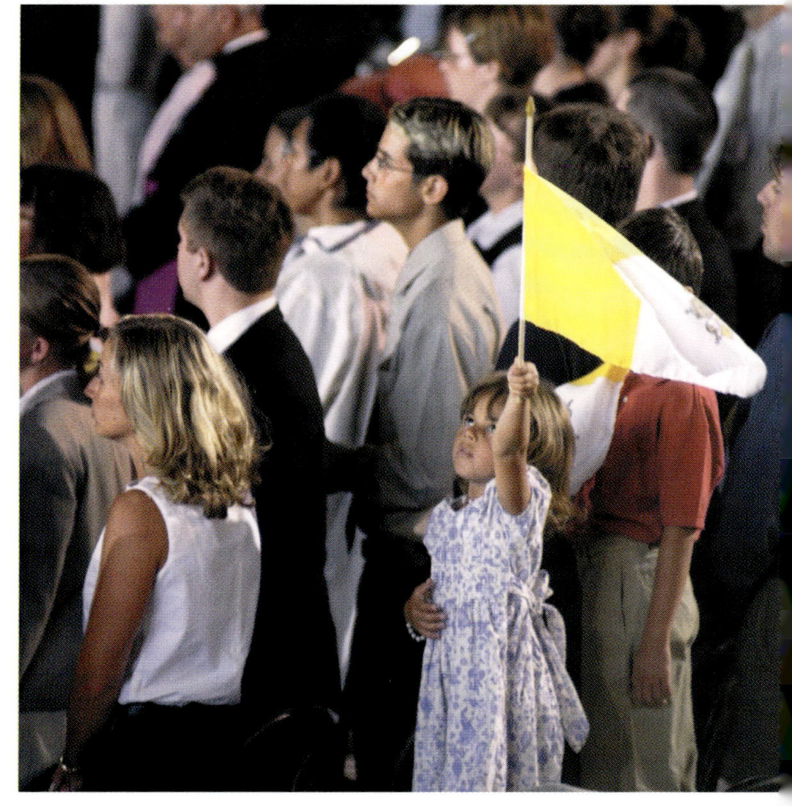

Mr. Prime Minister, dear friends: may the motto of World Youth Day echo throughout the land, reminding all Christians to be "salt of the earth and light to the world." God bless you all. God bless Canada.

JOHN PAUL II

World Youth Day 2002 Begins

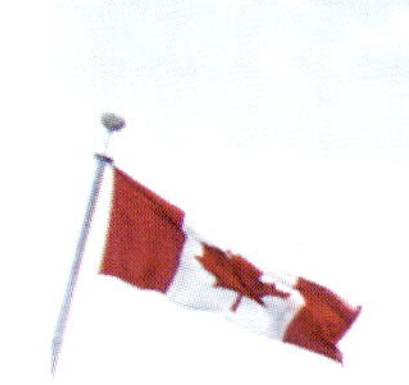

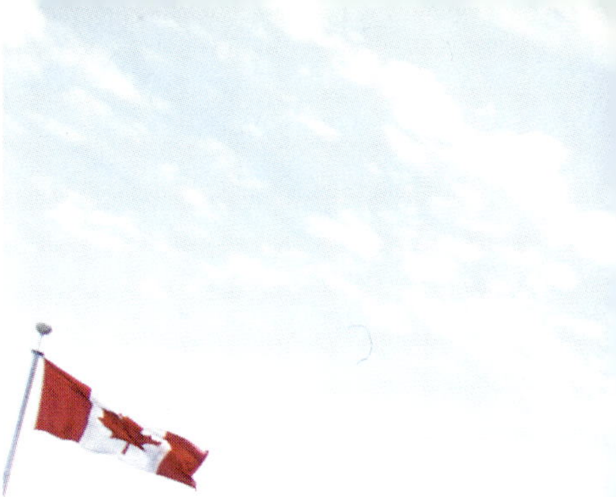

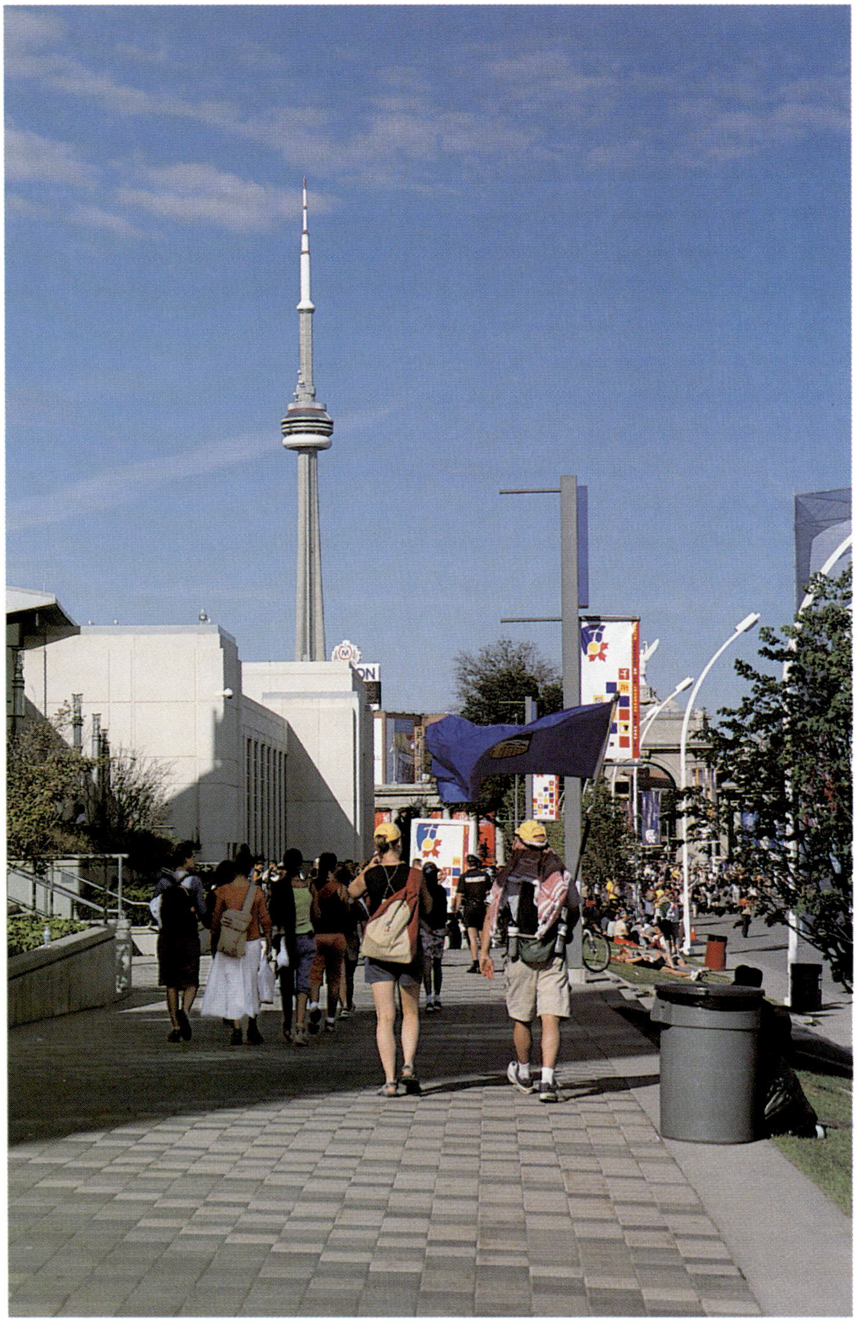

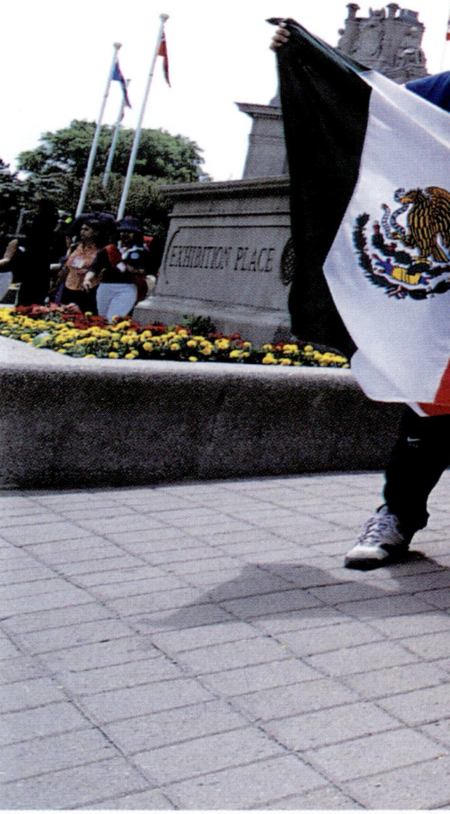

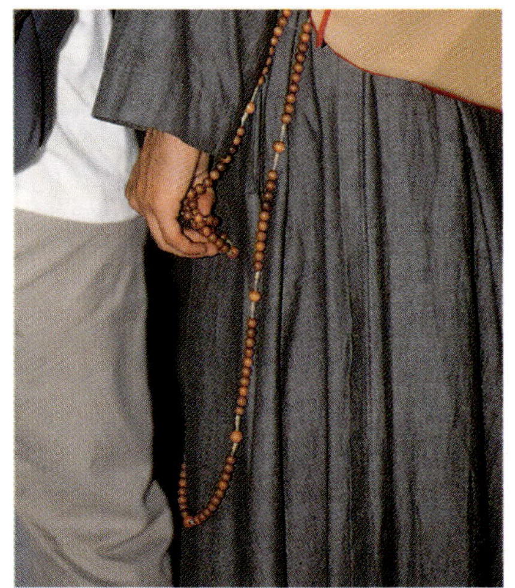

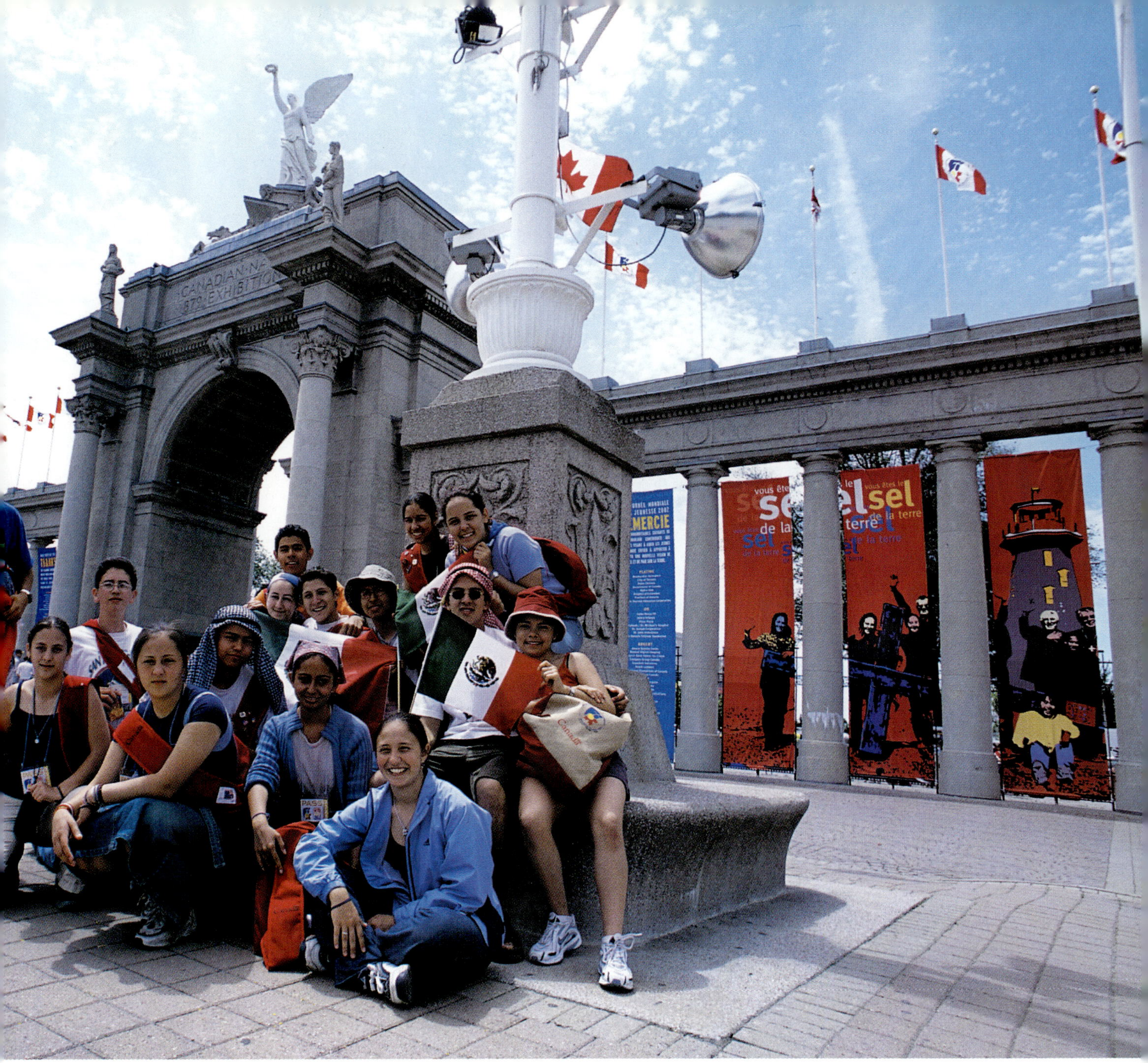

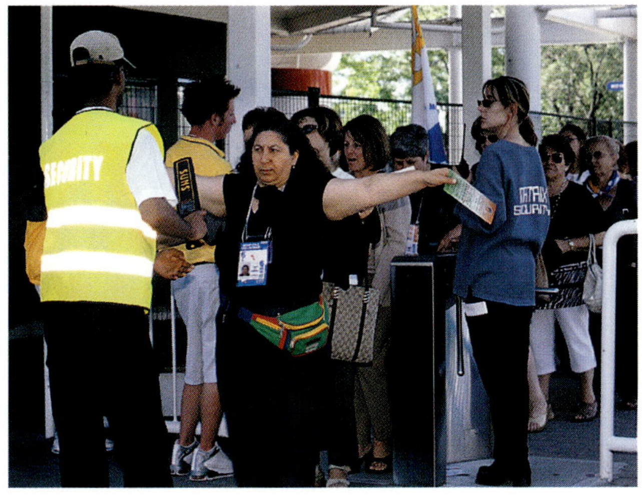

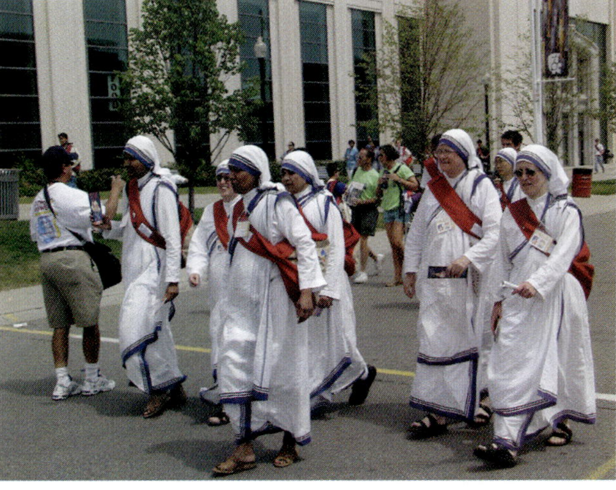

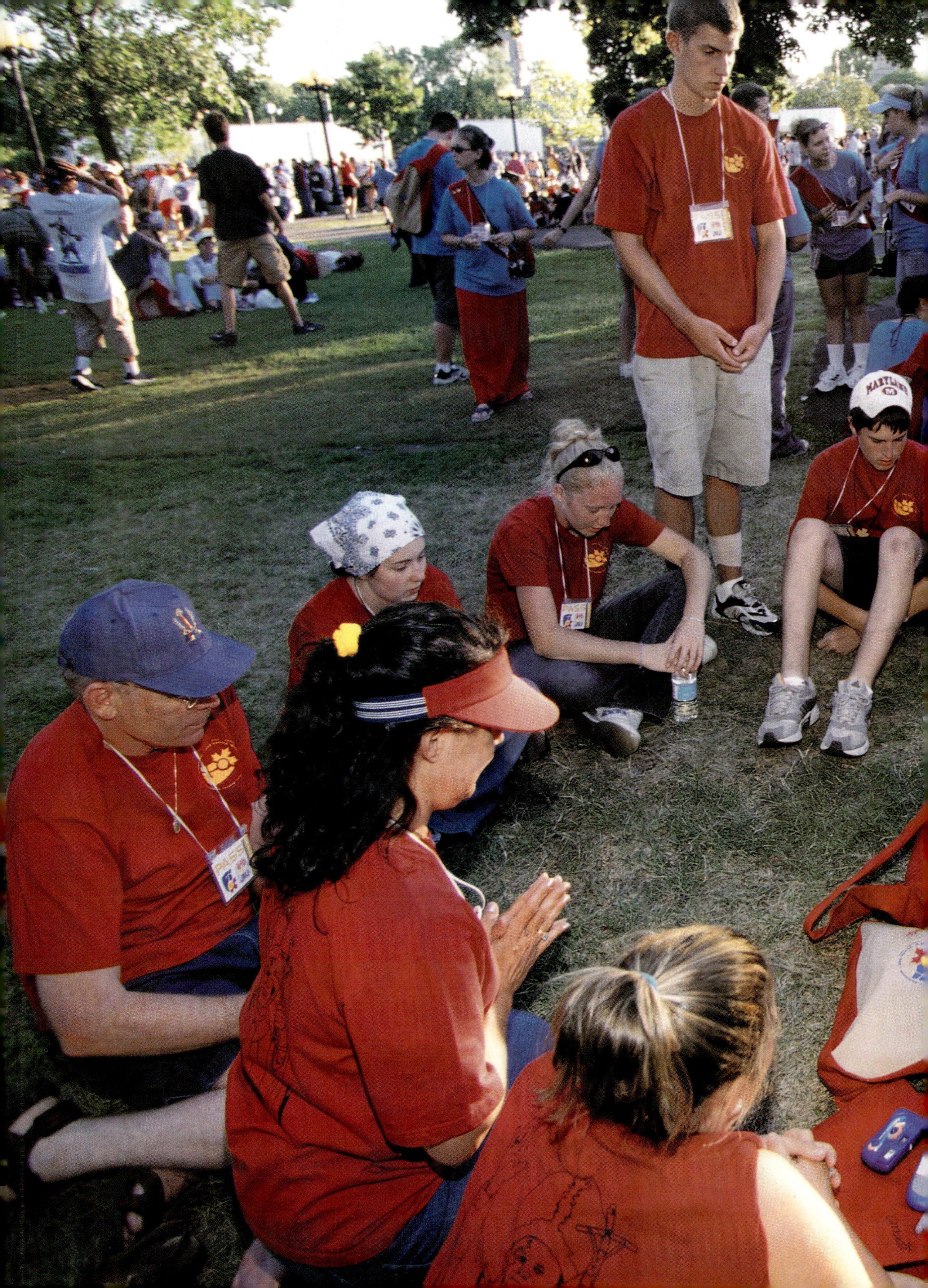

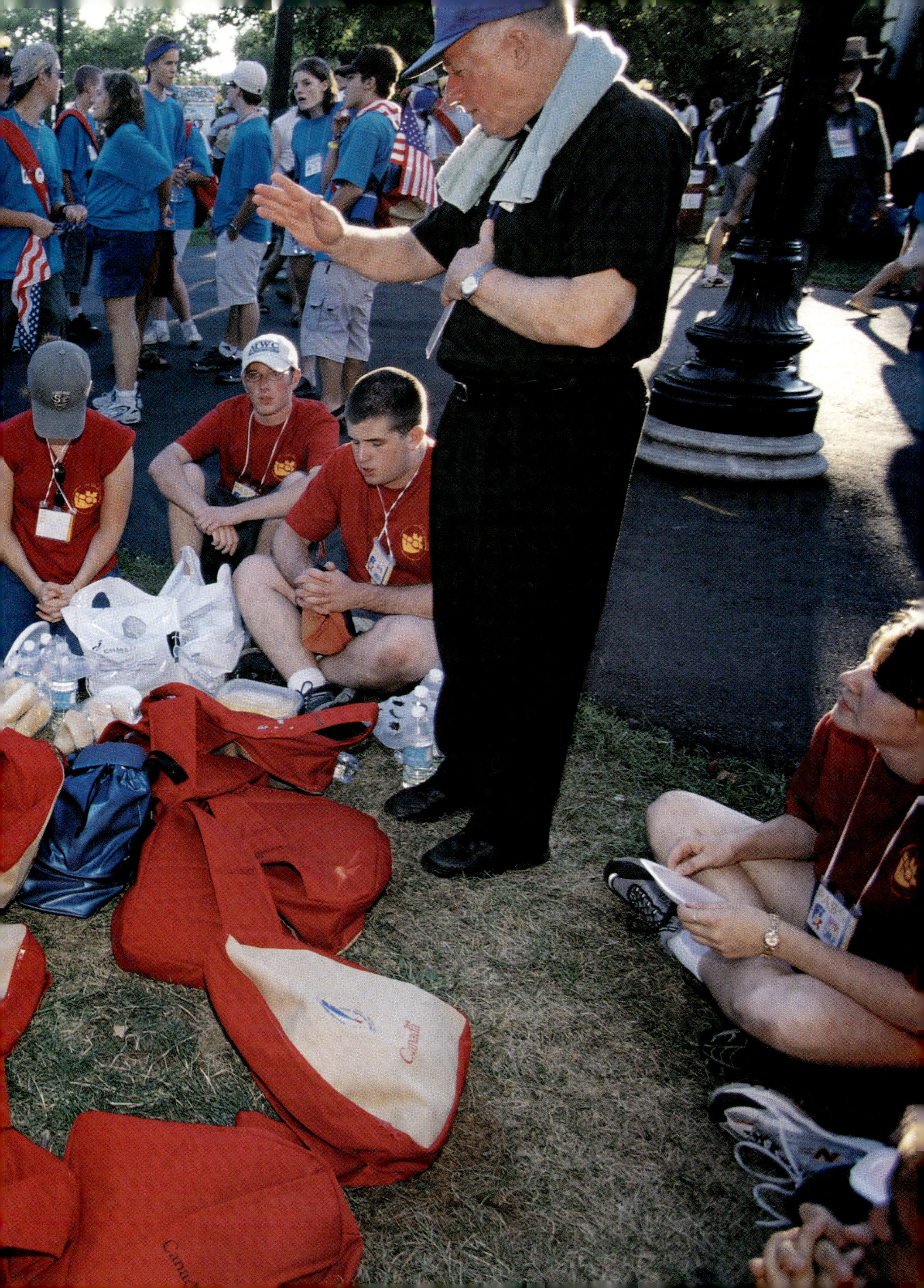

The great avenues of Toronto resound with the joyful tidings that Christ loves every person

The stage and the viewing areas at Exhibition Place were awash in the colourful flags from each of the 170 nations participating in WYD. This is where some 250,000 World Youth Day participants met together for the first time at the opening mass of welcome.

Youth on the Move, a group of about 40 young people from Toronto, opened the ceremony, singing a medley of theme songs from previous World Youth Days as footage from these events appeared on large screens all over the grounds. The same young people who had first received the World Youth Day Cross from Pope John Paul II on Palm Sunday, 2001 carried it onto the stage, in the culmination of an epic 43,000-kilometre journey to dioceses all across Canada.

The 500-member World Youth Day Choir and the choir of St. Michael's led the singing during the penitential rite and the reception of communion.

Cardinal Aloysius Ambrozic, Archbishop of Toronto, was the main celebrant at the mass, whose liturgical theme was the Transfiguration, when the apostles Peter, James and John were spiritually transformed by their encounter with Christ in his divine glory.

"By being with Jesus, by listening to him and following him, we become one with him," the cardinal said. "We become suffused with his own light. We become light ourselves 'You are the light of the world; You are the salt of the earth' (Matthew 5:13-14)."

While the homily and readings from the mass offered food for the hearts and minds of the pilgrims, it was the Eucharist that provided spiritual nourishment for their souls. Scores of bishops from around the world concelebrated the mass with the cardinal and helped distribute communion to the enormous international congregation. In the concluding rite, youths shared a brief reflection on the need to live the faith openly and without compromise, on the importance of setting a personal example, and on the challenge of building what Pope John Paul II describes as a new "civilization of love" in the third millennium.

Having been filled with food for the spirit during the three-hour mass, the participants then turned their attention to food for the body —and there was plenty available. About 15,000 meals were served at each meal period in each of the food service tents for a total of 3.5 million meals over the six days. Later that evening, a concert featuring Canadian talent allowed the exuberant World Youth Day pilgrims to burn off some excess energy.

Sharing a common unity in Christ, the pilgrims from different cultures developed an *esprit de corps* that endowed them with a strong sense of community during their short stay in Canada's most multicultural city. Together they sang, prayed, broke bread, laughed and shed tears. They exchanged badges, buttons, addresses—and even their hats. They bore one another's burdens and comforted each other.

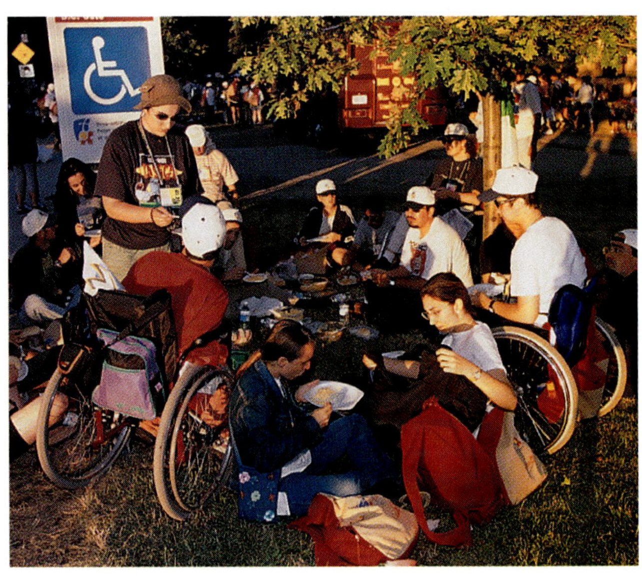

Behind each of you I have glimpsed the faces of all of your fellow young people whom I have met in the course of my apostolic travels and whom, in a way, you represent here. I have imagined you on a journey, walking in the shadow of the Jubilee Cross, on this great youth pilgrimage which, moving from continent to continent, is eager to hold the world in a close embrace of faith and hope.

JOHN PAUL II

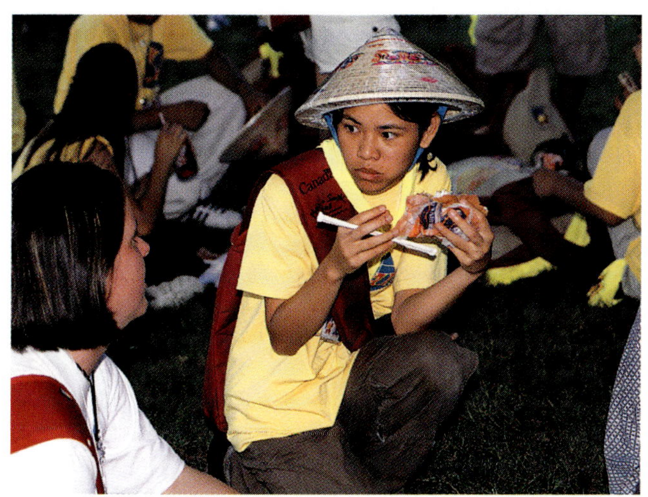

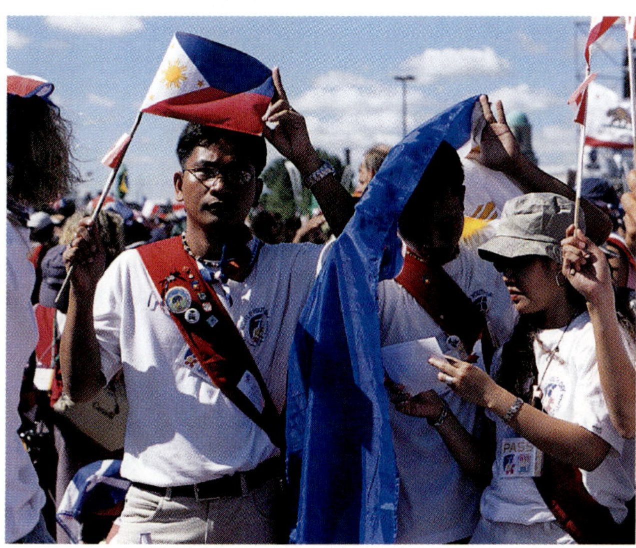

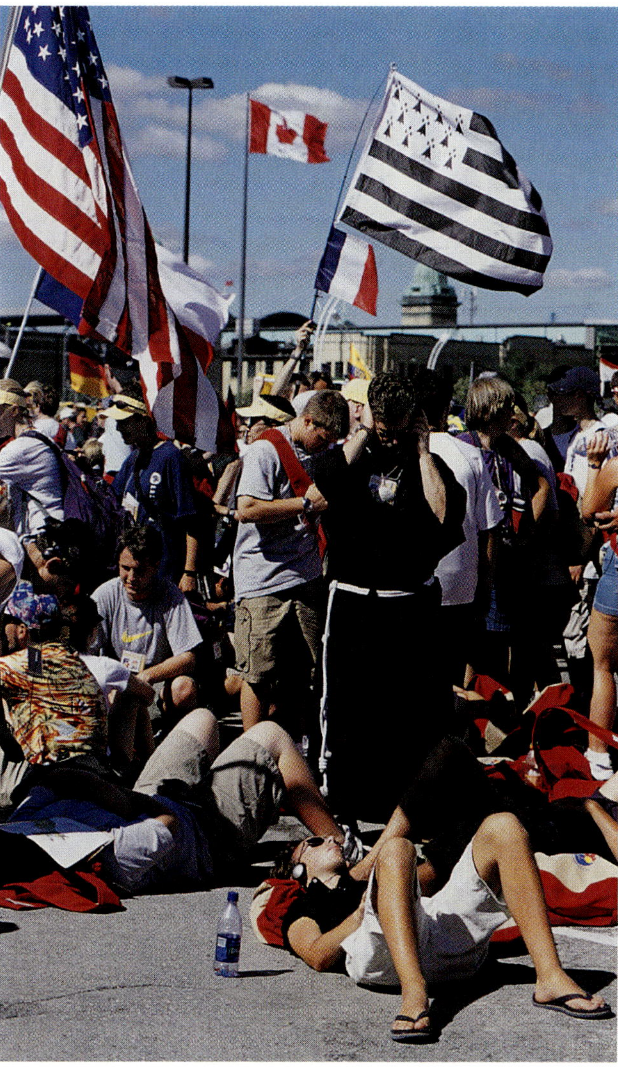

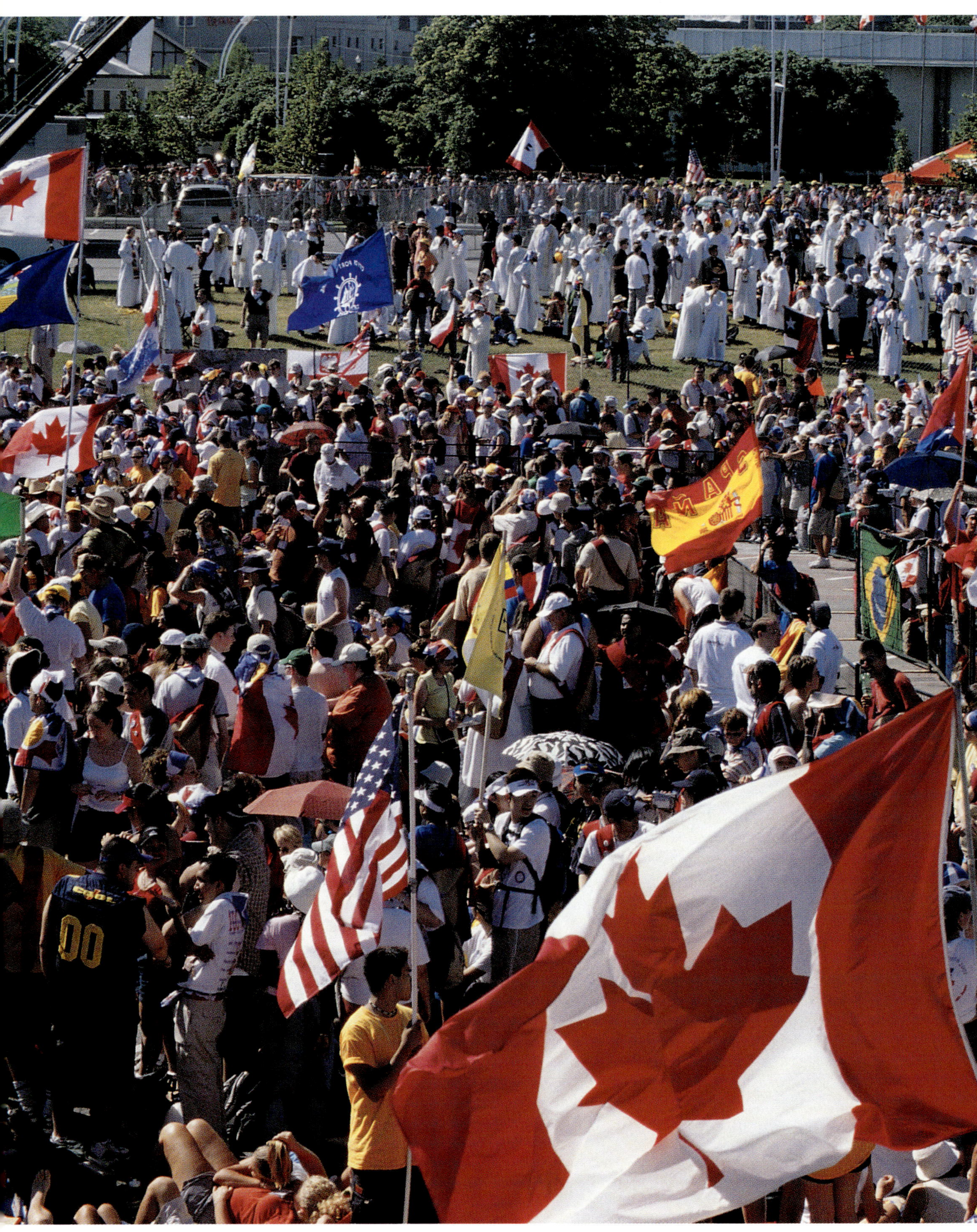

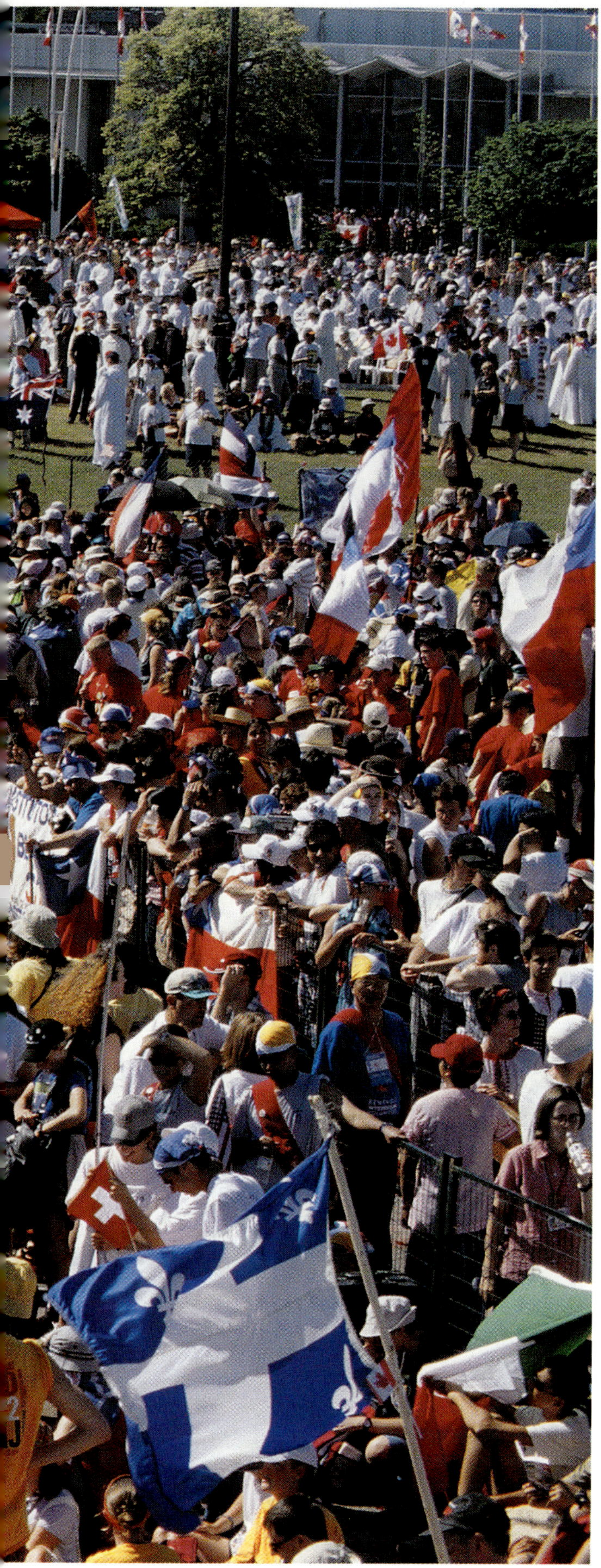

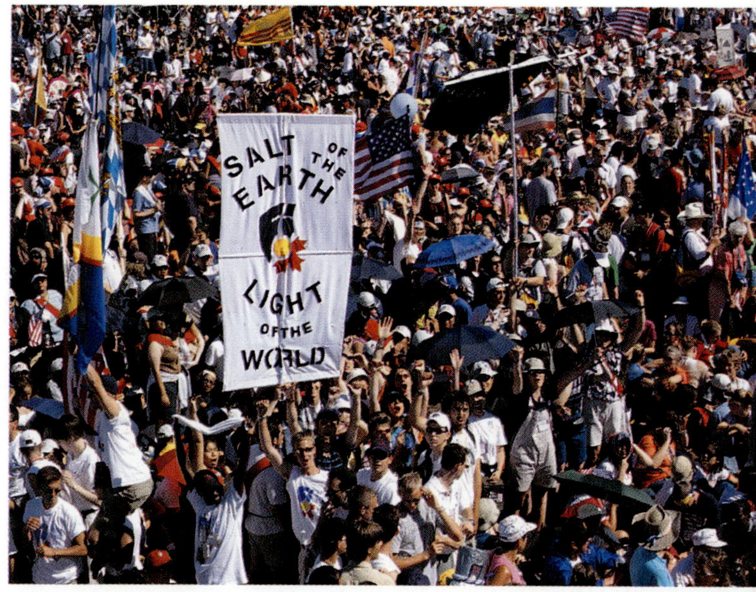

SALT OF THE EARTH
LIGHT OF THE WORLD

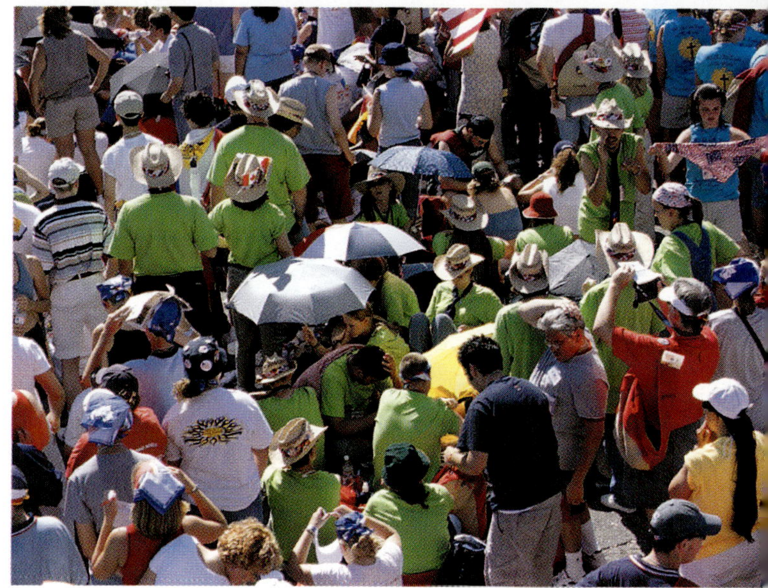

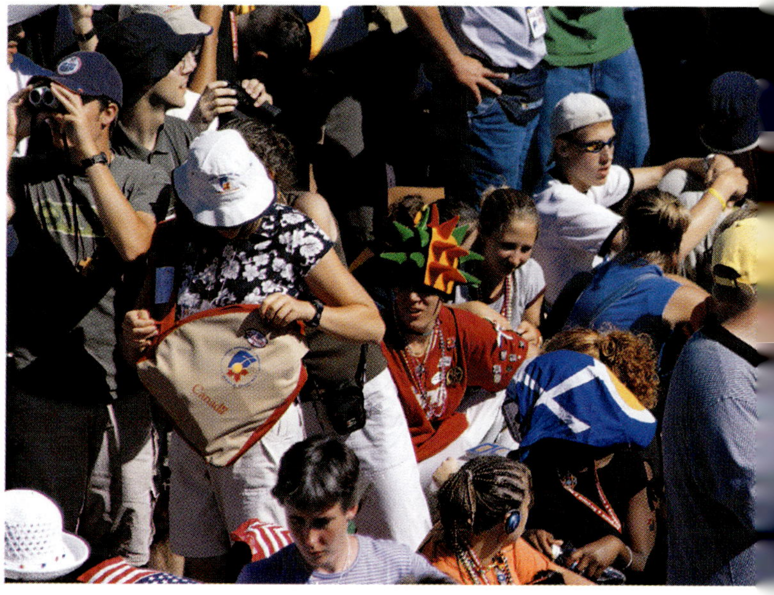

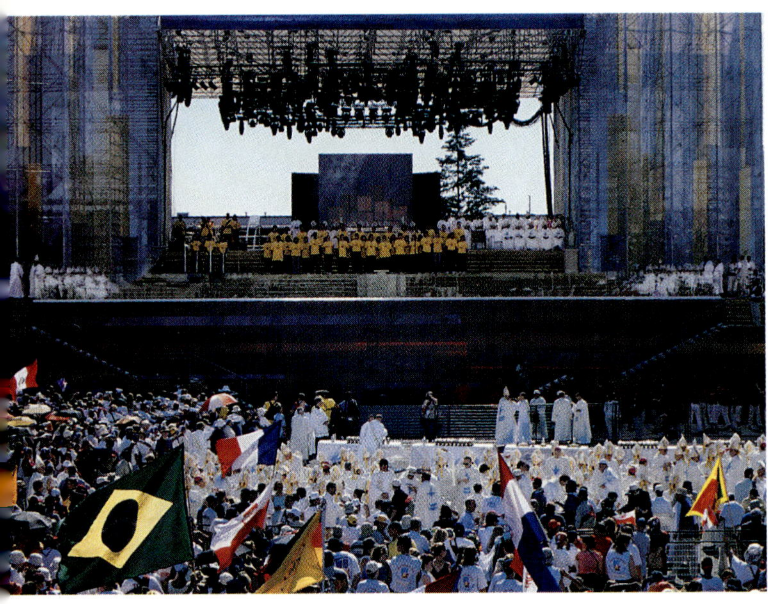

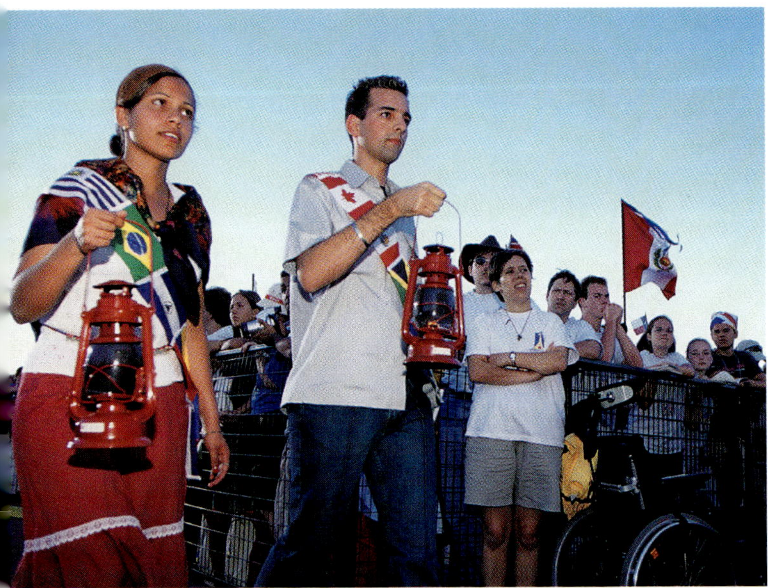

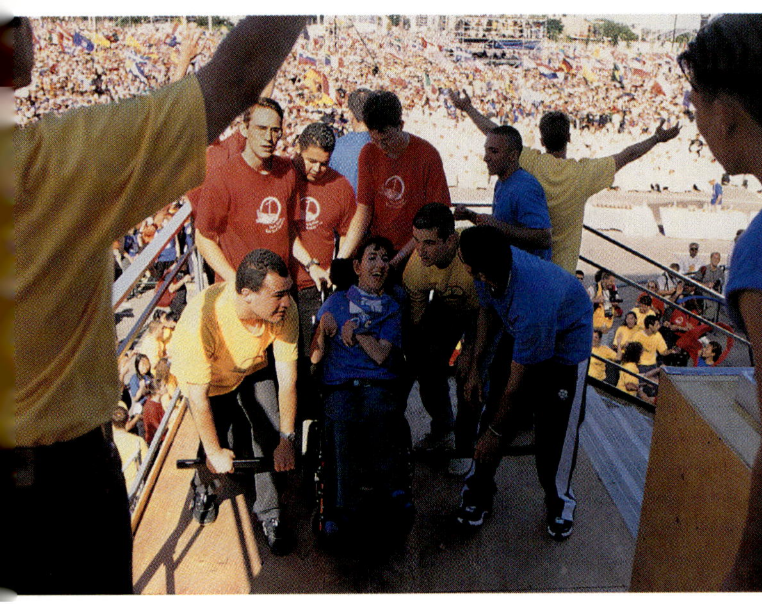

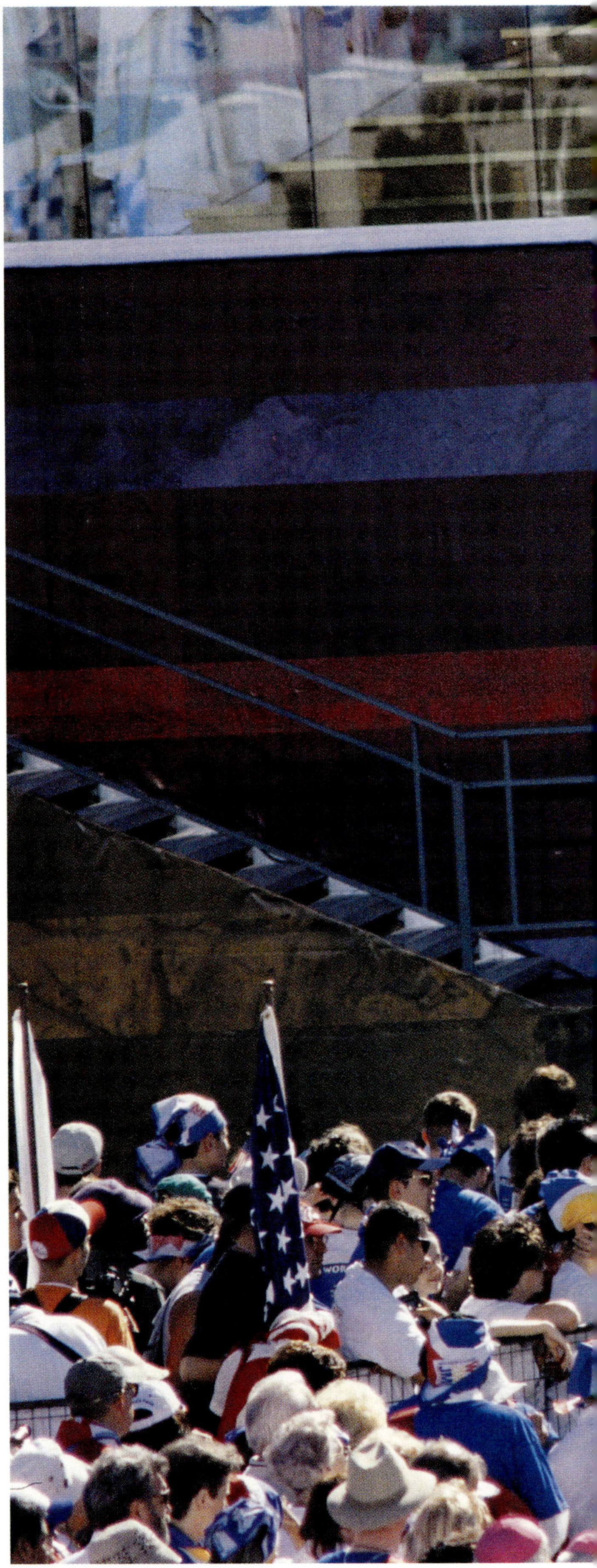

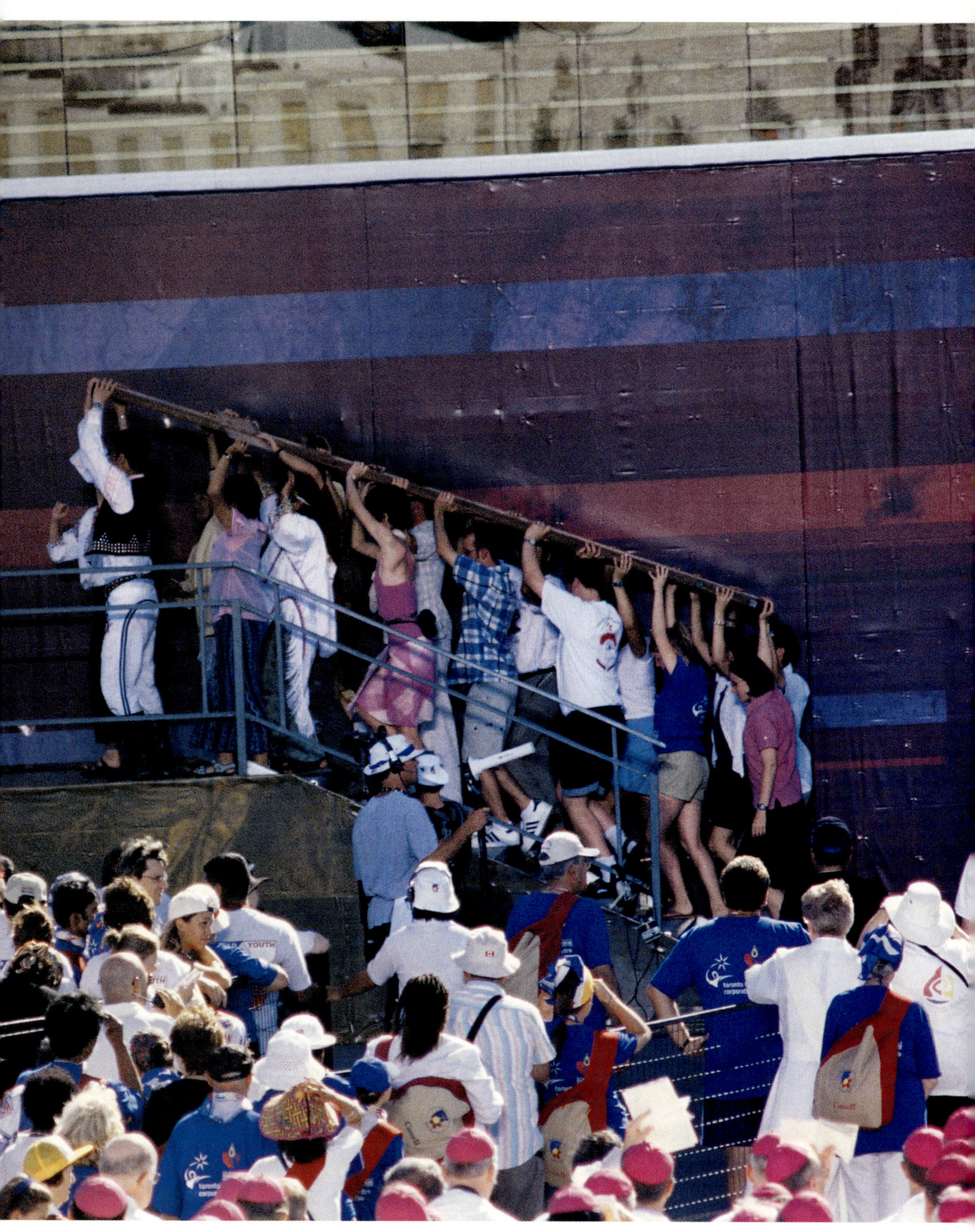

You are the light of the world

It's called Exhibition Place. The site usually hosts commercial events and is best known for the Canadian National Exhibition, held there during the month of August. A sprawling complex of immense exhibition halls with a huge midway, situated on the shores of Lake Ontario, tonight it is host to a very different kind of event. This monument to commerce has given way to a eucharistic celebration of the People of God. World Youth Day planted the cross in the middle of this symbol of power and money as tourists, residents and fairground staff looked on in amazement and wonder.

Under a beautiful, postcard-blue sky, groups of young people appear carrying the flags of their respective countries, all the while singing and dancing to their favourite rhythms. A joyful celebration is taking shape, the exuberance of the young contrasting with the serious demeanour of the clergy presiding over the Eucharist. And in the midst of this happy din, there is prayer as the crowd slowly assembles around the One they are here to celebrate. The cardinals, bishops and priests begin to relax as they become infected with the young people's enthusiasm and joy. The mass begins, and the 17th World Youth Day is officially off and running.

The chief pastor of the Church in Toronto welcomes the pilgrims who have come from every corner of the globe. "In our day-to-day life, in our words, in our most ordinary actions and our entire way of acting and reacting," says the cardinal, "we are asked to show God's countenance to the world. We are asked to be ready to make our defence to anyone who demands from us an accounting for the hope that is in us."

The sun is shining this Tuesday in July, but the clarity and brilliance are coming from the pilgrims assembled here, from the people of salt and light.

*In our day-to-day life, in our words,
in our most ordinary actions and our entire way
of acting and reacting, we are asked to show
God's countenance to the world.
Through us, the world is to be drawn to Jesus,
and with him to the Father.*

CARDINAL ALOYSIUS AMBROZIC

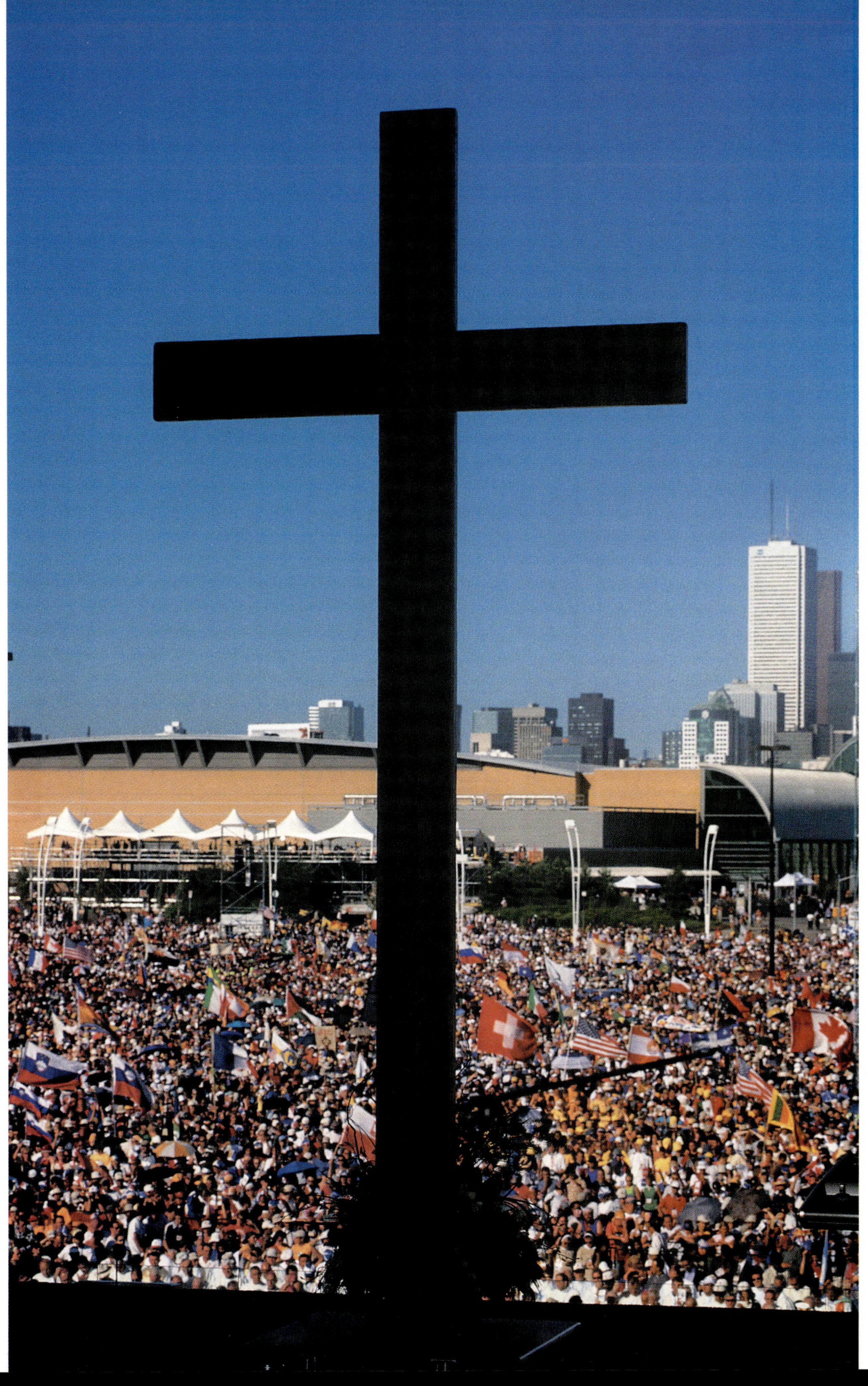

Welcoming Pope John Paul II

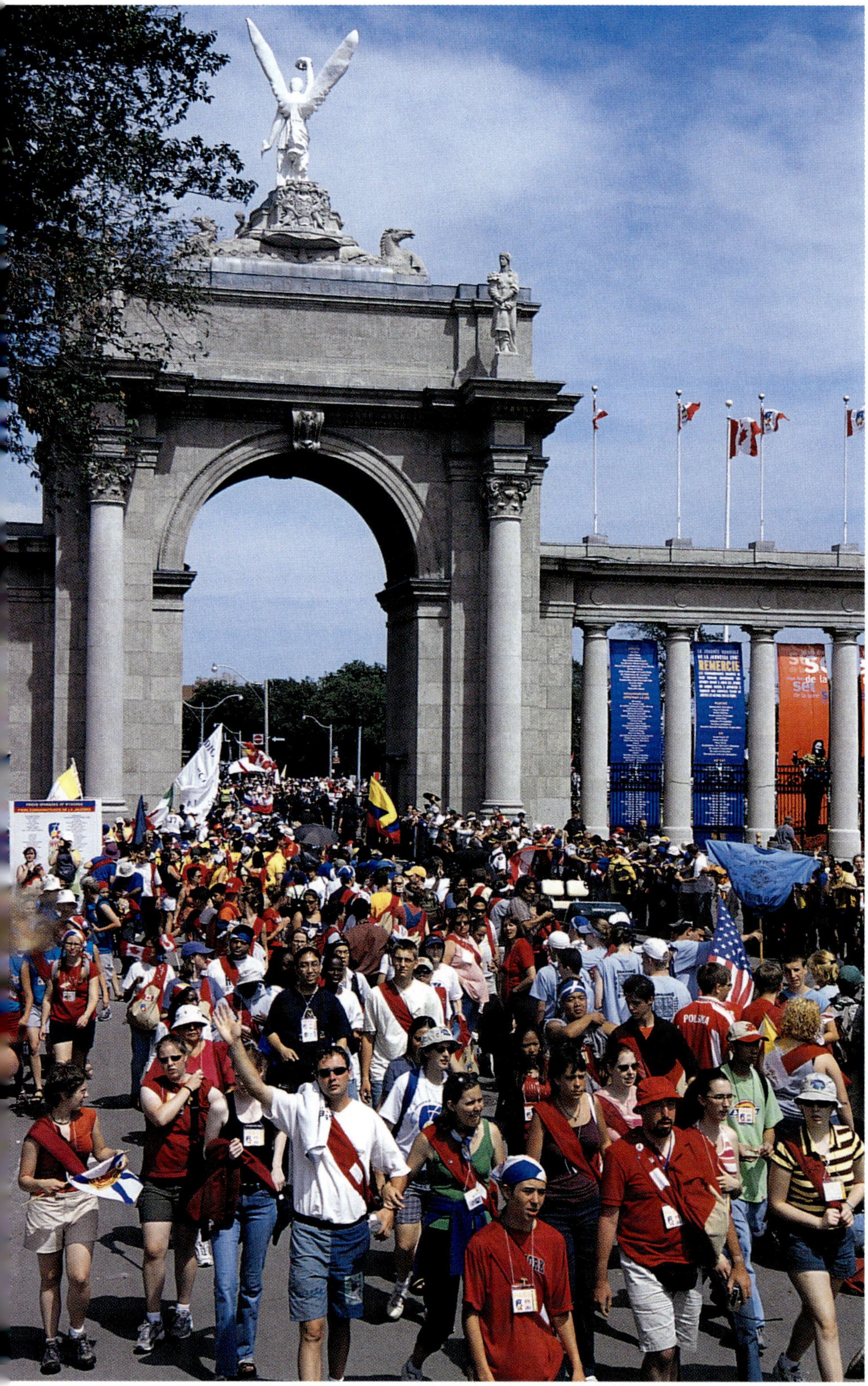

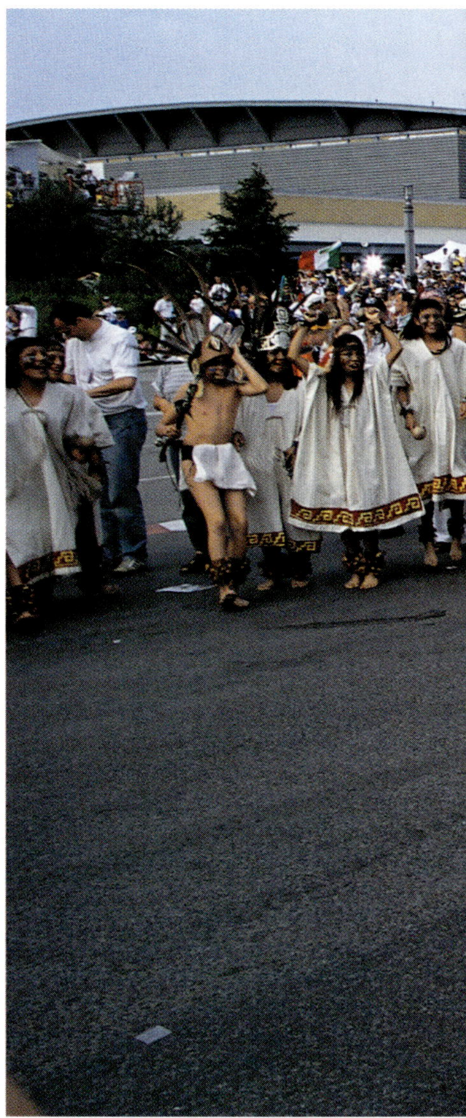

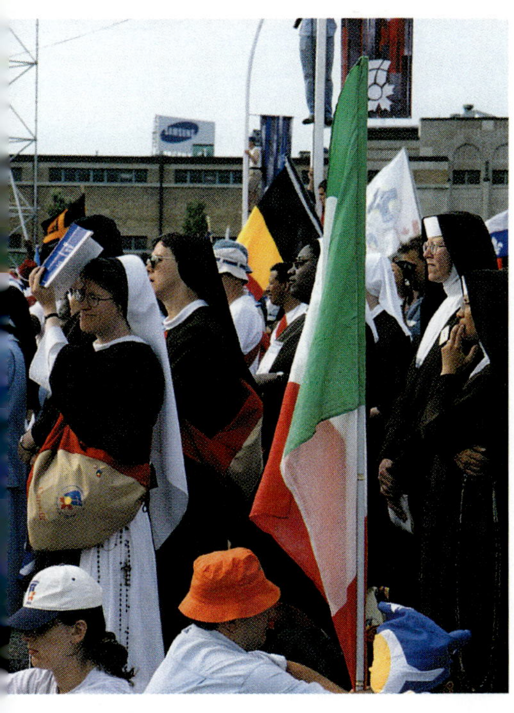
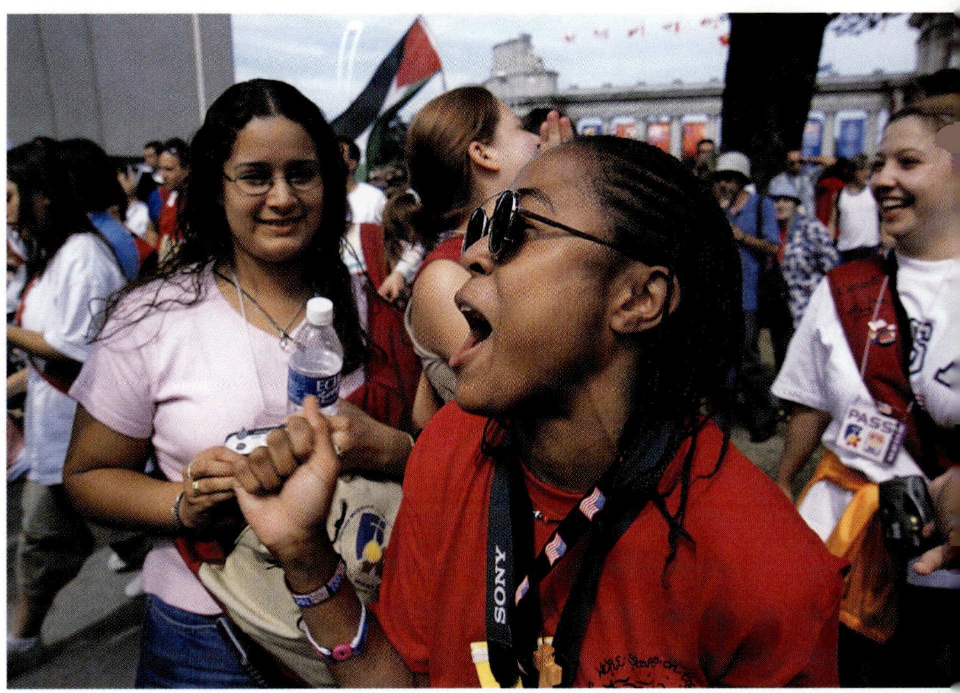

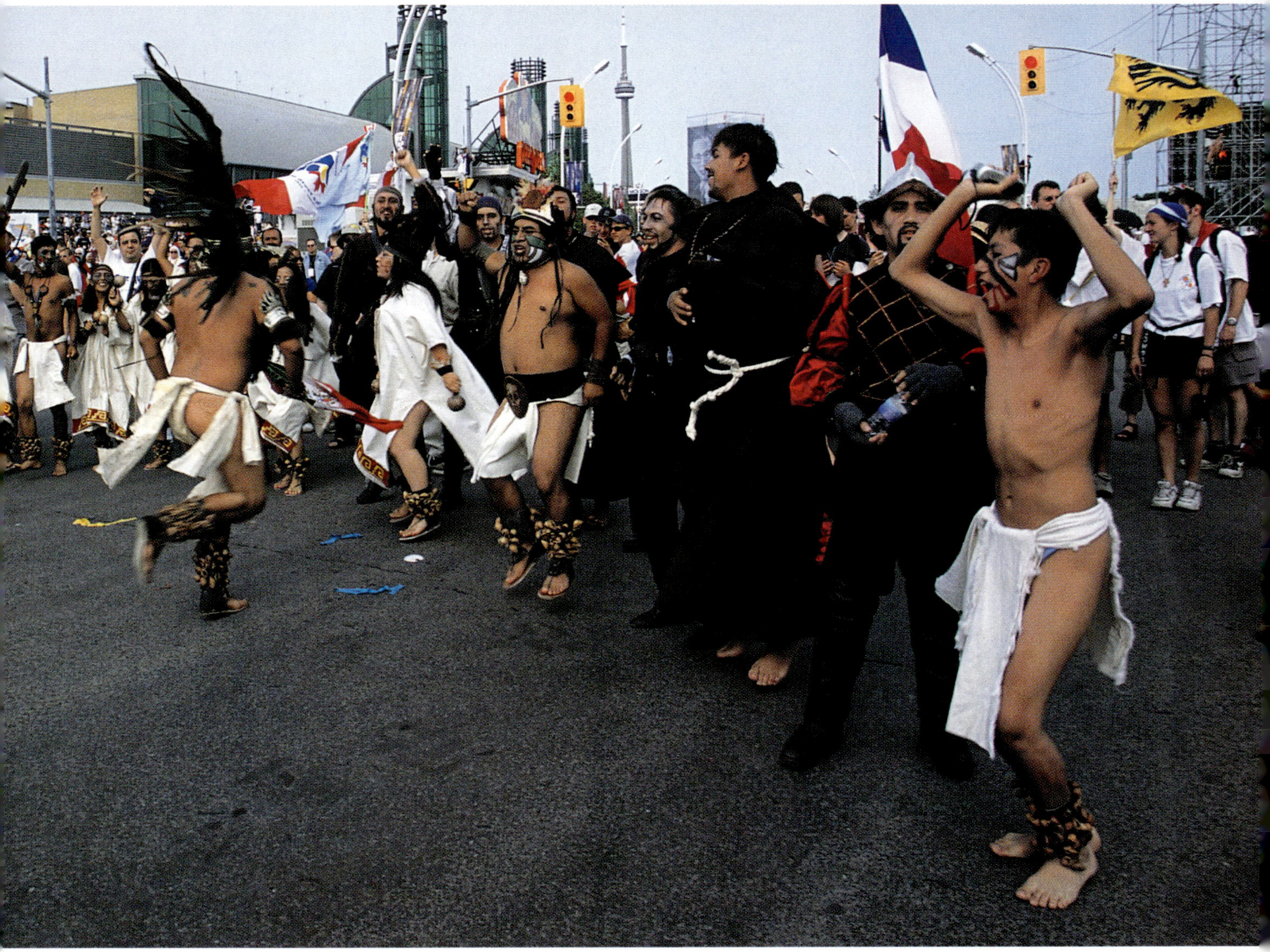

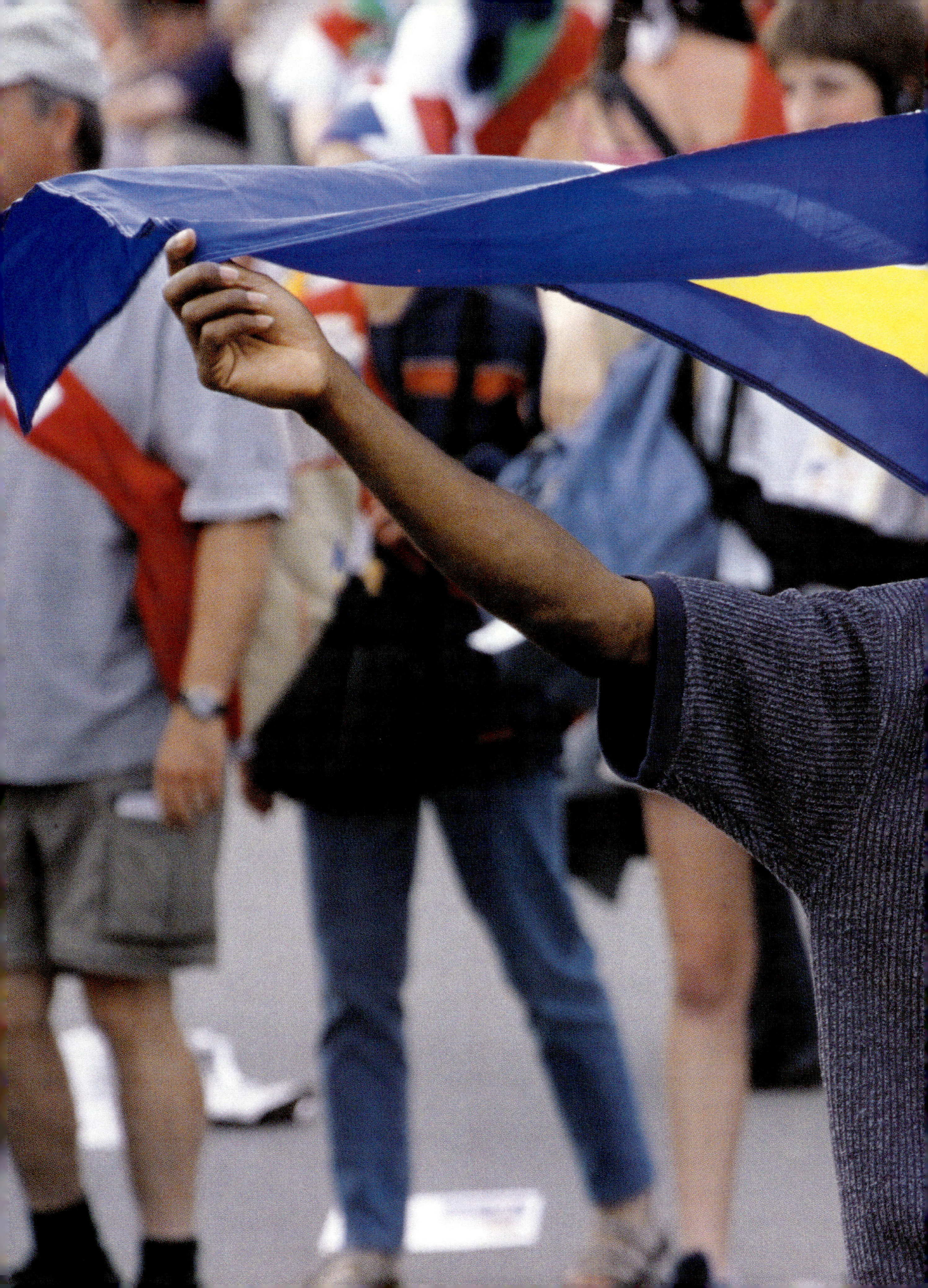

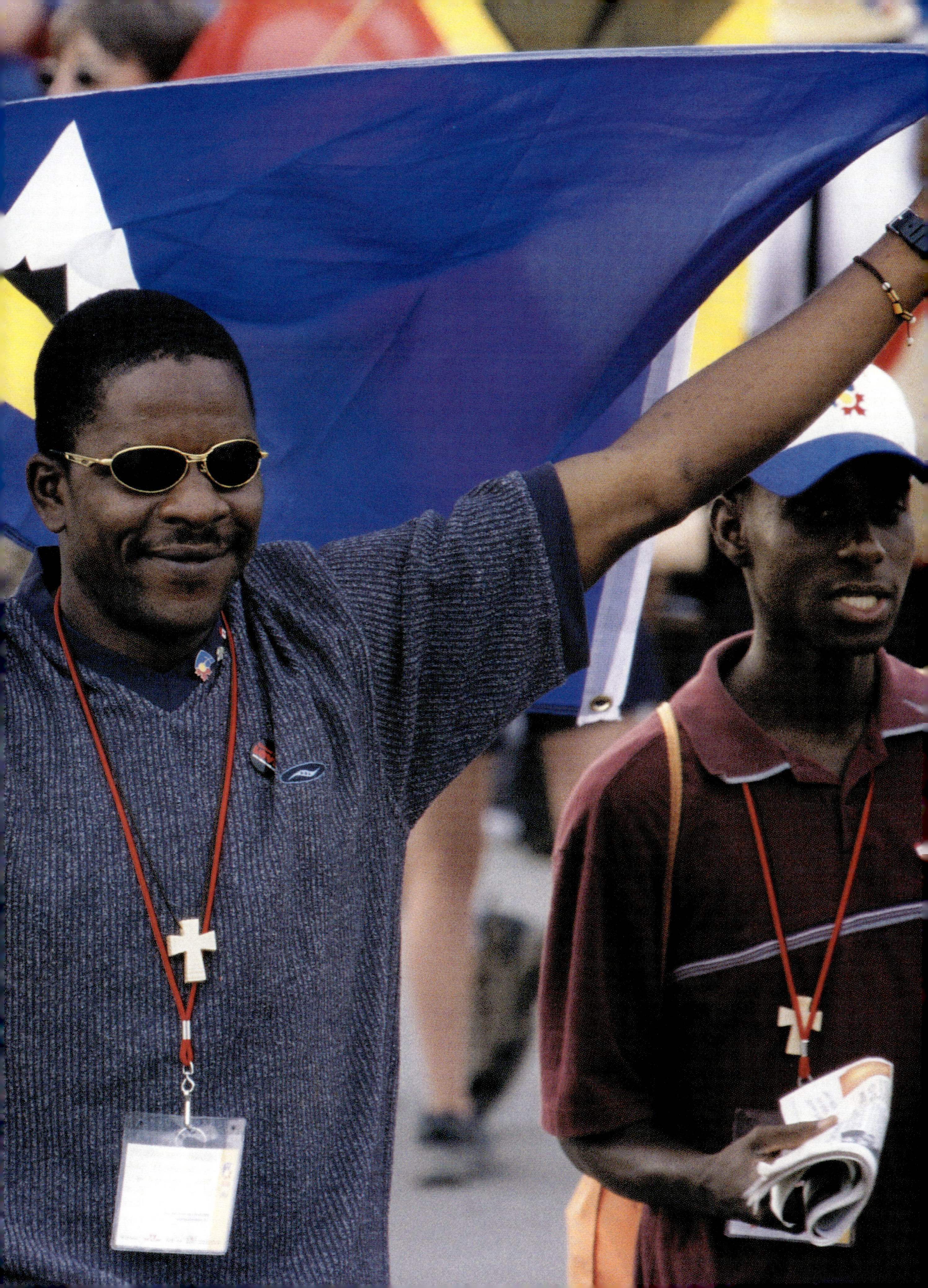

The pope who loves you dearly

The arrival of Pope John Paul II in Canada after a 15-year absence marked one of the most poignant moments of World Youth Day 2002. To many observers, the dramatic and unassisted descent of the pope from the aircraft—along with his later insistence that the helicopter fly over Exhibition Place before carrying him to an island retreat on Lake Simcoe—offered evidence that the stooped and tremulous 82-year-old pontiff remains resolutely at the helm of the Catholic Church.

After two days' rest, the Holy Father entered Exhibition Place in the popemobile to the thunderous applause of 400,000 Catholic faithful. Many of the pilgrims wept openly as he waved from the vehicle as it slowly wound its way to the main stage for the welcoming ceremony. They stretched and craned their necks for even a partial view of his waving hands. These wildly enthusiastic pilgrims gave him a five-minute ovation when he began his address to the crowd: "The pope, who loves you dearly ..." Some chanted a perennial WYD favourite: "JP2, we love you!"

Bishop Jacques Berthelet, president of the Canadian Conference of Catholic Bishops, welcomed the Pope on behalf of the WYD pilgrims and the bishops of Canada. "The youth of the world greet Your Holiness with affection," he said. Bishop Berthelet concluded his remarks with "Most Holy Father, thank you for being with us."

With the 500-member World Youth Day Choir singing "Jubilate Deo Omnis Terra," six young people representing the continents called out the names of all the participating nations as representatives of each joined a procession onto the main stage carrying their country's flag and wearing a national costume.

Nicolas Pappalardo, the Toronto youth who was chosen to thank the pope, told him, "You are our compass when we need guidance. You are a luminous beacon of hope in a world of darkness."

In his address, which was based on the Beatitudes, the Holy Father told the pilgrims that "the Church today looks to you with confidence and expects you to be people of the Beatitudes."

Referring to the September 11 terrorist attack in the United States, he said, "Last year we saw with dramatic clarity the tragic face of human malice. We saw what happens when hatred, sin and death take command. ... But today Jesus' voice resounds in the midst of our gathering. His is a voice of life, of hope, of forgiveness; a voice of justice and of peace. Let us listen to this voice."

A dance of thanksgiving featuring the Boston Liturgical Dance Ensemble followed the papal welcoming celebration, and a gala concert with the World Youth Day Choir, the Sacred Music Society and Sinfonia Sacra, along with other celebrations, brought the evening to a joyous conclusion.

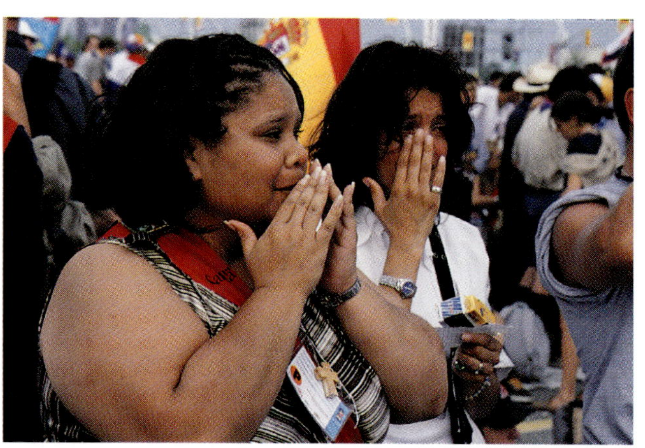

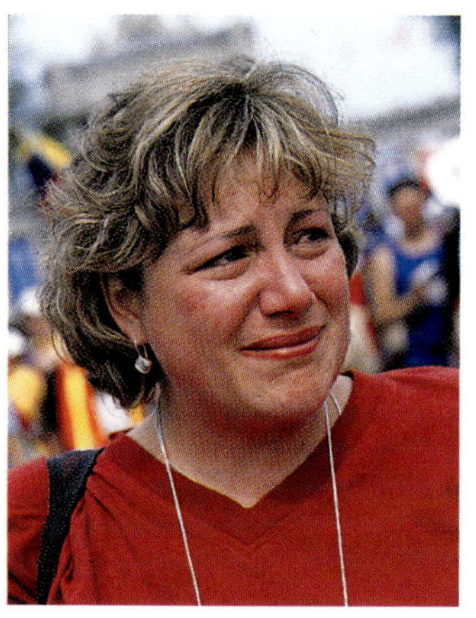

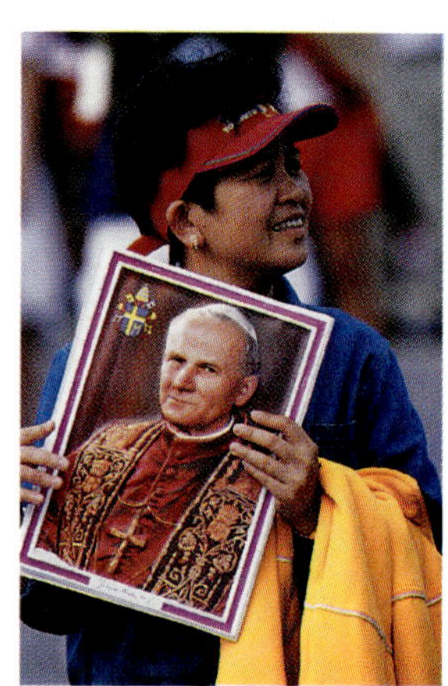

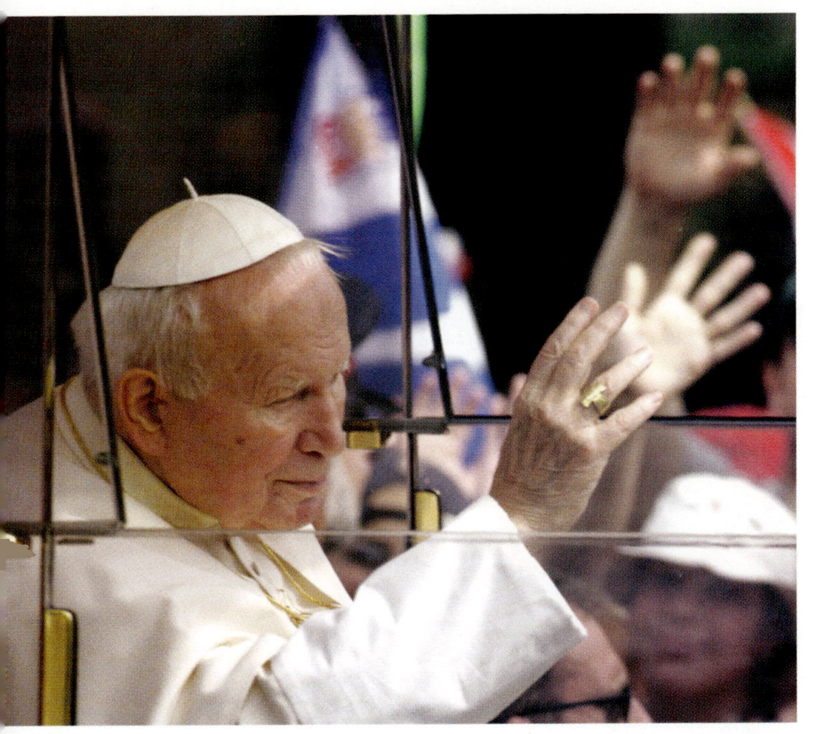

I have heard your festive voices, your cries, your songs, and I have felt the deep longing that beats within your hearts: you want to be happy!

John Paul II

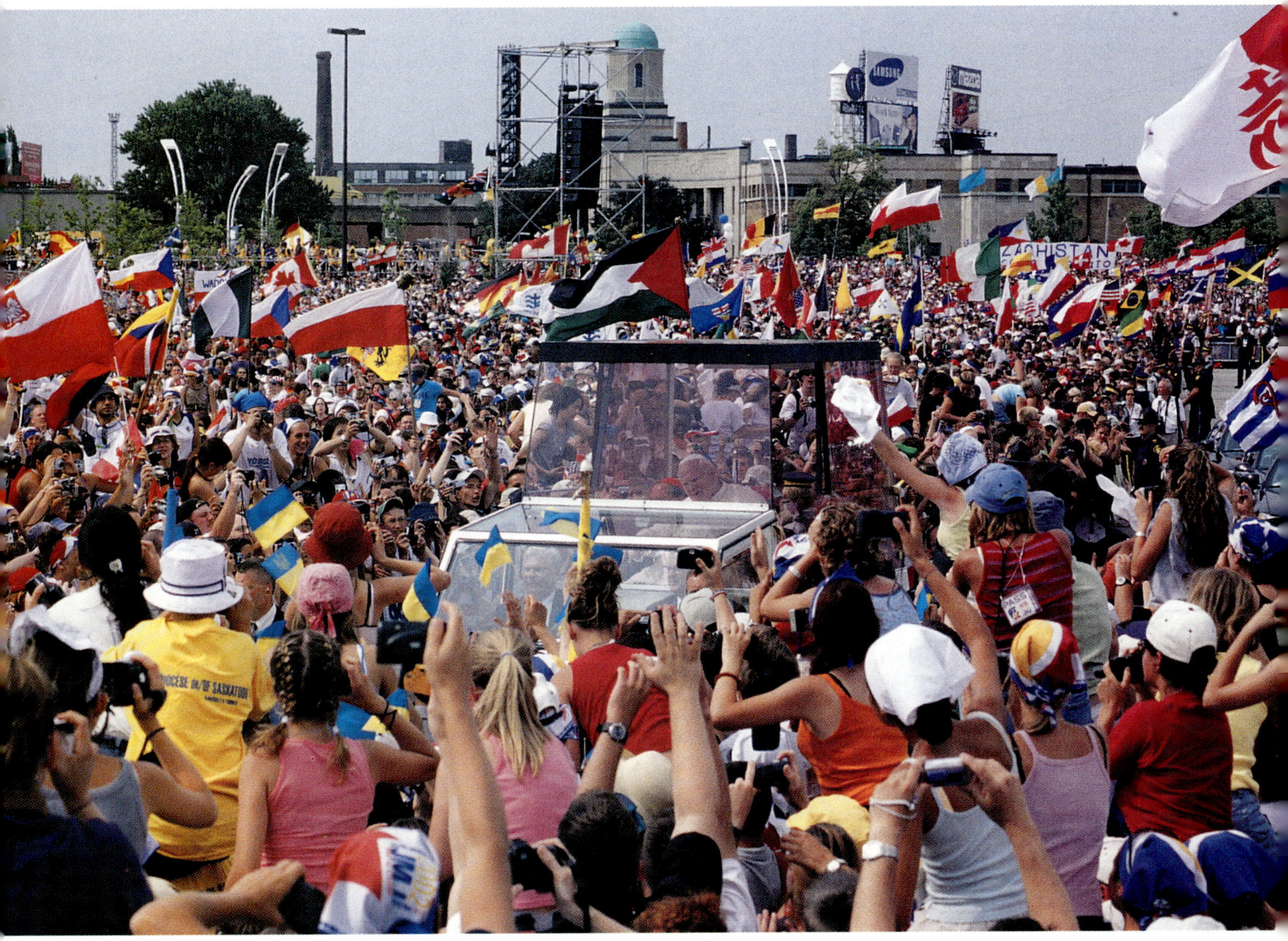

The aged pope, full of years but still young at heart, answers your youthful desire for happiness with words that are not his own. They are the words that rang out two thousand years ago: "Blessed are they…" The key word in Jesus' teaching is a proclamation of joy: "Blessed are they…"

JOHN PAUL II

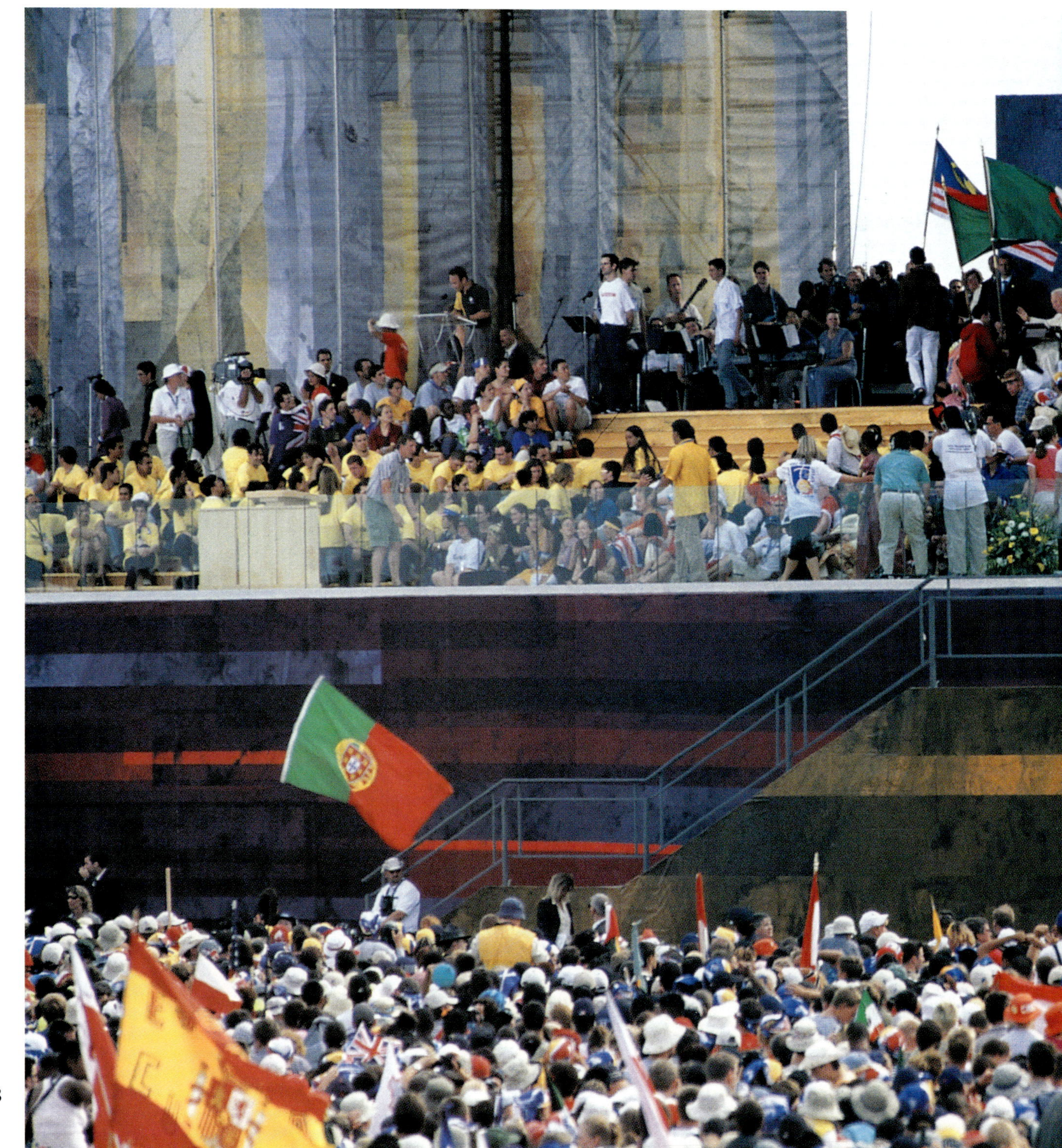

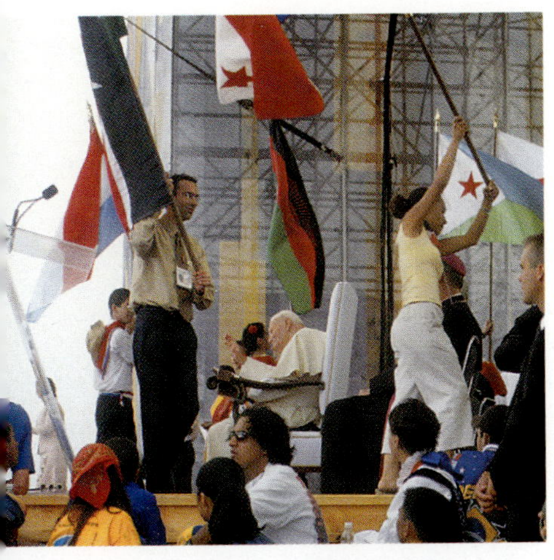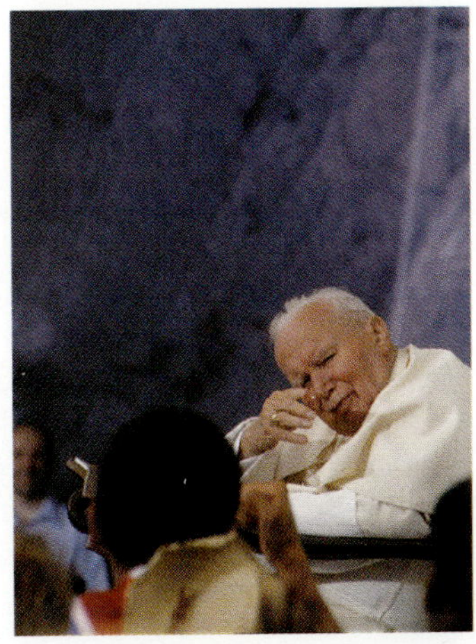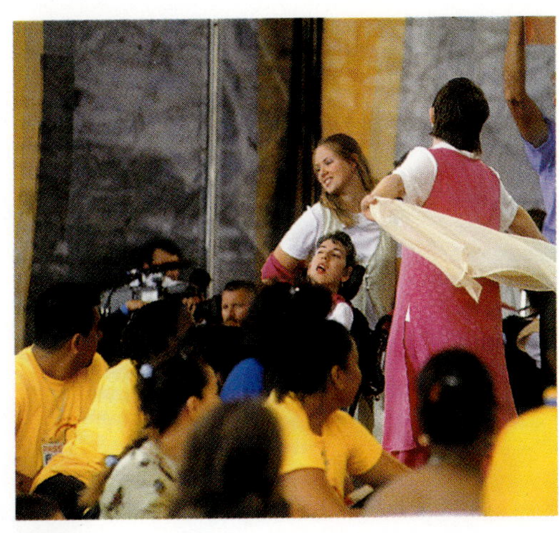

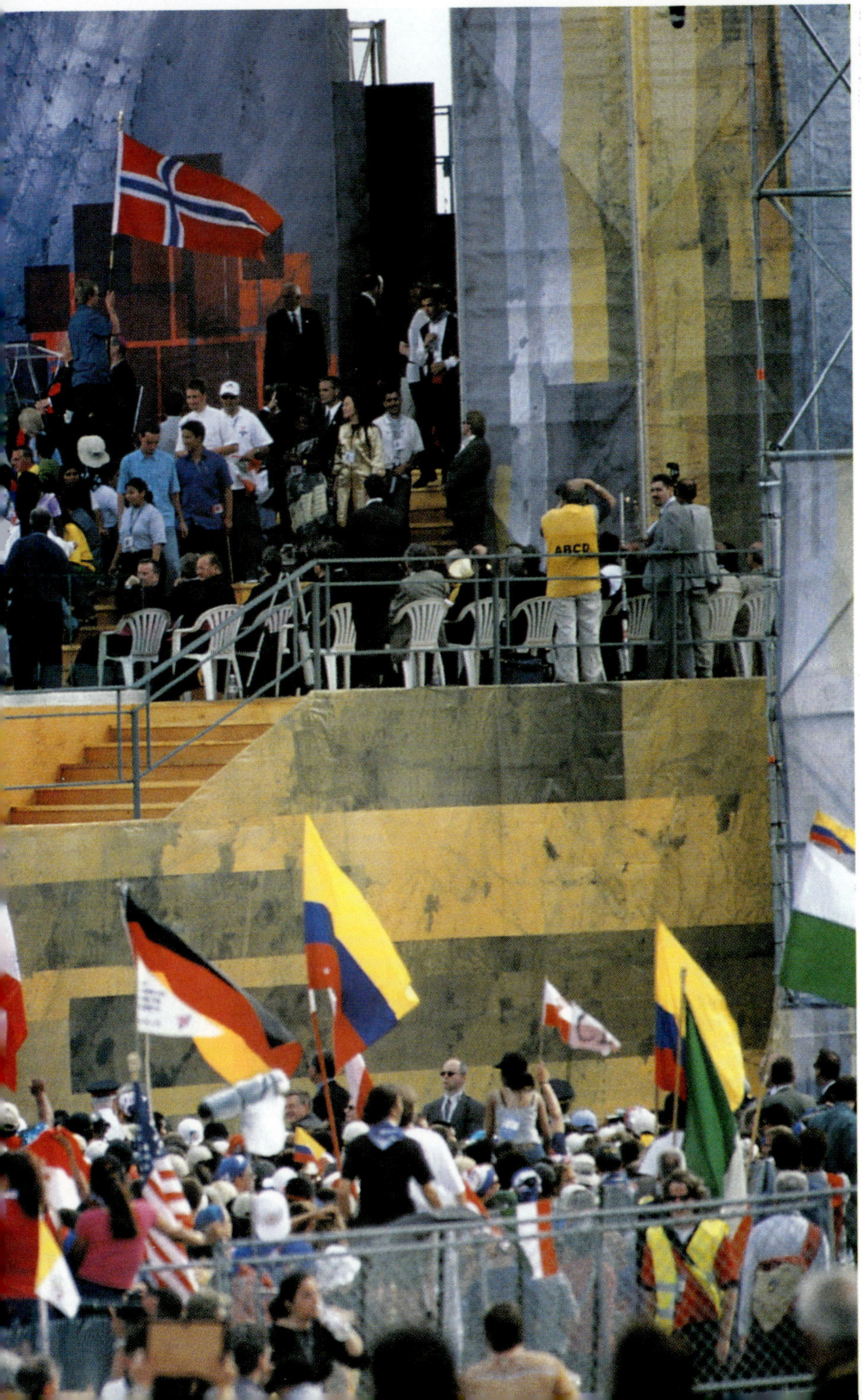

*With your gaze
set firmly on him,
you will discover
the path of
forgiveness and
reconciliation in a
world laid waste by
violence and terror.*

JOHN PAUL II

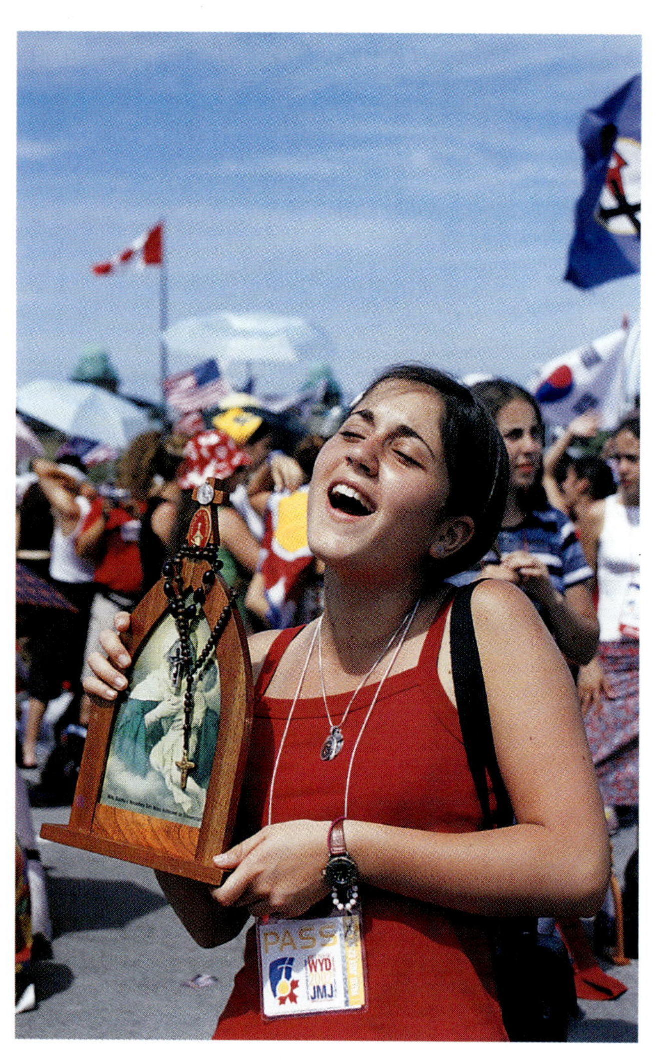

*Blessed are you if, like Jesus,
you are poor in spirit,
good and merciful;
if you really seek what is
just and right;
if you are pure in heart,
peacemakers, lovers of the
poor and their servants.
Blessed are you!*

JOHN PAUL II

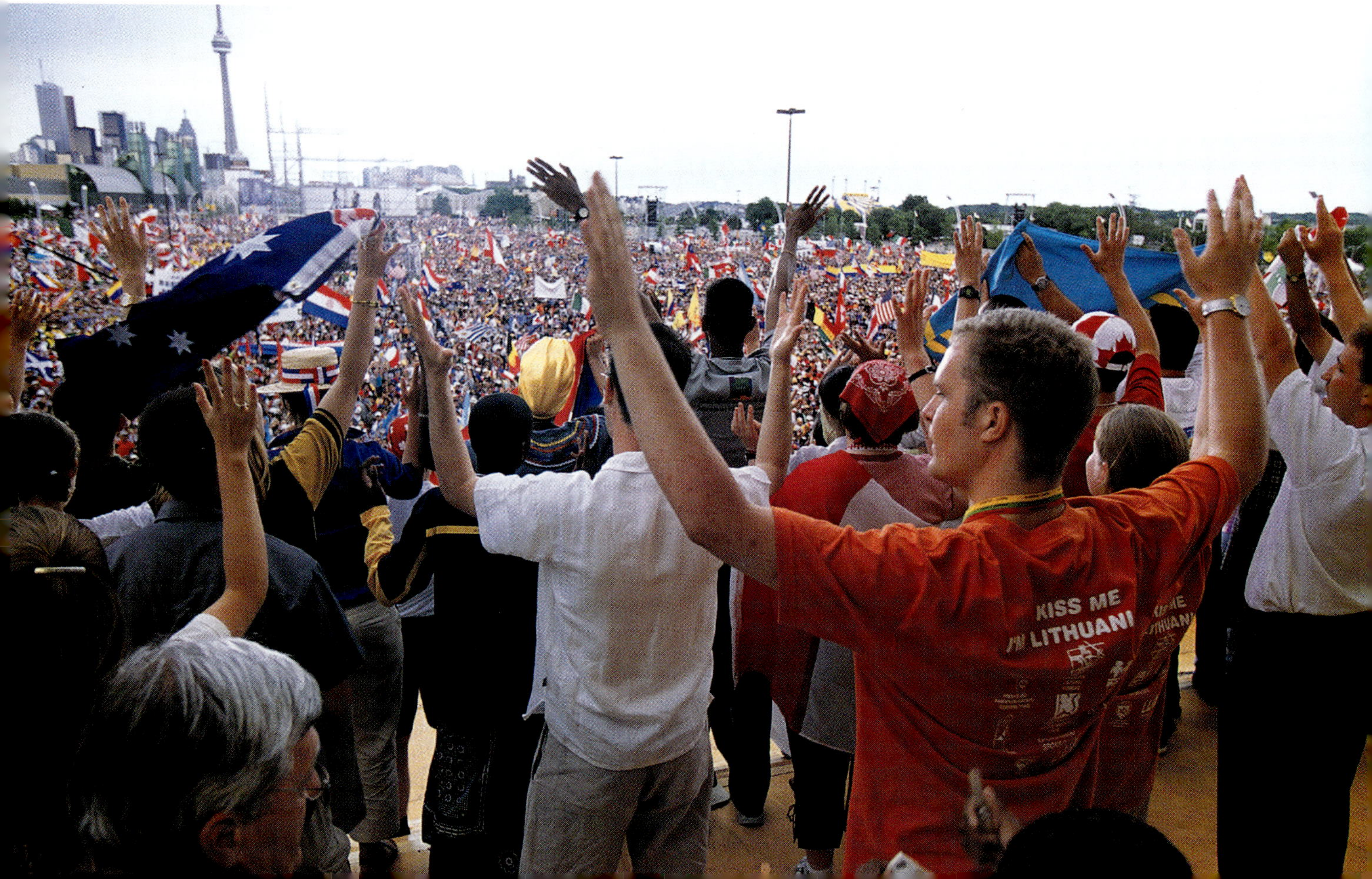

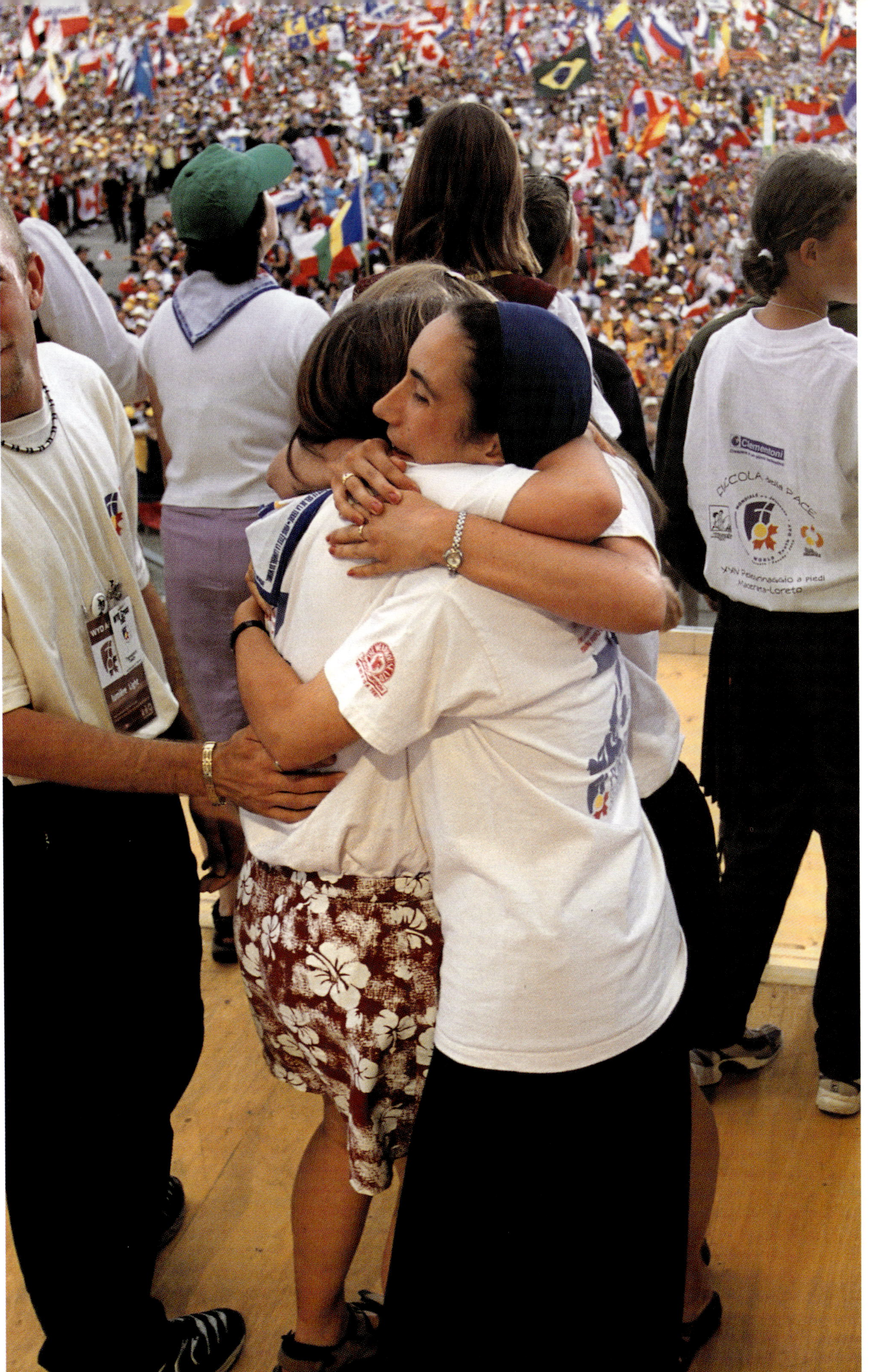

I couldn't see him!

They are like a huge flock of Canada geese: the first takes off and the rest immediately fly in the same direction. One individual moves and a swarm of banner waving, T-shirted pilgrims makes a beeline for the security barriers. John Paul II is coming! Finding the perfect spot to see the pope is a real challenge. It doesn't matter how well situated you are before his arrival: other pilgrims equally keen and determined to see the Holy Father invade your space.

Like prayer, neck craning is an integral part of this gathering, and for good reason. The two-storey buddy system—one pilgrim on the shoulders of another, usually with upraised arms holding a camera and a flag for good measure—is sure to block your hitherto unobstructed view. And as the pope nears, the cheering is deafening. Suddenly you detect movement. John Paul, maybe. No, it's only the television van. Then you spy the roof of a moving vehicle. The jubilant crowd chants, "JP2, we love you." A few seconds pass ... it's too late. You miss your chance, you don't see him. But your smiling neighbour triumphantly informs you, "I saw the popemobile!"

Smiles are everywhere, and rivers of tears too. You see a young girl clinging high up a lamppost, a Polish group singing Marian hymns, indigenous people from South America clad in traditional costume, American priests hearing confessions right in the middle of the crowd, Italians from Venice who welcome you as one of their own.

Lots of joy. Lots of emotion. And an immense love for the elderly pope whose unwavering belief in the youth of the world is a model for us all.

Maybe you don't see the pope, but that's okay, because in the hundreds of thousands of faces, you will surely meet him.

Lord Jesus Christ, proclaim once more your Beatitudes in the presence of these young people, gathered in Toronto for the World Youth Day. Look upon them with love and listen to their young hearts, ready to put their future on the line for you.

JOHN PAUL II

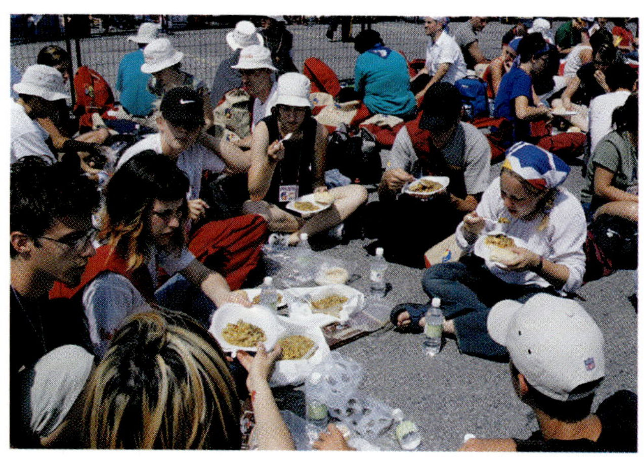

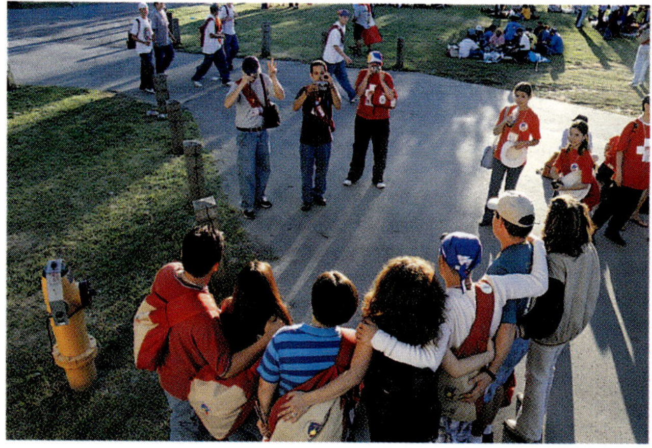

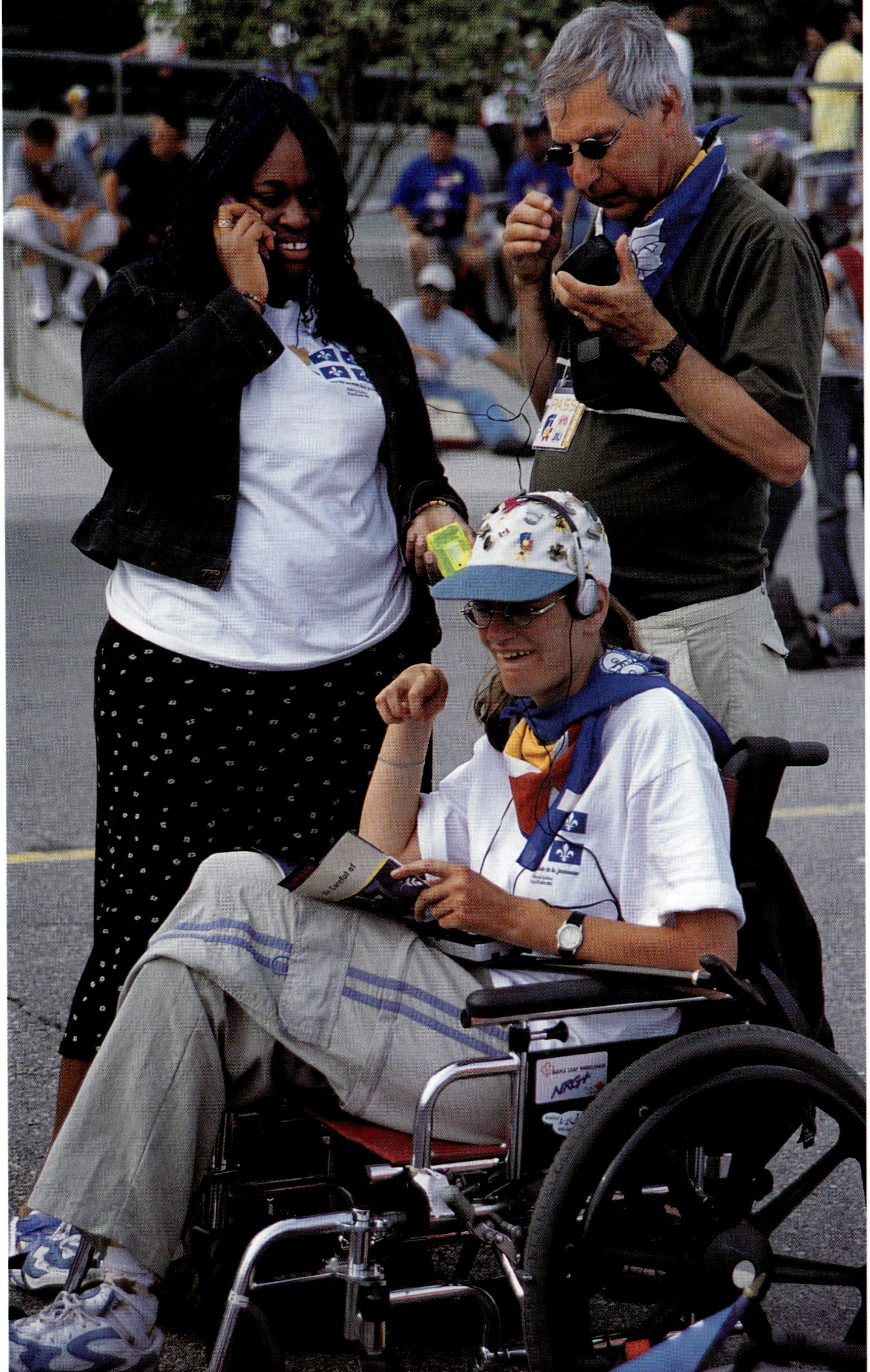

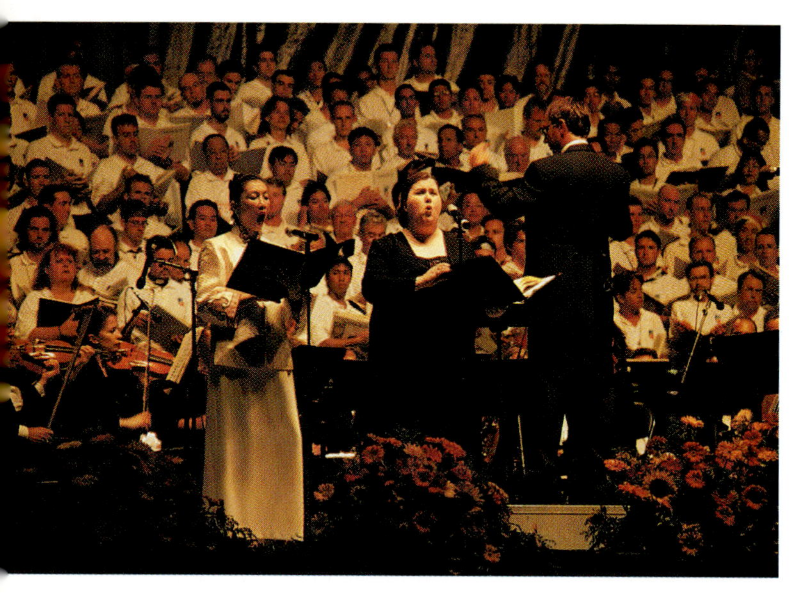
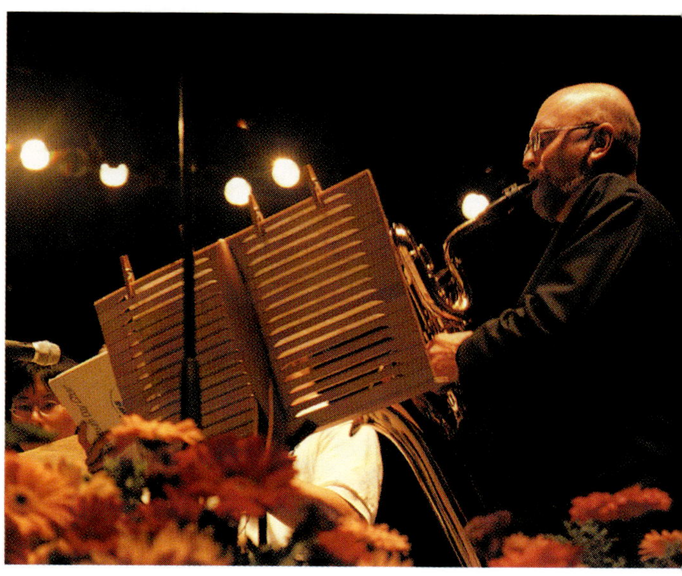

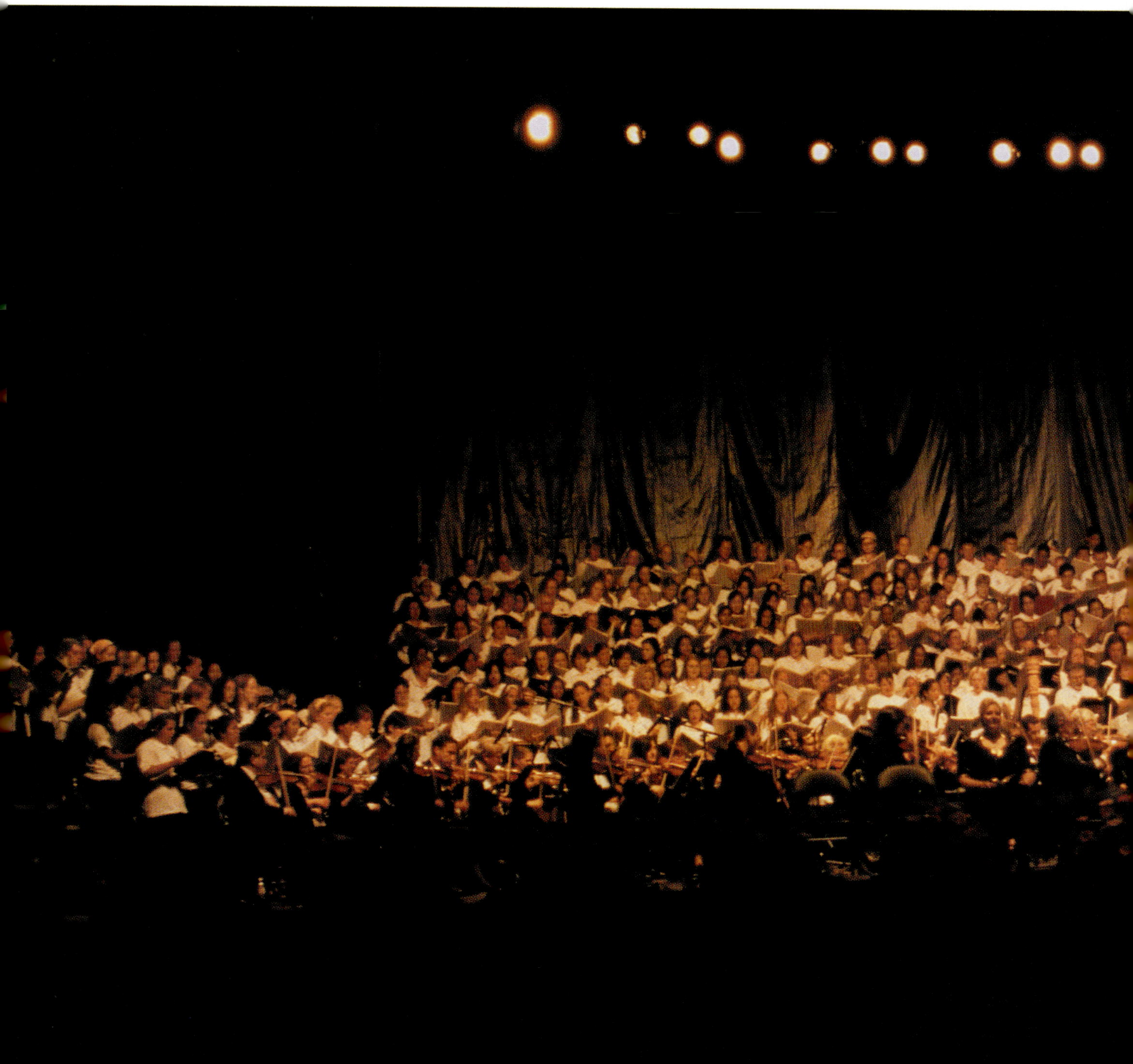

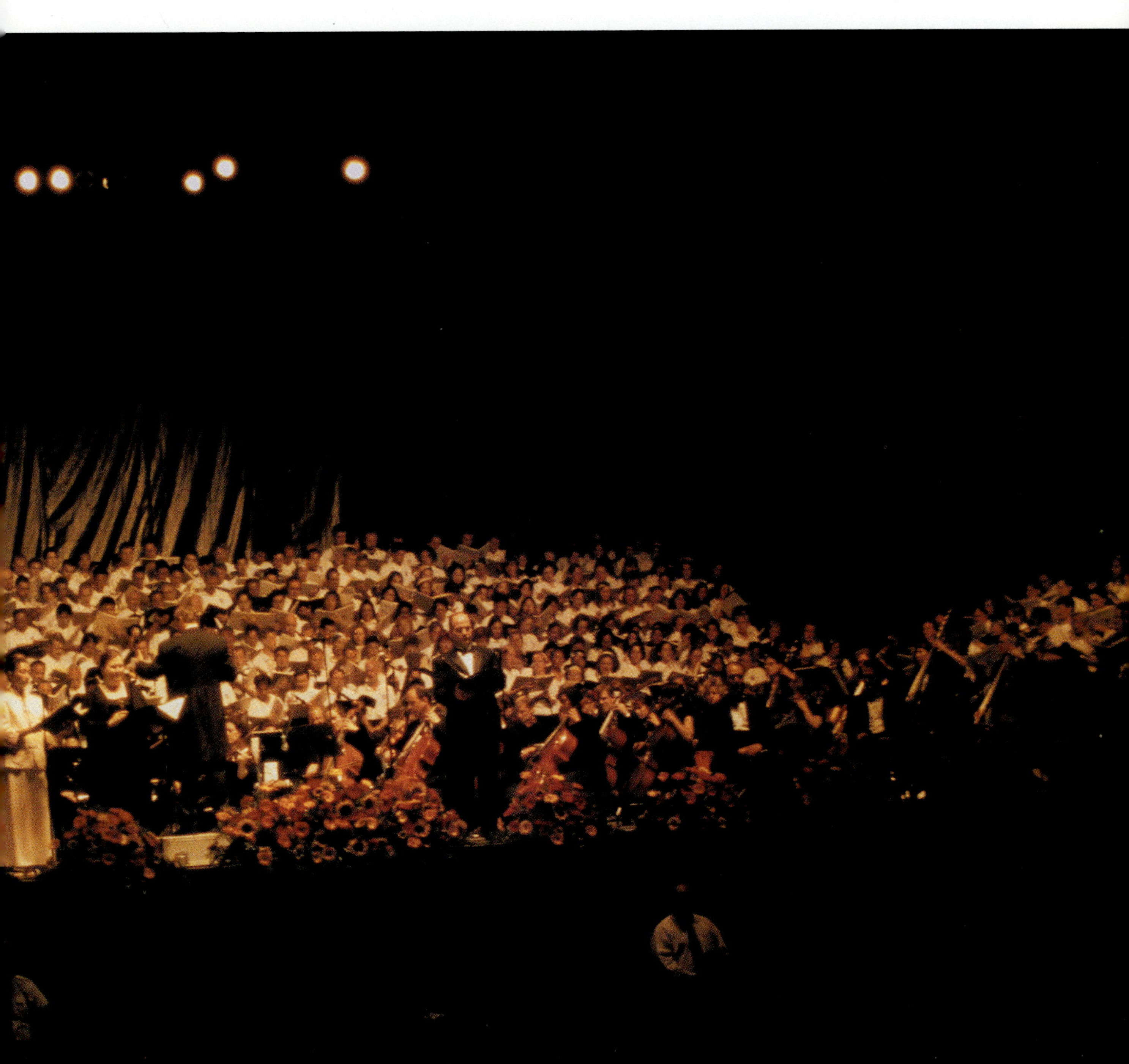

*Make them men and women of the Beatitudes.
Let the light of your wisdom shine upon them, so that in word
and deed they may spread in the world the light and the salt of
the Gospel. Make their whole life a bright reflection of you,
who are the true light that came into this world, so that
whoever believes in you will not die, but will have eternal life.*

JOHN PAUL II

A Festival of Learning

Discover your Christian roots, learn about the Church's history, deepen your knowledge of the spiritual heritage which has been passed on to you, follow in the footsteps of the witnesses and teachers who have gone before you!

JOHN PAUL II

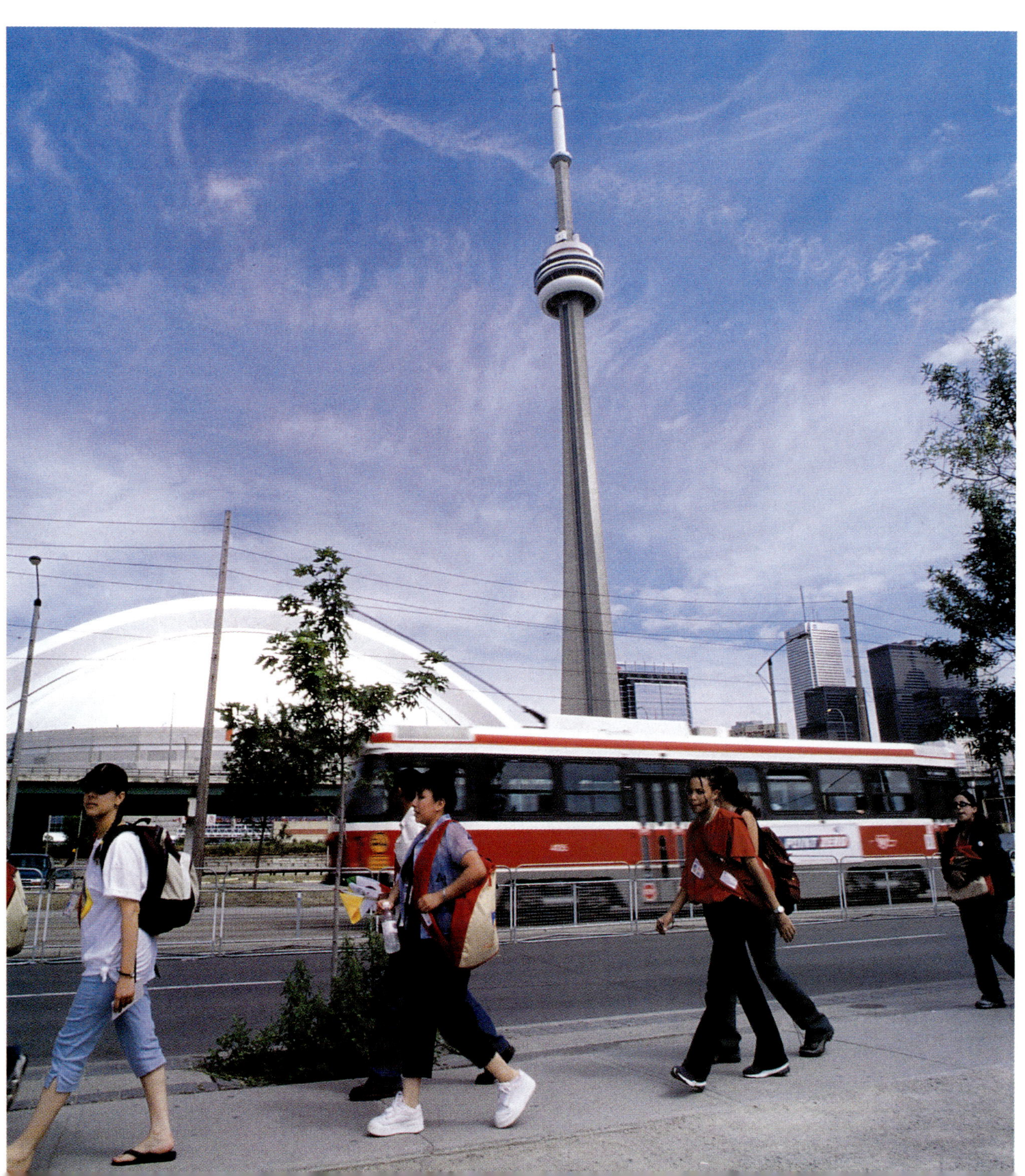

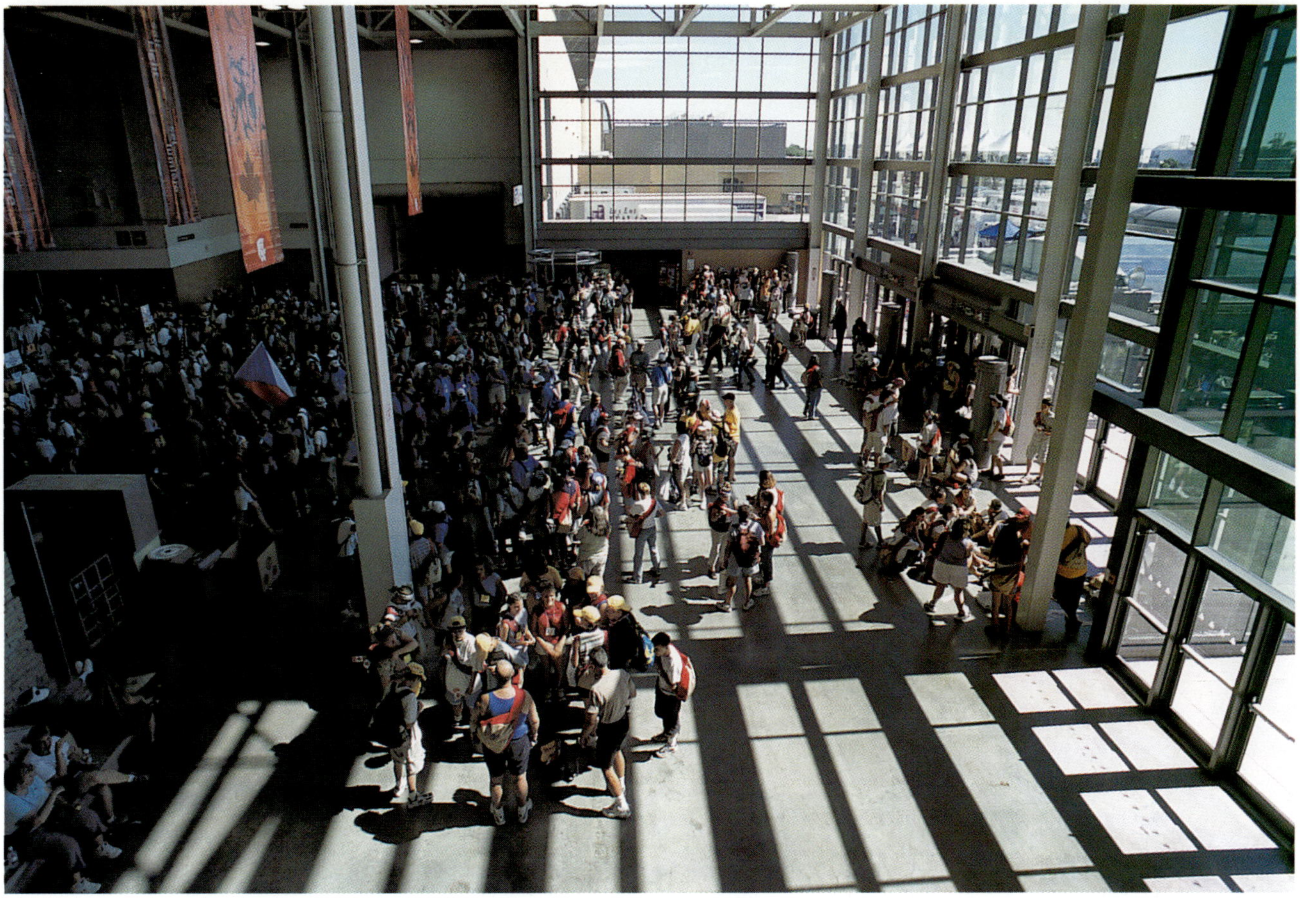

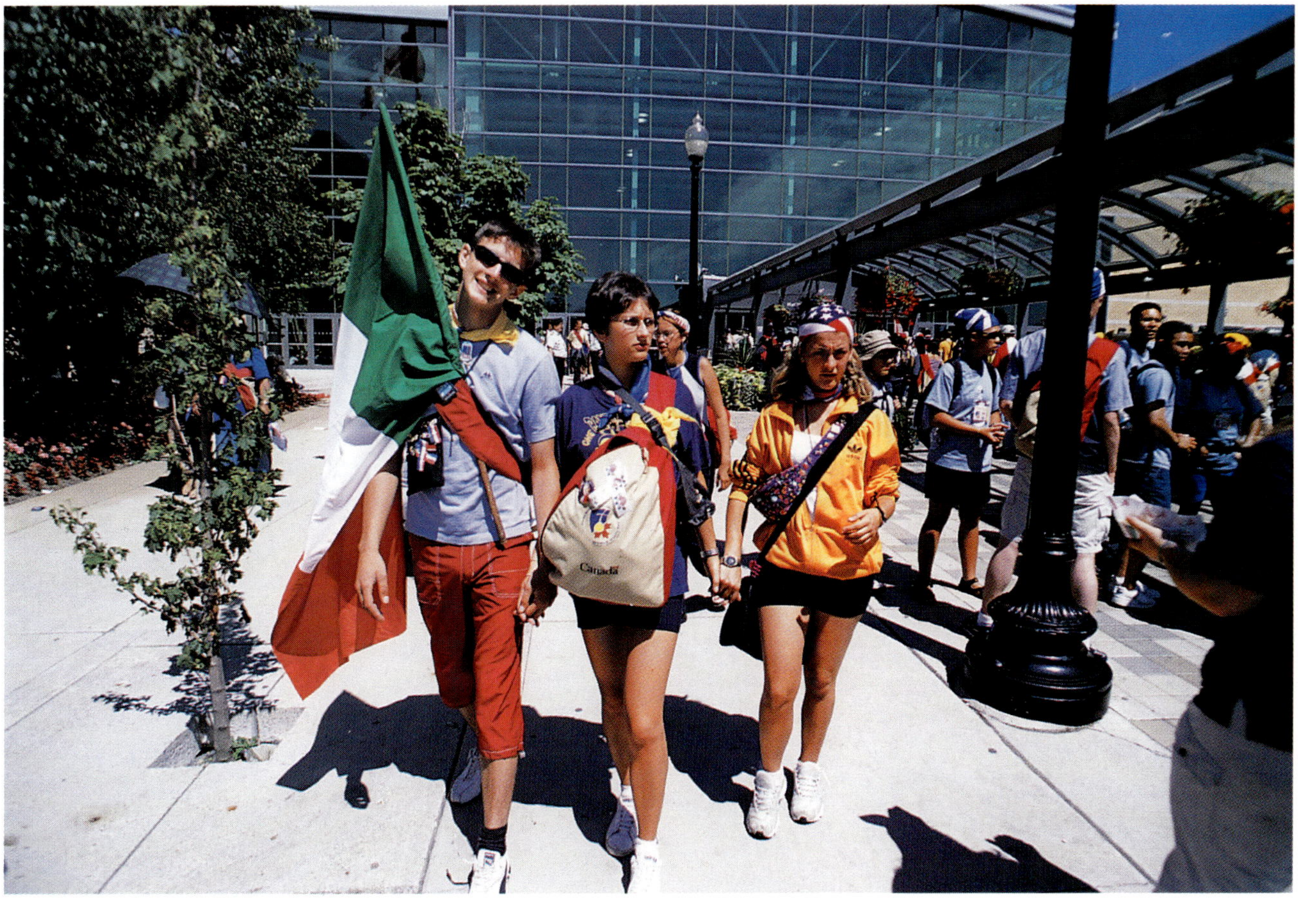

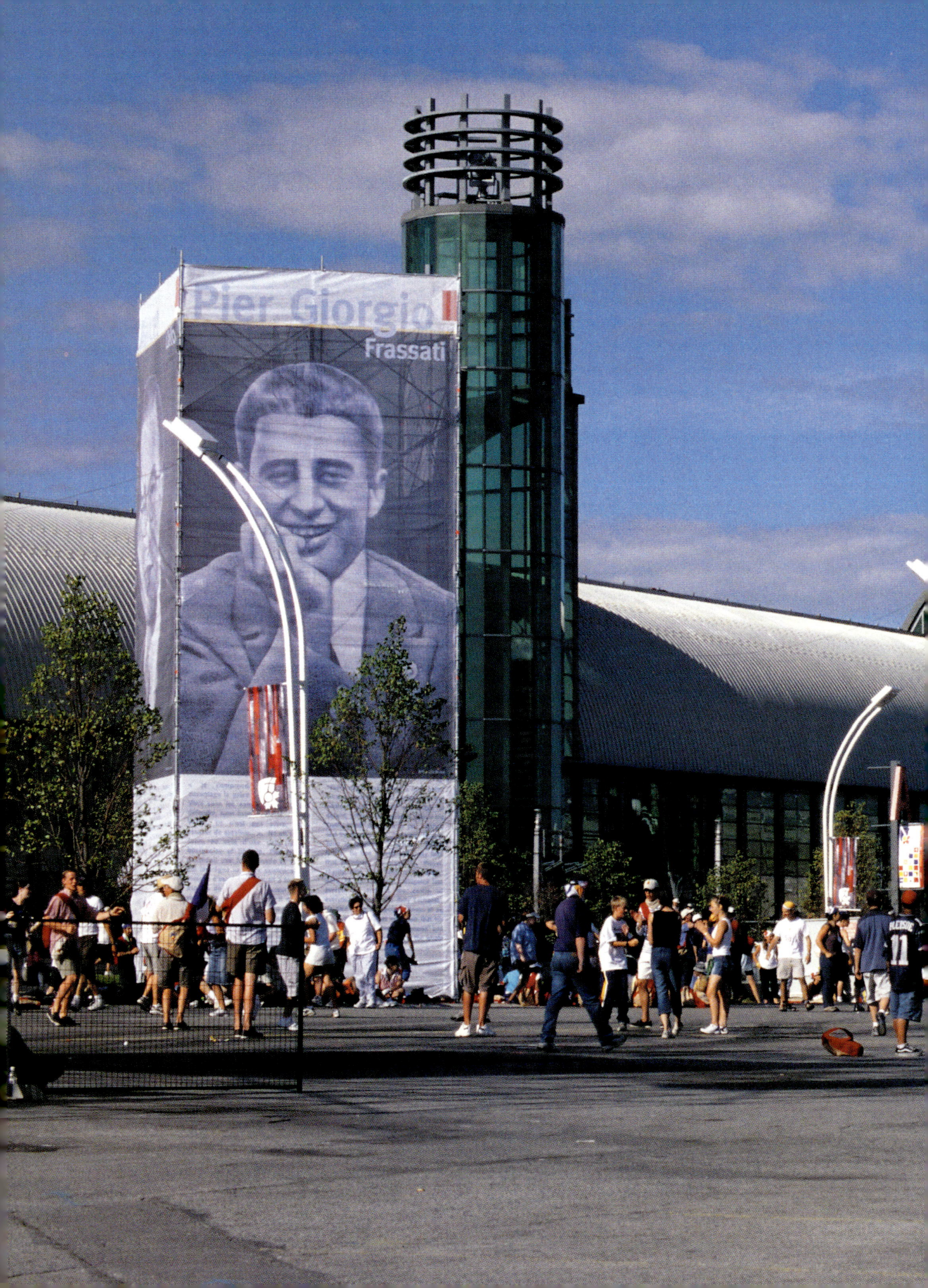

Pier Giorgio
Frassati

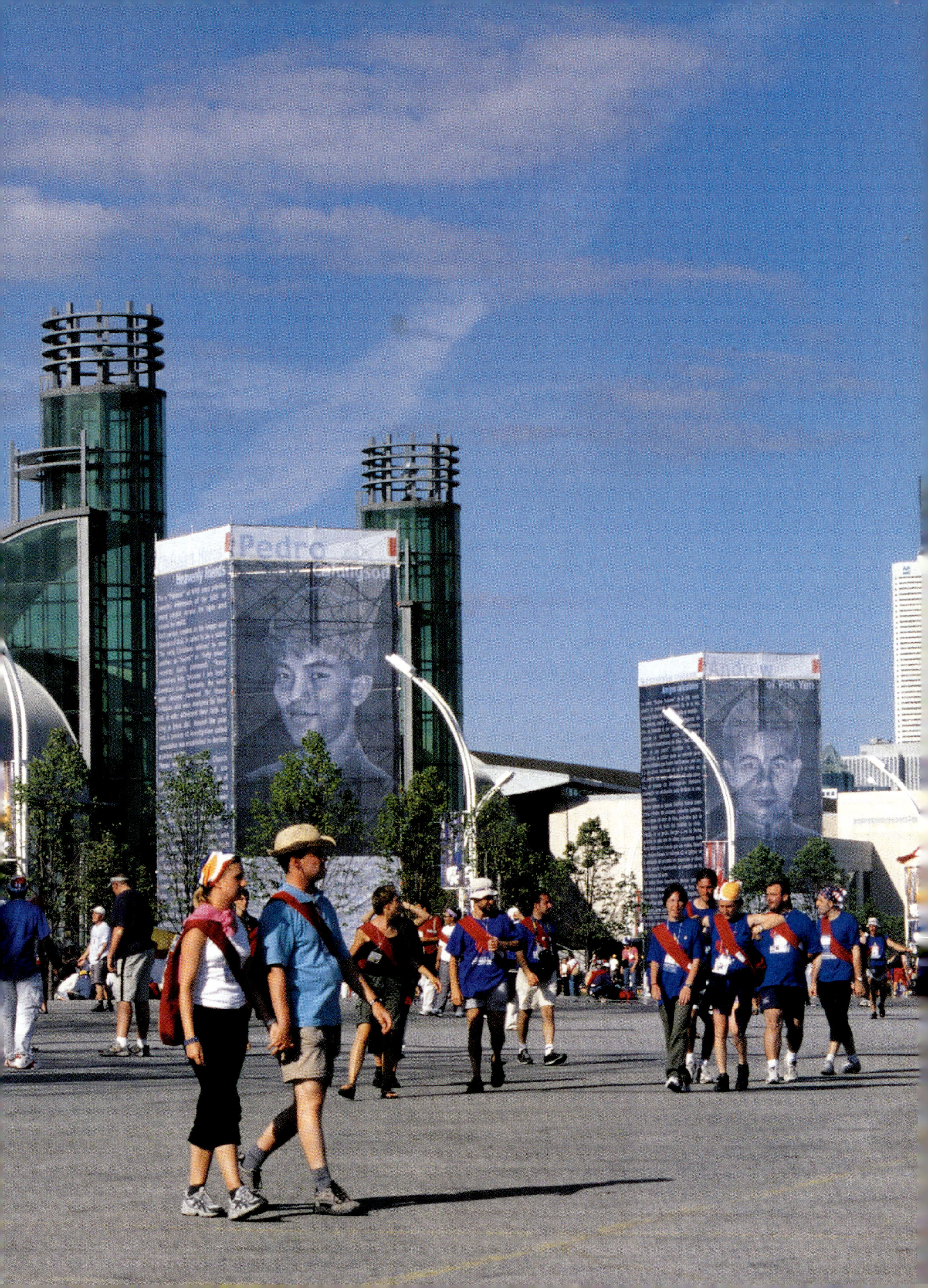

In the heart of a multicultural and multifaith city, we shall speak of Christ

World Youth Day 2002 was not only a celebration of faith from the Catholic perspective. It was also a festival of learning for the young pilgrims from around the world.

More than 260 bishops, archbishops and cardinals presented catechetical sessions in 24 languages at 129 churches in the Toronto area and in seven giant halls at Exhibition Place. Polish, Korean, Ukrainian, Italian, German, French, Filipino—no matter their language, pilgrims could find a welcoming parish community in the Toronto area. Cardinal Lustiger of France and Poland's Cardinal Glemp were just two of the senior clerics who generated a strong rapport in their catechetical sessions. (Catechesis is the process by which Christians are nourished and educated in the faith.)

Each day senior clerics preached and taught on one of the key themes for WYD 2002: becoming "the salt of the earth," becoming "the light of the world" and being reconciled with God.

Jean Vanier, the Canadian-born founder of L'Arche, an international organization of communities for people who have developmental disabilities, was invited to meet with youth and talk to them about their spiritual journey. A gifted speaker who is neither a bishop nor a priest, he had a powerful impact on his listeners. Many pilgrims also took part in sessions of prayer and song organized by the Taizé community from France.

The catecheses involved several rites, including the Ukrainian Catholic, which often uses icons, a form of sacred art that is used in worship. The WYD Icon, *The Adoration of the Magi*, was on display at St. Nicholas Ukrainian Catholic Church on July 23 for the Eastern Catholic encounter and on July 24 for the evening Byzantine Vespers. The icon was then transported to Downsview Lands for the overnight vigil on July 27 and was carried onstage toward the end of the closing mass with Pope John Paul II.

Aboriginal involvement in WYD 2002 was extensive and imparted to the event a uniquely Canadian flavour. First Nations participants from many countries led performances and prayer experiences at the Youth Festival, an aboriginal village was constructed and other events and ceremonies celebrated indigenous cultures. St. Ann's church in Toronto, which has a life-sized statue of Blessed Kateri Tekakwitha, the

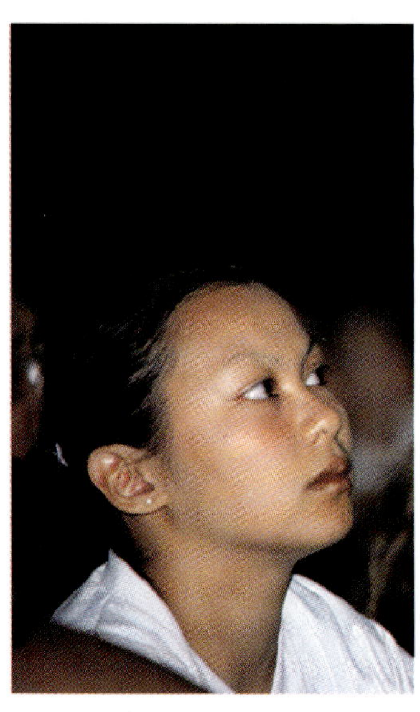
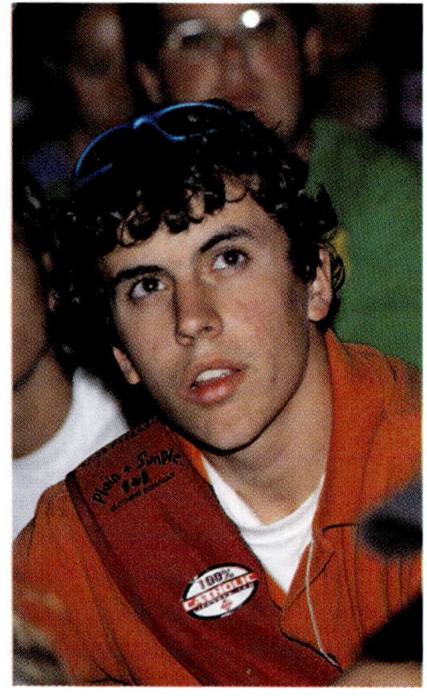
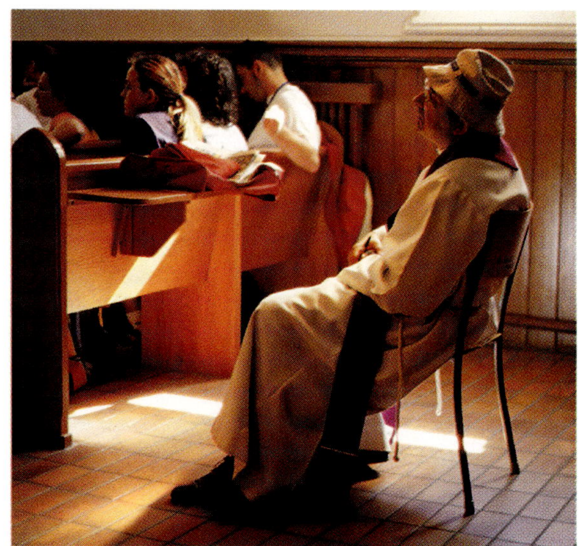

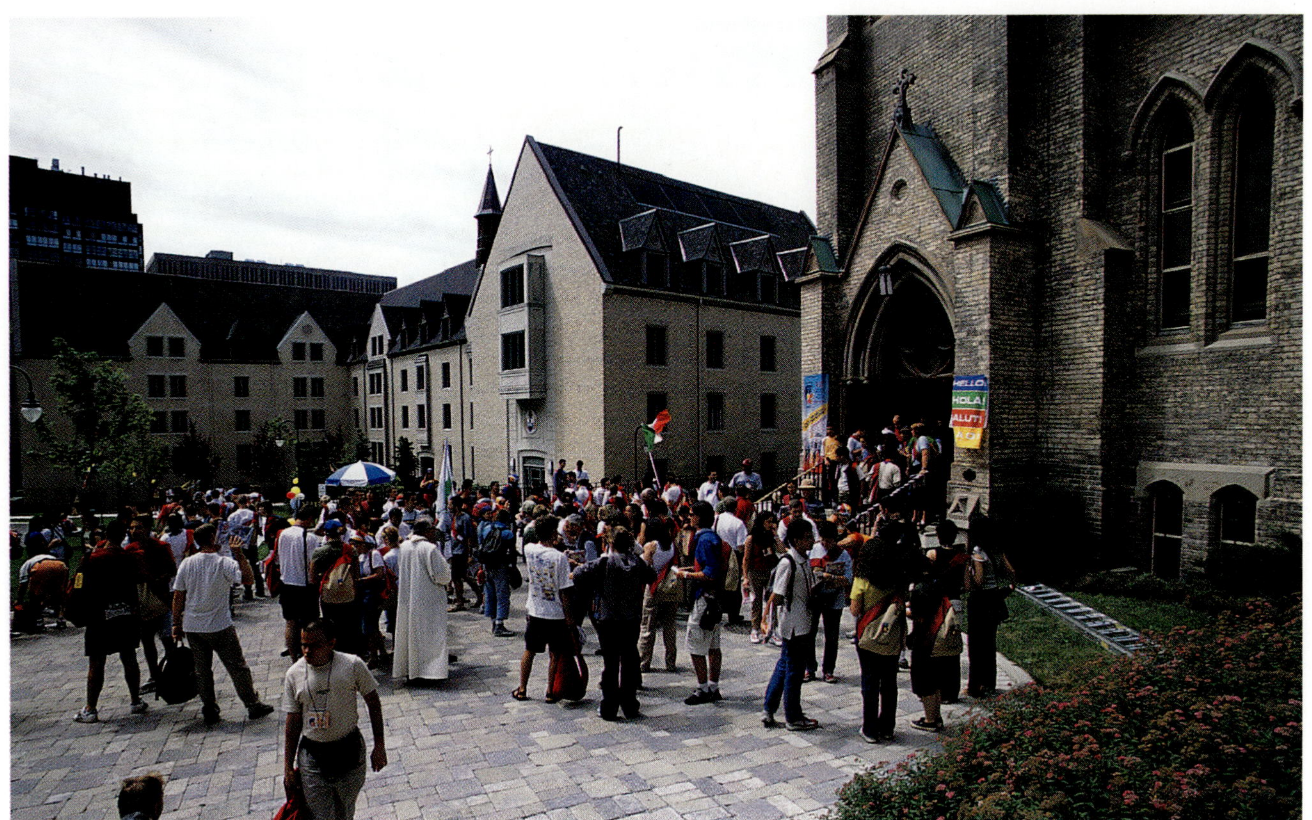

"Lily of the Mohawks," hosted aboriginal prayer groups and gatherings. She is one of ten saints and blesseds who are the patrons of World Youth Day. Her image, as well as those of St. Thérèse of Lisieux, St. Josephine Bakhita, St. Agnes of Rome, Blessed Andrew of Phù Yen, Blessed Pier Giorgio Frassati, Blessed Pedro Calungsod, Blessed Marcel Callo, Blessed Francisco Castellò Aleu and Blessed Gianna Beretta Molla, were featured on giant banners at the entrance to Exhibition Place.

The Nunavut Performers entertained with Inuit music that included traditional throat singing. The native dancers from the Tohono O'odham Nation from Arizona thrilled audiences at Exhibition Place and in Nathan Phillips Square, in front of Toronto's city hall. Canada's First Nations were also involved in the opening and closing ceremonies and in the vigil with the pope.

Hundreds of other performers from scores of nations delighted audiences wherever they performed. The popular Youth Festival boasted ten stages and involved 3,000 people from 35 countries. In all, some 173 performing arts groups presented over 300 performances. The festival also offered pilgrims a chance to take in 30 different seminars and workshops, ten prayer experiences, and ten cultural gatherings. They could also visit displays from over 300 vocational and service groups at Exhibition Place.

World Youth Day is partly about seeing faith in terms of service to the community. Hundreds of international participants spent time with young children and senior citizens. Some worked in food banks, while others took up tools to paint or repair various community centres. A house was constructed for a Toronto family over the course of the week, with the help of many WYD volunteers working under the direction of Habitat for Humanity, a charitable organization that uses donated materials and labour to create housing for the poor.

Pilgrims kept in touch with family and friends at home through a variety of means, including cell phones and e-mails sent from onsite Internet cafés. Others relied on letters and postcards, while some were just too tired to do much else but sleep at the end of such busy days.

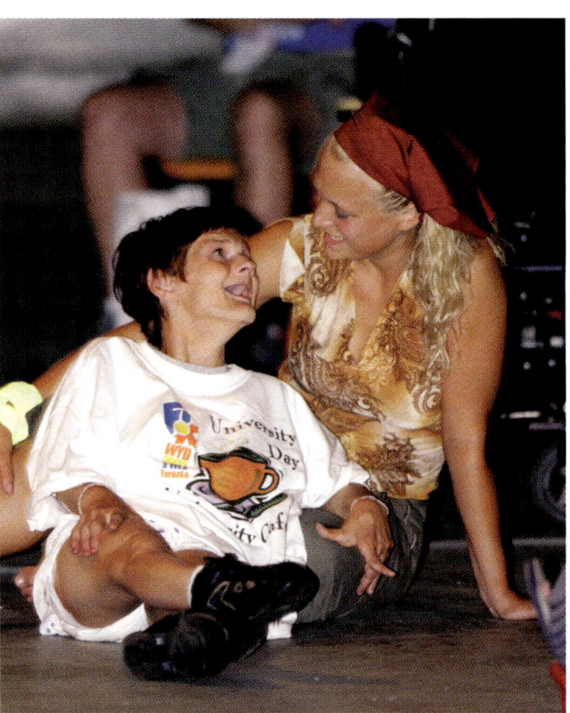

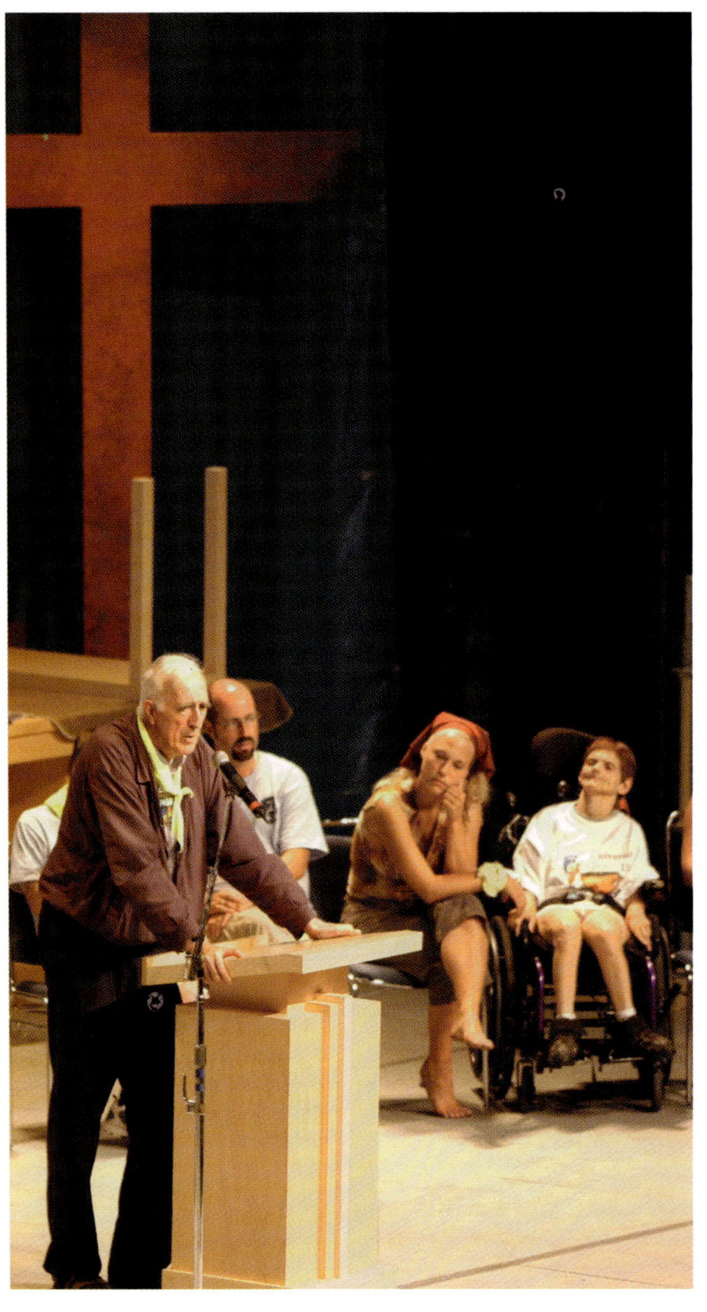

Jesus did not limit himself to proclaiming the Beatitudes, he lived them!

JOHN PAUL II

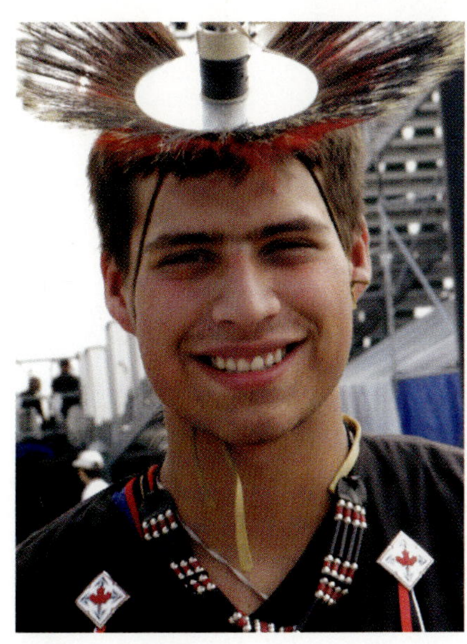

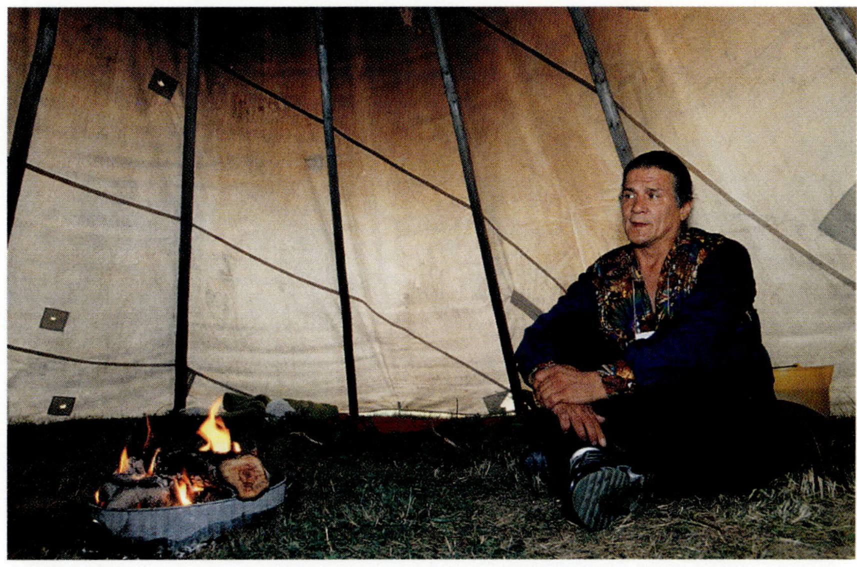

*I am happy to meet the young people
of the First Nations of the land of Blessed Kateri
Tekakwitha. You rightly call her* kaiatano
*(most noble and worthy person). May she be
an example to you how Christians are to be
the salt and light of the earth.*

JOHN PAUL II

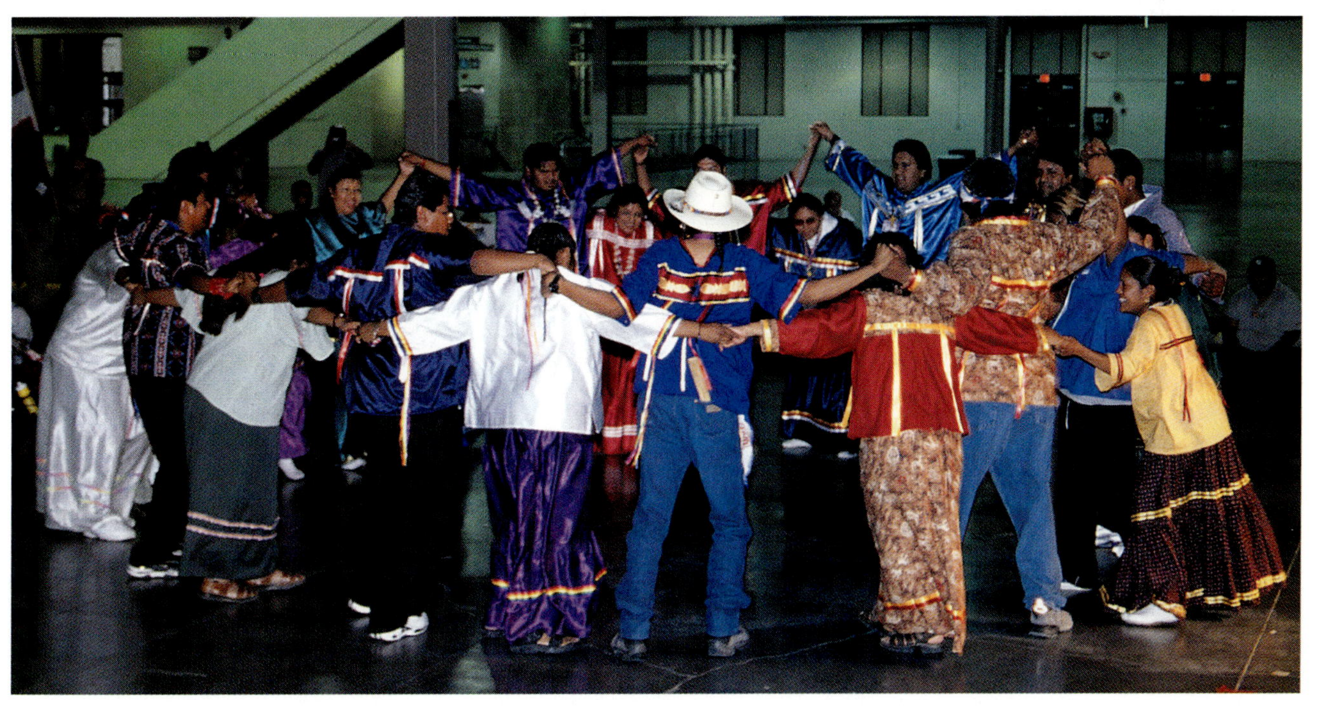

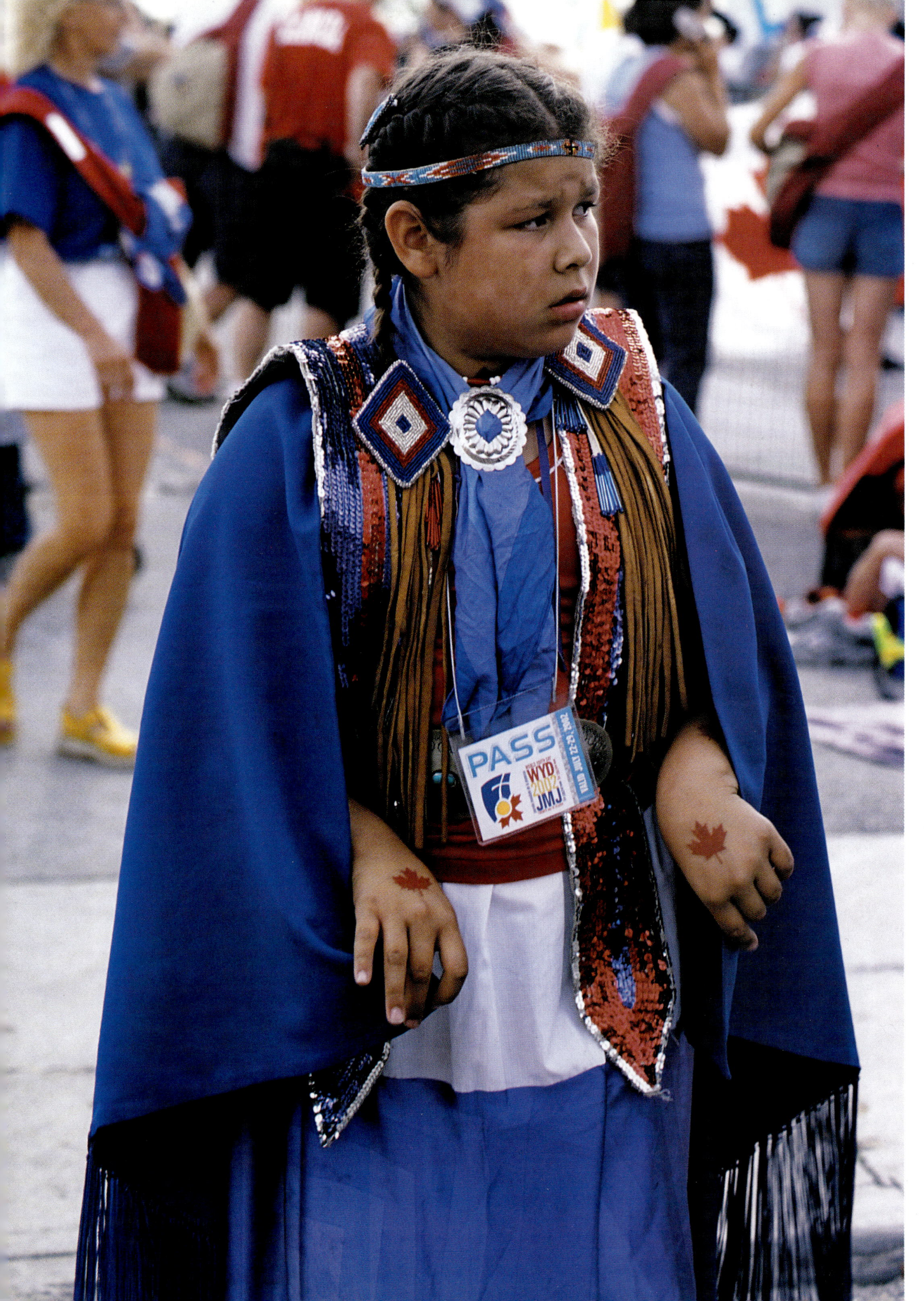

PASS
WYD
2002
JMJ

*Each one of us belongs to a great family,
in which he has his own place and his own role to play.
Selfishness makes people deaf and dumb; love opens eyes
and hearts, enabling people to make that original and
irreplaceable contribution which, together with the thousands
of deeds of so many brothers and sisters, often distant and
unknown, converges to form the mosaic of charity
which can change the tide of history.*

JOHN PAUL II, WYD 1996

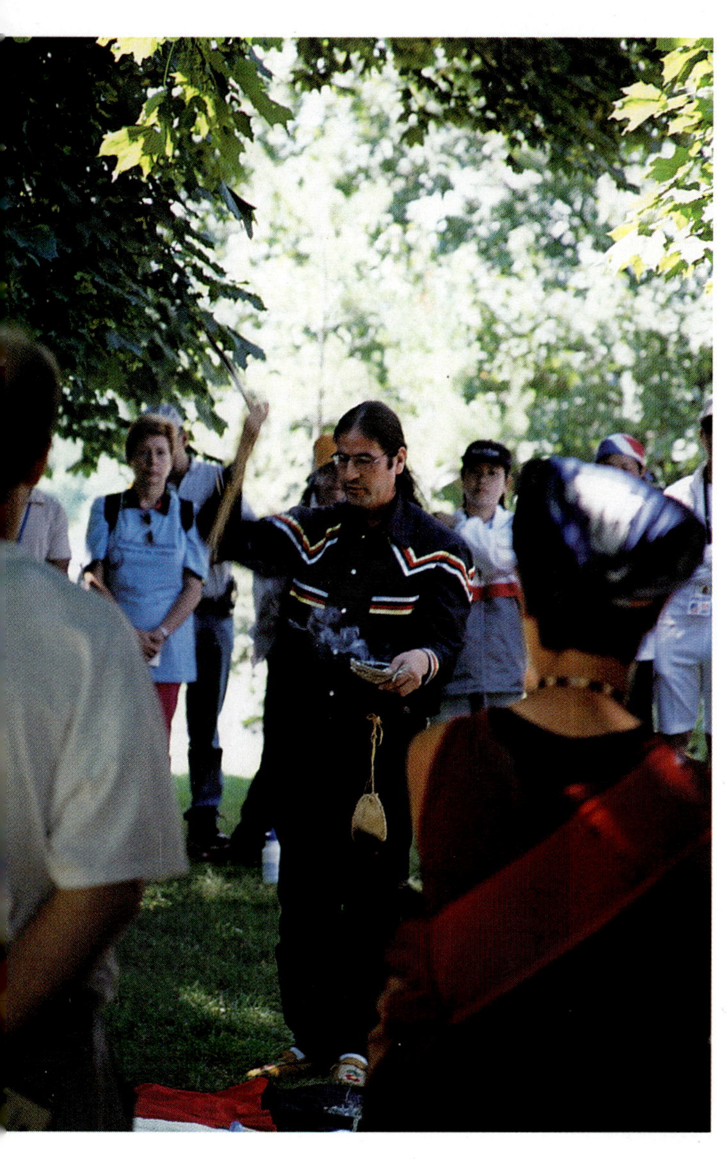

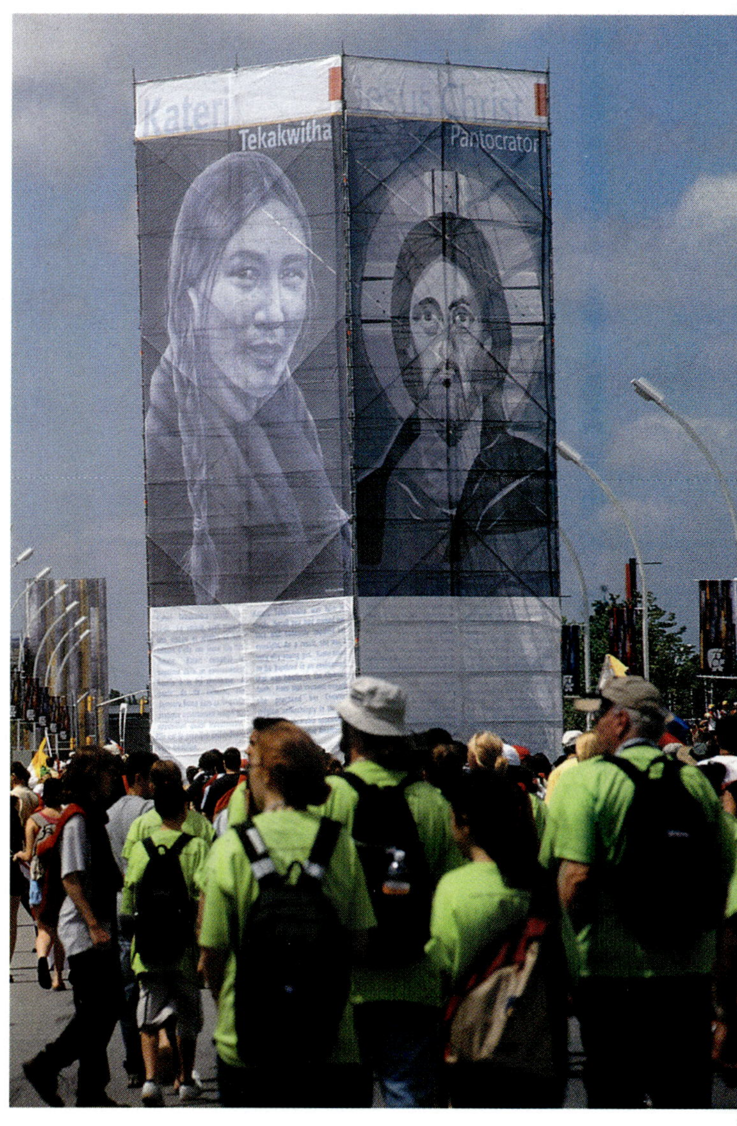

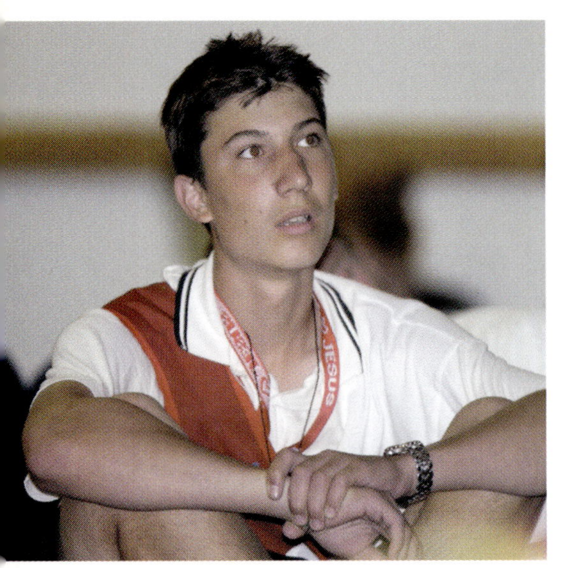

Come, and make the great avenues of Toronto resound with the joyful tidings that Christ loves every person and brings to fulfilment every trace of goodness, beauty and truth found in the city of man.

JOHN PAUL II

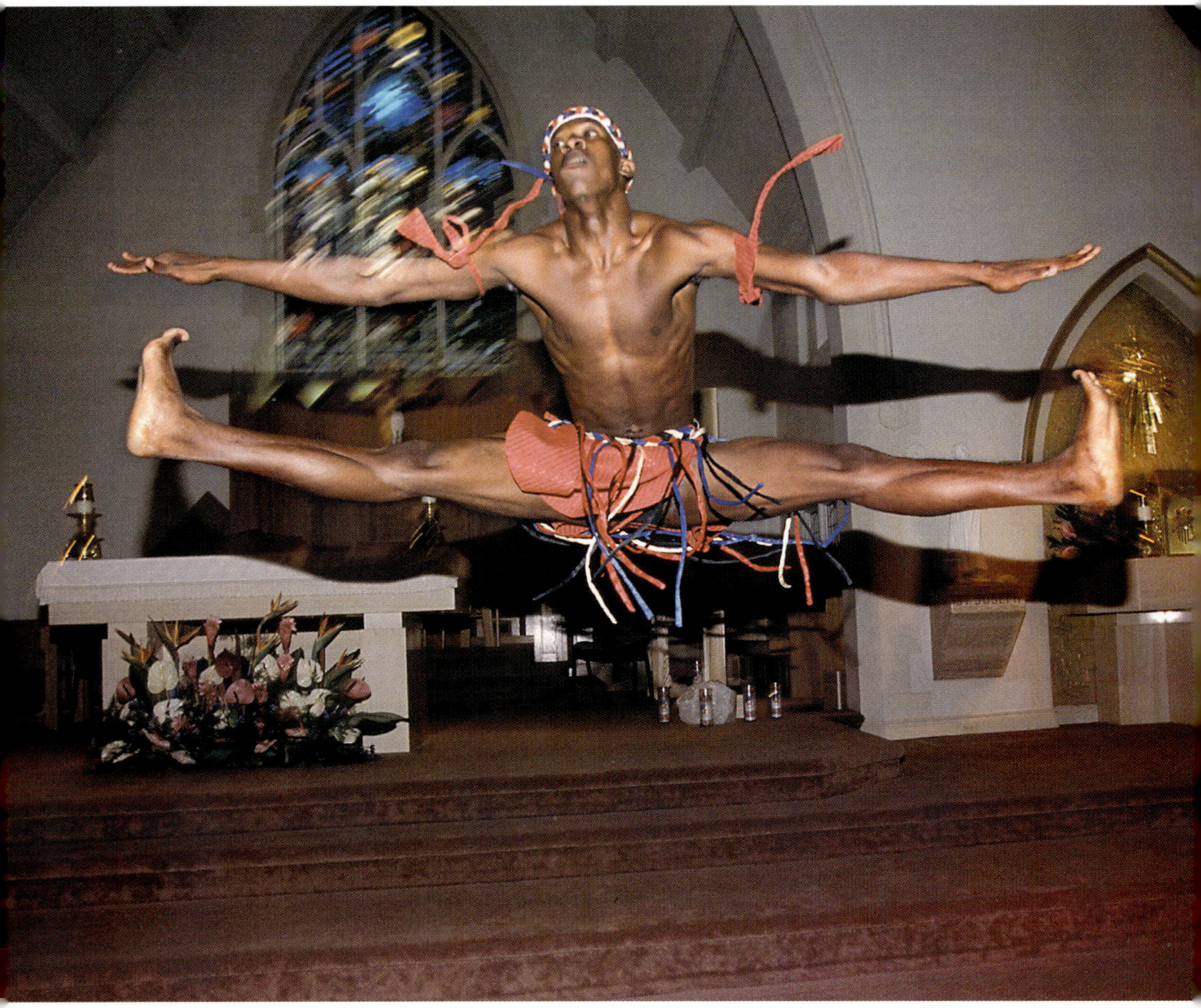

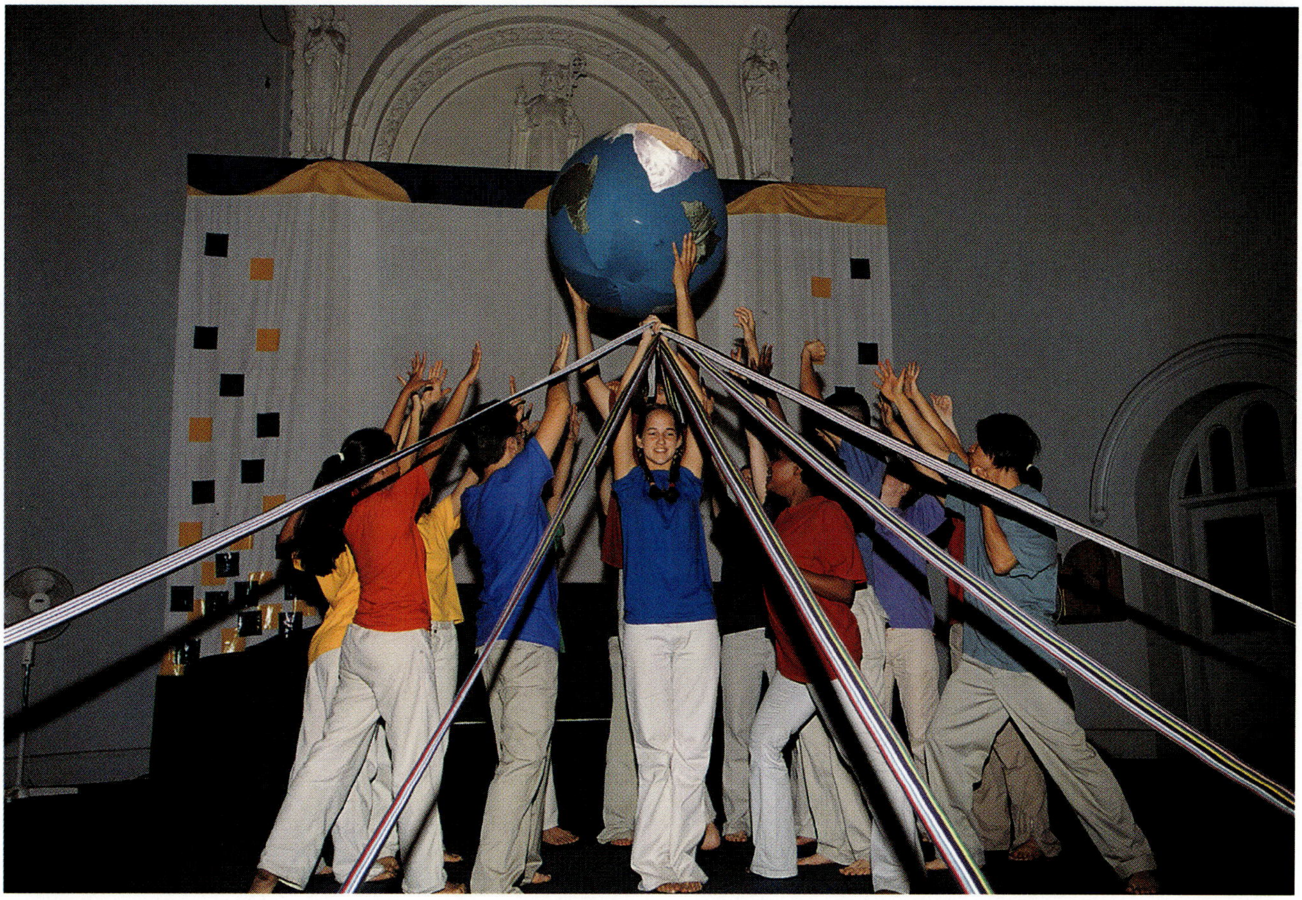

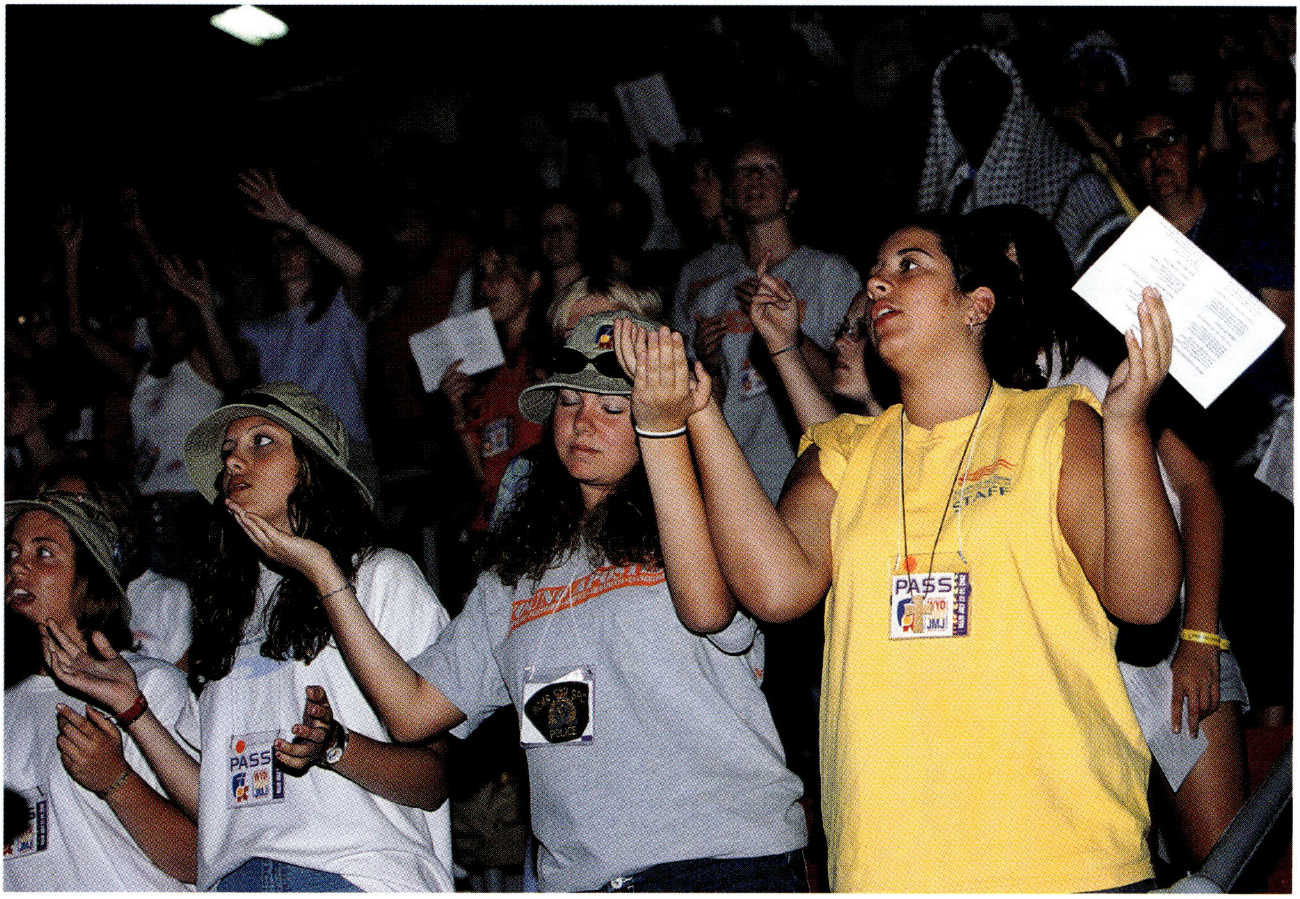

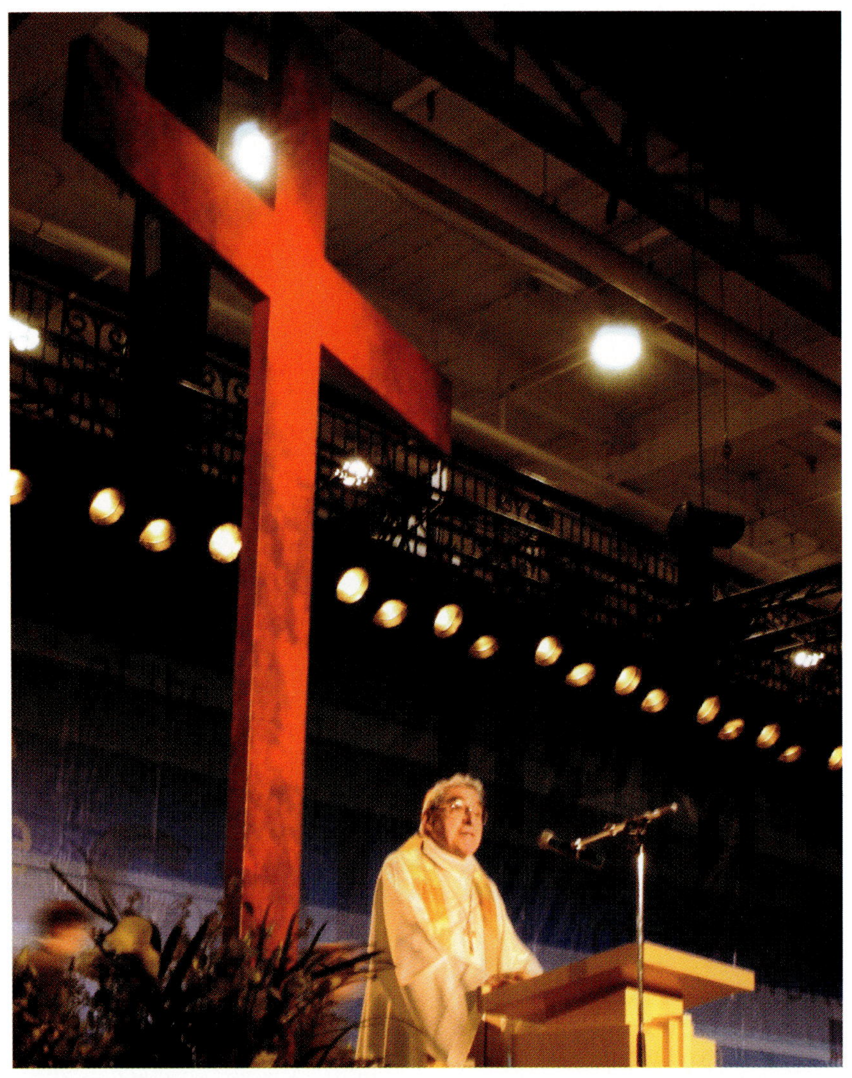

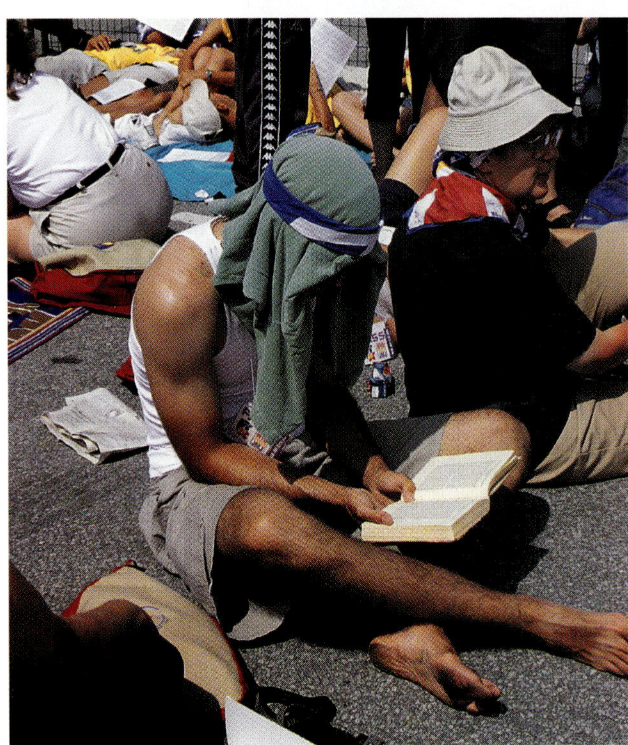

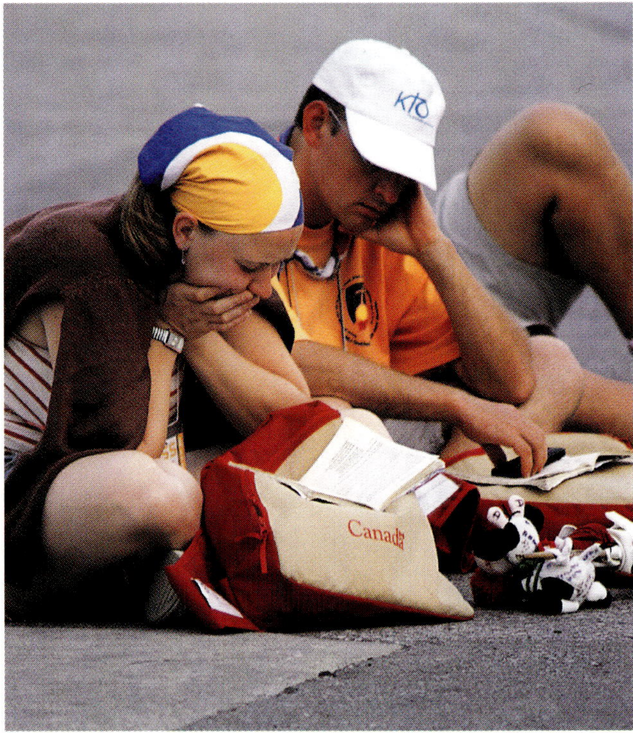

Come, and tell the world of the happiness you have found in meeting Jesus Christ, of your desire to know him better, of how you are committed to proclaiming the Gospel of salvation to the ends of the earth!

JOHN PAUL II

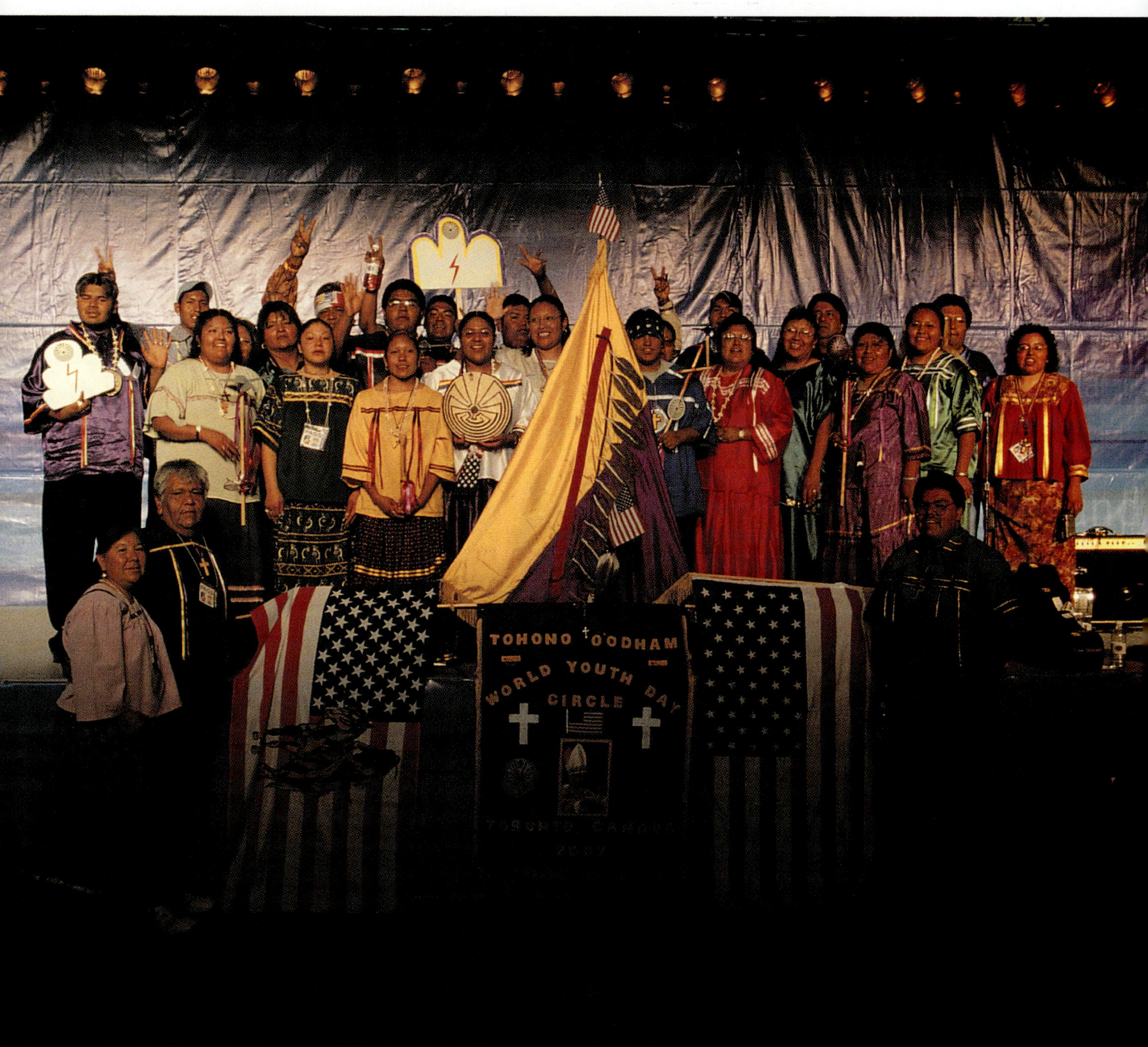

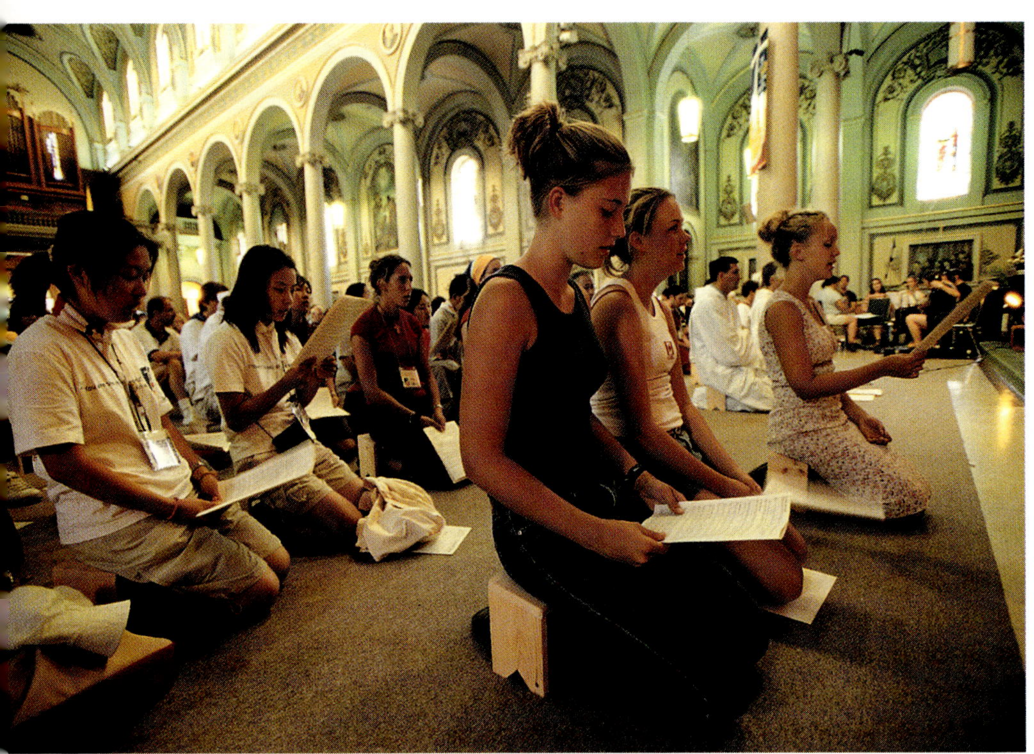

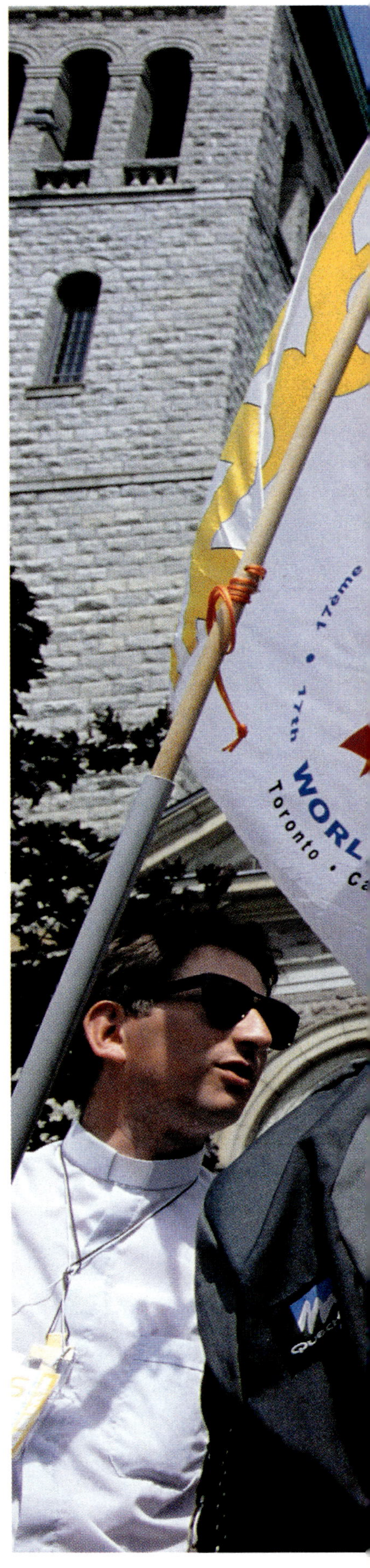

By contemplating the light radiant on the face of the Risen Christ, you will learn to live as "children of the light and children of the day" (1 Thessalonians 5:5), and in this way you will show that "the fruit of light is found in all that is good and right and true" (Ephesians 5:9).

JOHN PAUL II

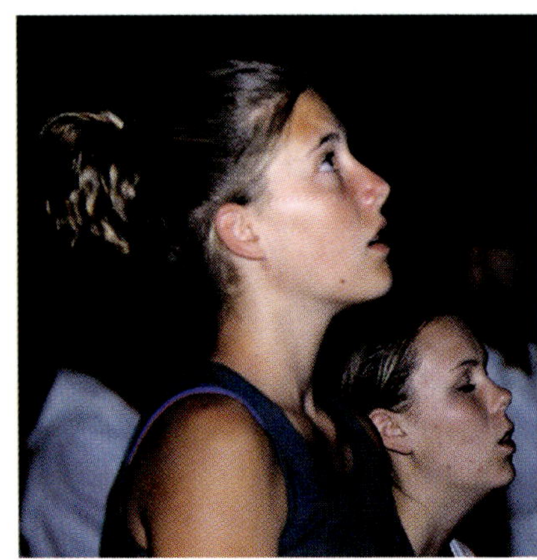

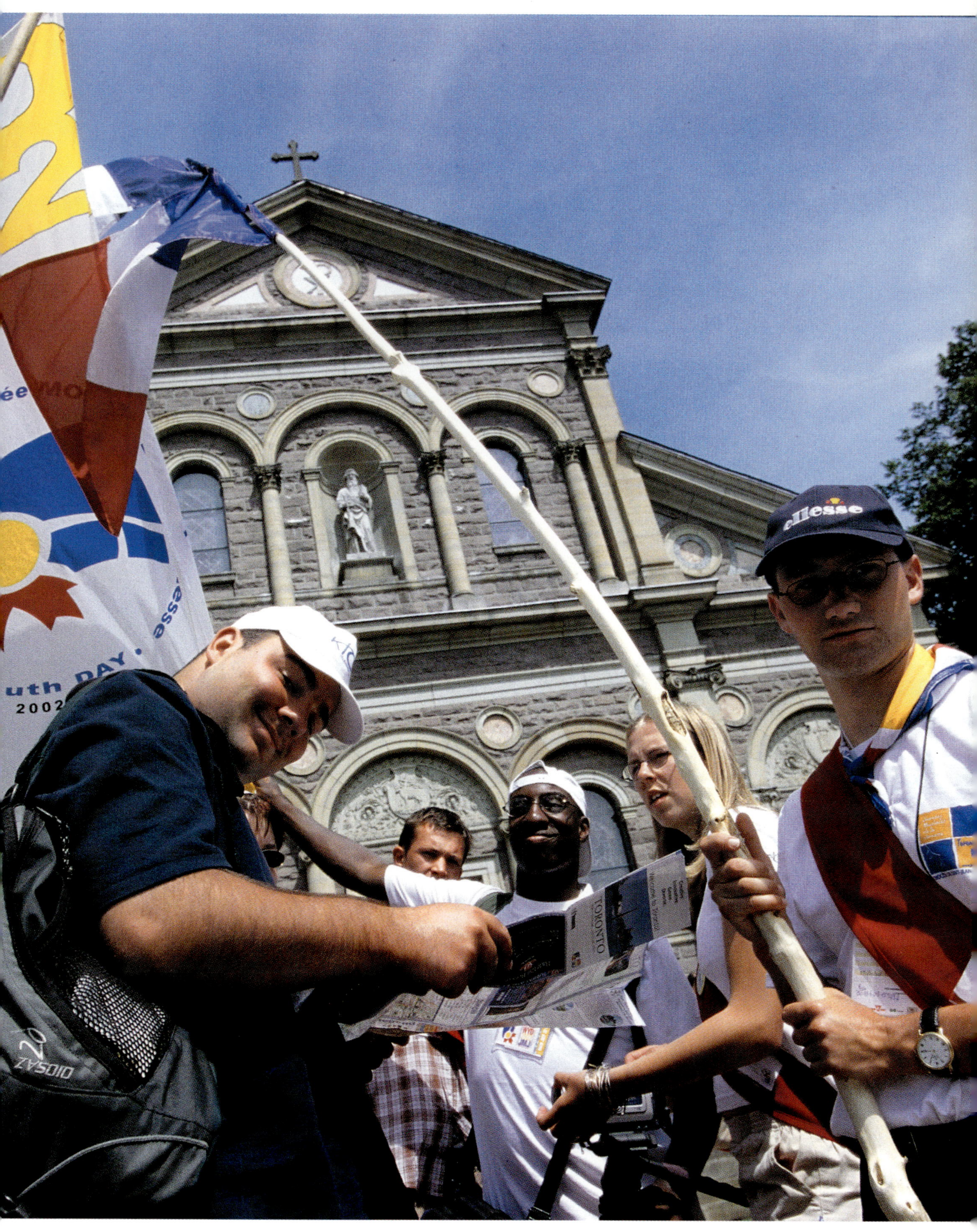

*In the heart of a multicultural and multifaith city,
we shall speak of Christ as the one Saviour
and proclaim the universal salvation of which
the Church is the Sacrament.*

JOHN PAUL II

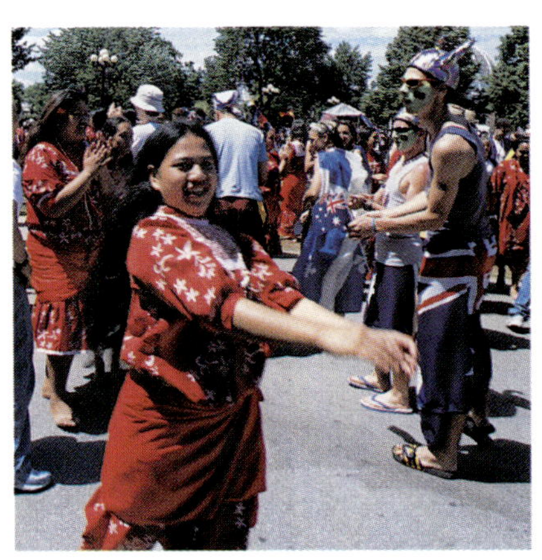

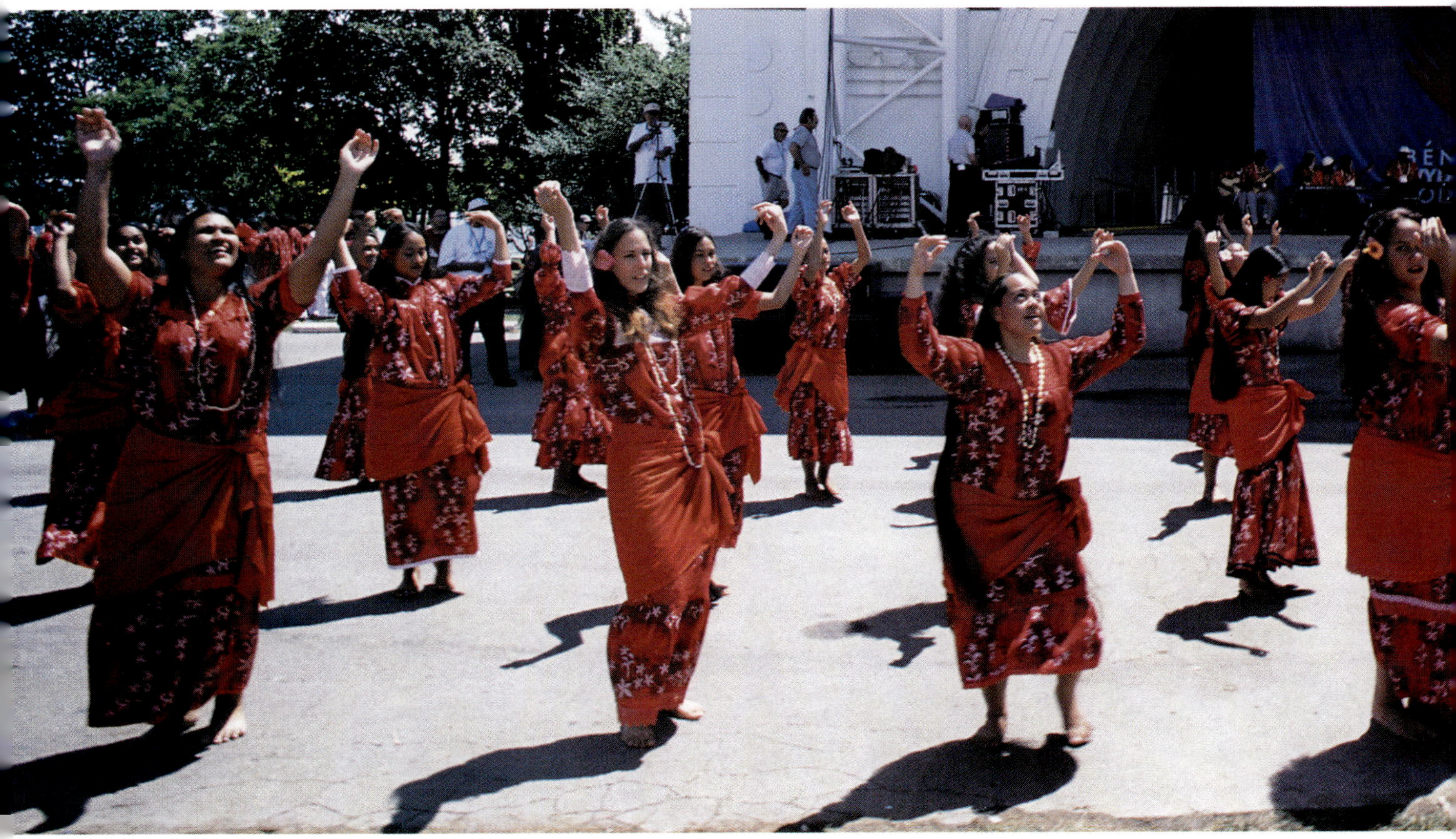

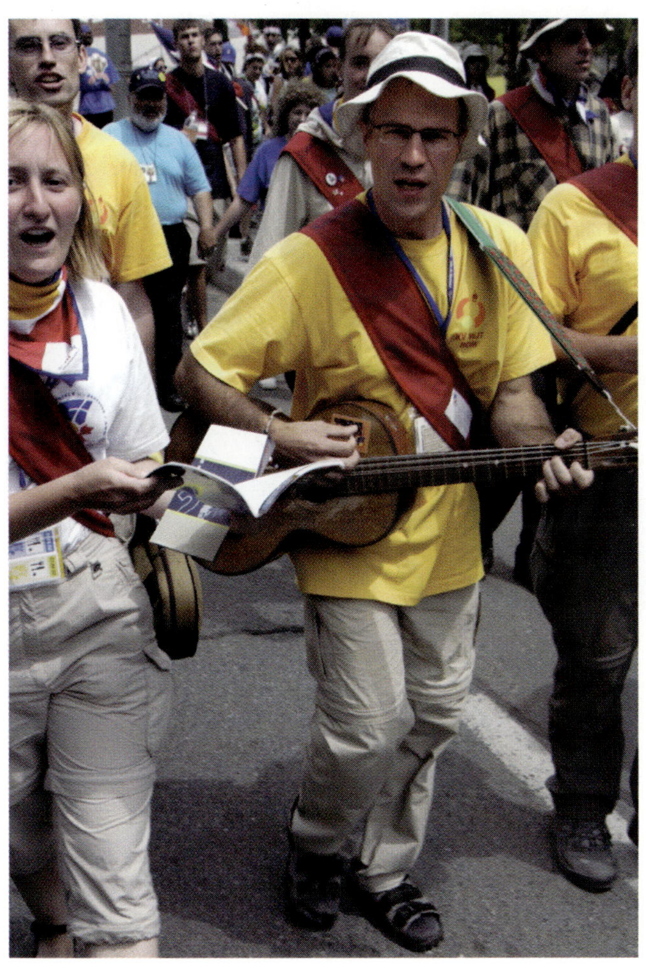

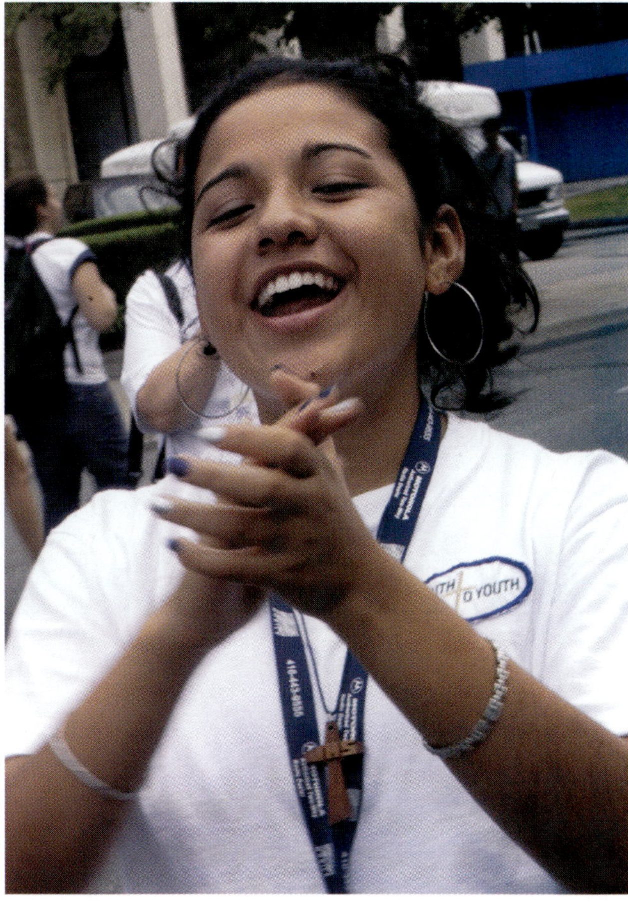

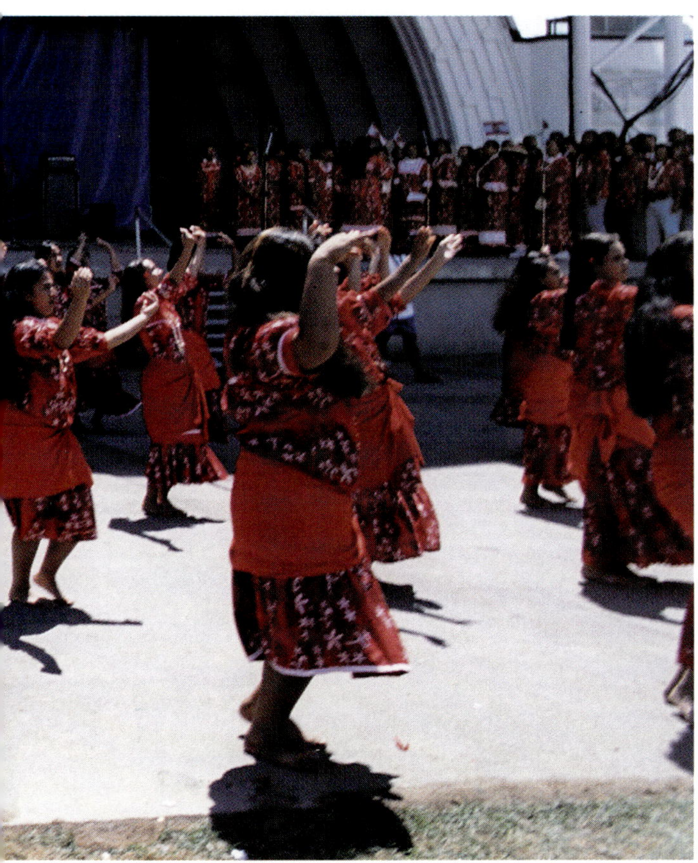

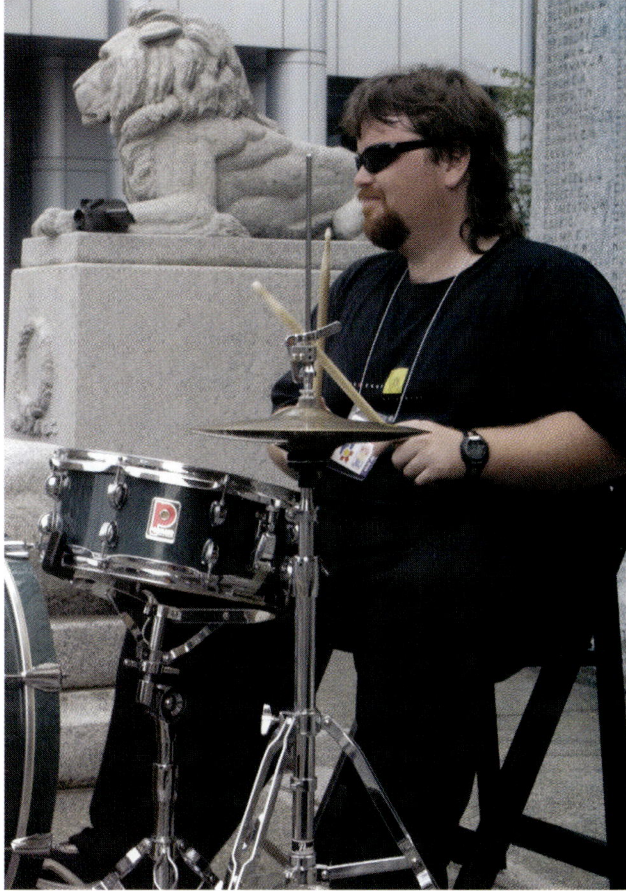

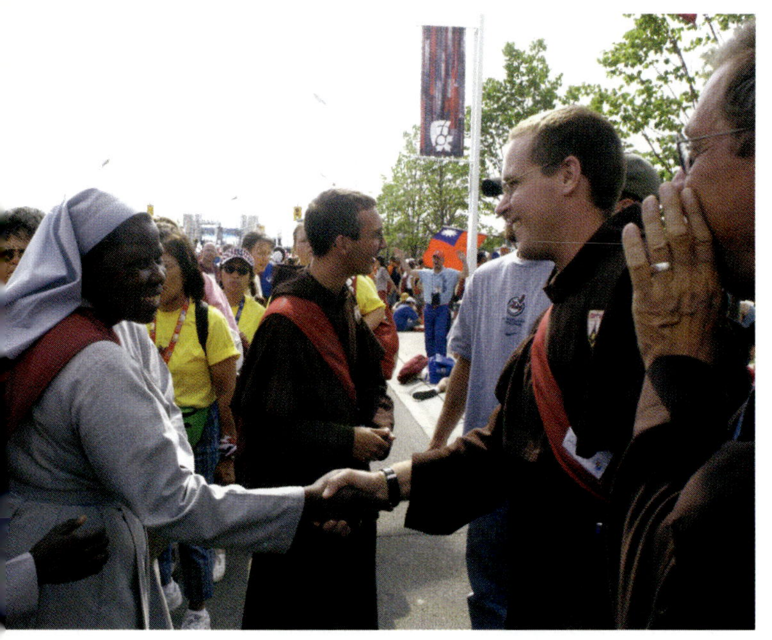

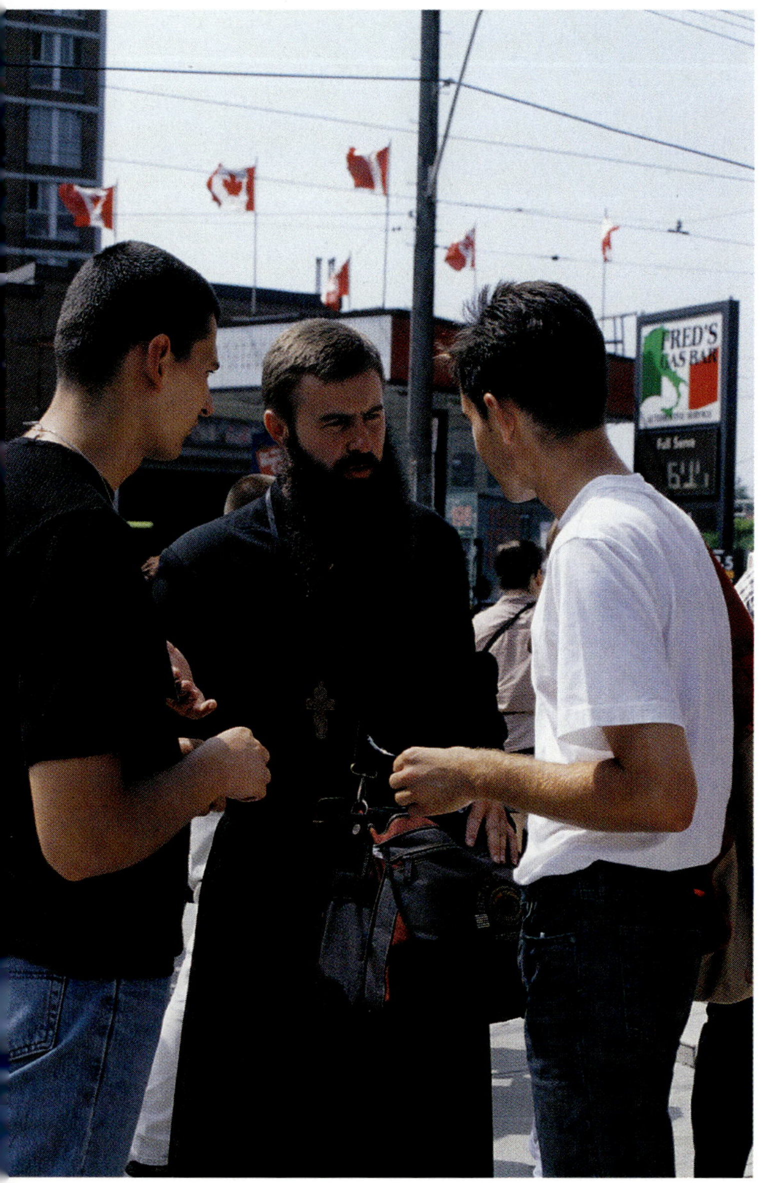

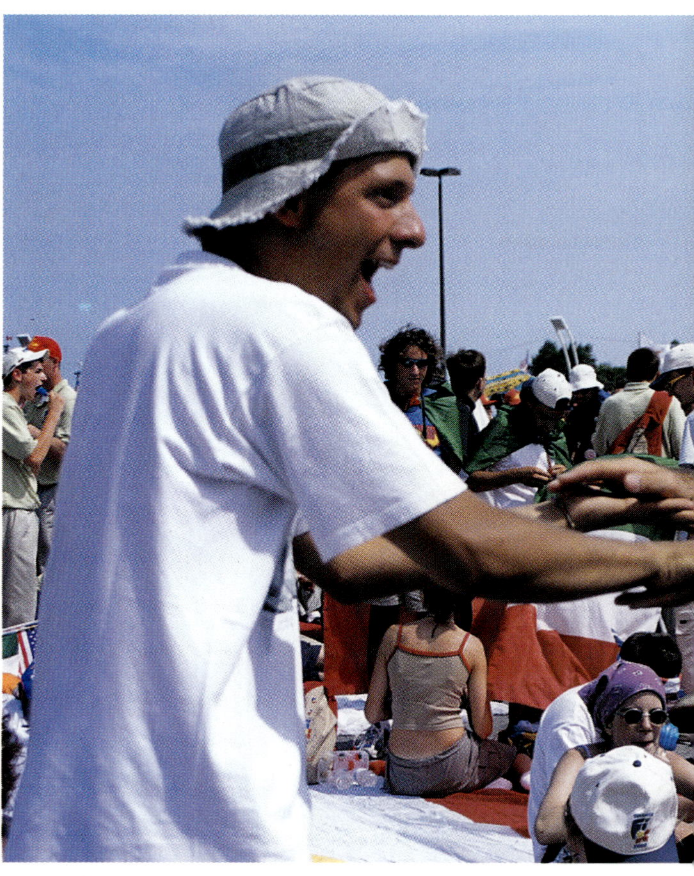

To all of you I say: may your contacts with your pastors help you discover and appreciate more and more the beauty of the Church, experienced as missionary communion.

JOHN PAUL II

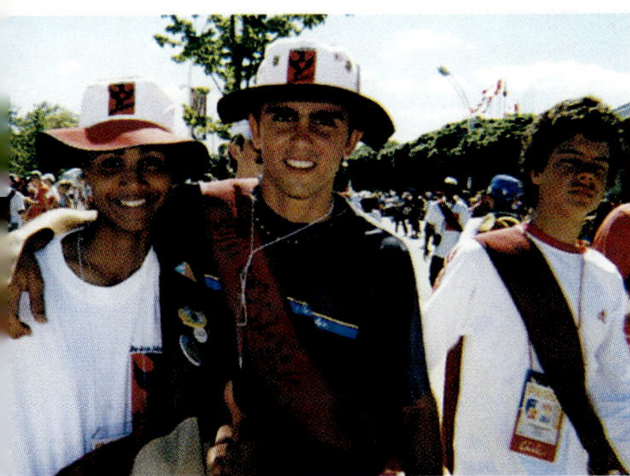

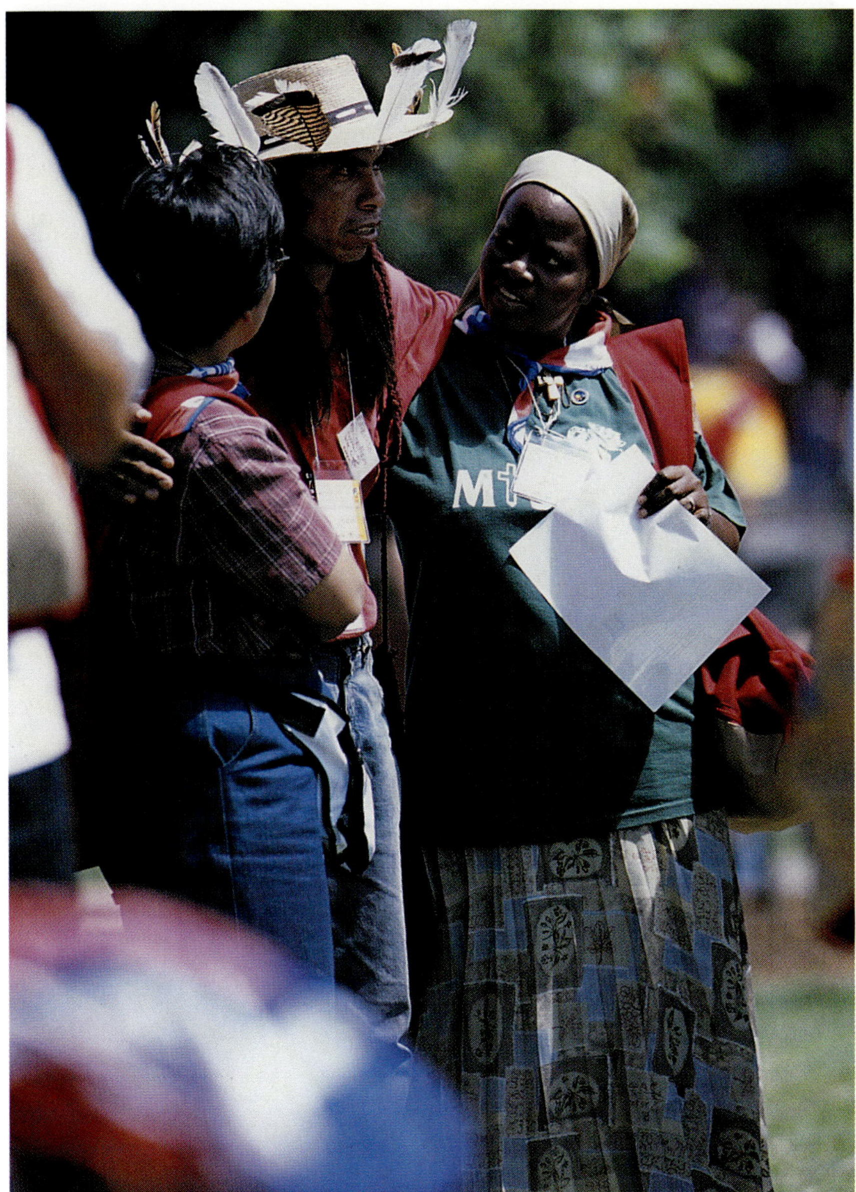

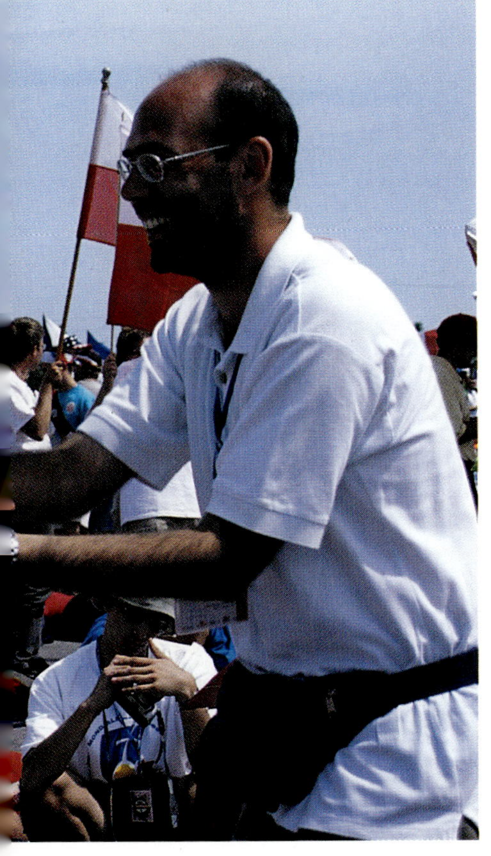

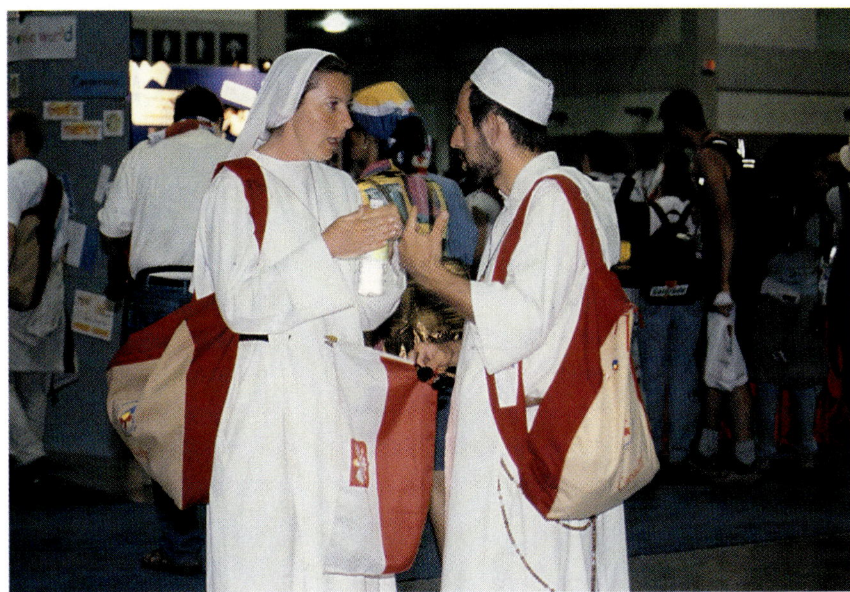

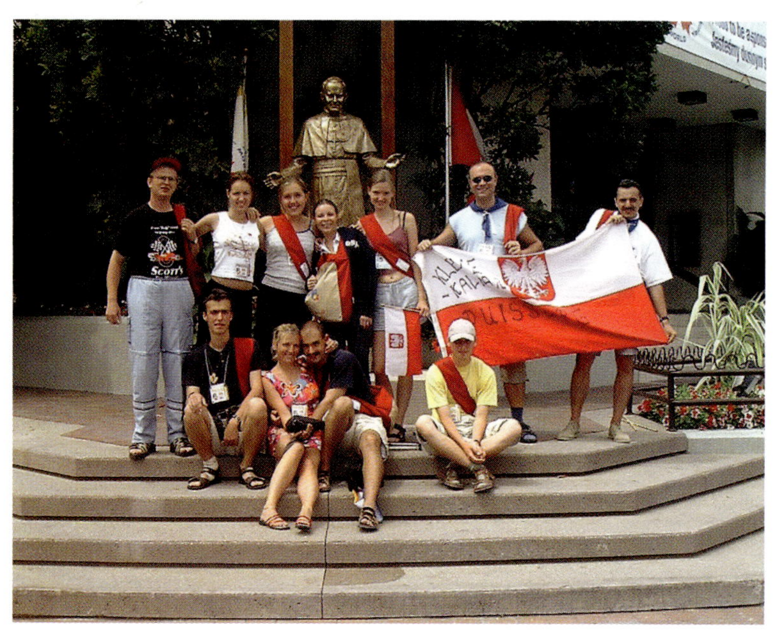

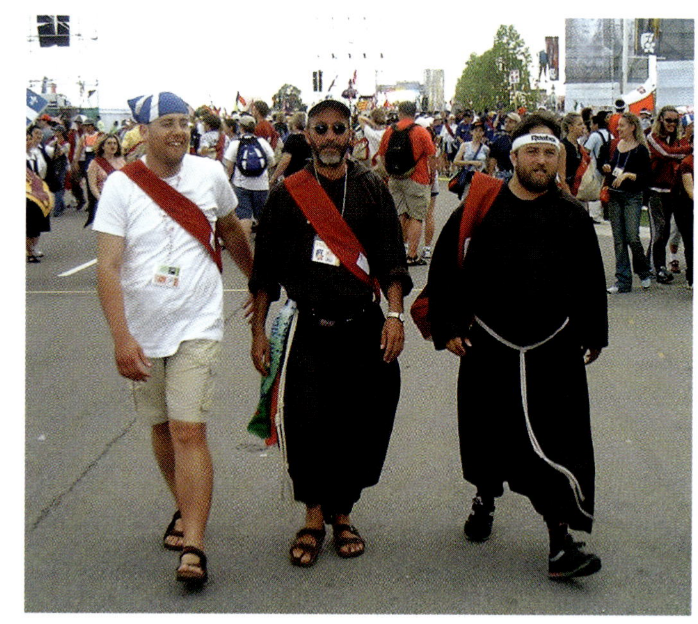

I greet my fellow countrymen who have come to Toronto from Poland.

John Paul II

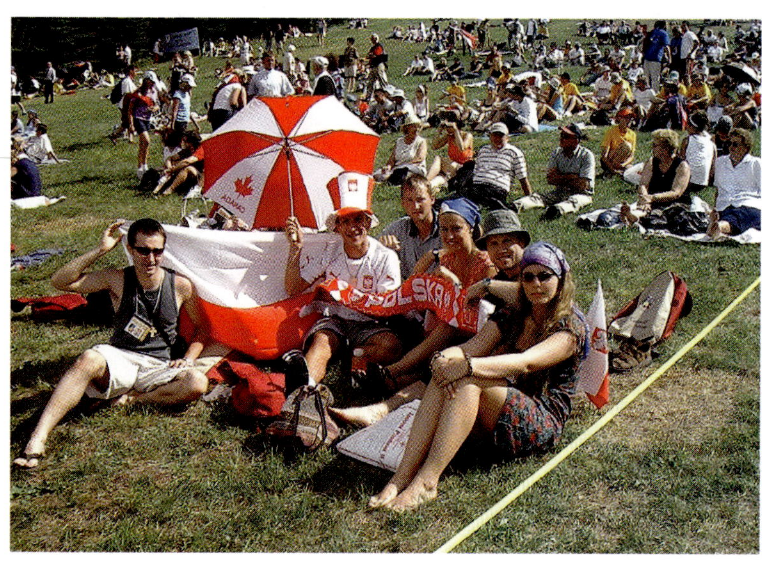

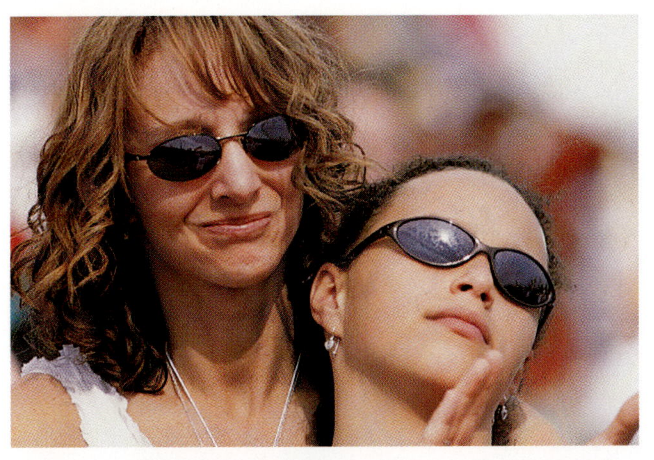 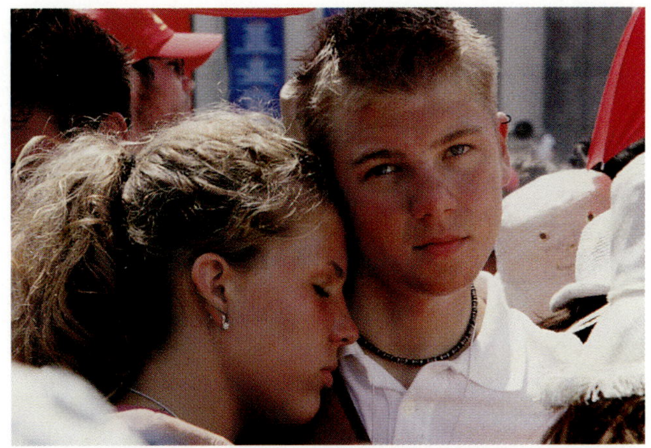

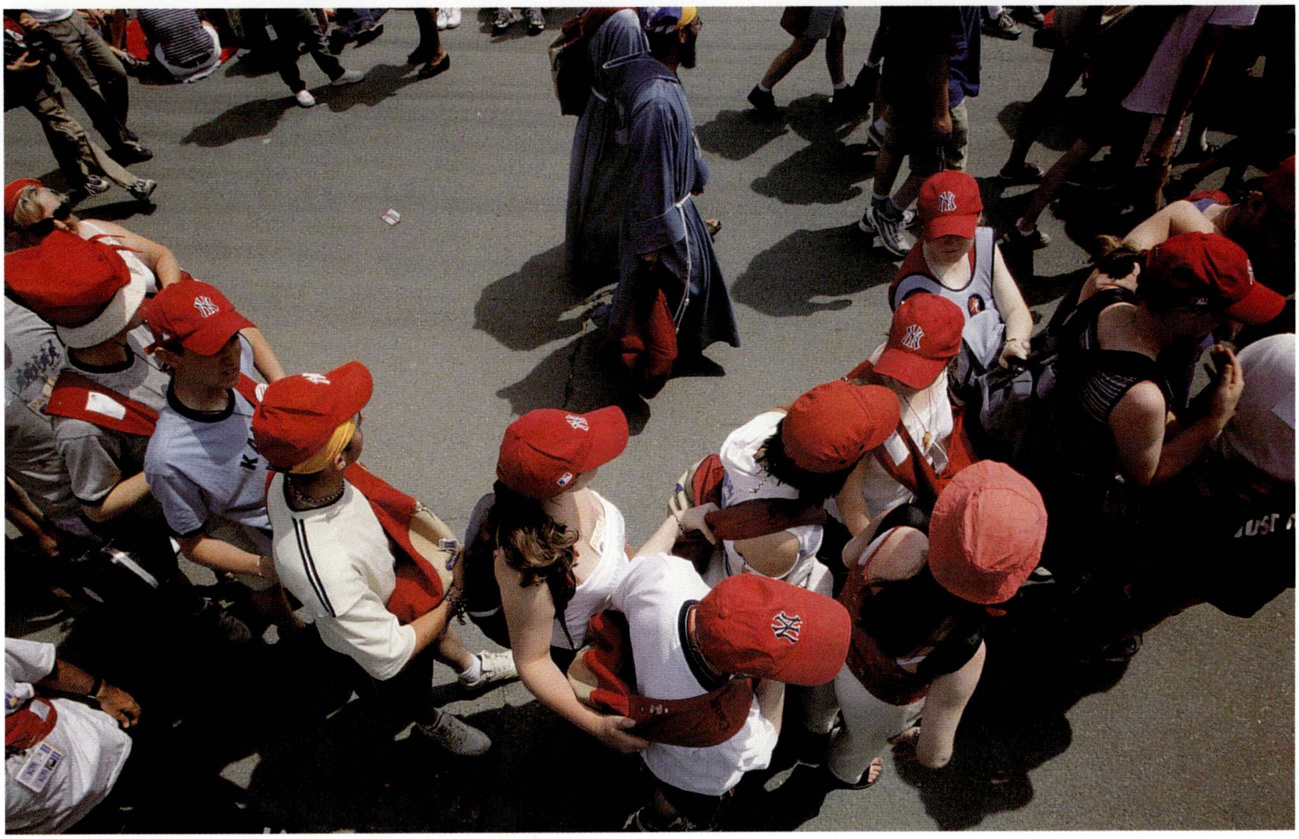

*Young people listening to me, answer the
Lord with strong and generous hearts!
He is counting on you...*

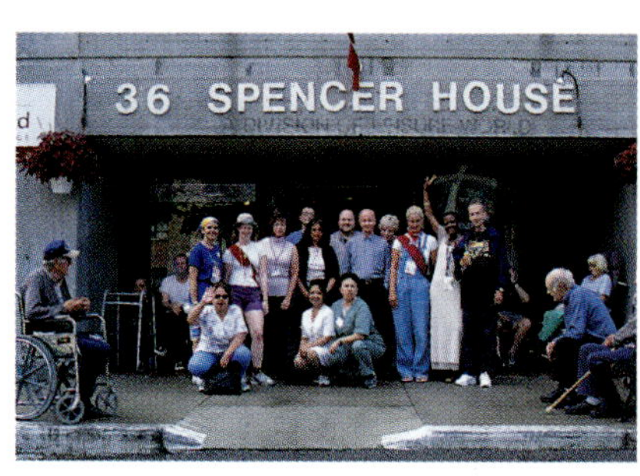 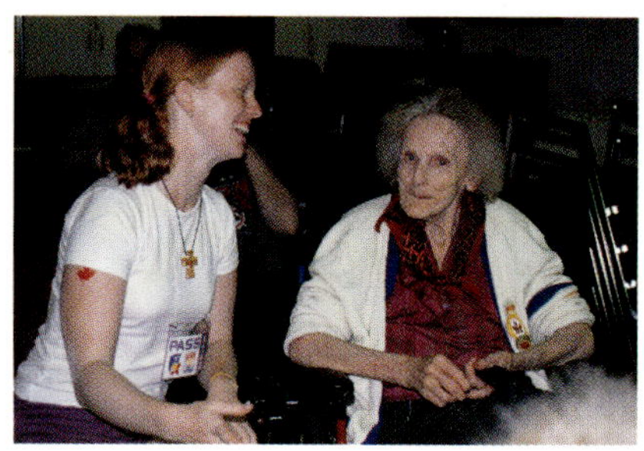 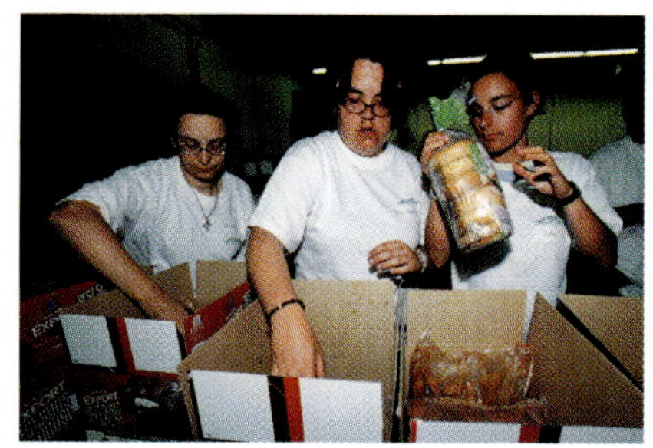

*… Never forget: Christ needs you to carry out his plan
for salvation! Christ needs your youth and your
generous enthusiasm to make his proclamation
of joy resound in the new millennium.*

JOHN PAUL II

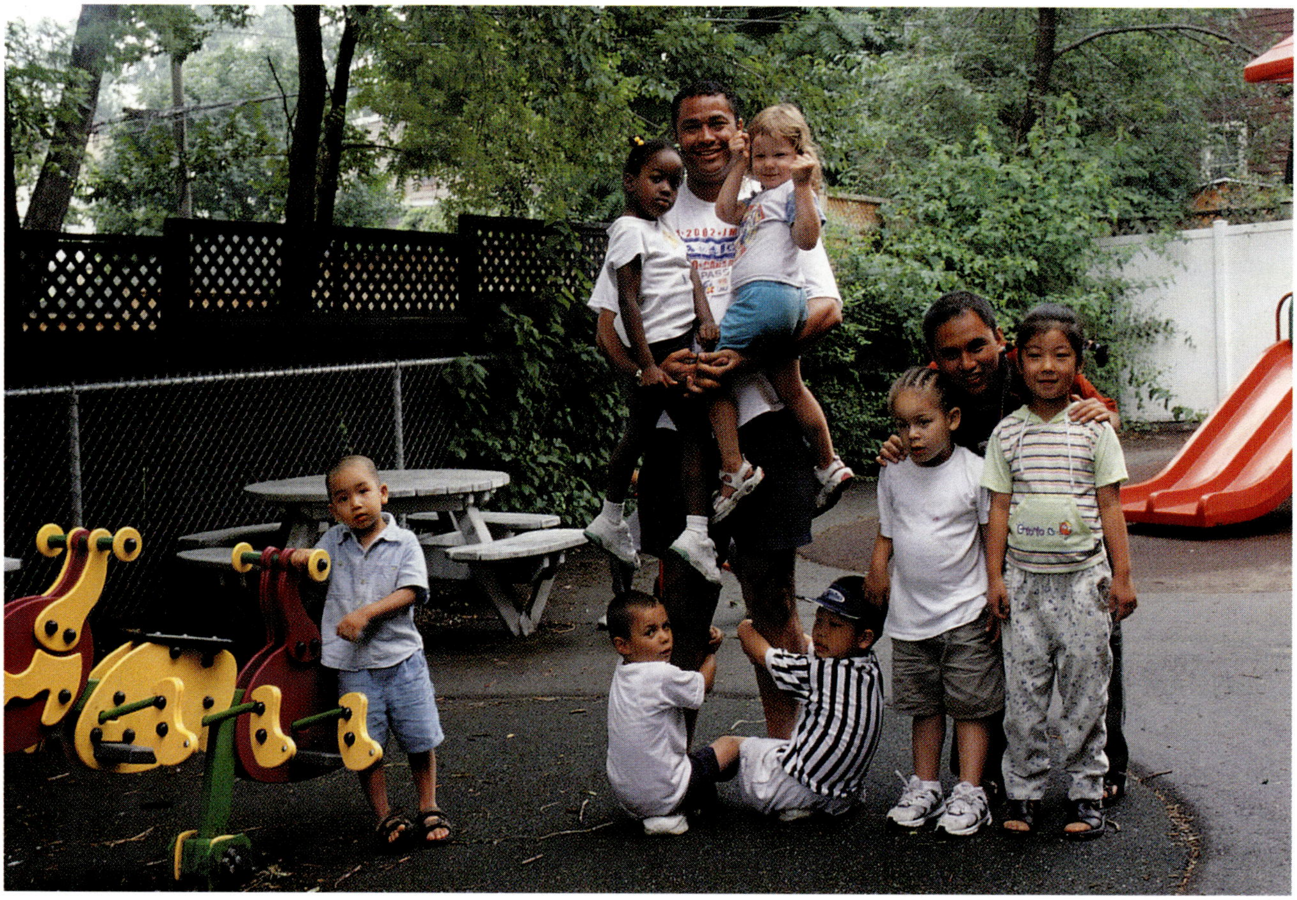

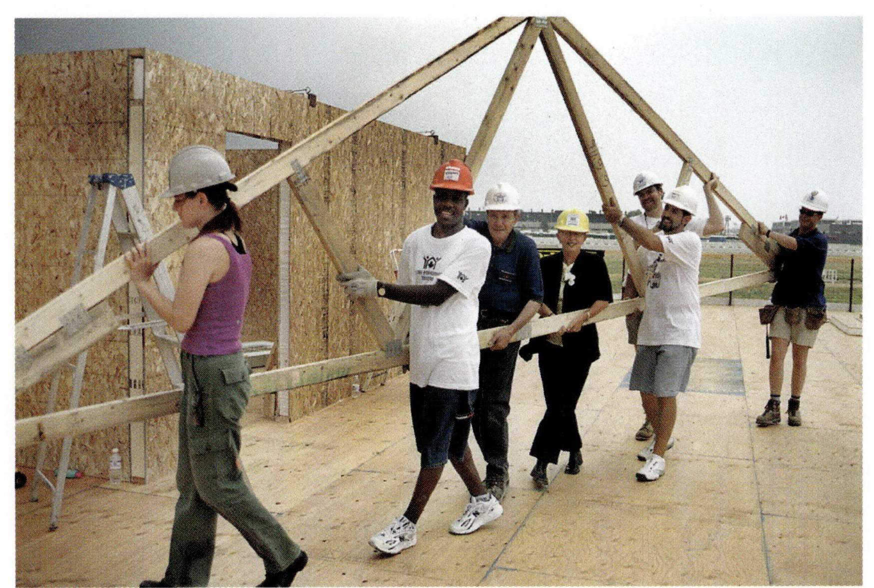

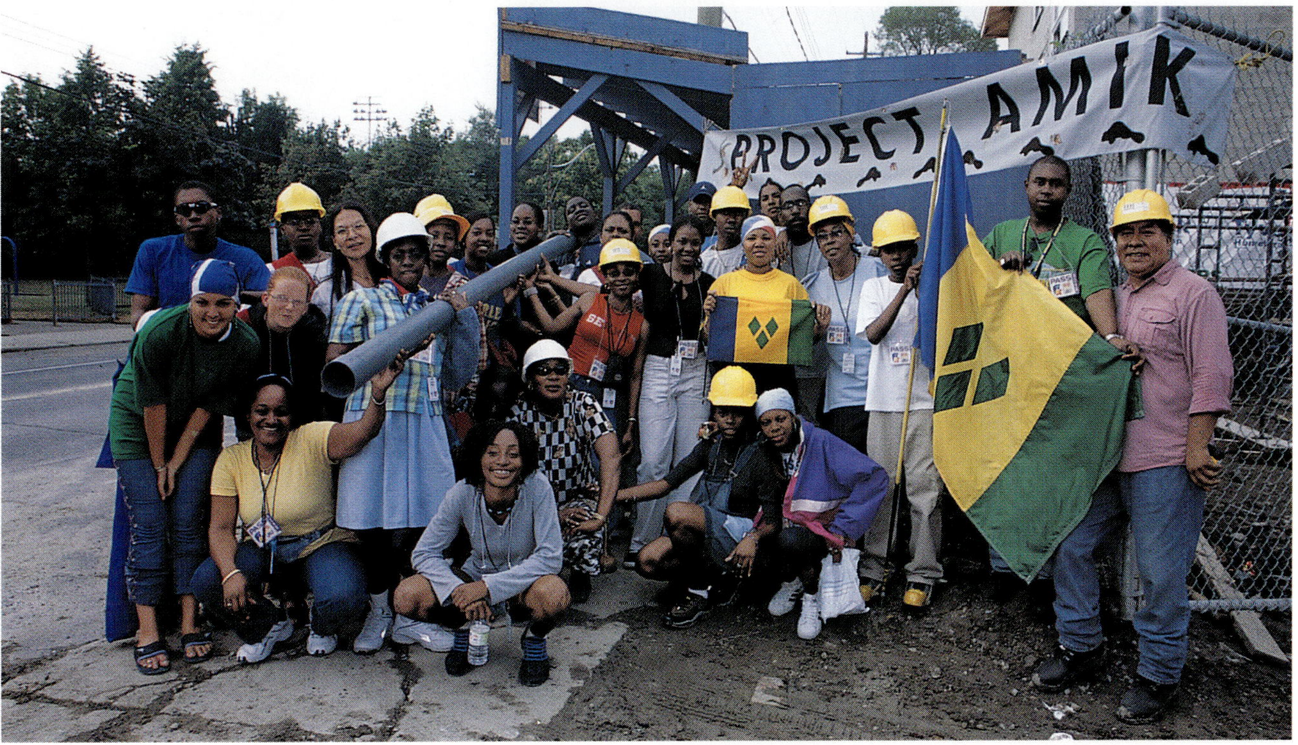
PROJECT AMIK

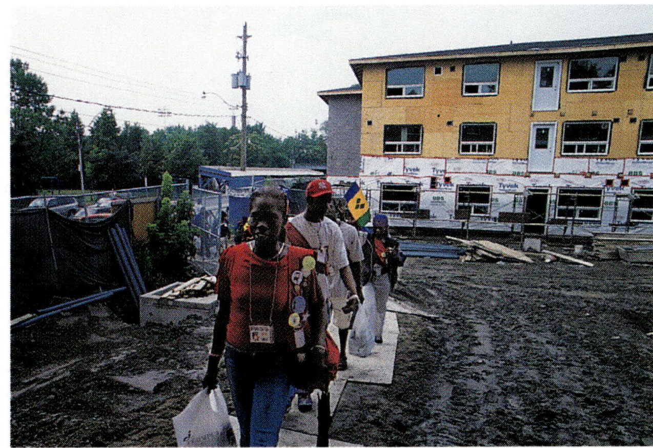

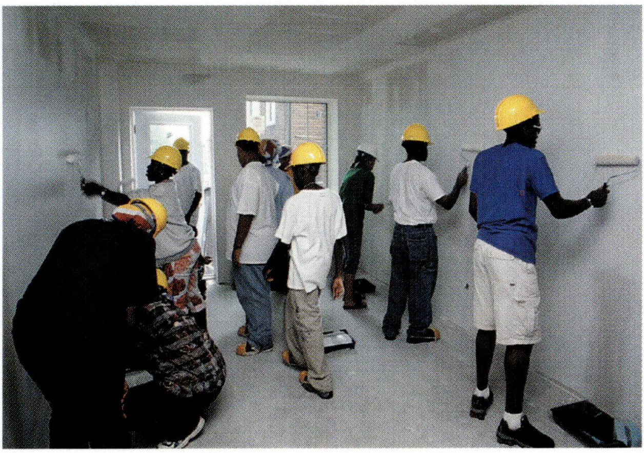

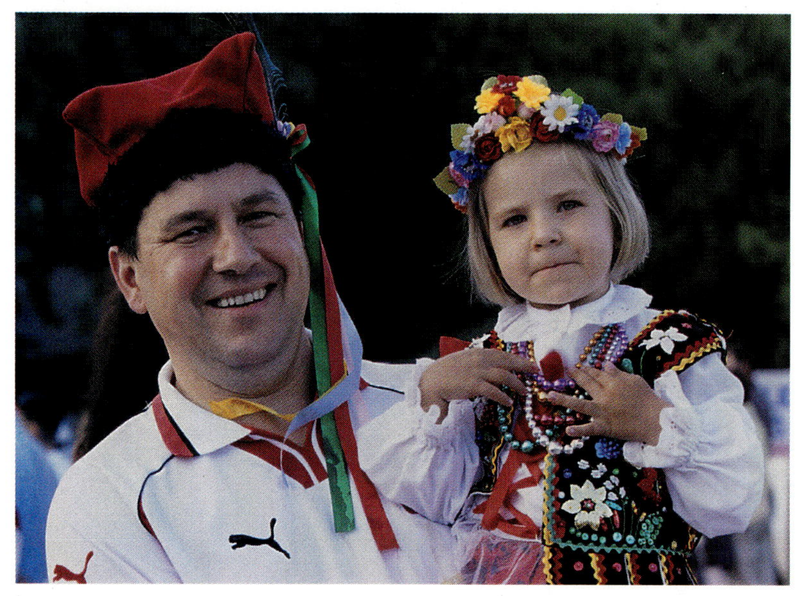

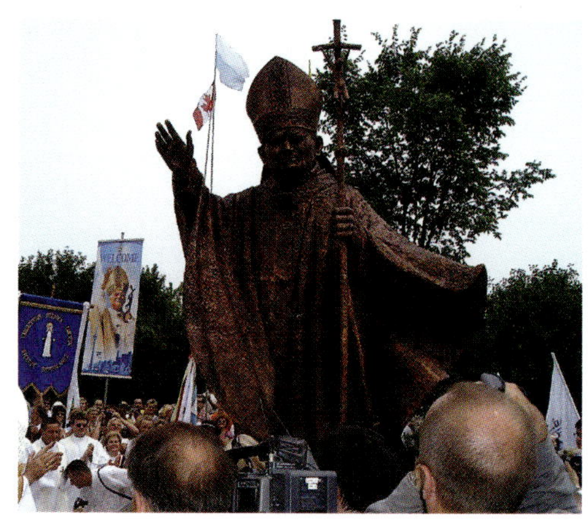

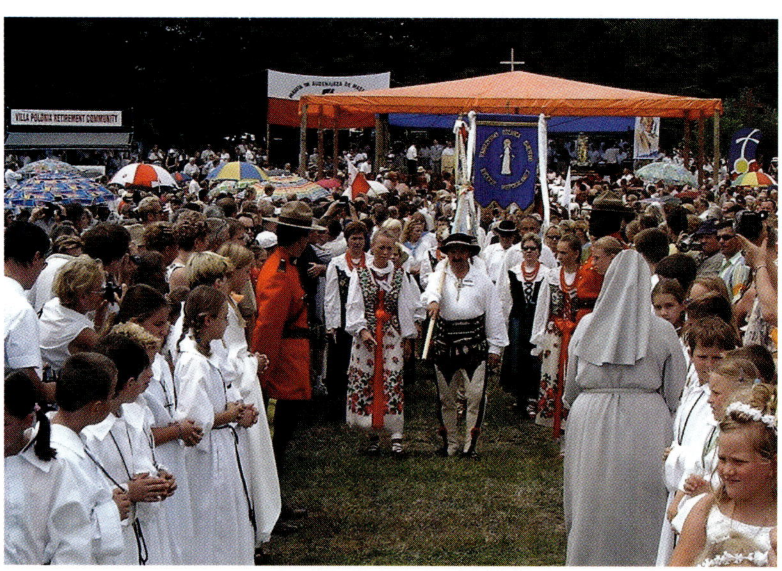

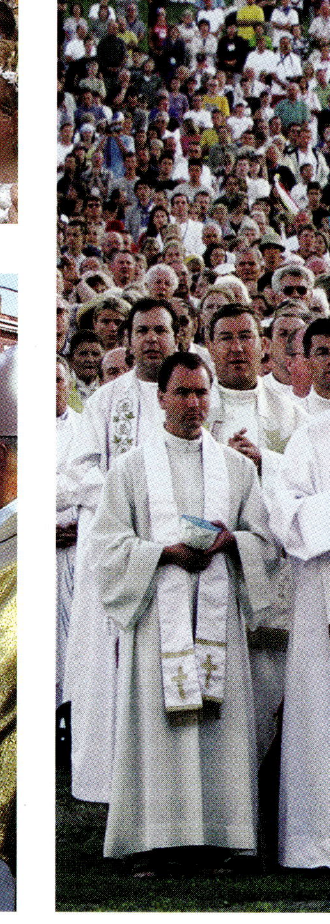

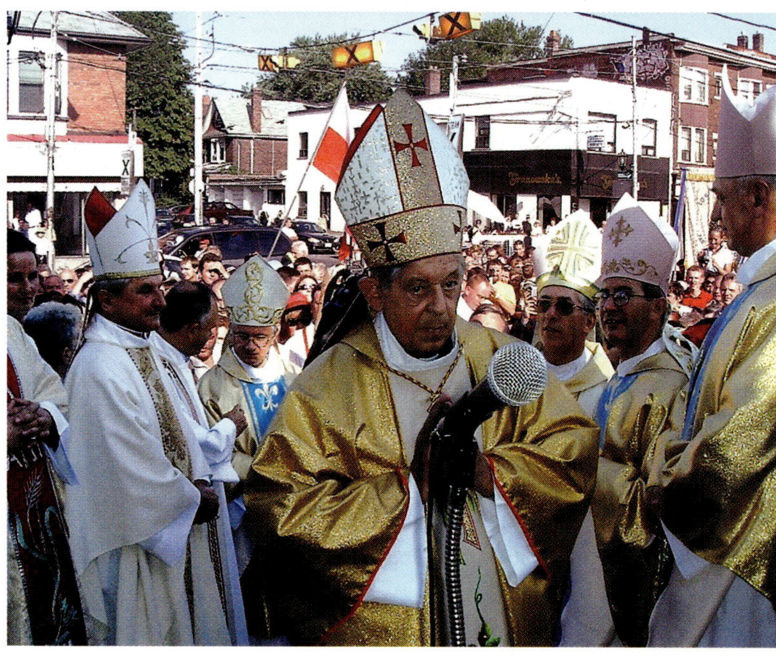

My thoughts turn to our Polish homeland, which I will soon visit again. Never lose sight of your Christian heritage. It is there that you will find the wisdom and courage you need to meet the great moral and ethical challenges of our times. I entrust you all to the protection of Our Lady of Jasna Góra.

JOHN PAUL II

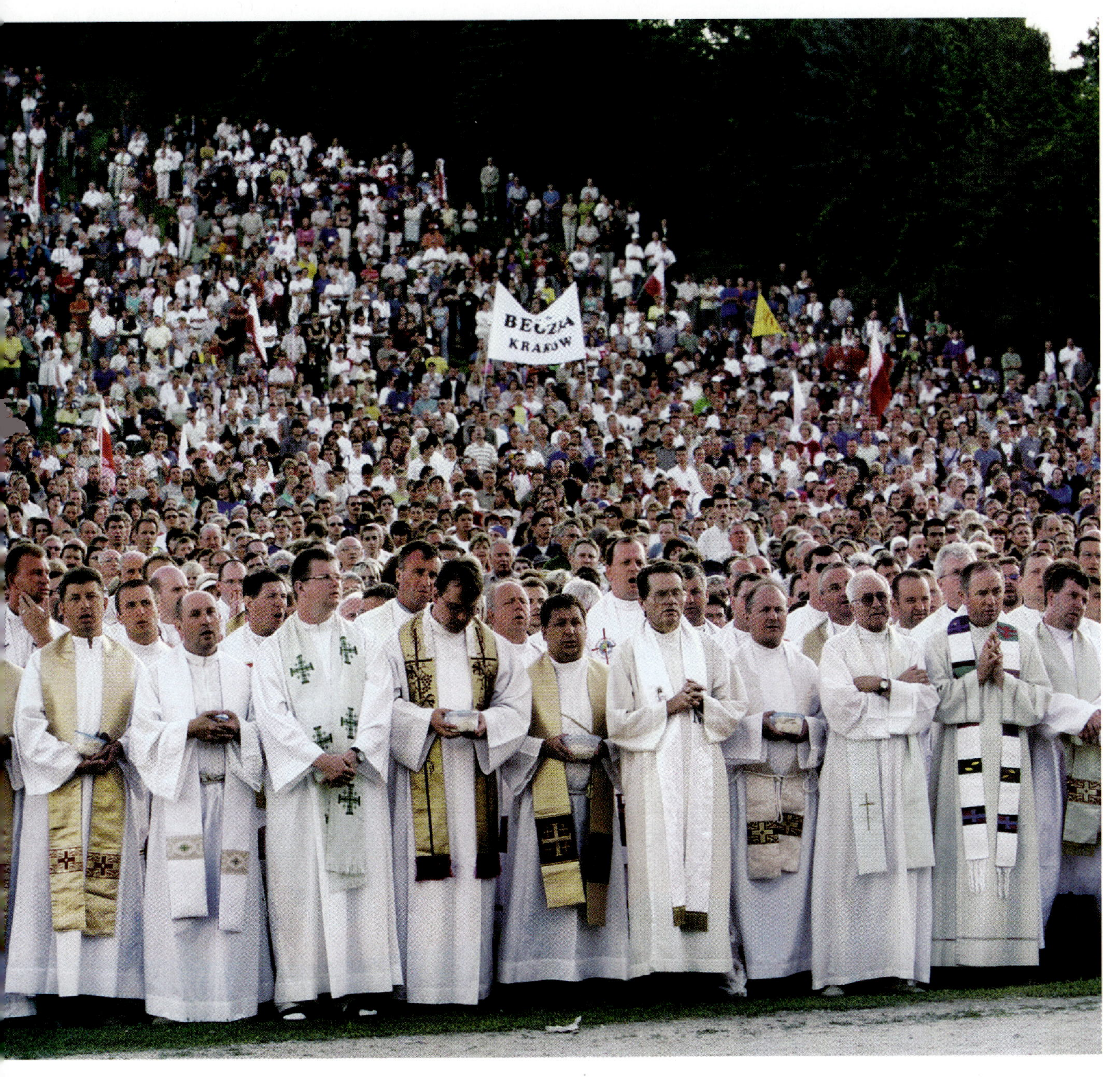

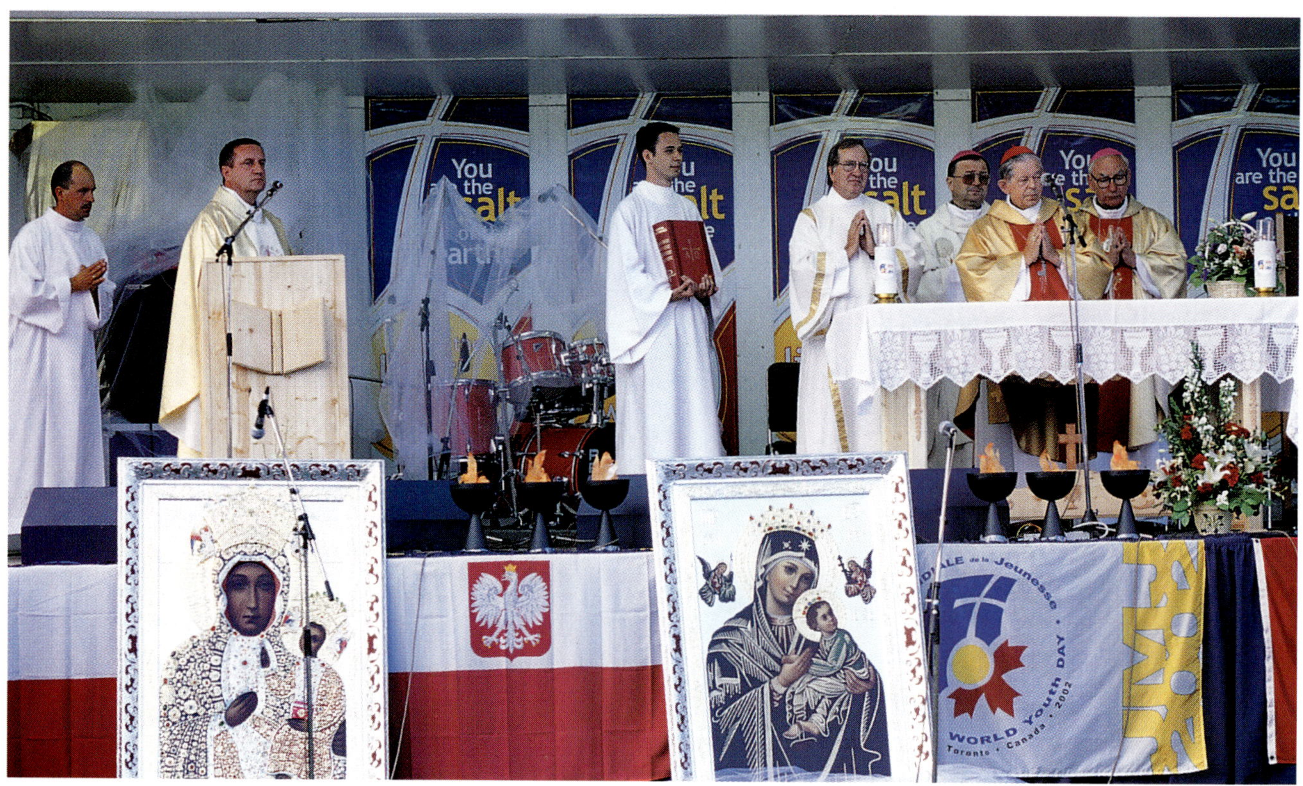

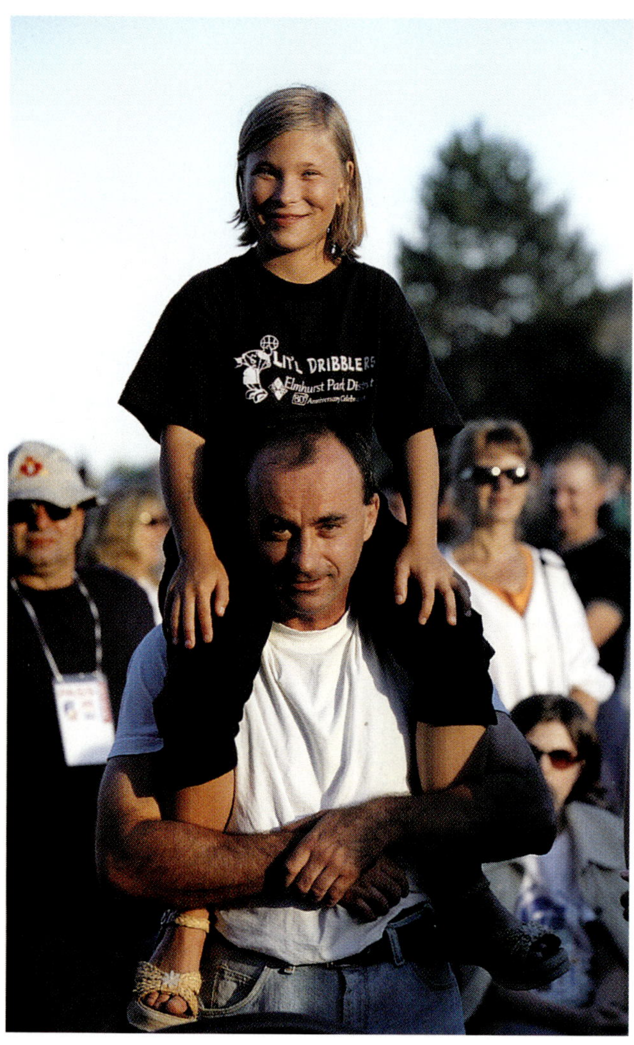

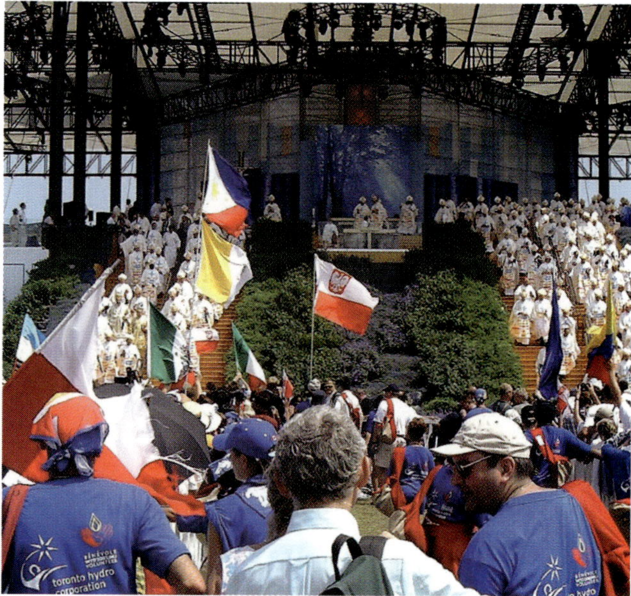

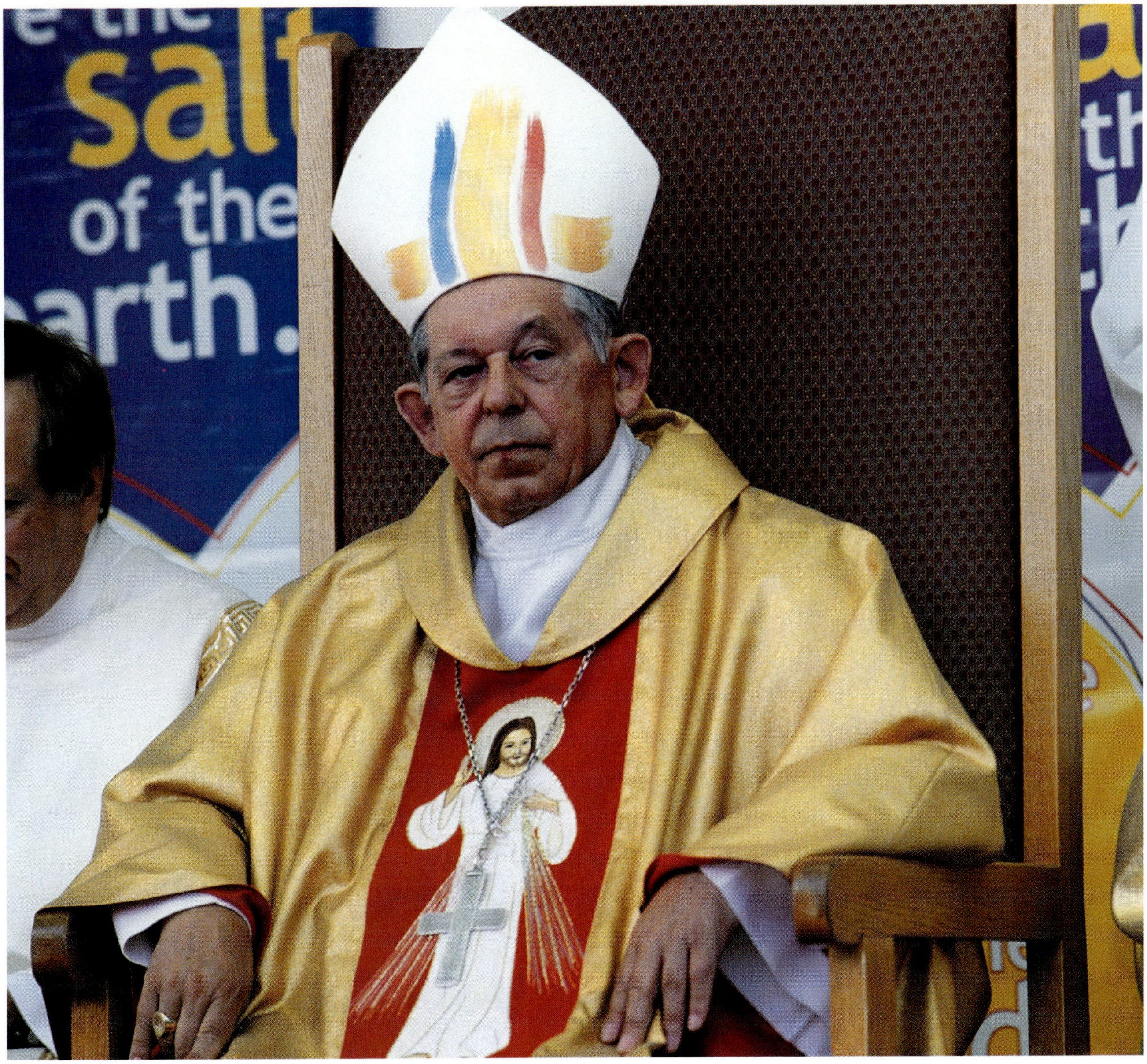

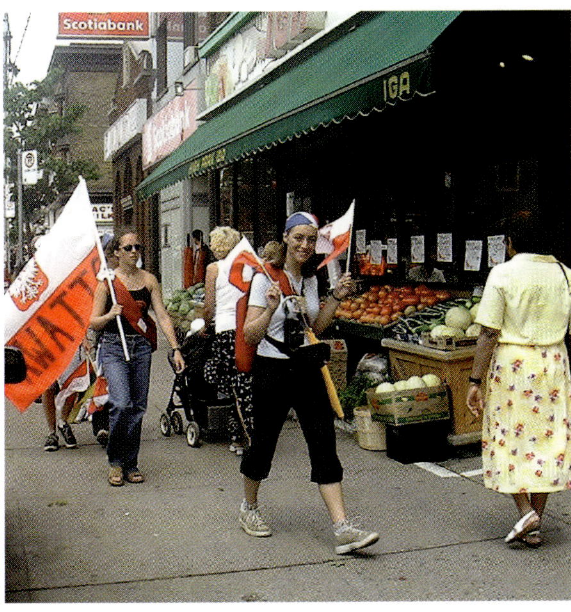

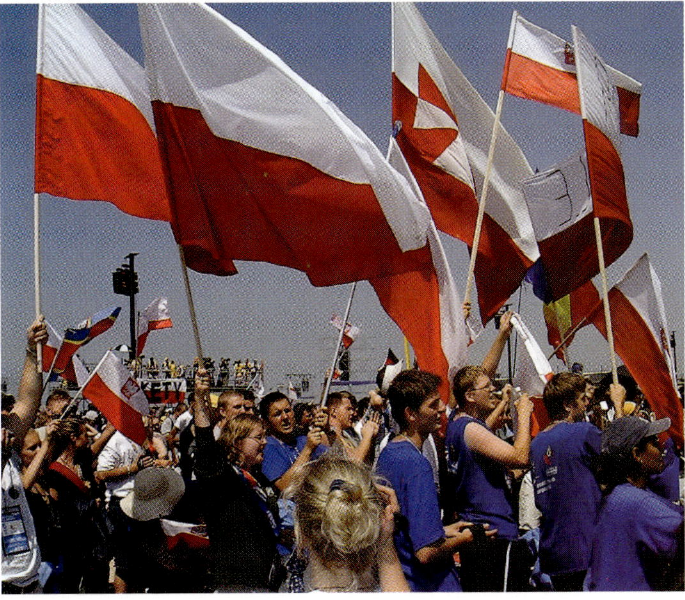

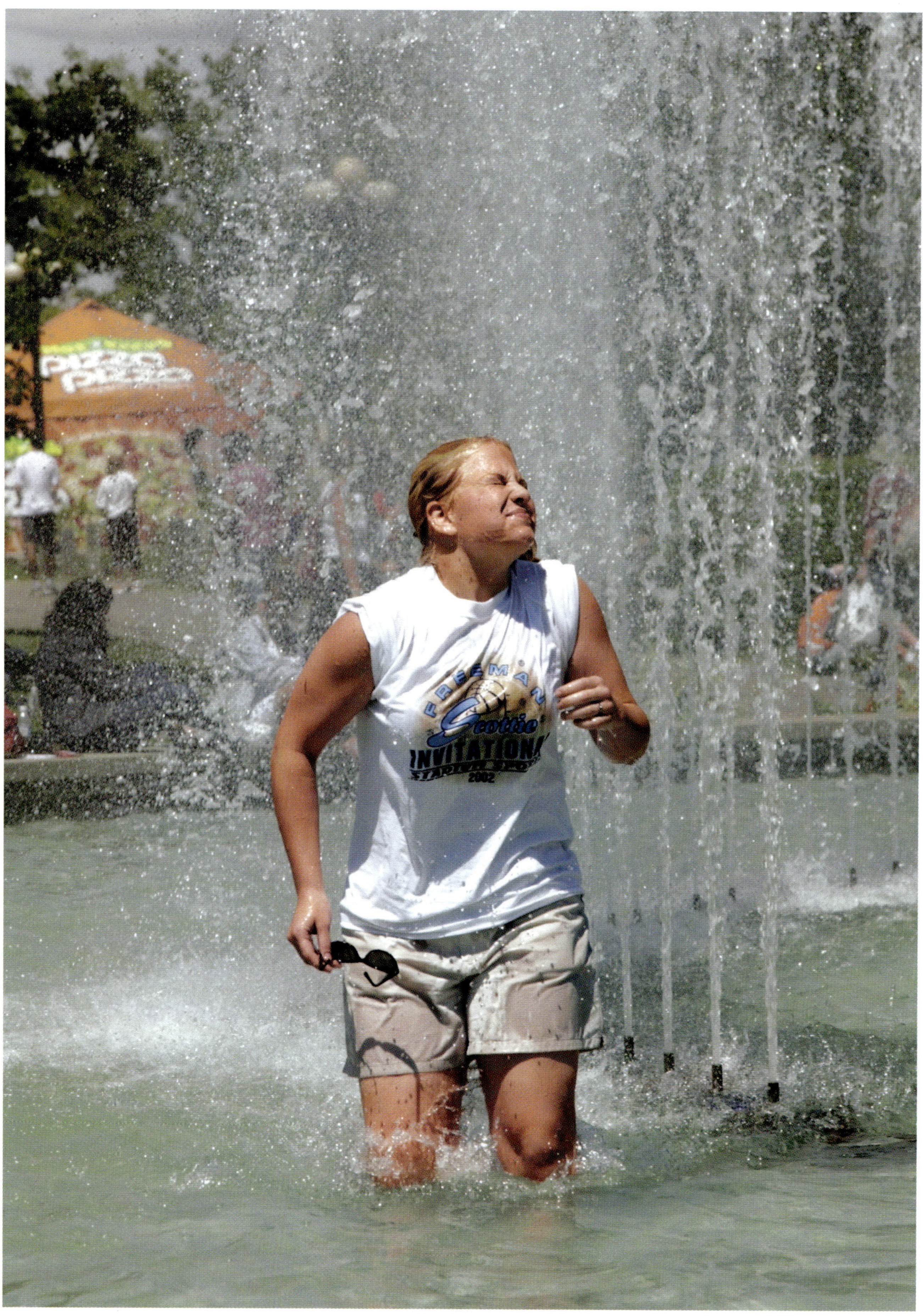

FREEMAN
Scottie
INVITATIONAL
2002

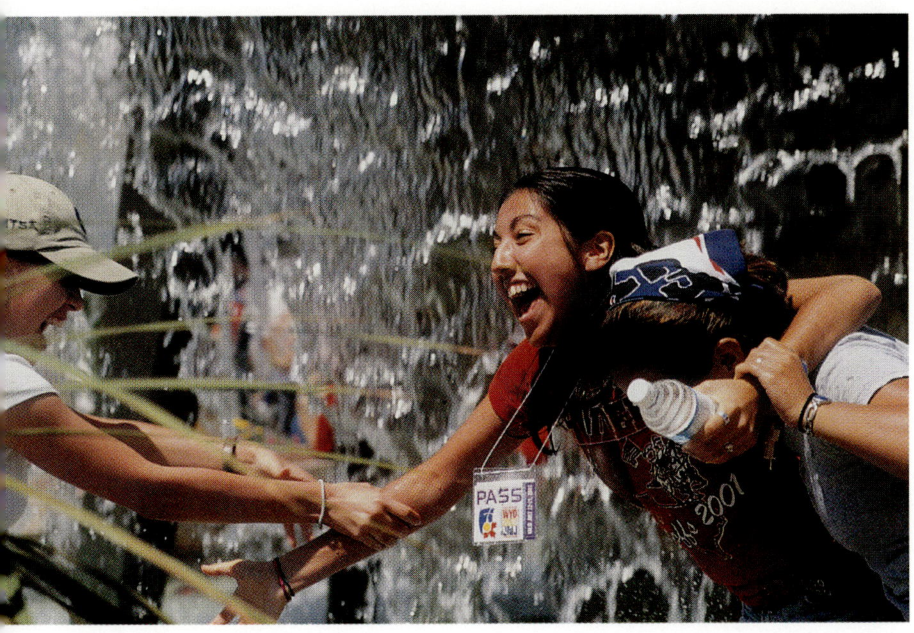

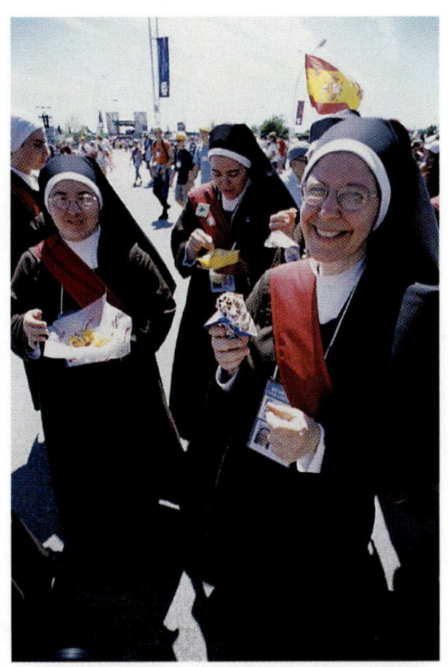

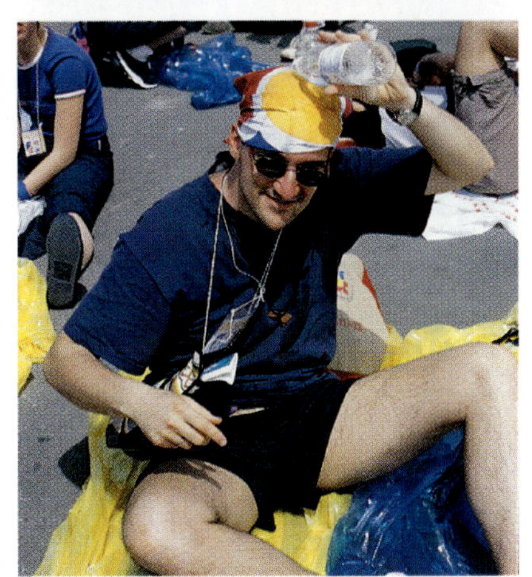

Our personal encounter with Christ bathes life in new light, sets us on the right path and sends us out to be his witnesses.

JOHN PAUL II

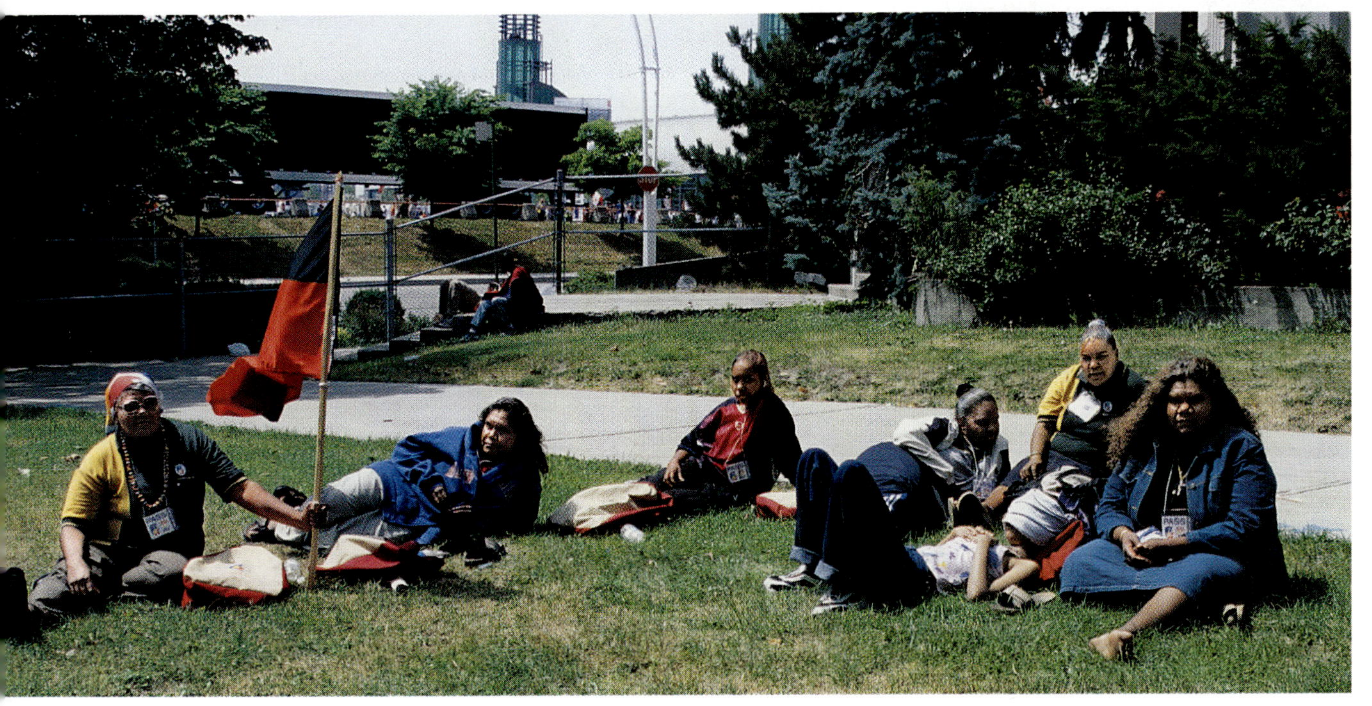

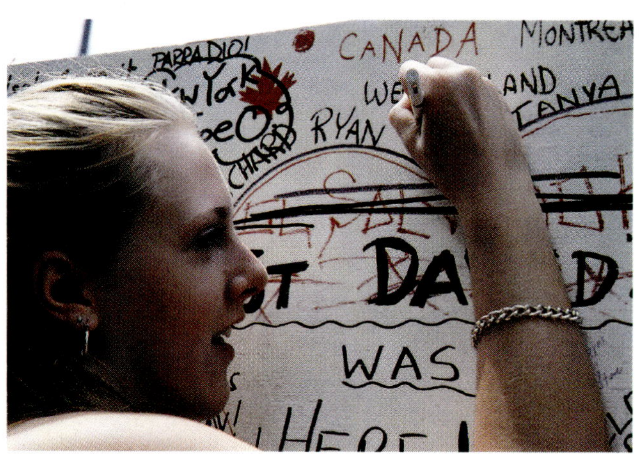 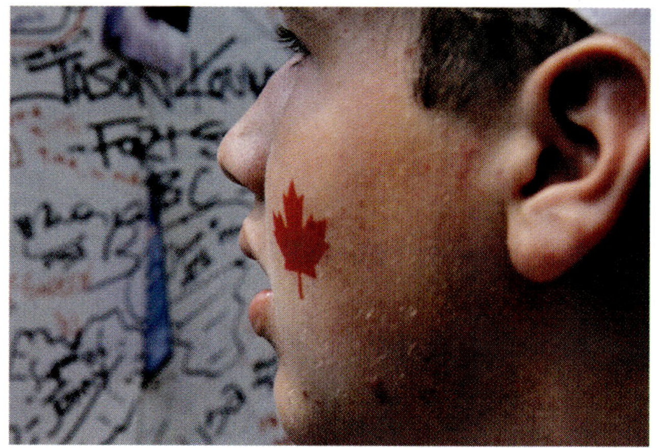

Day after day, from all parts of the world, I received in the Vatican good news about all the initiatives that have marked your journey here. And often, even without having met you, I commended you one by one in my prayers to the Lord. He has always known you, and he loves each one of you personally.

John Paul II

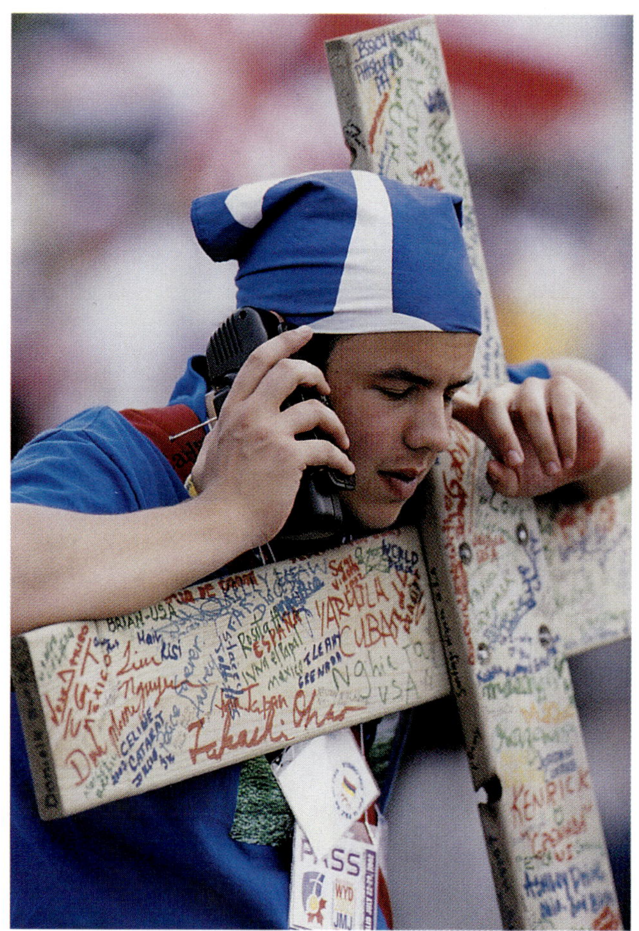 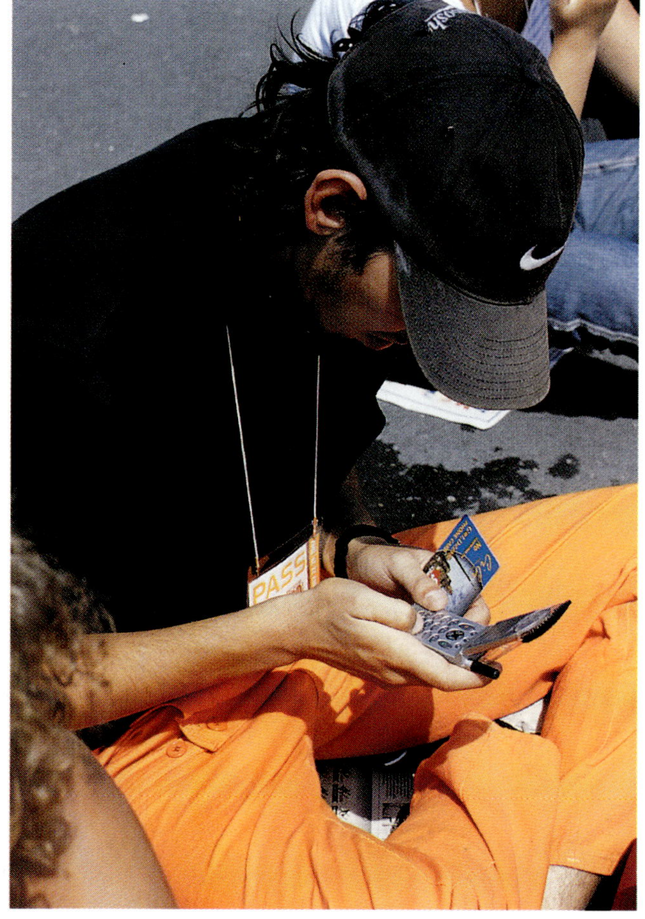

A meeting place of cultures

Getting to the rooms reserved for the discussion groups proves to be a challenge as you run a gauntlet of entertaining distractions. Along the way you pass through concert areas where you can hear performances covering every musical taste from Christian rock to Marian hymns, and in just about any language that comes to mind. You walk around hundreds of pilgrims seated on the floors of the exhibition halls eating their lunch. You spot a group of Mexicans in a hallway praying with their bishop, or see priests hearing confessions in the midst of this happy confusion. You breeze past sandwich vendors, vocation information booths, and kiosks full of books and magazines. You look upon thousands of faces, many showing traces of fatigue but still smiling.

When you finally get settled in your assigned place in the discussion group, you must be prepared for the unexpected. At one session, ten people in a huge room are talking quietly about how they try to live the Gospel in their daily lives. During the often animated discussion, the door opens and a dozen or so people come in and sit down in silence at the far end of the room. This happens again and again. By an hour later the late arrivals number about 50. Some sleep, others pray or read. Obviously these young people prefer the peace and quiet of this room to the hustle and bustle outside the door.

All the while the discussion group keeps on talking, without any embarrassment. Who are these latecomers? They are exhausted pilgrims just arriving from the Philippines for World Youth Day. They enter the room discreetly to rest and to listen and to be. They later thank the discussion leader for the hospitality they have received.

A small incident, to be sure, but one full of significance: a marriage between speech and silence, sharing and rest, discussion and prayer. Perhaps this is a foretaste of what it is to be a gathering of what John Paul II describes as the "people of the Beatitudes."

Only Jesus speaks the unchanging message that responds to the deepest longing of the human heart, because he alone knows "what is in each person" (John 2:25).

JOHN PAUL II

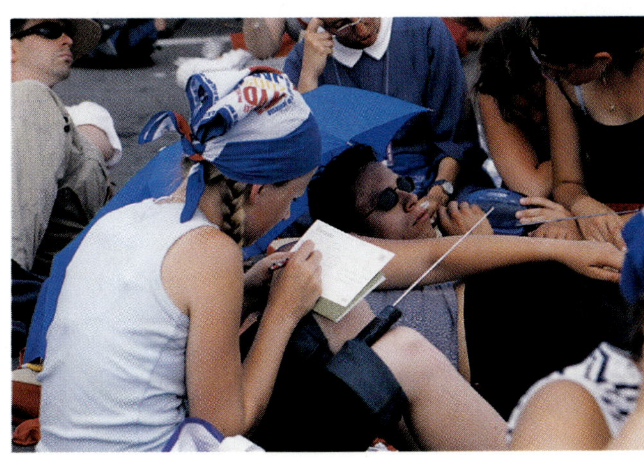

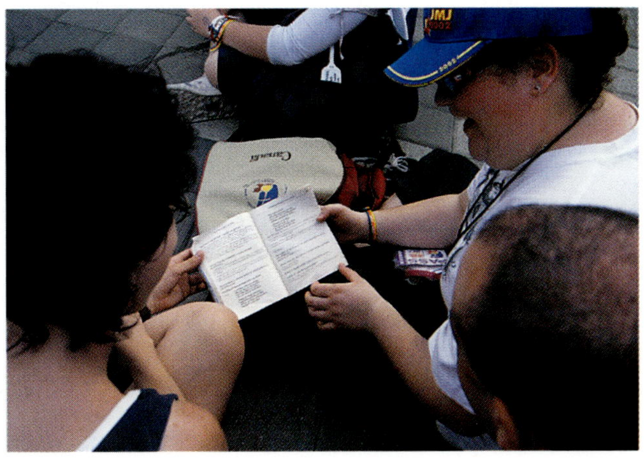

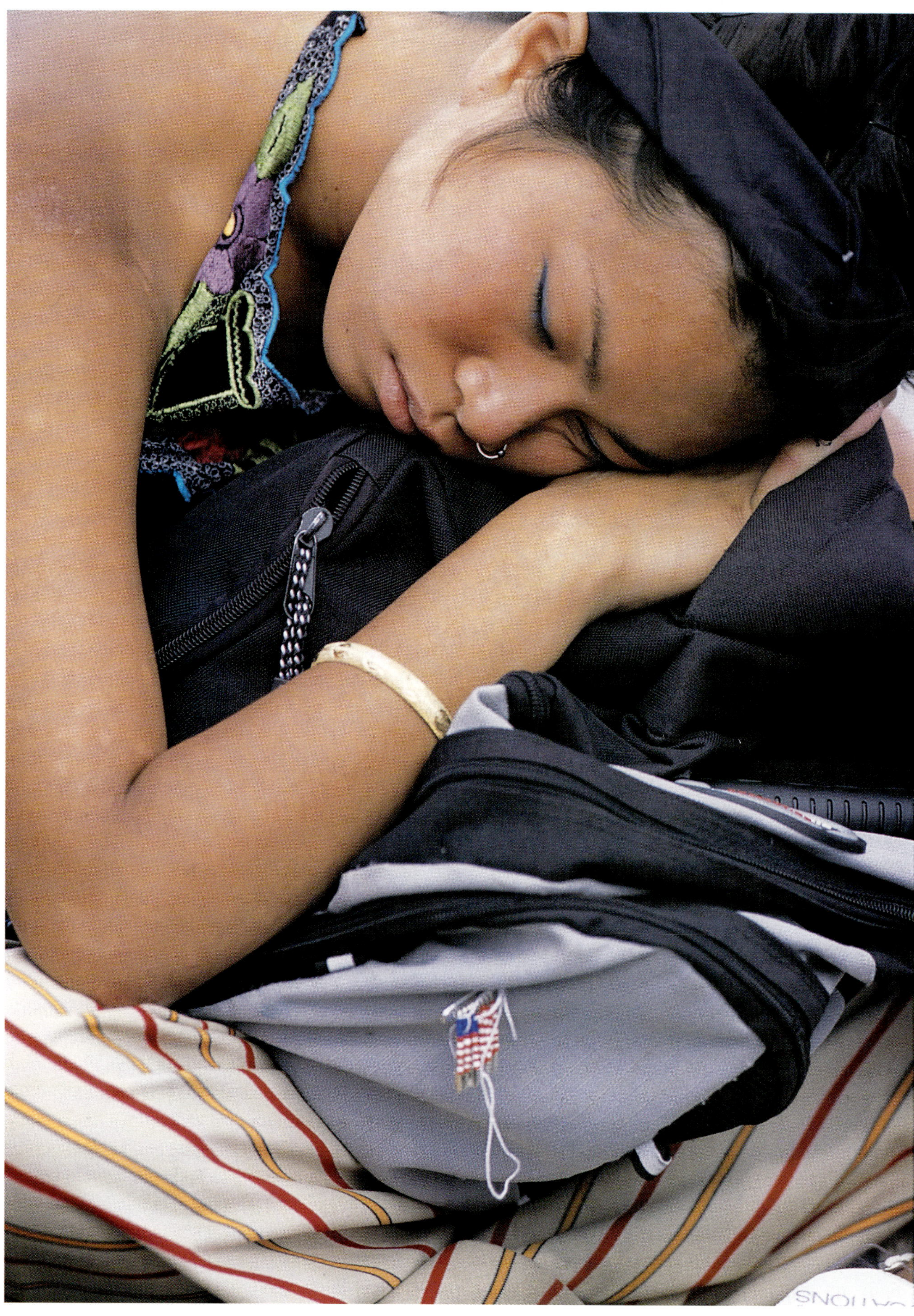

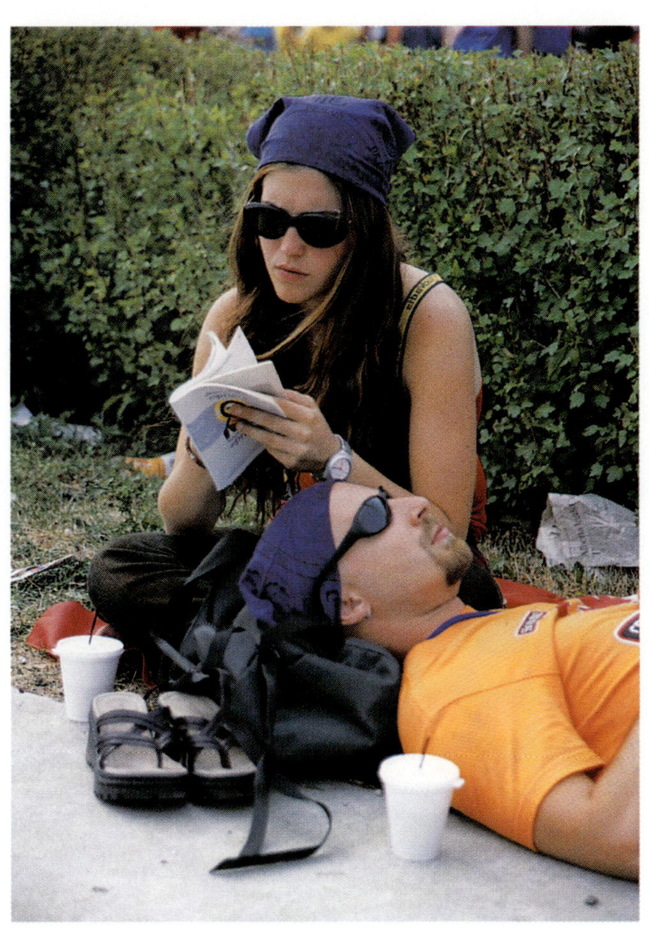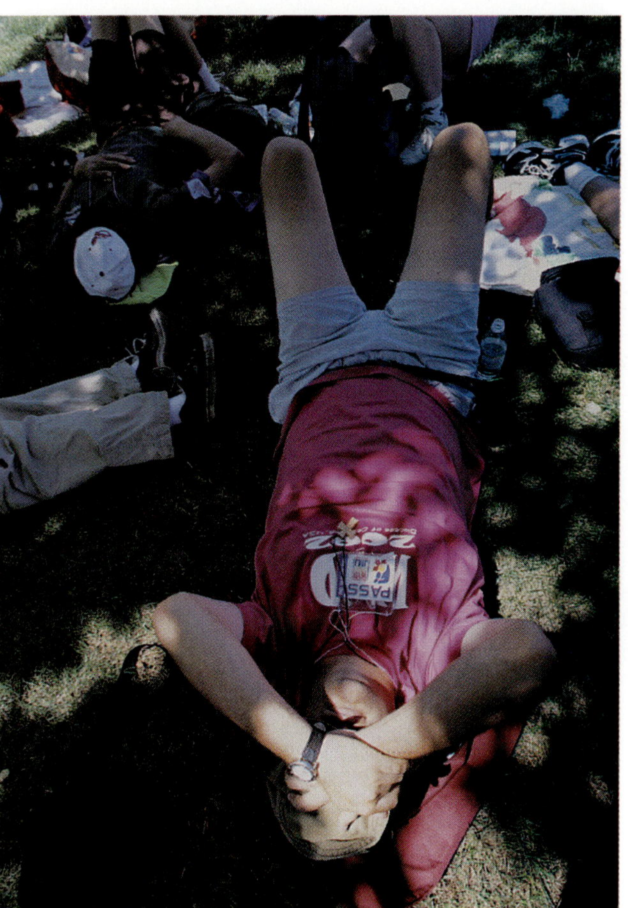

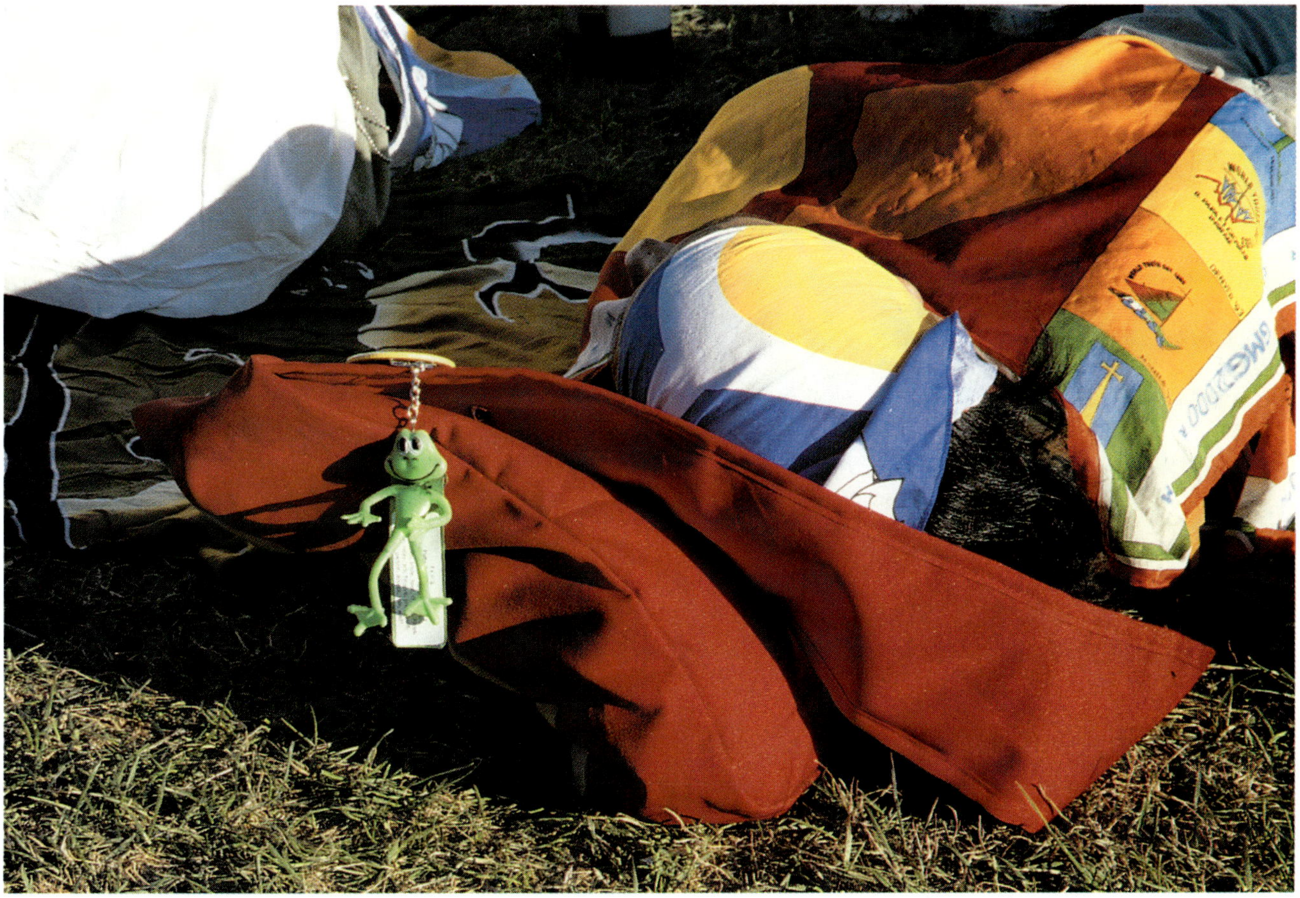

The Way of the Cross

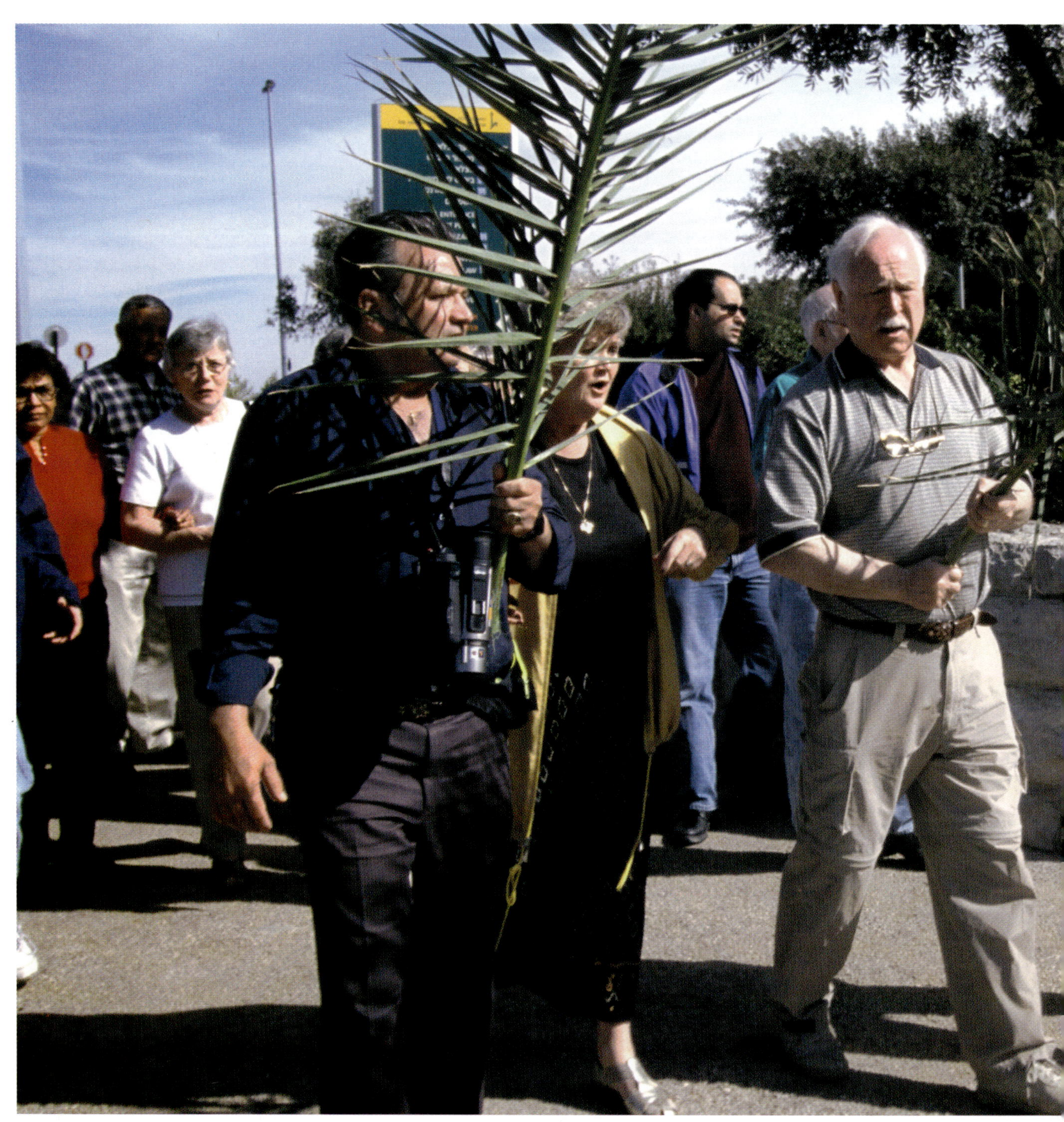

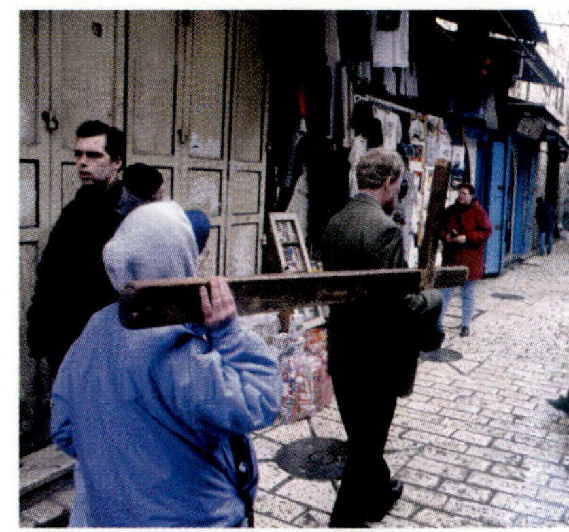

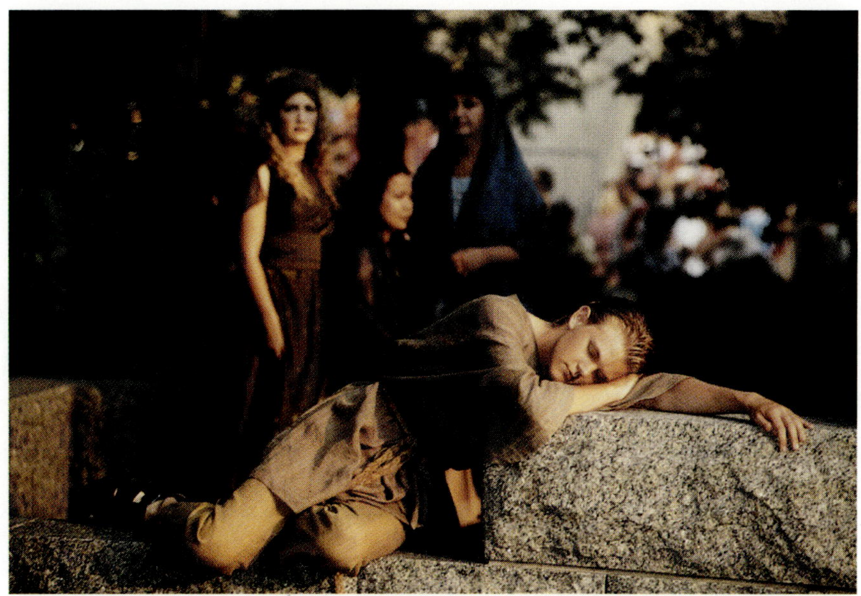

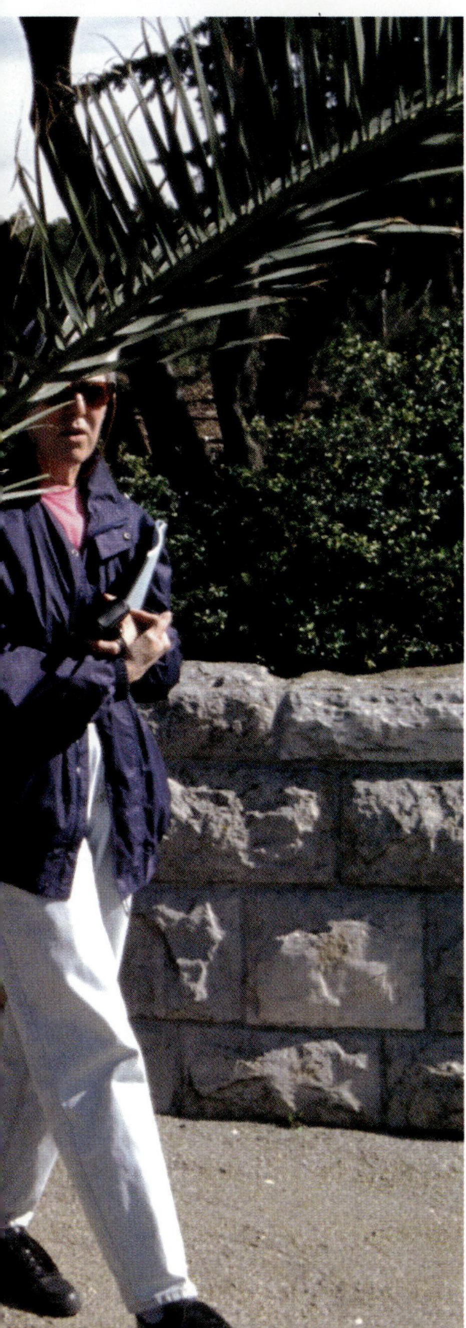

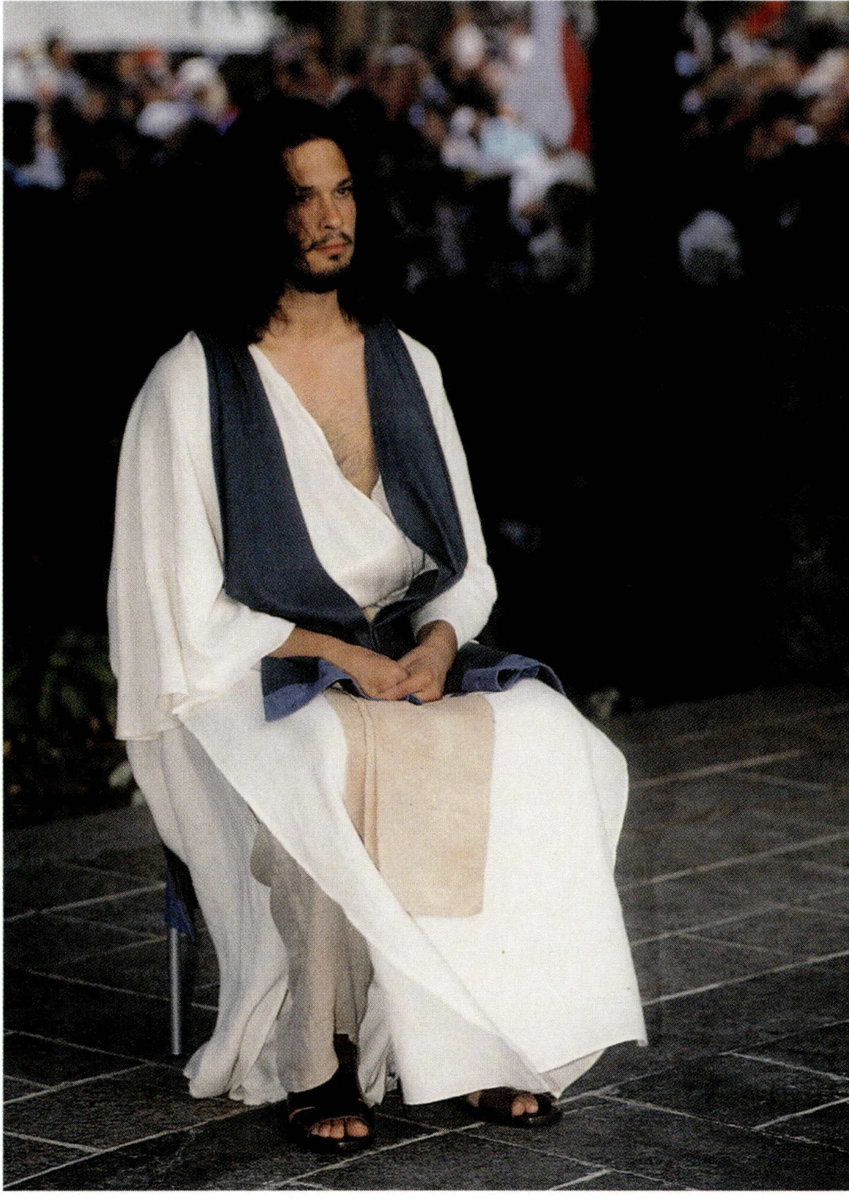

"If any want to become my followers"
(Matthew 16:24)

Finding prayerful ways to follow the story of Christ's passion and resurrection has long been part of the Christian tradition. There was a time when Christians retraced the actual steps of Jesus by going on pilgrimage to Jerusalem. Because such a trip was beyond the means of most people, many of the faithful retraced Christ's journey along the Via Dolorosa by following a series of "stations" in their local church. Thus the tradition of the Way of the Cross was established.

For one night in July, streets in the very heart of Toronto were transformed into a giant theatre with 14 stages where the passion was enacted and interpreted in a version of the Way of the Cross written by Pope John Paul II himself. Light rain added to the sombre mood as hundreds of thousands of WYD pilgrims and others gathered to witness this enactment of the suffering and death of Christ.

Following an opening prayer and brief address by Cardinal James Francis Stafford, the 50-member volunteer cast left Nathan Phillips Square in front of Toronto City Hall on a highly emotional journey up University Avenue to Queen's Park, site of the Ontario Legislature.

This event was open to the public and pilgrims alike, and all were able to follow the drama on large video screens. The Taizé Community choir encouraged the crowd in song to "stay here, watch and pray" at the first station, where Christ was condemned to death.

Hundreds of thousands viewed the live broadcast of the Way of the Cross, including the author, Pope John Paul II himself, who was resting at Strawberry Island on Lake Simcoe. At the sixth station, members of L'Arche community joined with the actors and chorus.

The World Youth Day Cross, which had travelled to all corners of Canada since April 2001, was the focus of the Way of the Cross. At the outset of the procession, four youths ignited torches from the eternal flame in the Peace Garden in Nathan Phillips Square. The flame was lit originally by Pope John Paul II in 1984, during his visit to Canada. In turn, that flame had come from an ember taken from the Hiroshima Peace Park. The torches followed Jesus throughout his journey up University Avenue.

At the eleventh station, pilgrims winced, cried out or held each other's hands in prayer as they watched the crucifixion scene unfold. Jesus, portrayed by Robert Légère, 25, originally from St. Louis de Kent in New Brunswick, was nailed to the cross. The role of Mary was portrayed by Ursula Fiedorczuk, who was born in Bialystok, Poland and moved to Canada ten years ago.

The concluding song, performed by Janis Clark during the walk to the fourteenth station where Jesus is laid in the tomb, was the powerful lament "Were You There When They Crucified My Lord?"

The following day, at the vigil with the pope at Downsview Lands, the pilgrims prayed with the Holy Father and remembered the time that Christ spent in his tomb. On Sunday, they celebrated the joy of the resurrection together at the concluding mass.

Grant to us and to all the men and women of our time the grace to remain faithful to the truth.

JOHN PAUL II

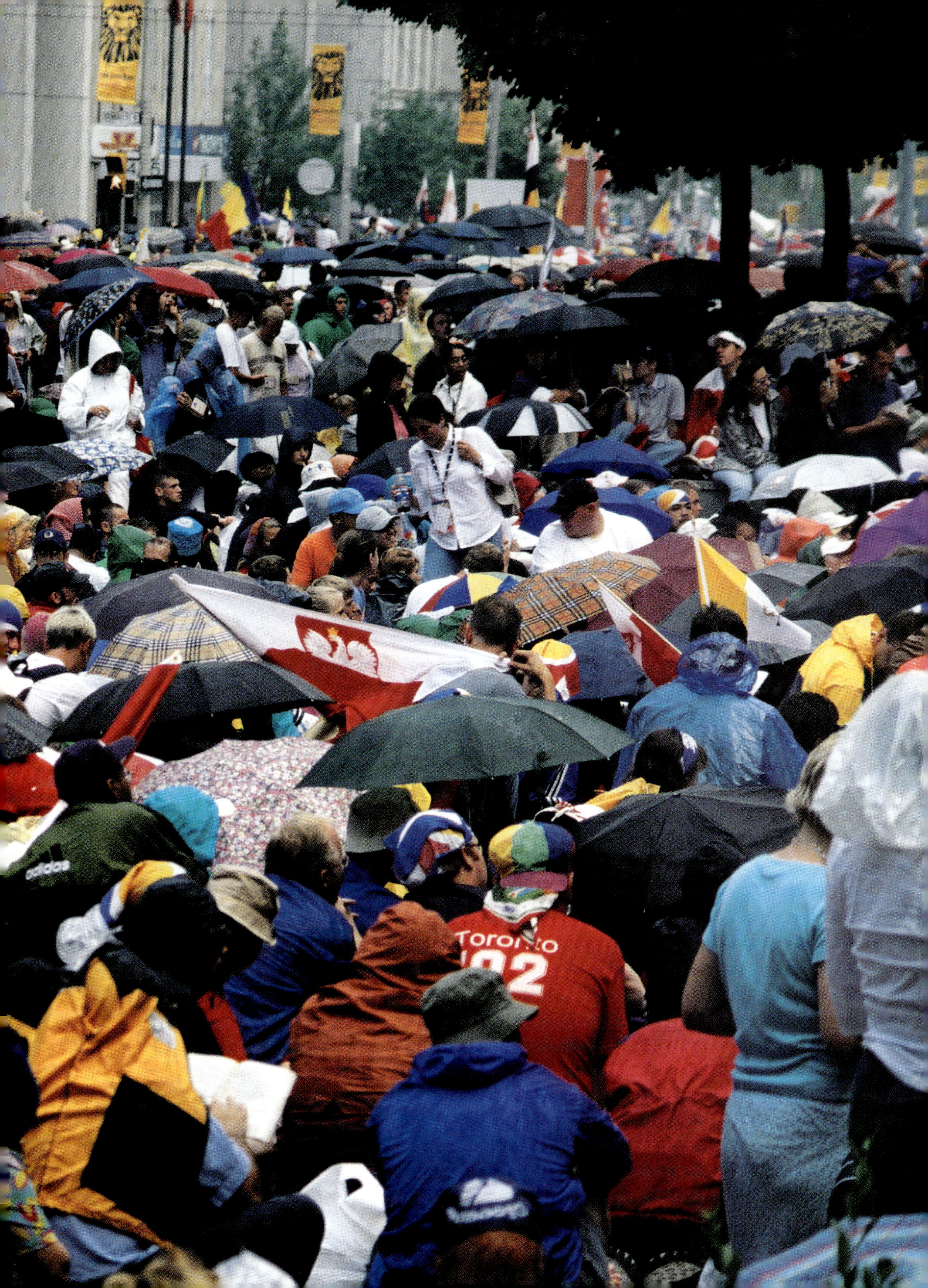

Jesus is condemned to Death

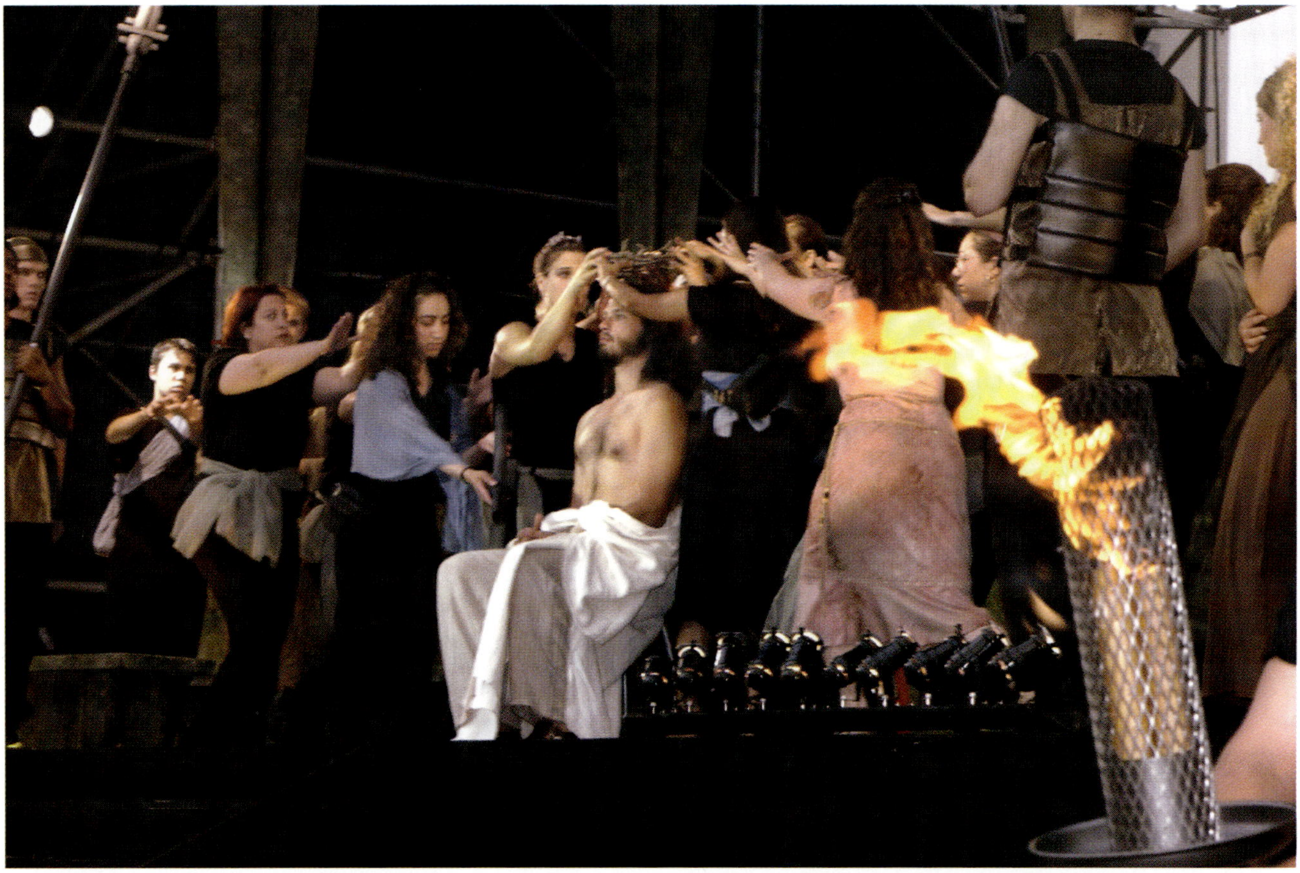

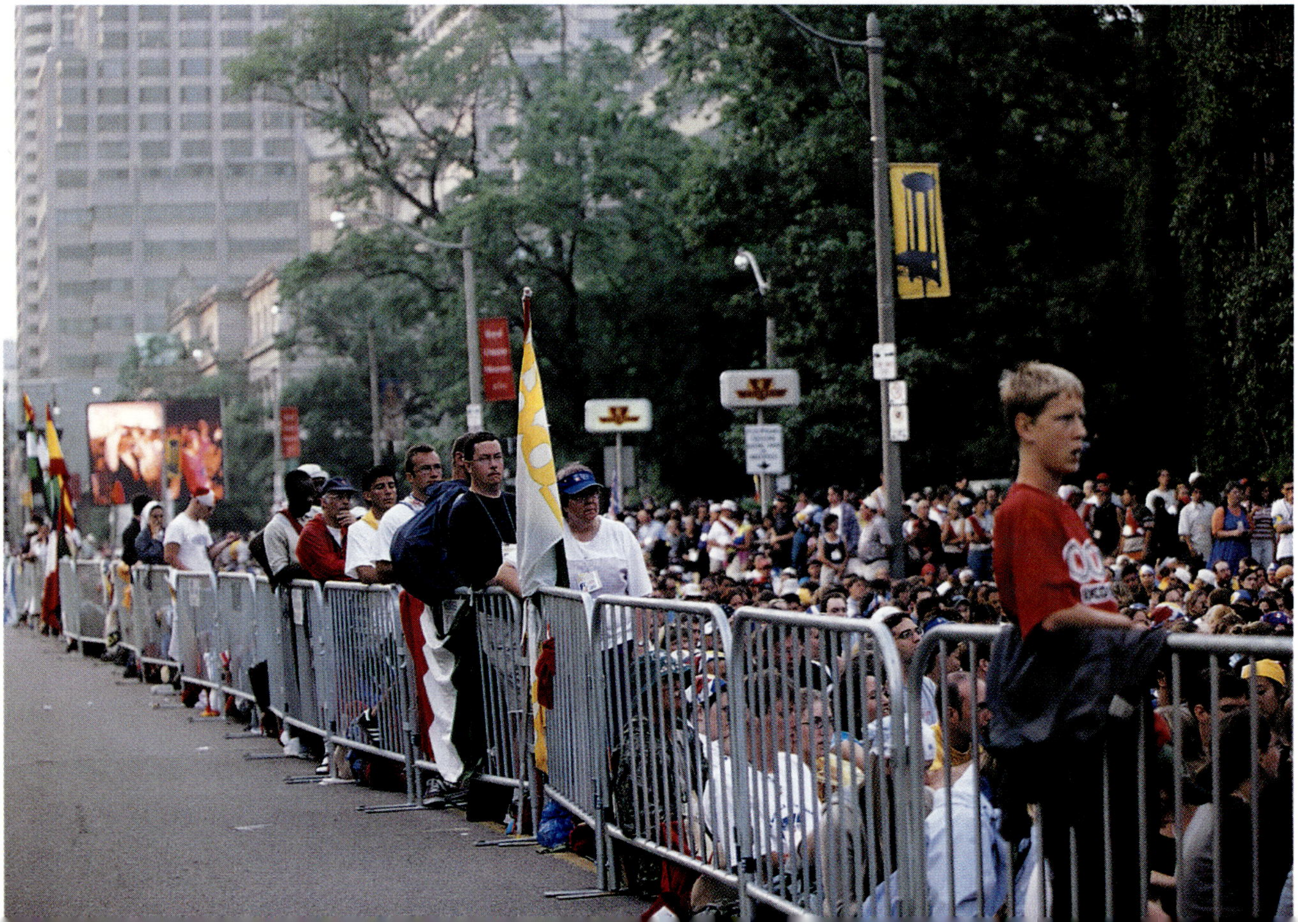

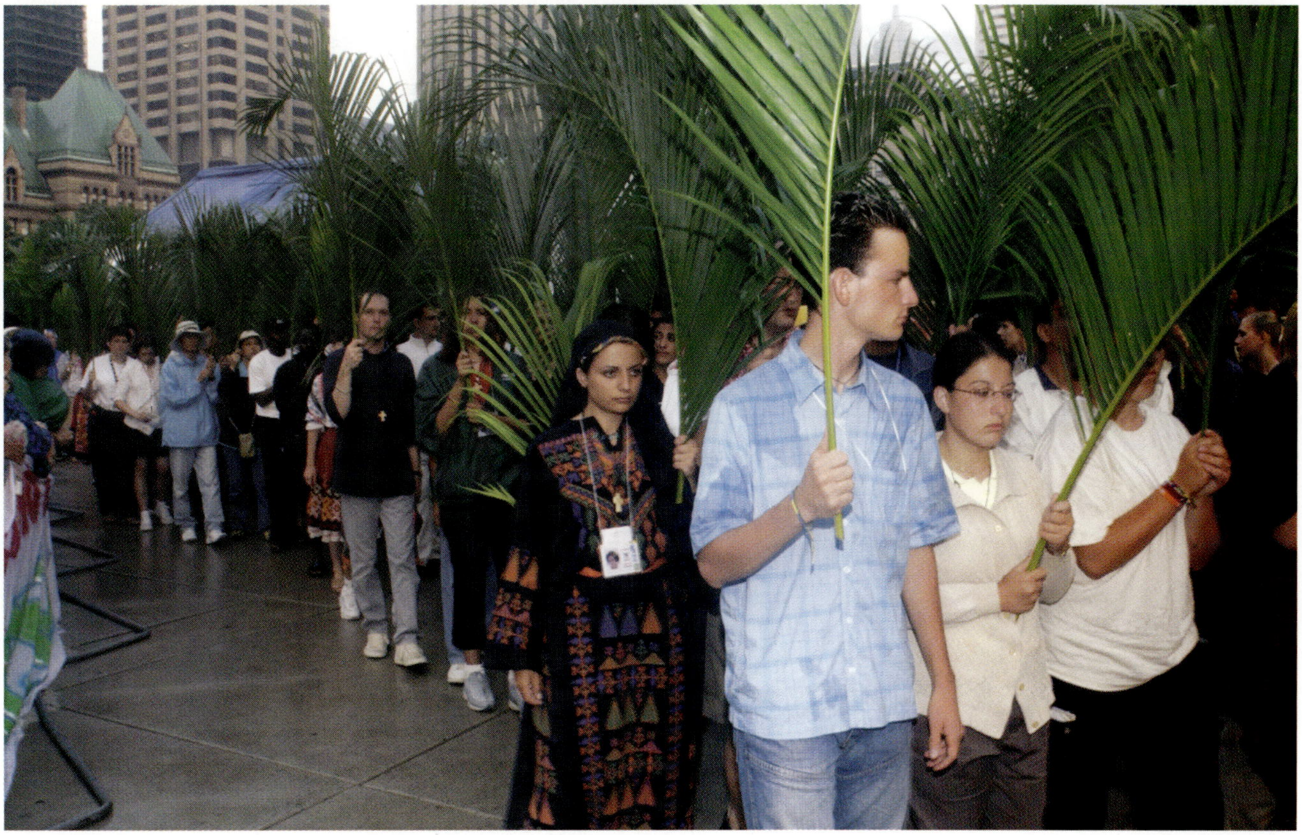

Jesus takes up his Cross

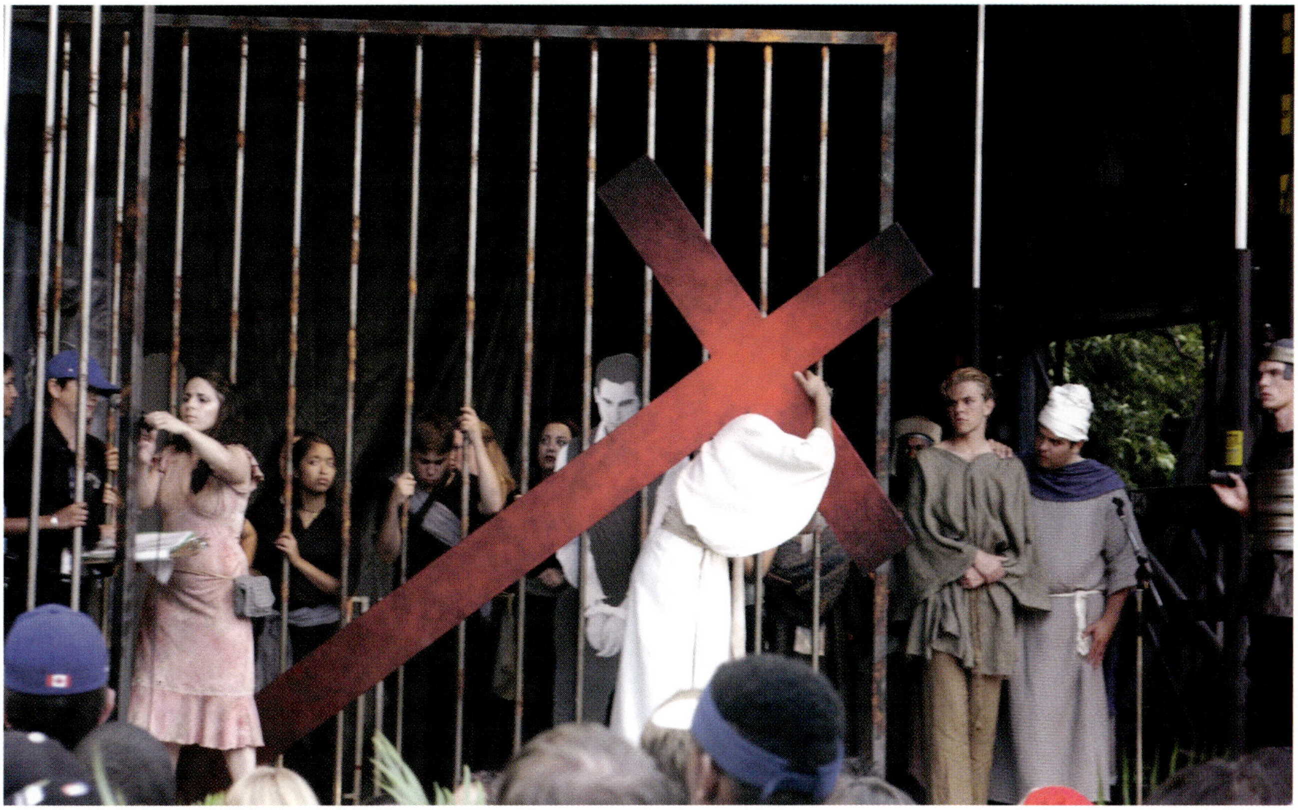

Jesus falls the first time

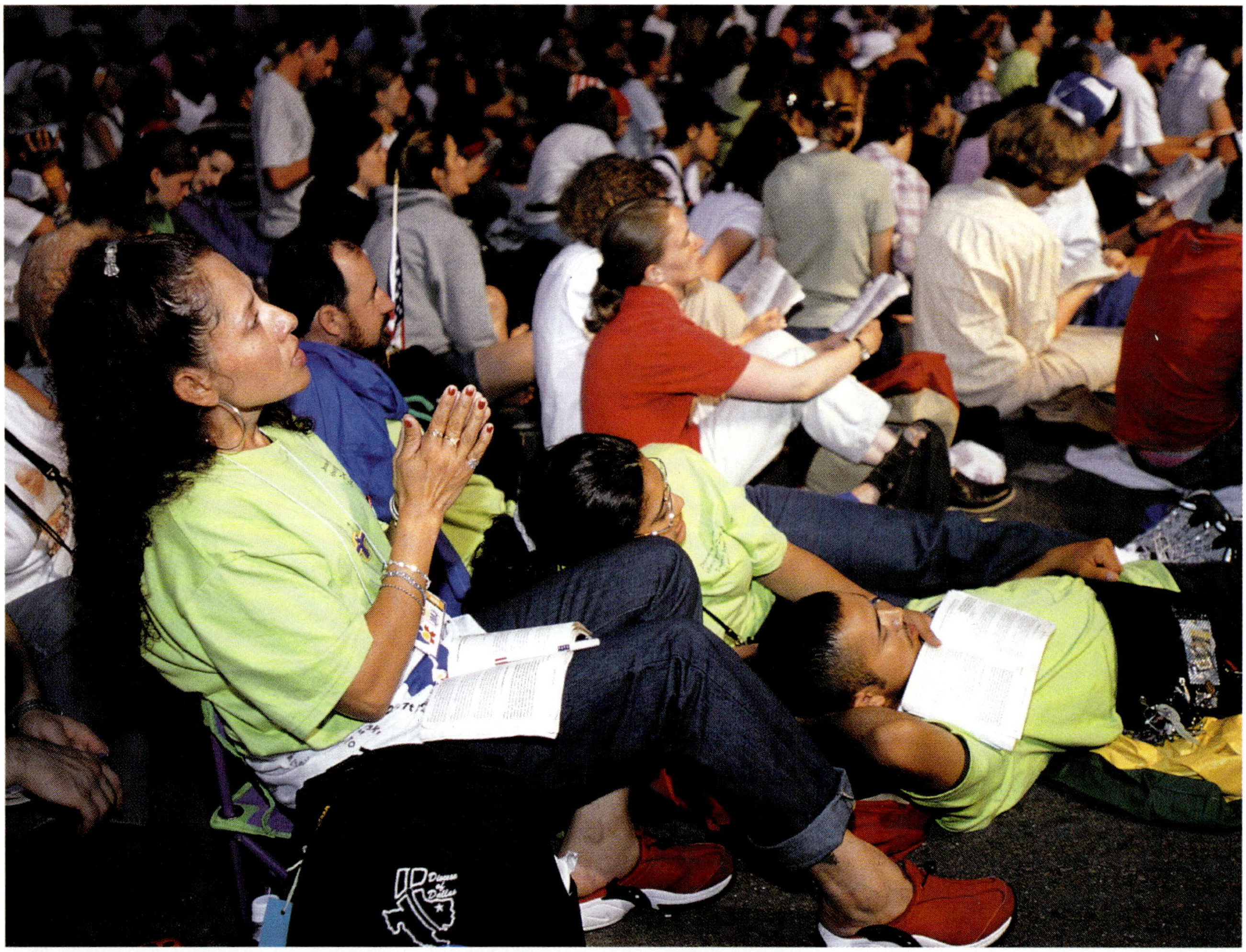

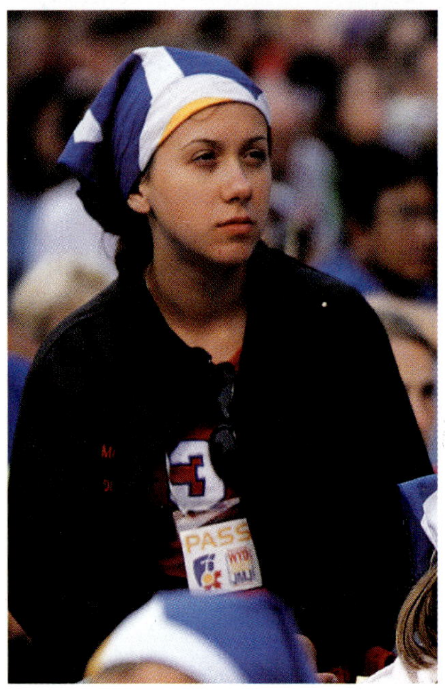

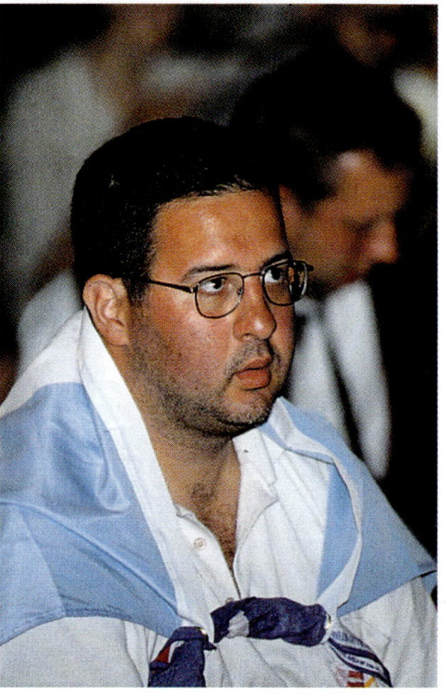

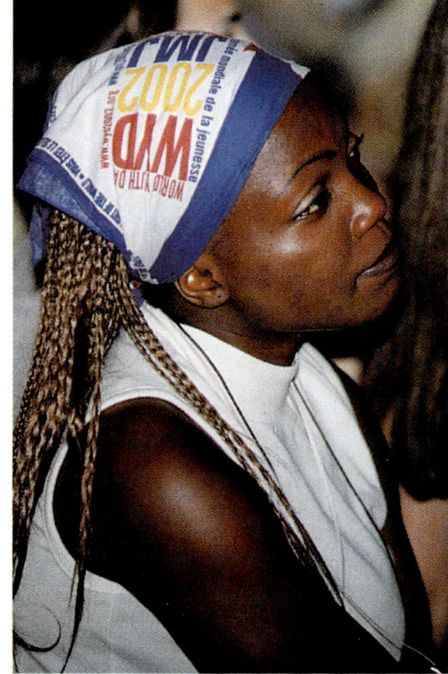

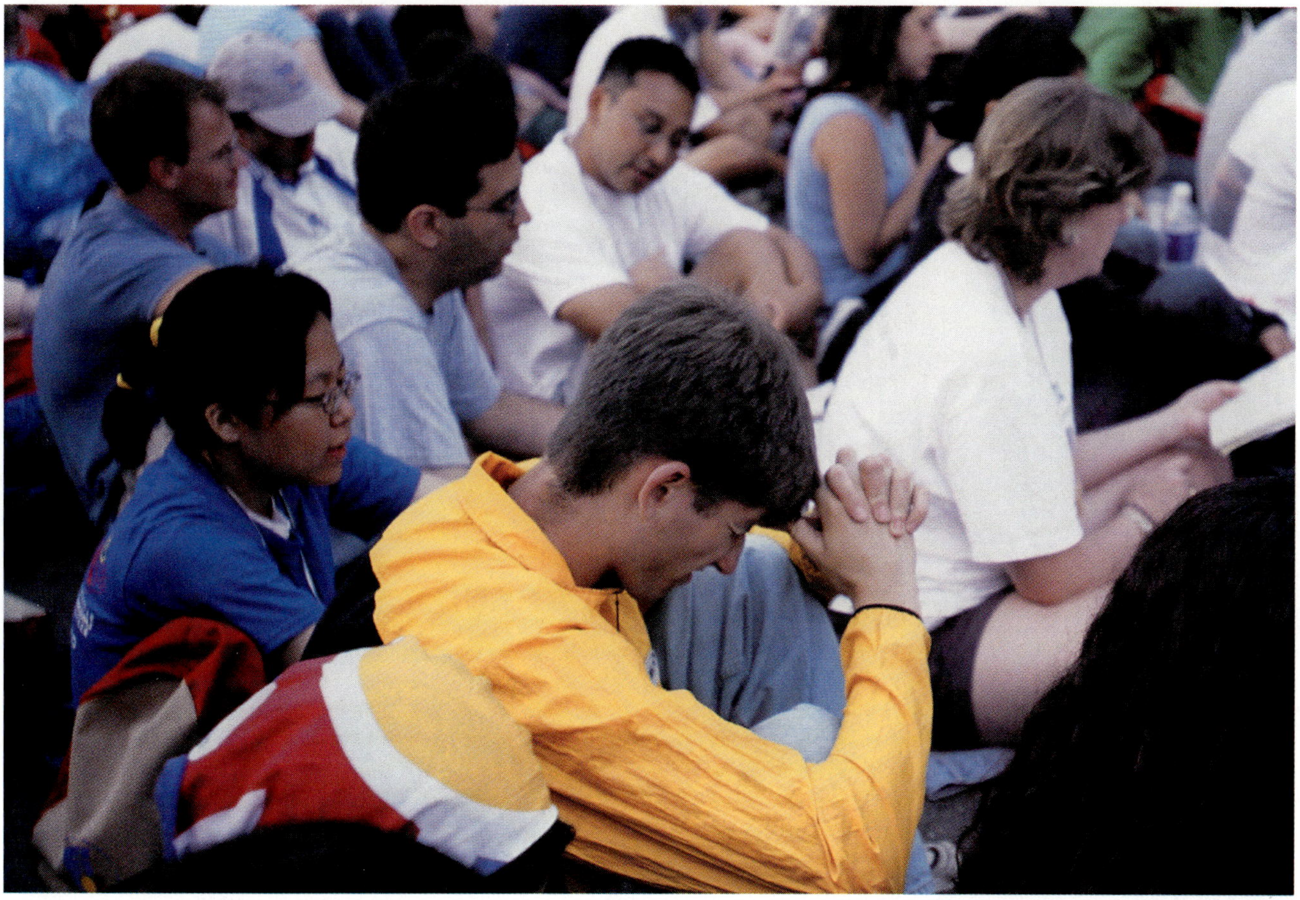

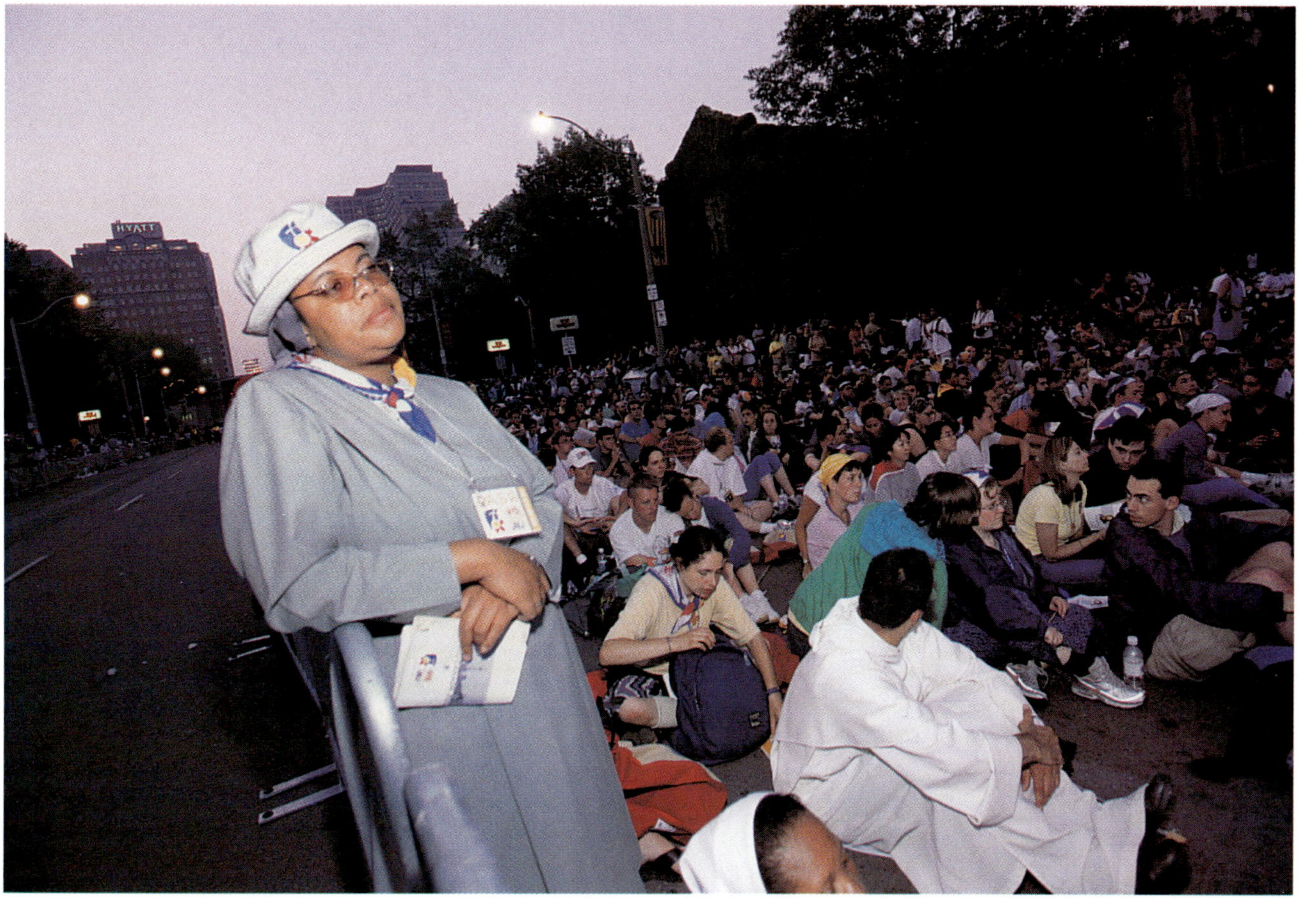

Jesus meets his mother

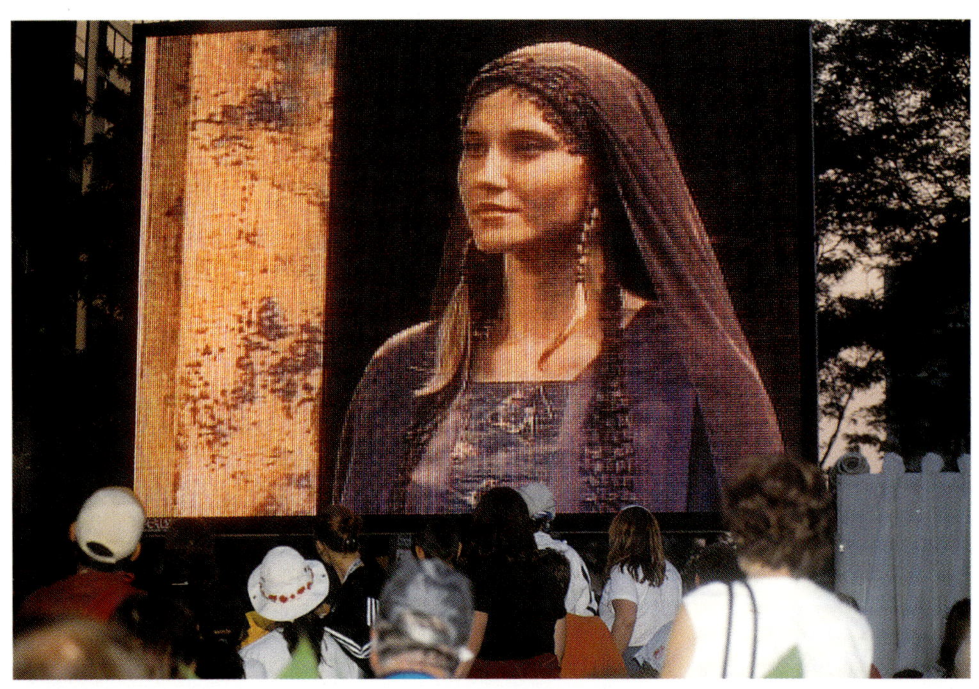

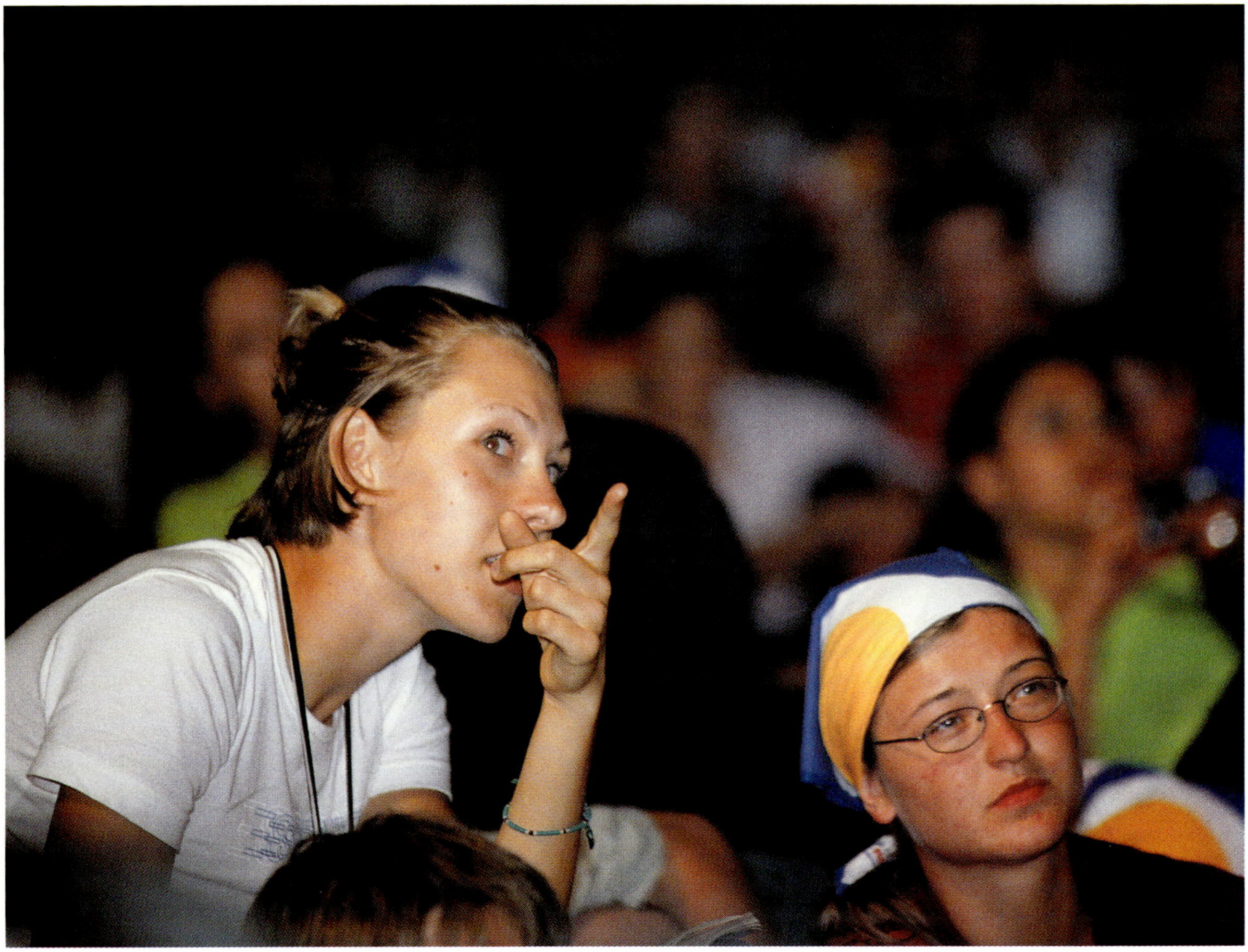

Simon of Cyrene helps Jesus to carry his Cross

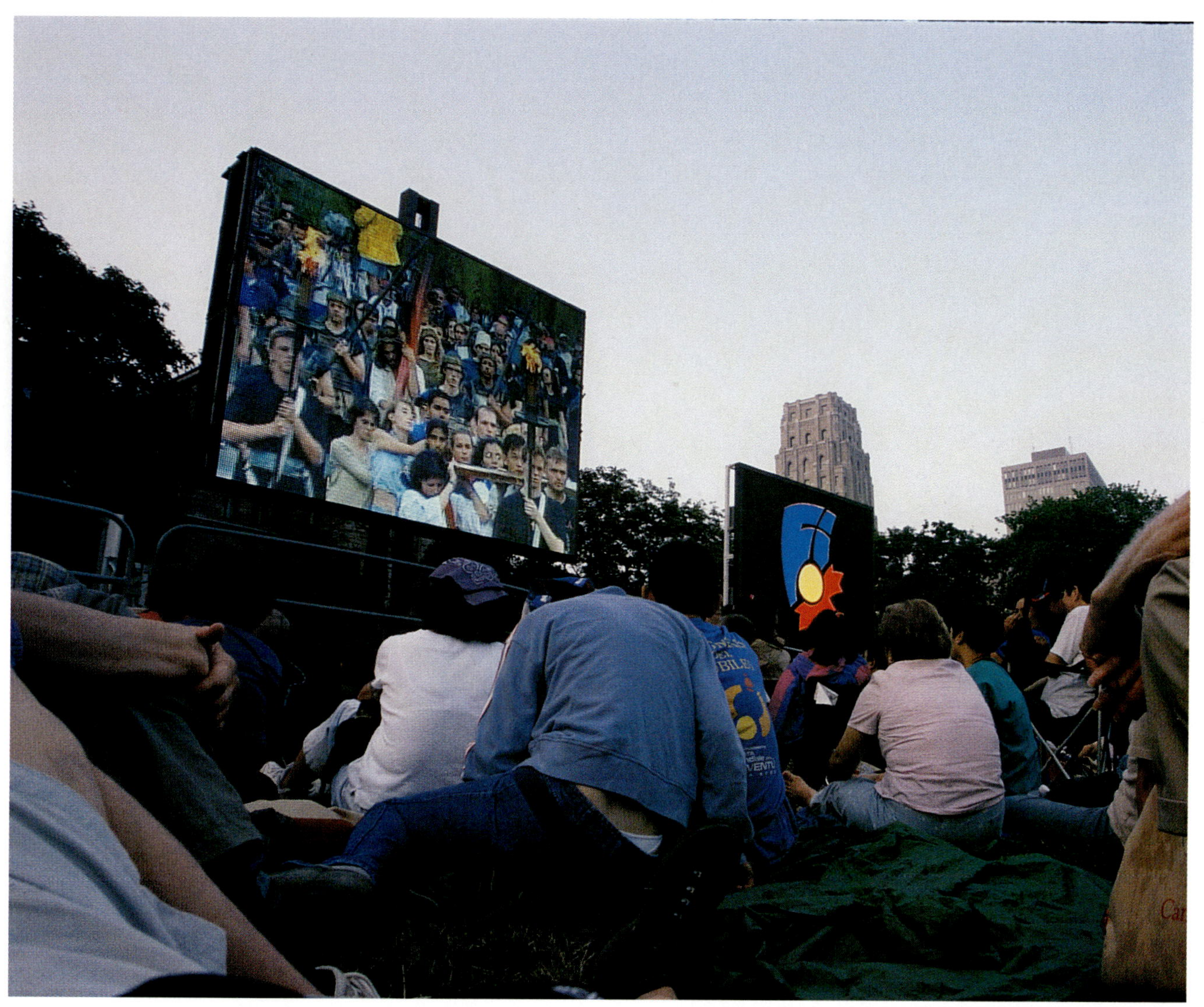

Do not permit that we should turn away from those who are crushed by the cross of illness, loneliness, hunger or injustice.

JOHN PAUL II

Veronica wipes the face of Jesus

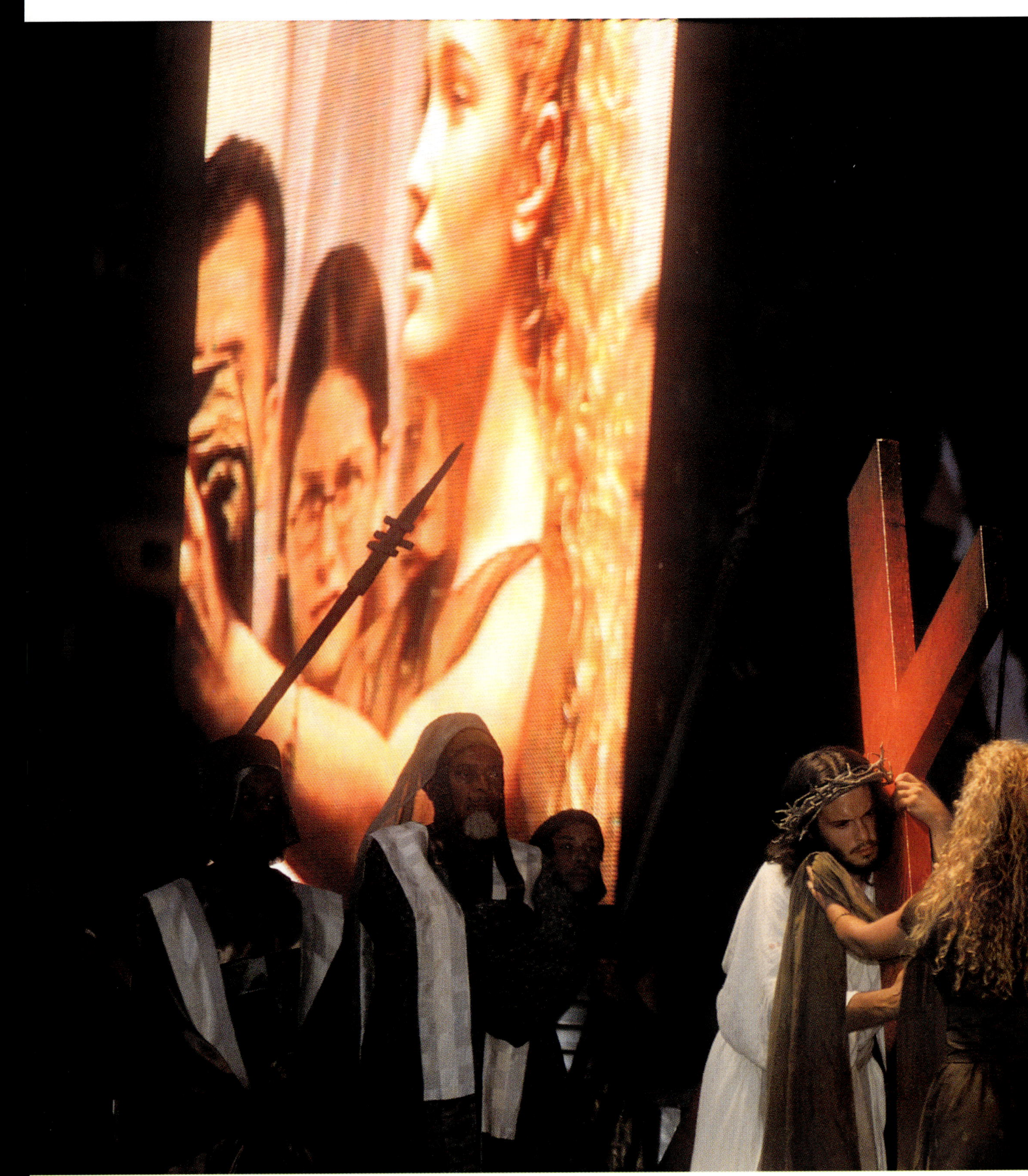

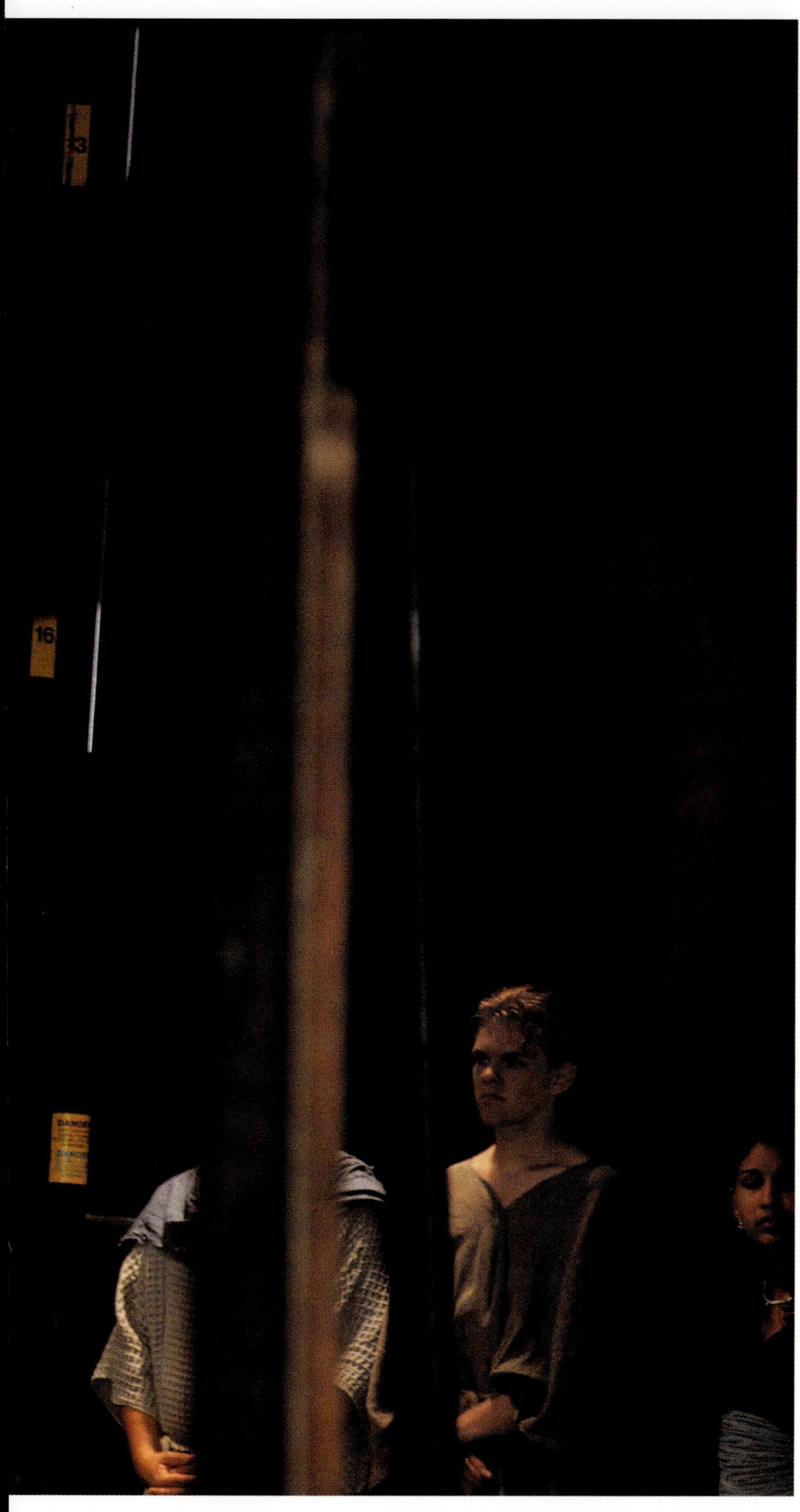

*Grant that
our works and
the works of all
who will come after
us will make us
like unto you
and will leave in
the world the
reflection of your
infinite love.*

JOHN PAUL II

Jesus falls the second time

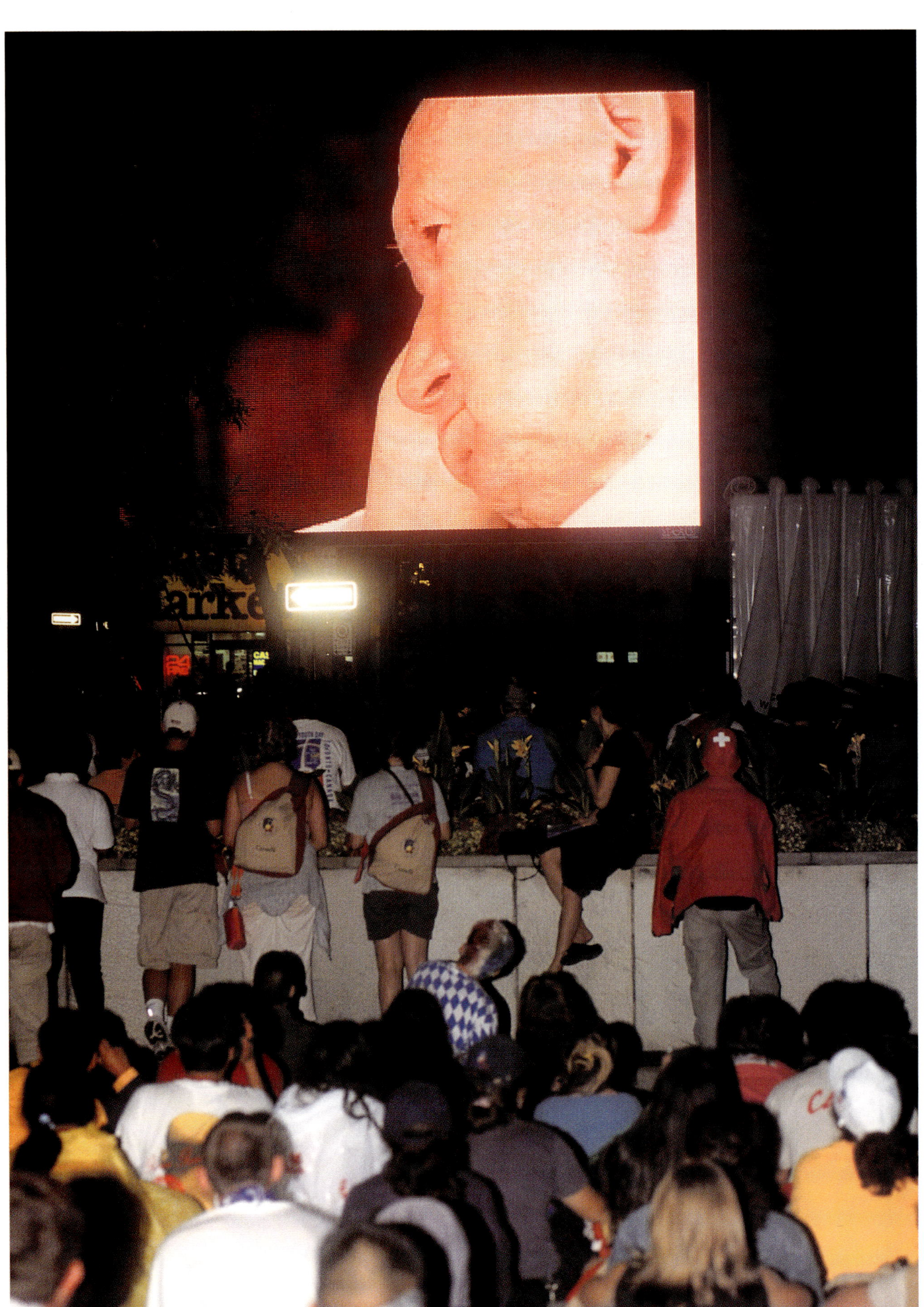

O Christ, as you fall under the weight of our faults and rise again for our justification, we pray, help us and all who are weighed down by sin to stand up again and continue the journey. Give us the strength of the Spirit to carry with you the cross of our weakness.

JOHN PAUL II

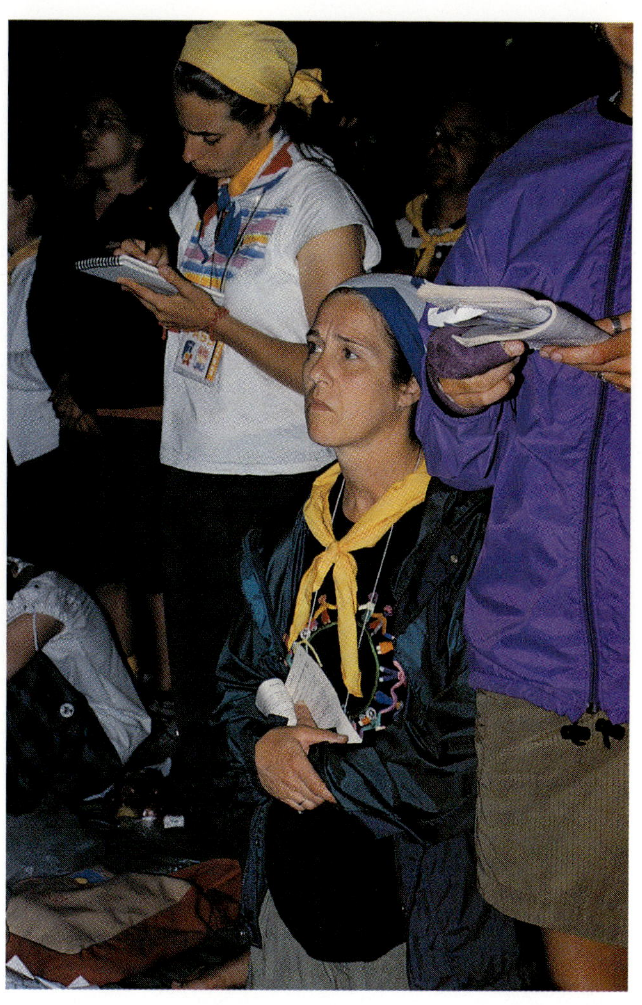

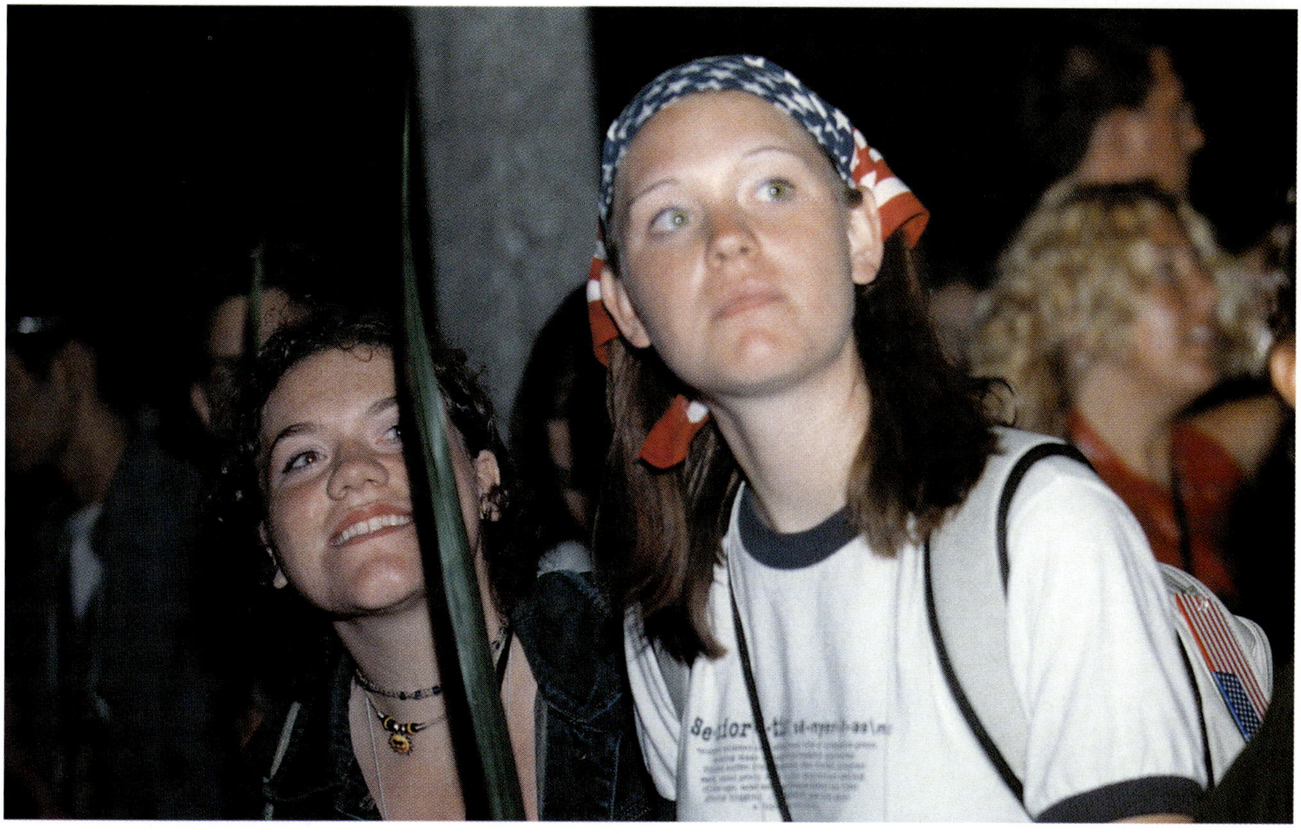

Jesus consoles the women of Jerusalem

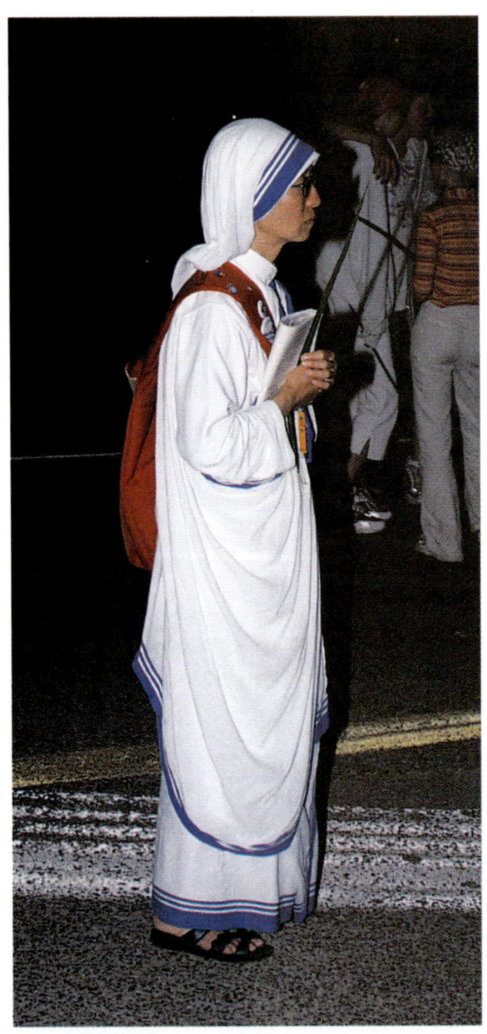

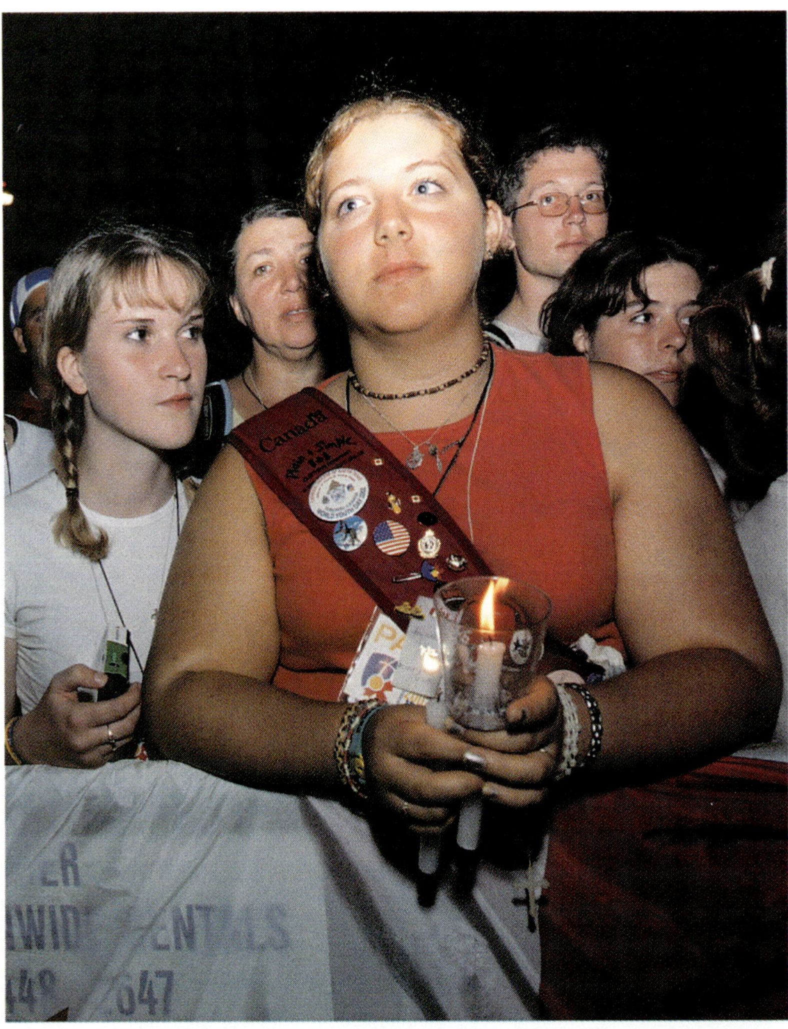

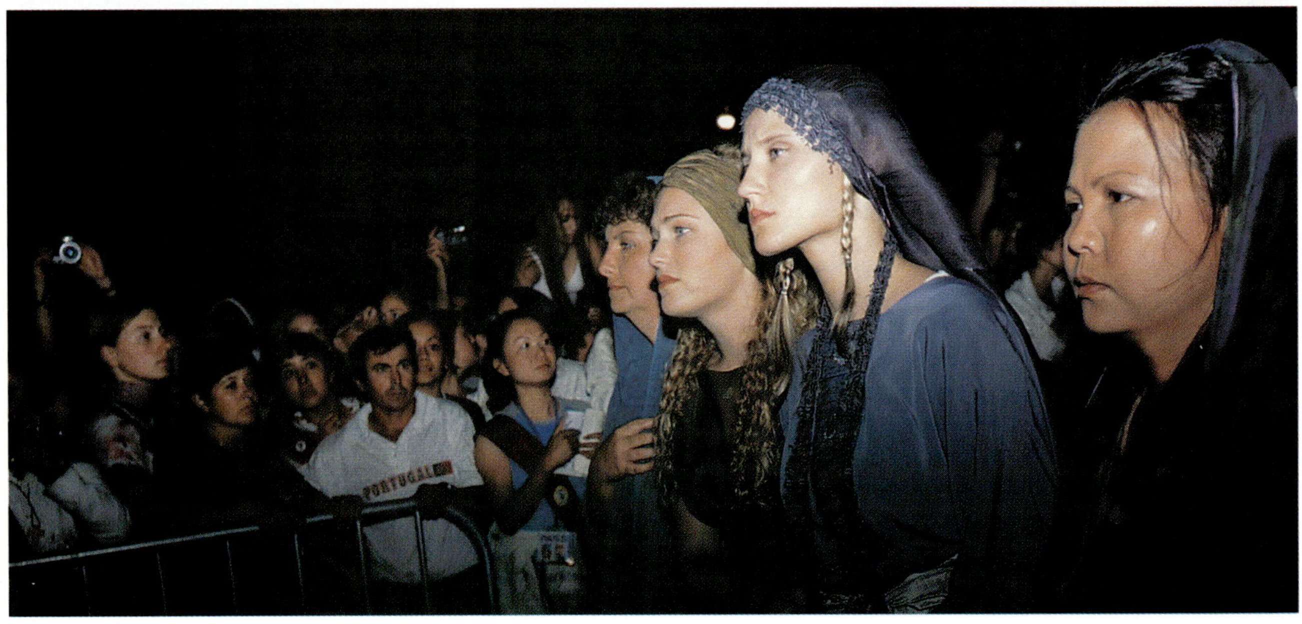

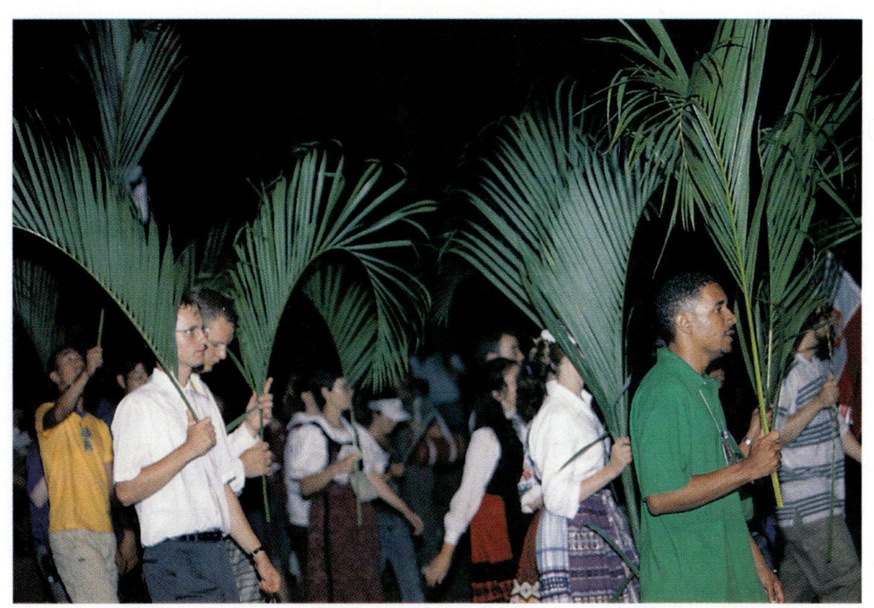

Jesus falls the third time

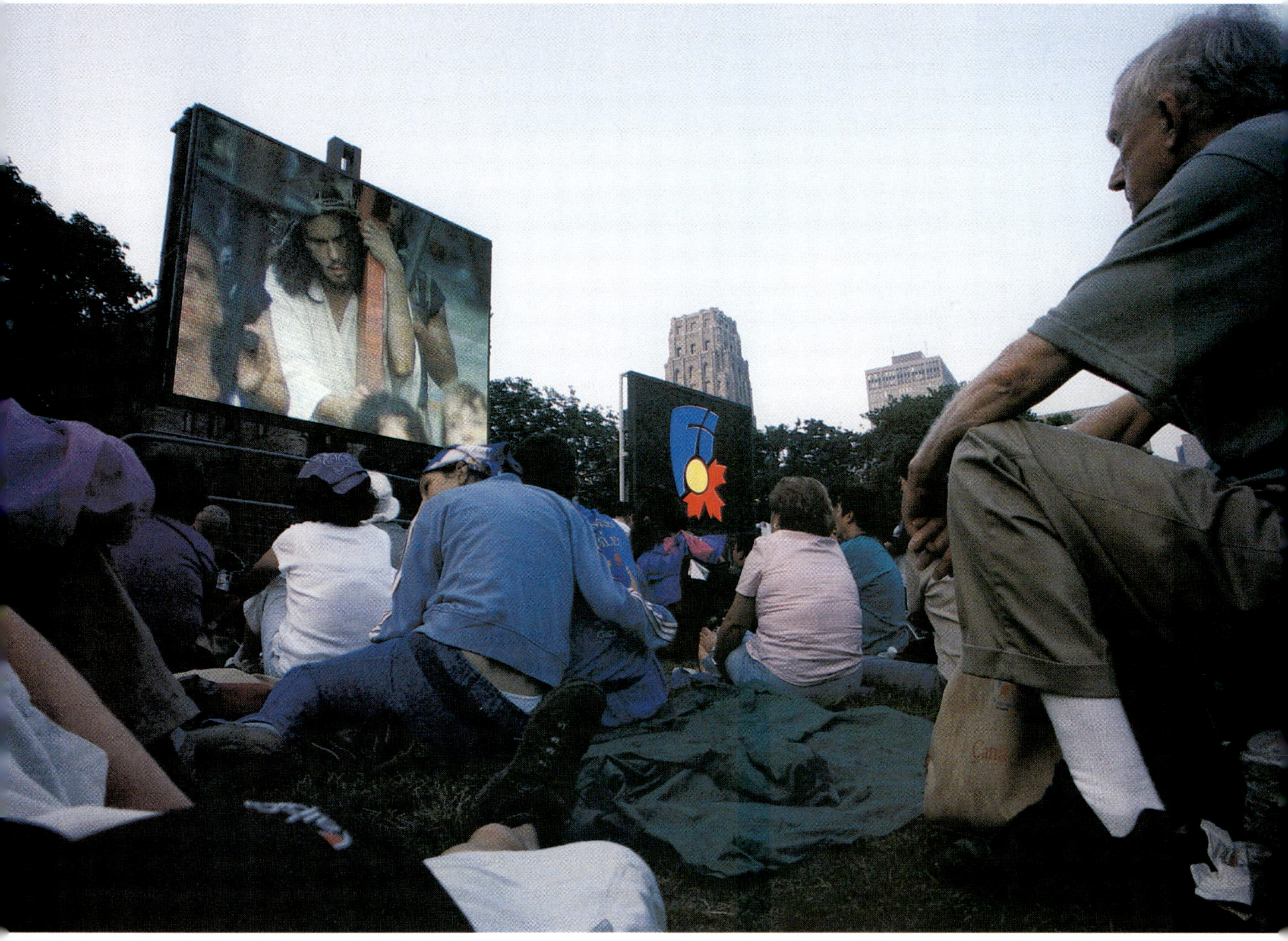

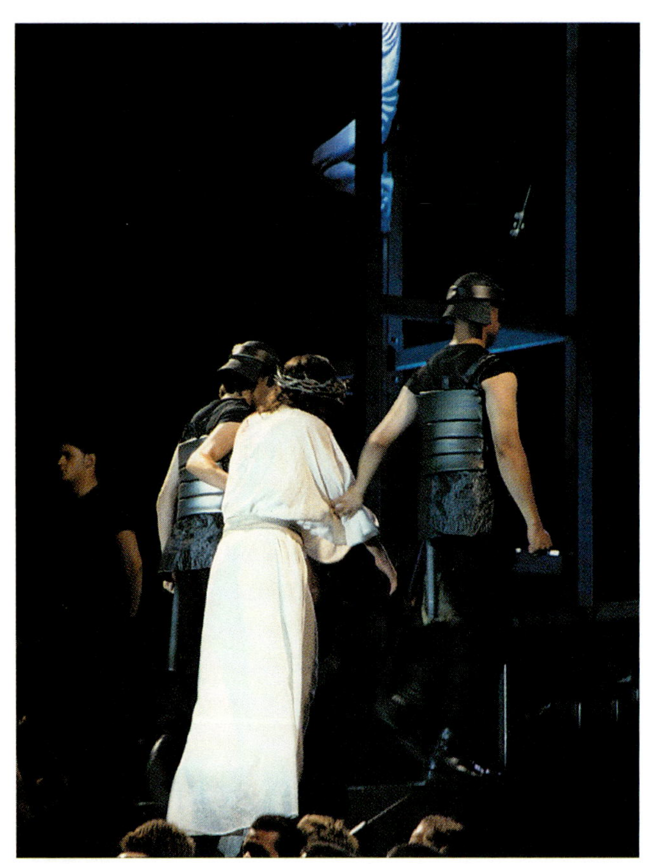

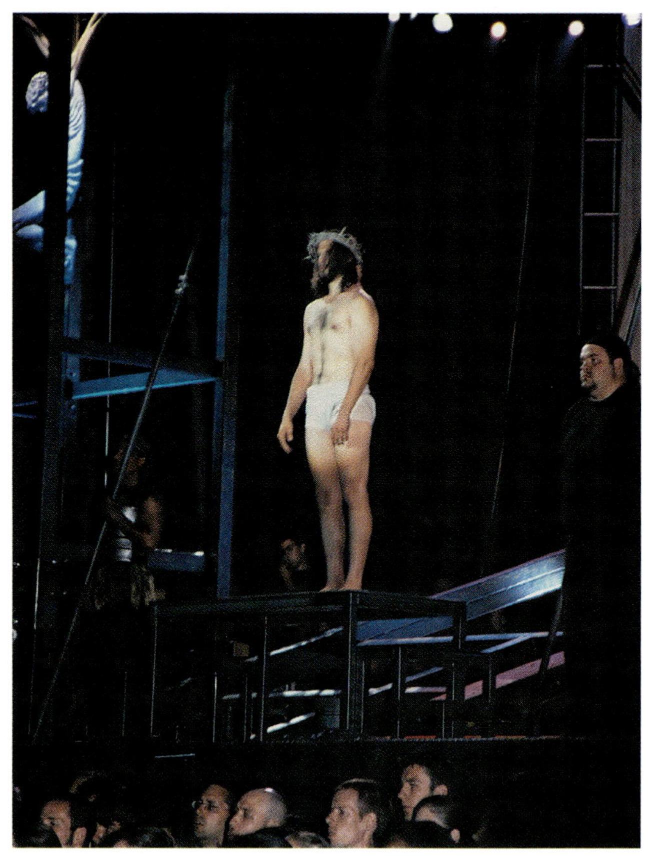

*Jesus
is stripped
and offered gall
and vinegar
to drink*

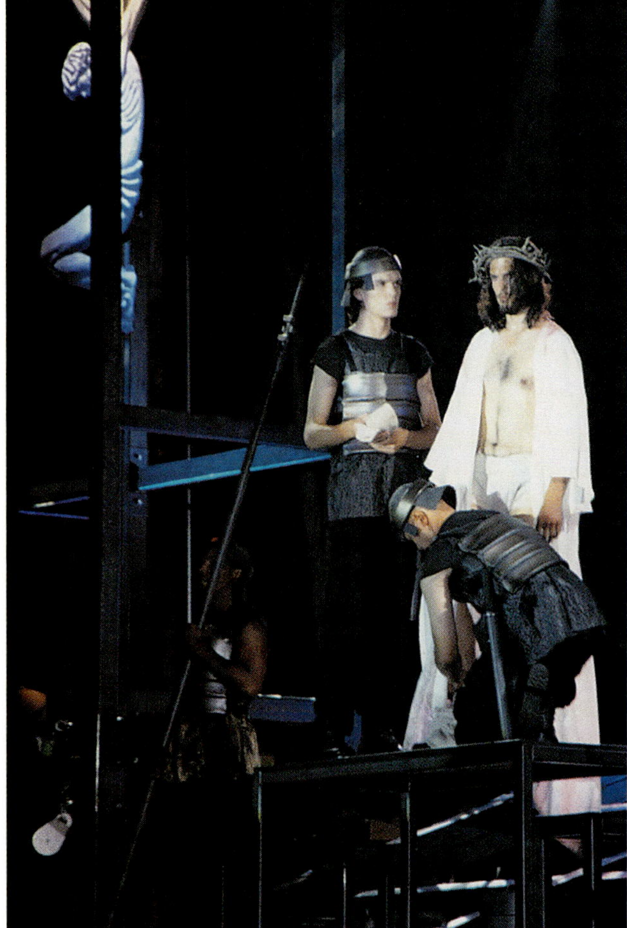

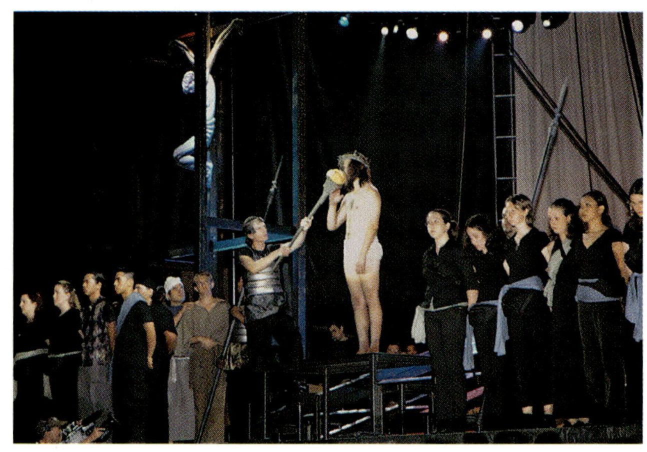

Jesus is nailed to the Cross

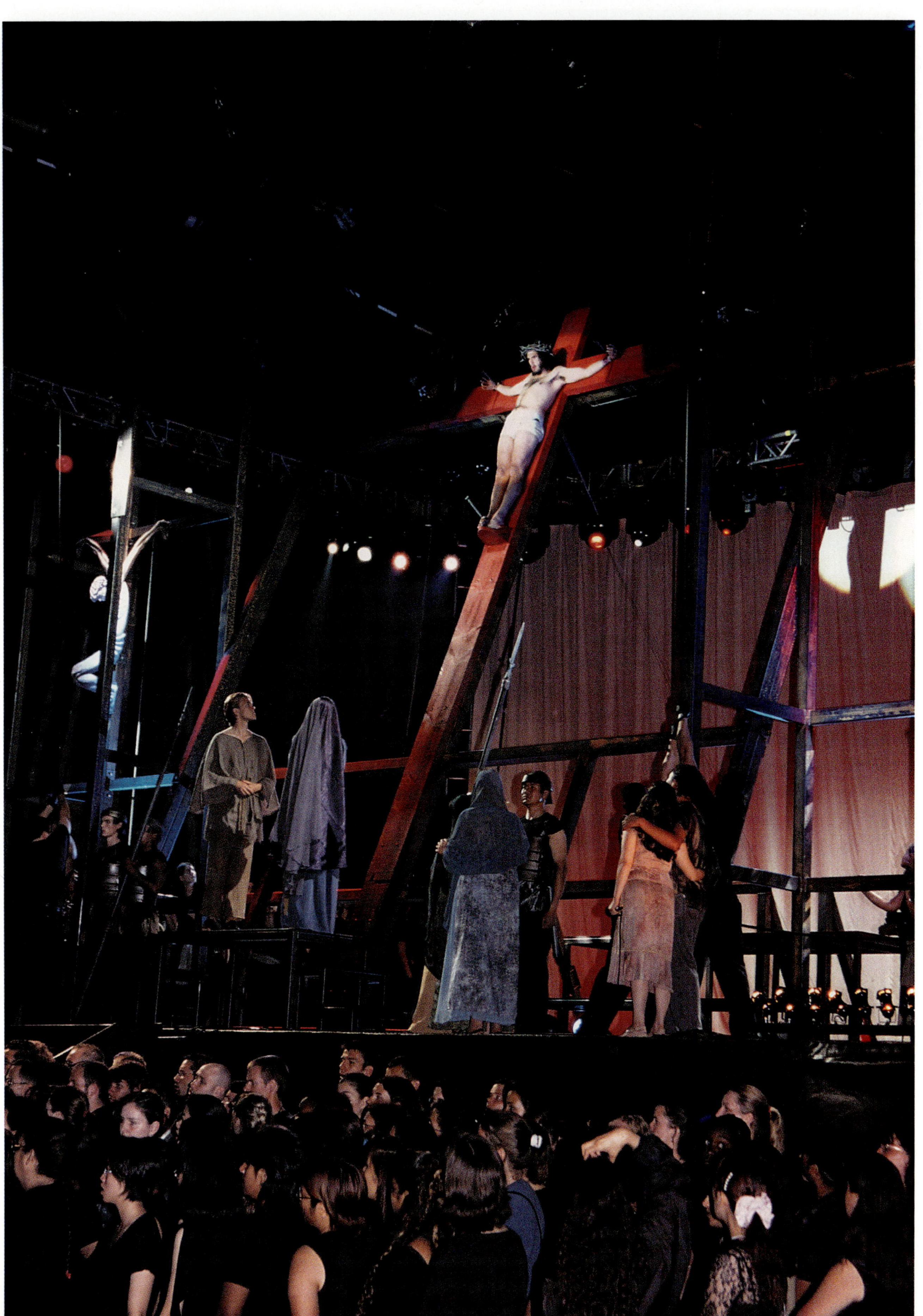

Jesus dies on the Cross

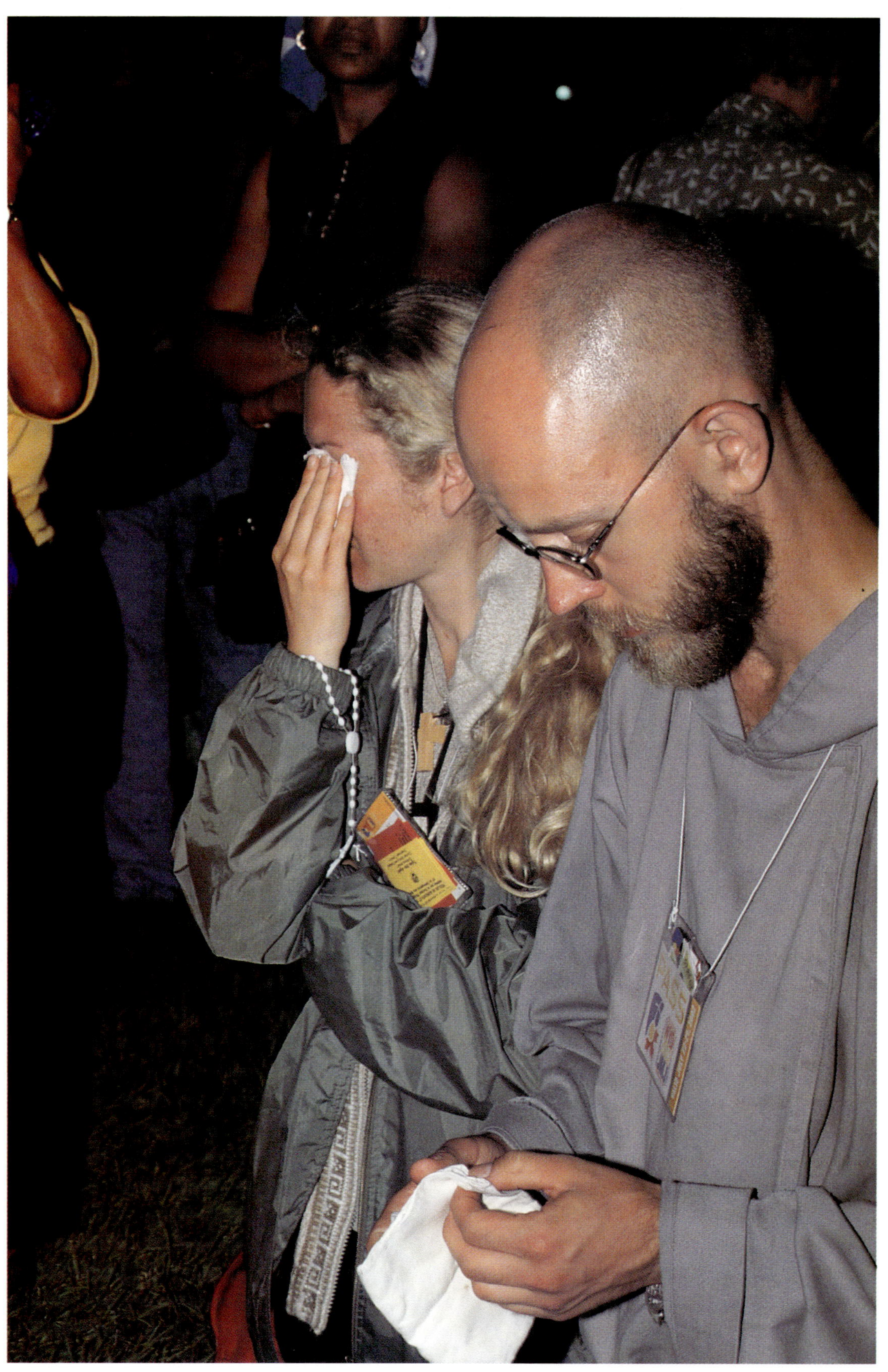

Jesus is taken down from the Cross and given to his mother

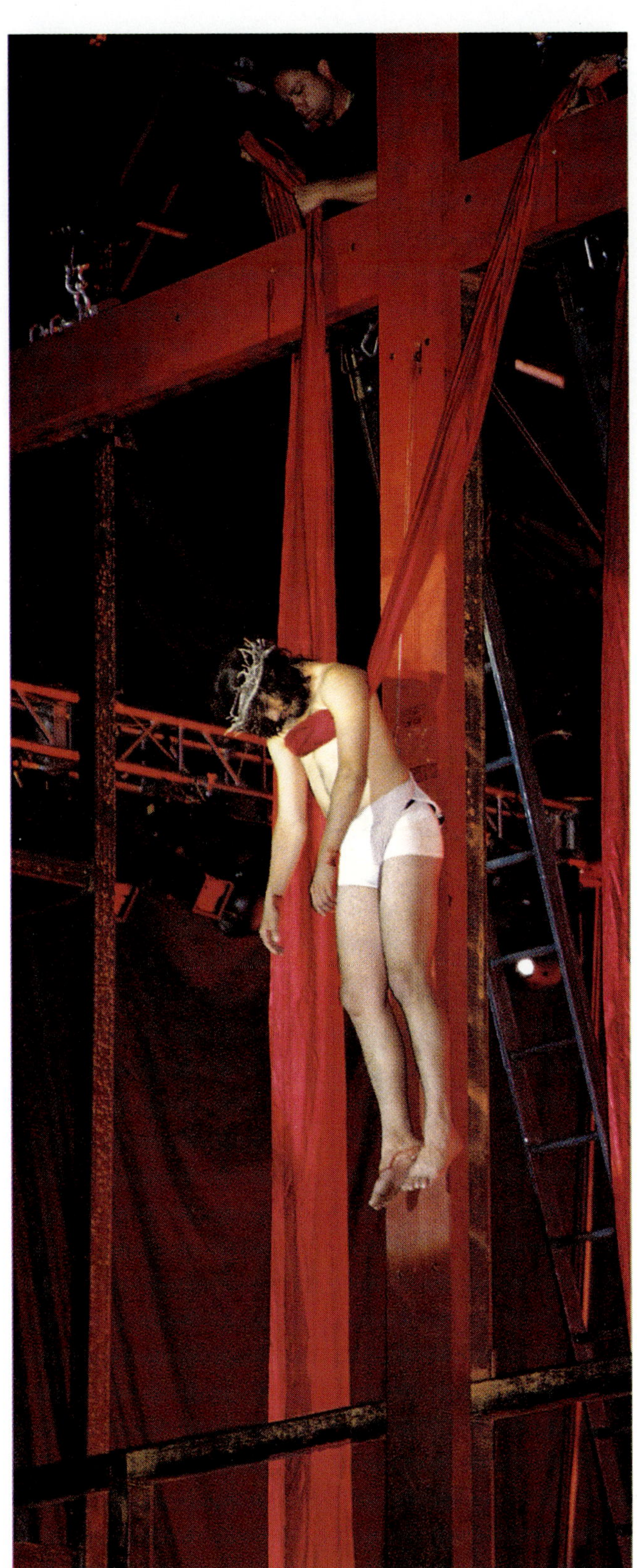

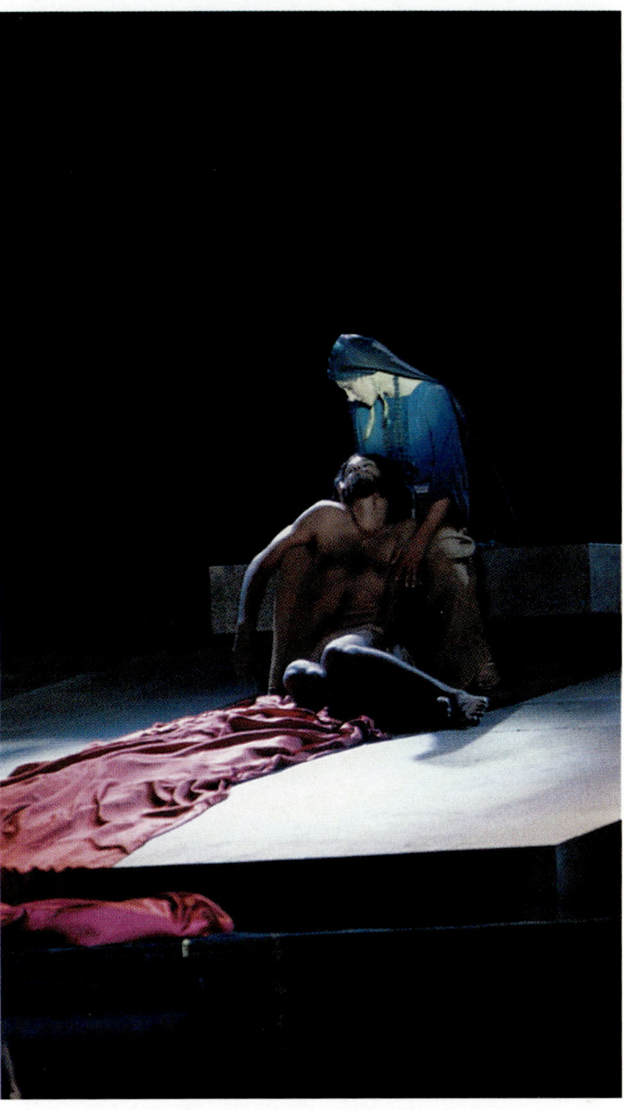

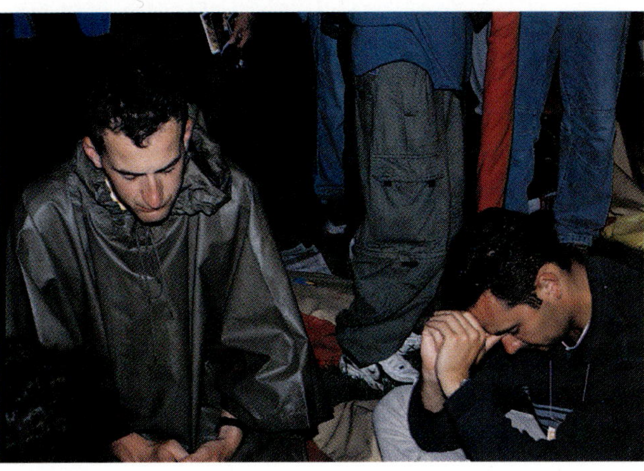

Jesus is laid in the tomb

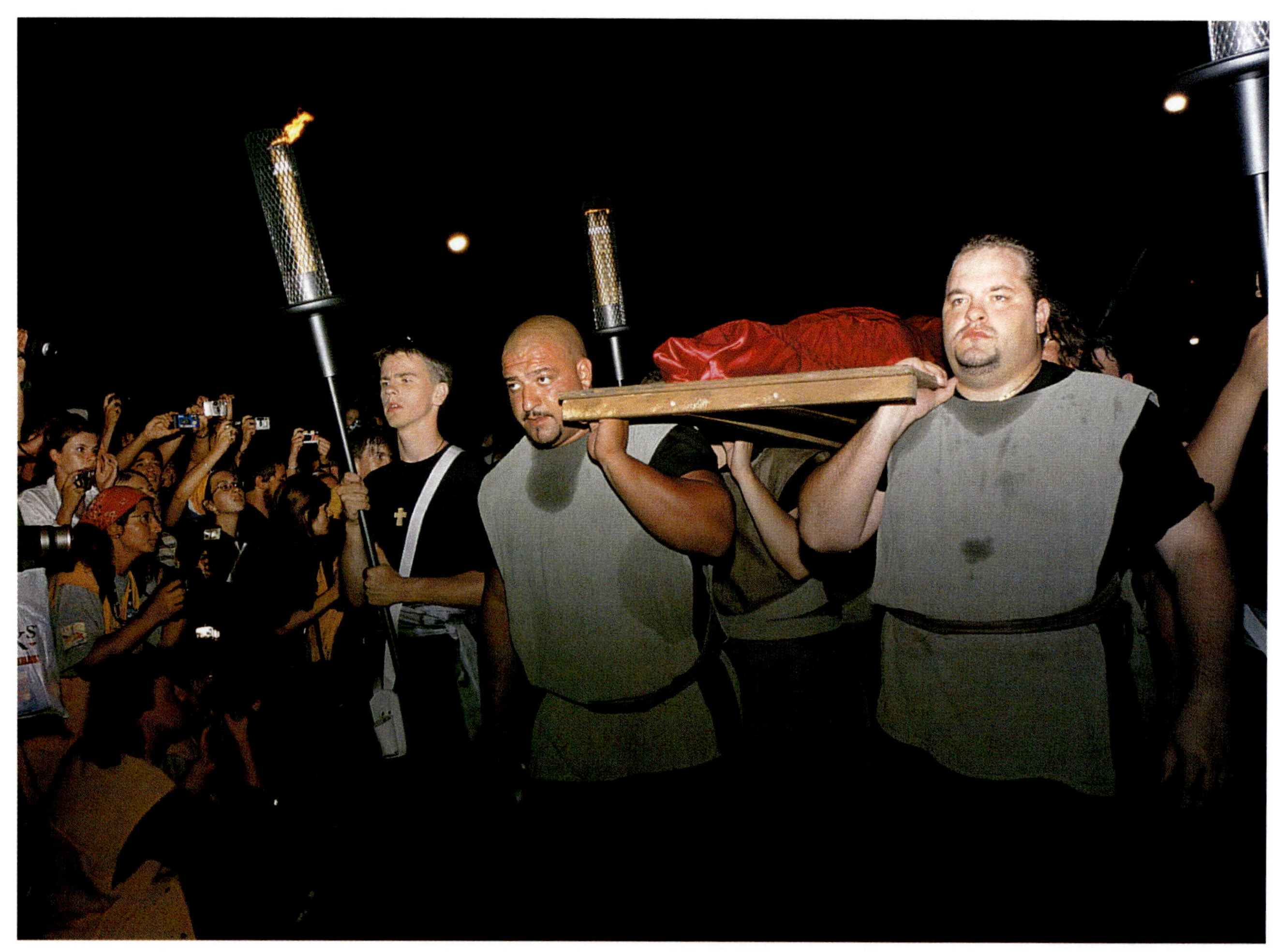

*Grant that the sign of the empty tomb
may speak to us and to future generations and
become a wellspring of living faith, generous love,
and unshakeable hope.*

JOHN PAUL II

He walked among us

Few people have ever seen the likes of this before—or at least not since the Middle Ages. Then, players wandered through the streets of European cities and retold Bible stories in the form of mystery plays. Performing the Way of the Cross in a large modern city and on a major thoroughfare lacking any explicitly religious symbols is a truly unique event.

Jesus, Mary, the women, the soldiers, Pilate, Simon of Cyrene, the apostles, and all the others pass by City Hall, enormous hospitals, corporate headquarters and the provincial legislature. They walk along streets of concrete and asphalt, along the tree-lined boulevard that is University Avenue with its adjoining parks and tiny gardens, from the fading light of sunset to the darkness of night. And an immense crowd, hundreds of thousands strong, peaceful yet excited, line the route to watch and wonder and pray. Pilgrims without borders, pilgrims of the night, they come together to relive with Jesus his suffering and death.

Jesus moves through the heart of the city. He carries the Cross past air-conditioned skyscrapers filled with the busy and the powerful. He walks past the sick in the hospitals that line University Avenue. He shares their suffering, the young and old, male and female.

He makes his way, station after station, through the believers and the atheists, the hopeful and the despairing, the rich and the poor, the happy families and the forlorn individuals. He is the object of scrutiny by curious onlookers, excited children, contemplative crowds. He passes through a gathering of nations, languages and cultures, sowing on his way the question that every Christian must answer: "And you, who do you say that I am?" He is nailed to the cross, then placed in the tomb. The crowd disperses into the night, each person looking for the last station—the station that manifests itself in life's many twists and turns.

Tonight Jesus passes among us on the Way of the Cross—just as he does every day on the streets of the world.

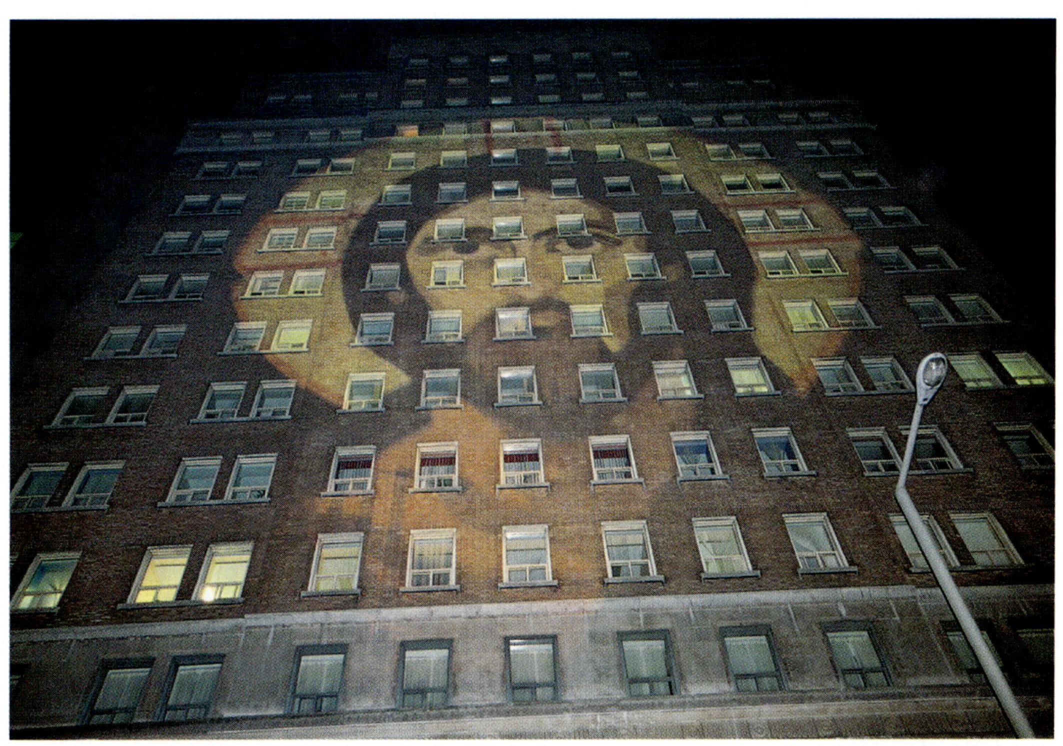

Reconciliation

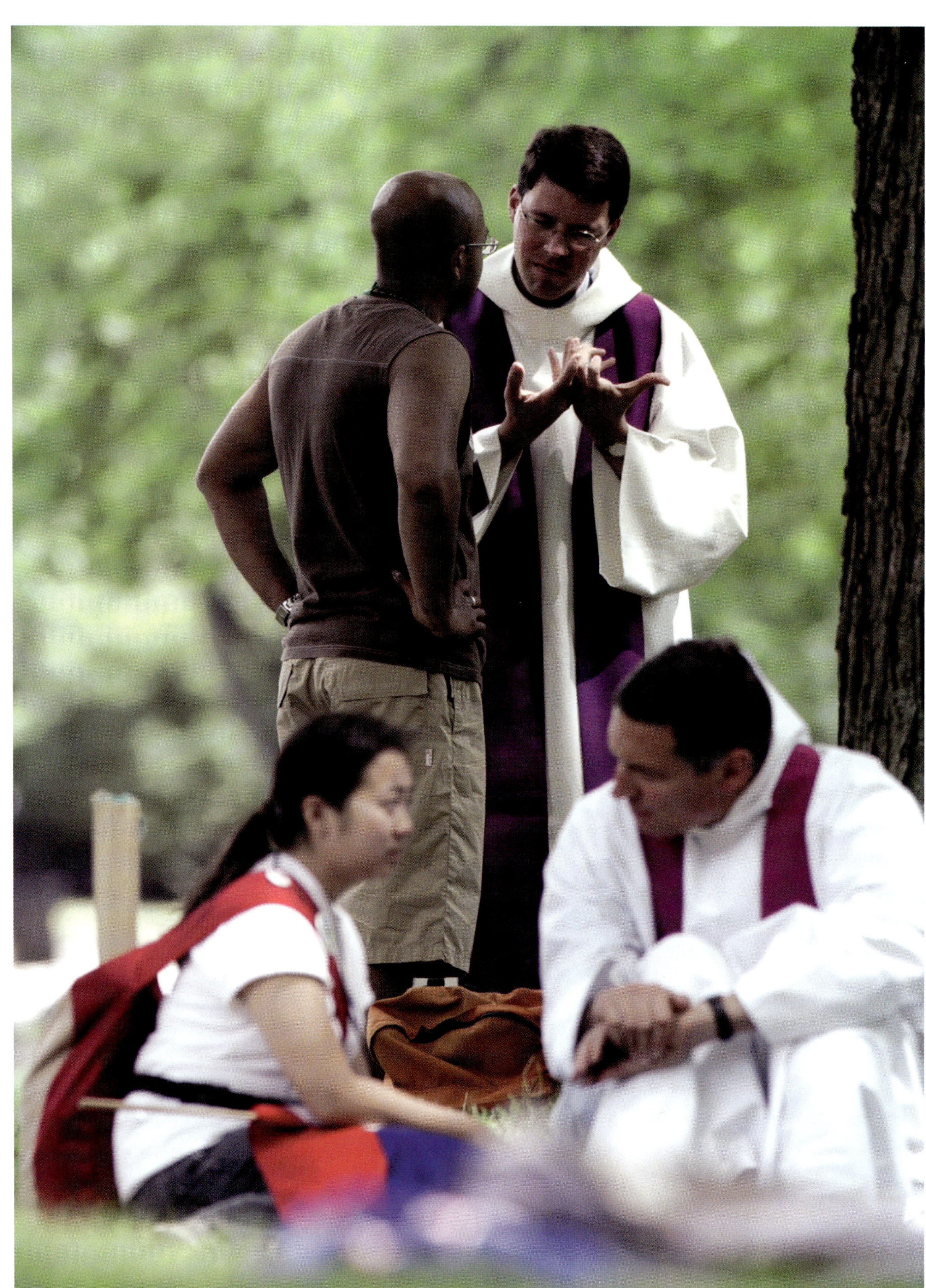

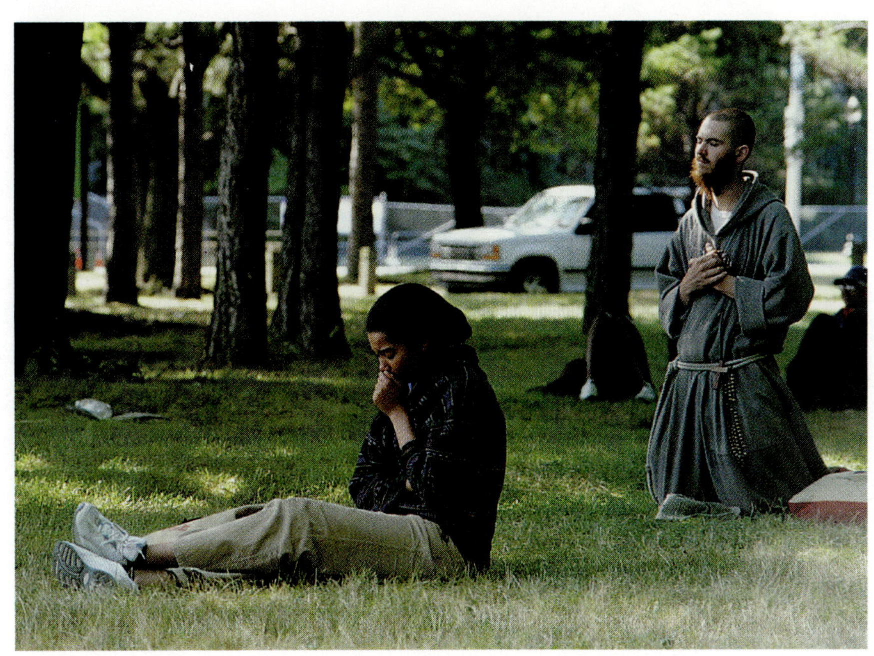

*Draw strength from the sacramental grace
of Reconciliation and Eucharist.*

JOHN PAUL II

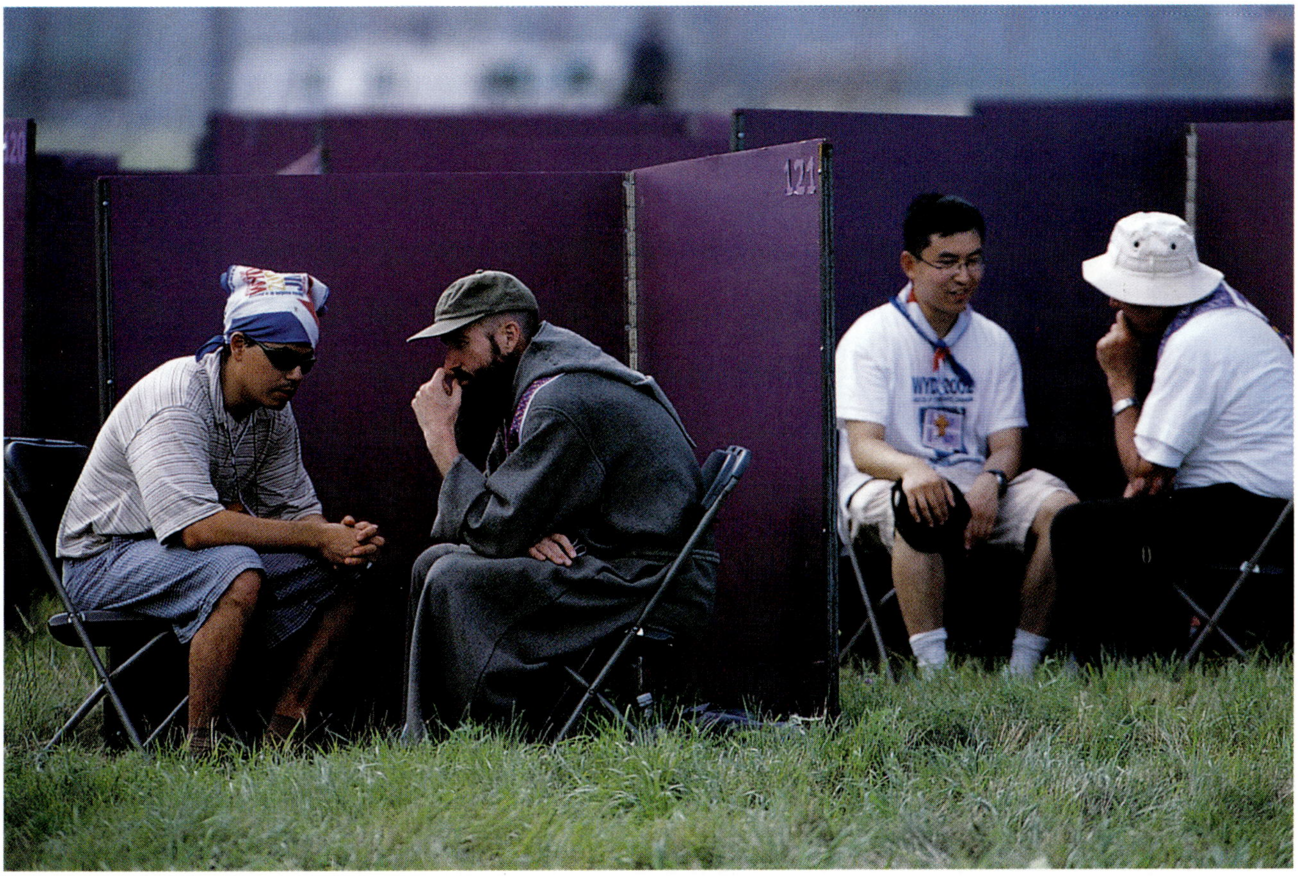

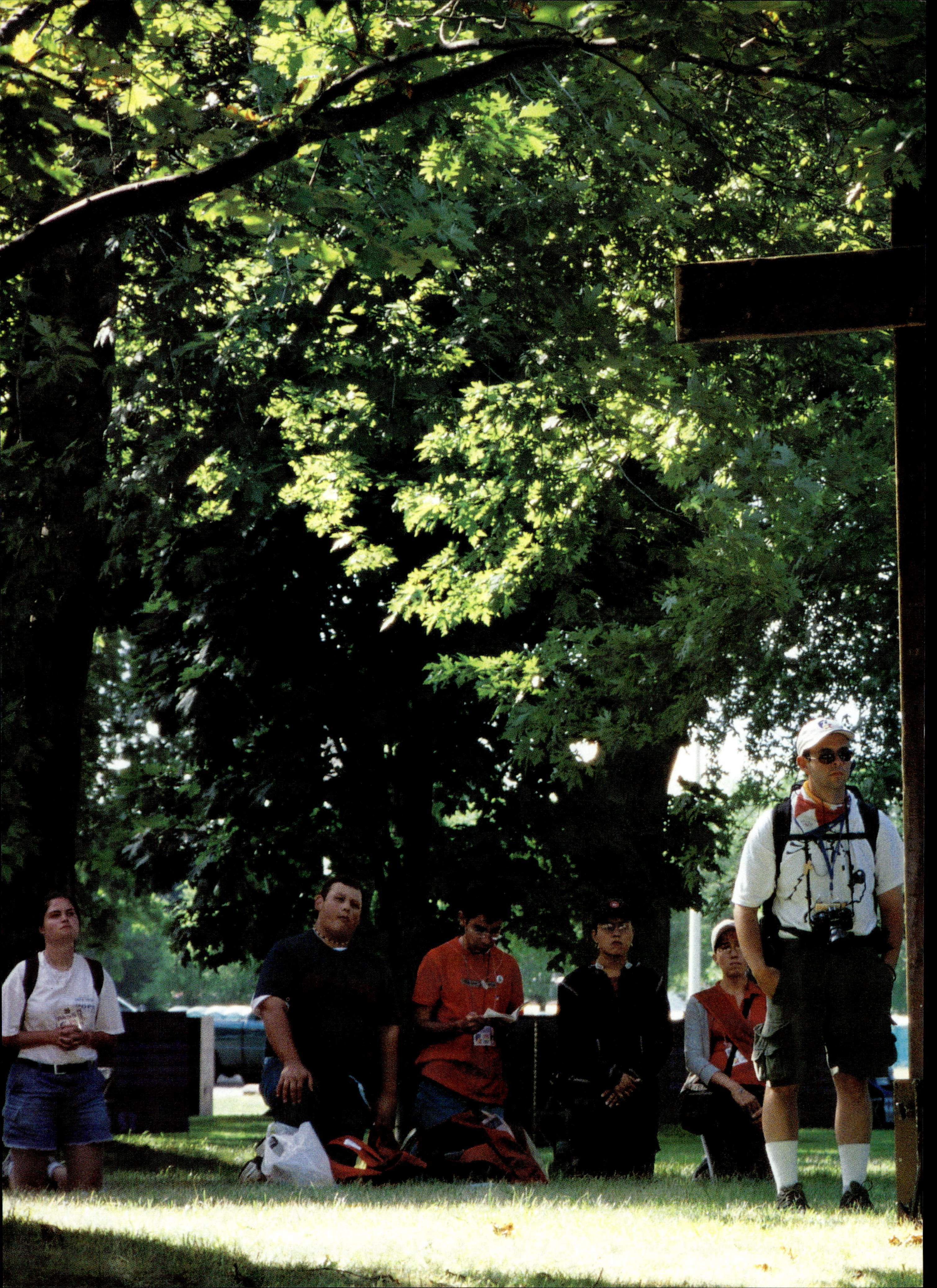

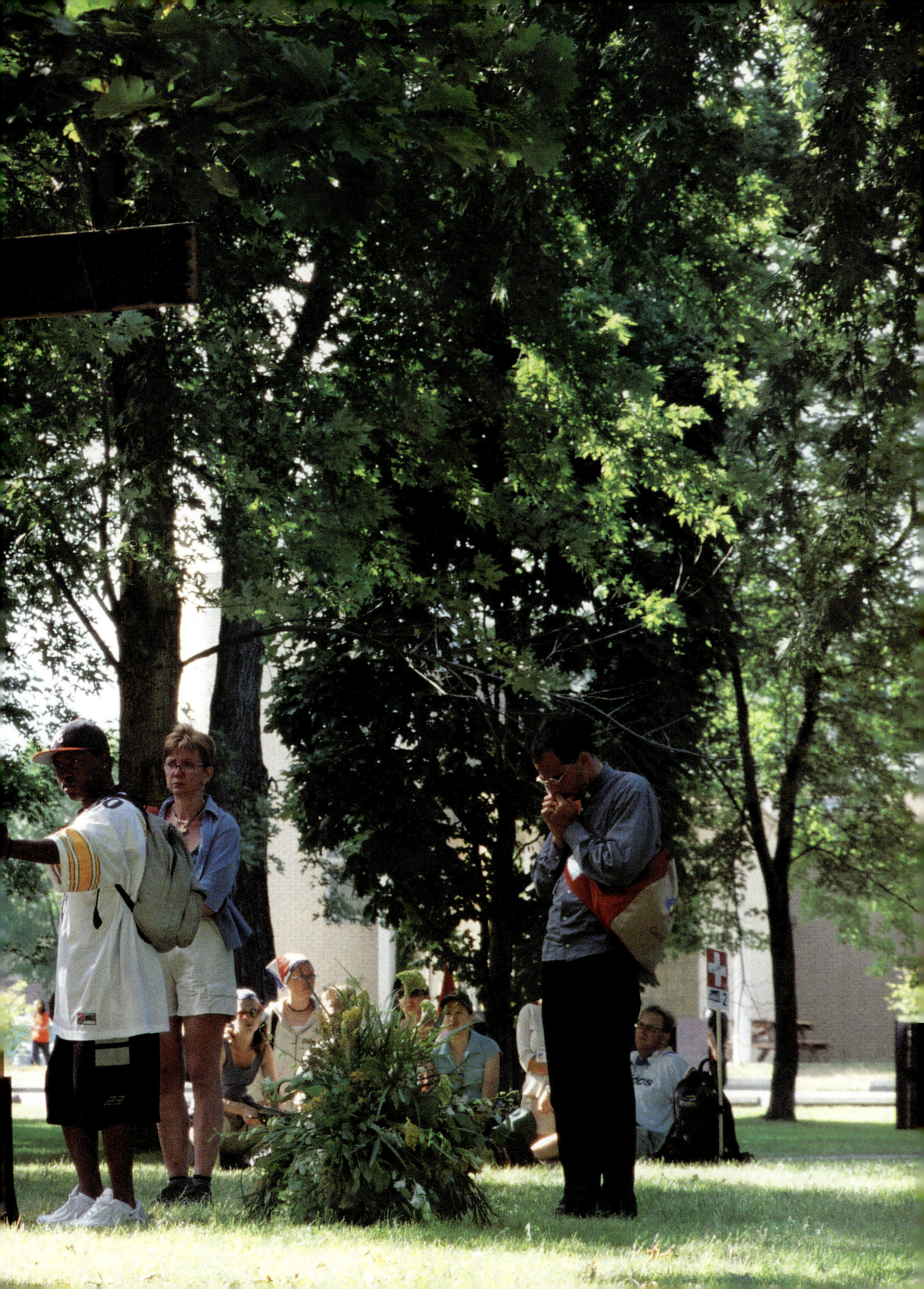

"Set out into the deep"

"Confession is good for the soul" goes the old saying. If true—and Catholics believe it is—many thousands of World Youth Day pilgrims did their souls good by contritely confessing their sins and receiving God's forgiveness.

About 1,000 priest-confessors were available, 200 or so at any given time. The main venue for the Sacrament of Reconciliation was Coronation Park, adjacent to Exhibition Place, which was renamed Duc in Altum Park for the week. "Duc in altum" is Latin for "set out into the deep," a reference to the words of Jesus to his first disciples (Luke 5:4) and a phrase used by John Paul II in his apostolic letter *Novo Millennio Ineunte*, issued on January 6, 2001.

In preparation for receiving the sacrament of reconciliation, volunteers guided the pilgrims seeking forgiveness to an area of the park set aside for reflection. Here they were asked to meditate and pray before receiving the Eucharist. Many pilgrims shed tears of sorrow for having damaged their relationship with God and with those closest to them.

When the pilgrims felt ready for confession, they entered the sacrament of reconciliation area with its 200 temporary confessionals. Beside each simply constructed confessional stood two chairs, one for the priest, the other for the penitent.

Once cleansed of their sins and forgiven, many of the young people spent time in prayer in front of the World Youth Day Cross before beginning the act of penance assigned to them by their confessor according to the nature of their confessed sins. A common penance was to make the sign of the cross with holy water from a large baptismal font near the WYD Cross. Contributing alms to the poor, performing good deeds, fasting and prayer were other prescribed penances.

The parable of the prodigal son was the theme for the sacrament of reconciliation. In the biblical story, the son renounces his father and leaves home, an action that is interpreted to symbolize the separation of mankind from God through sin. The son comes back years later, after realizing that his father had loved him but that he had betrayed that love. The father showers his son with gifts and has a party to celebrate his return. The unconditional love the father offers his repentant son symbolizes the desire of God to forgive the sins of humanity.

Reconciliation has always been a part of World Youth Day, but Pope John Paul II gave it special emphasis during WYD in Rome in the Jubilee Year 2000. The ancient Roman Circo Massimo was transformed into a giant confessional. The pope was reportedly "very keen" to continue this tradition in Toronto, and the International Knights of Columbus donated CAN$1 million toward the expenses related to mounting the sacrament of reconciliation. Confessions were also heard at Downsview Lands during the evening of the vigil with the pope, which preceded the closing mass.

God, the Father of mercies, through the death and resurrection of his Son, has reconciled the world to himself and sent the Holy Spirit among us for the forgiveness of sins...

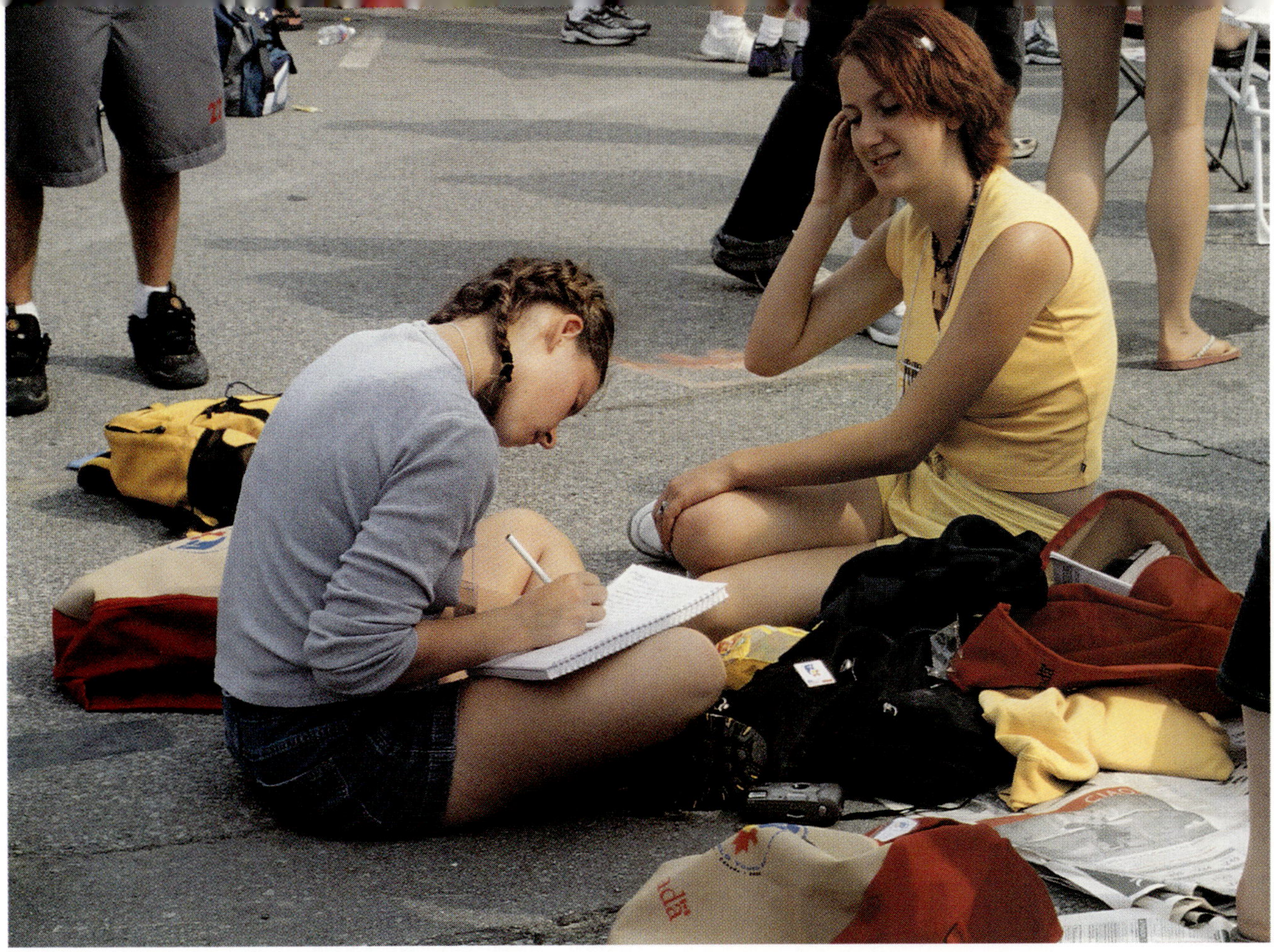

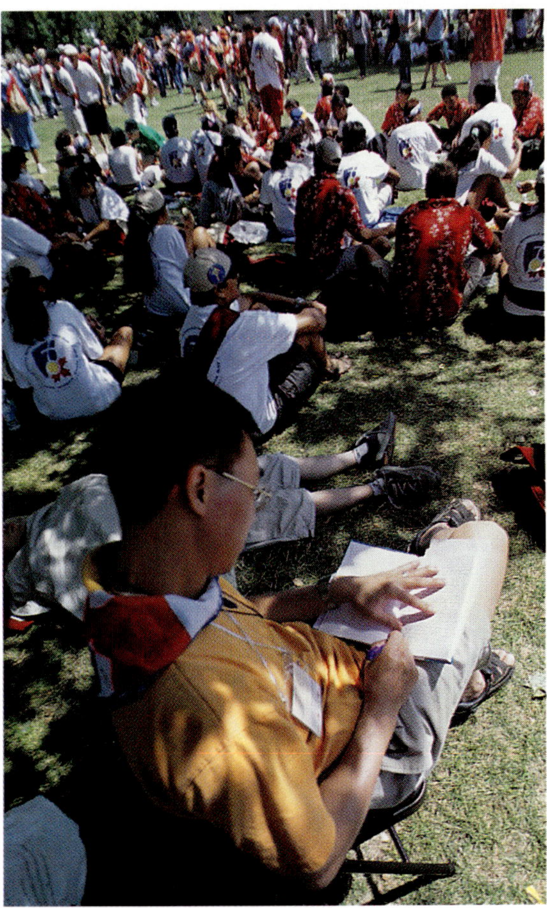

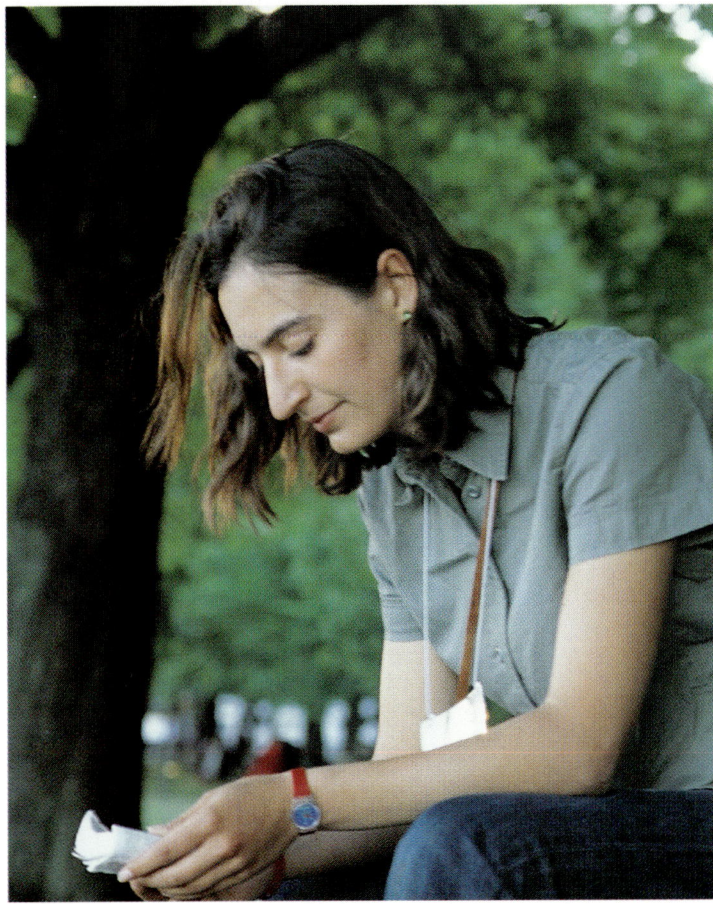

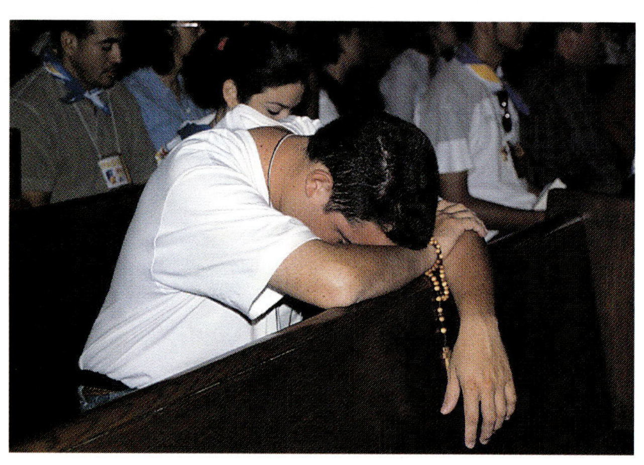

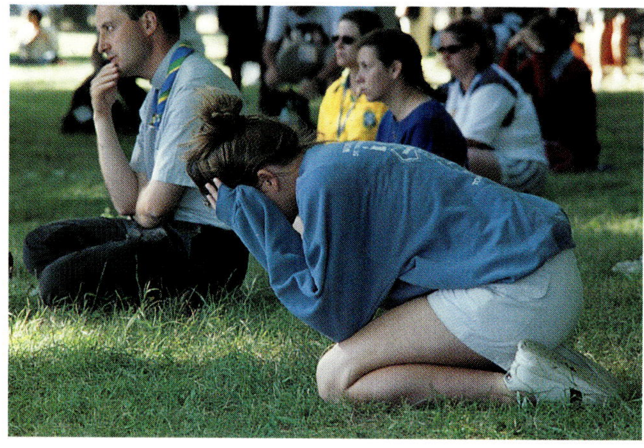

*... through the ministry of the Church
may God give you pardon and peace*

YOUNG PEOPLE AT PRAYER

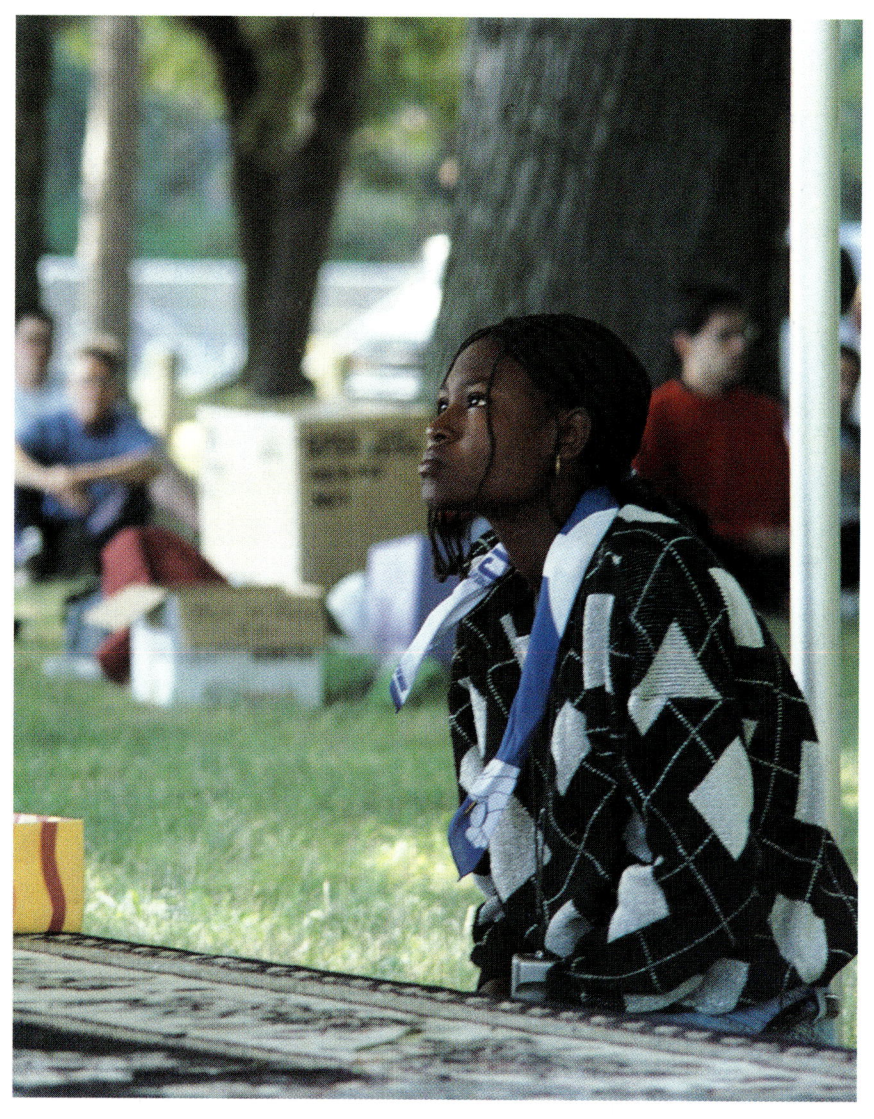

More than just a place

At first one might think that the young penitents could use a little more privacy. In a park on the shores of Lake Ontario, organizers have set up a place where pilgrims can celebrate the sacrament of Reconciliation. This calm, quiet space houses scores of two-sided, folding polling booths that have been converted to confessionals. From morning to night hundreds of priests hear the confessions of countless pilgrims.

Little by little this activity permeates the WYD celebrations. During the opening mass, several priests on the fringes of the crowd hear confessions. Right in the middle of the bustling activities of the youth festival itself, in the packed corridors of the National Trade Centre, people celebrate a sacrament. A rather crude confessional is even set up between an ice cream cart and an information panel! During the ceremony to welcome the pope, amidst all the excitement and pent-up emotion in the crowd, priests continue to hear confessions and dispense God's forgiveness.

The night of the Way of the Cross, in spots lit up by the giant screens, you can make out the silhouettes of priests and penitents. For six days, this scene, surprising at first glance, plays itself out thousands of times in the most unexpected and public places.

Duc in Altum Park is more than a place; it is above all an invitation to take a step in the direction of the love that goes by the name of forgiveness. Many of the young and not-so-young respond. Most significantly, it is the sacrament of pardon that also sets out "into the deep," taking root in the middle of the crowd and of the city, as if to announce the beginnings of John Paul II's "civilization of love."

Our relationship with God is strongly connected to our relationship with each other. Just as our relationships with others can be hurt and damaged, so too with our relationship with God.

YOUNG PEOPLE AT PRAYER

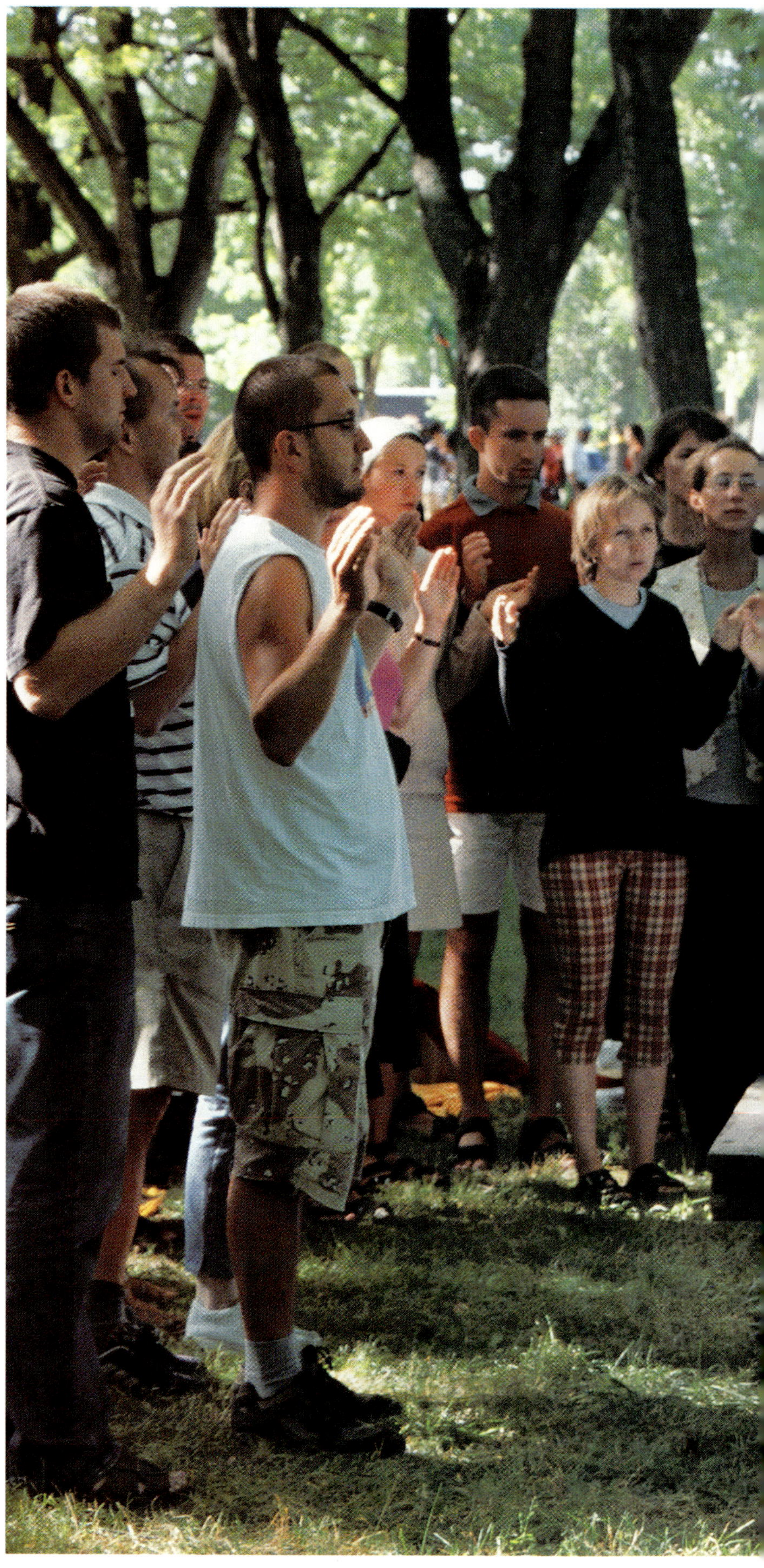

*"Duc in altum!"
These words ring
out for us today,
and they invite us
to remember the
past with gratitude,
to live the present
with enthusiasm
and to look to the
future with
confidence:
"Jesus Christ is
the same yesterday,
today and forever"
(Hebrews 13:8).*

Young People at Prayer

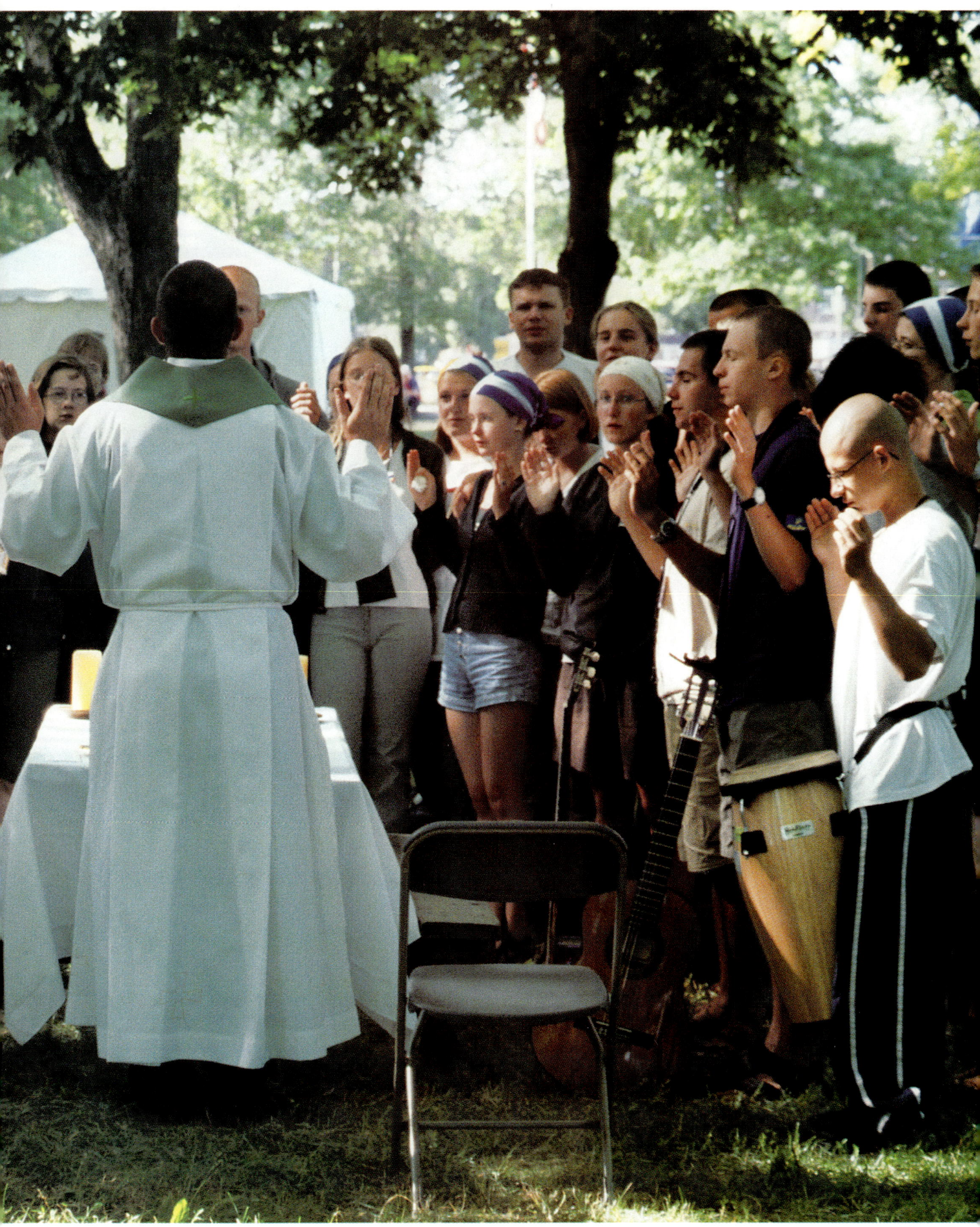

The Liturgy of Solemn Vespers

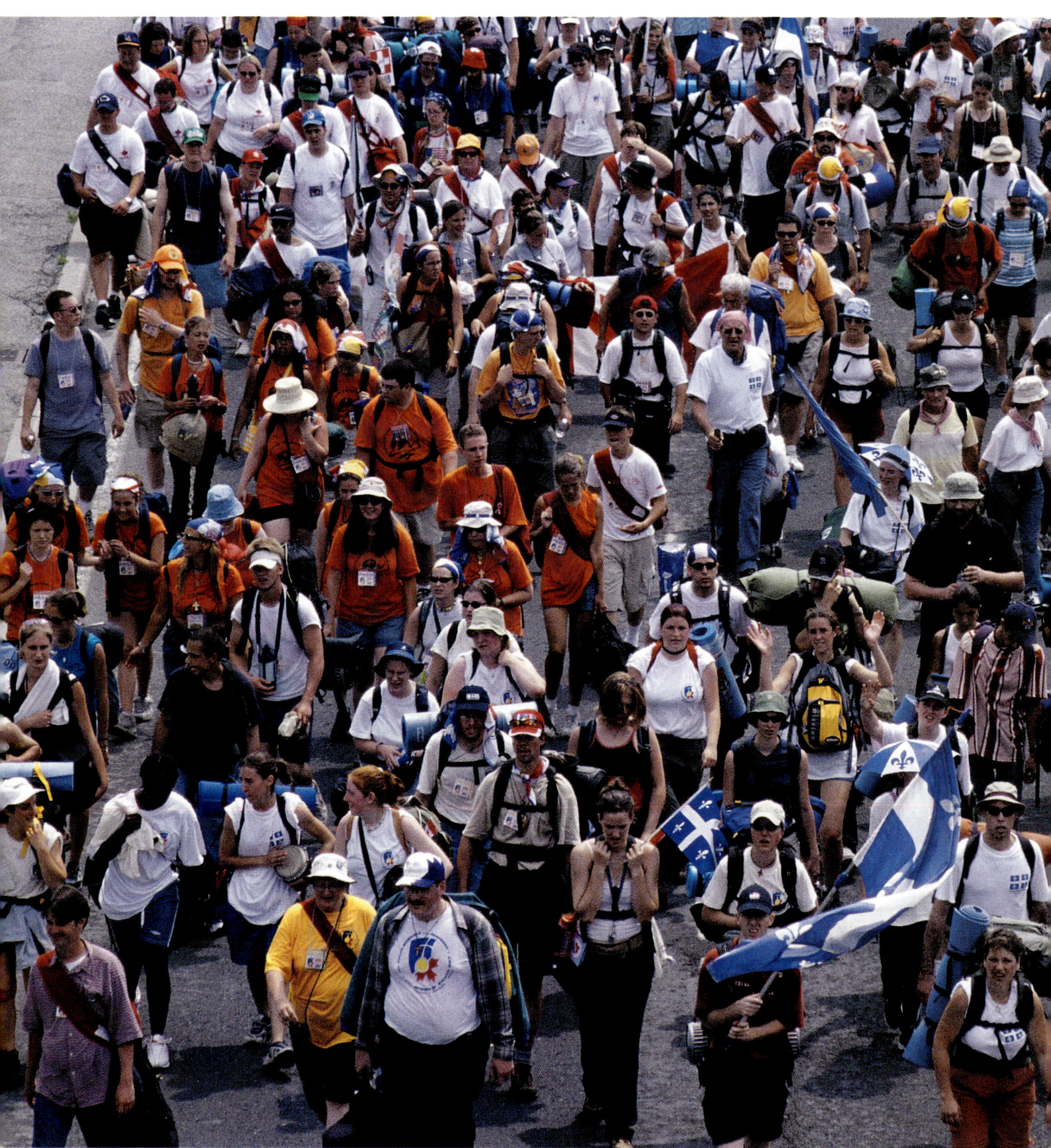

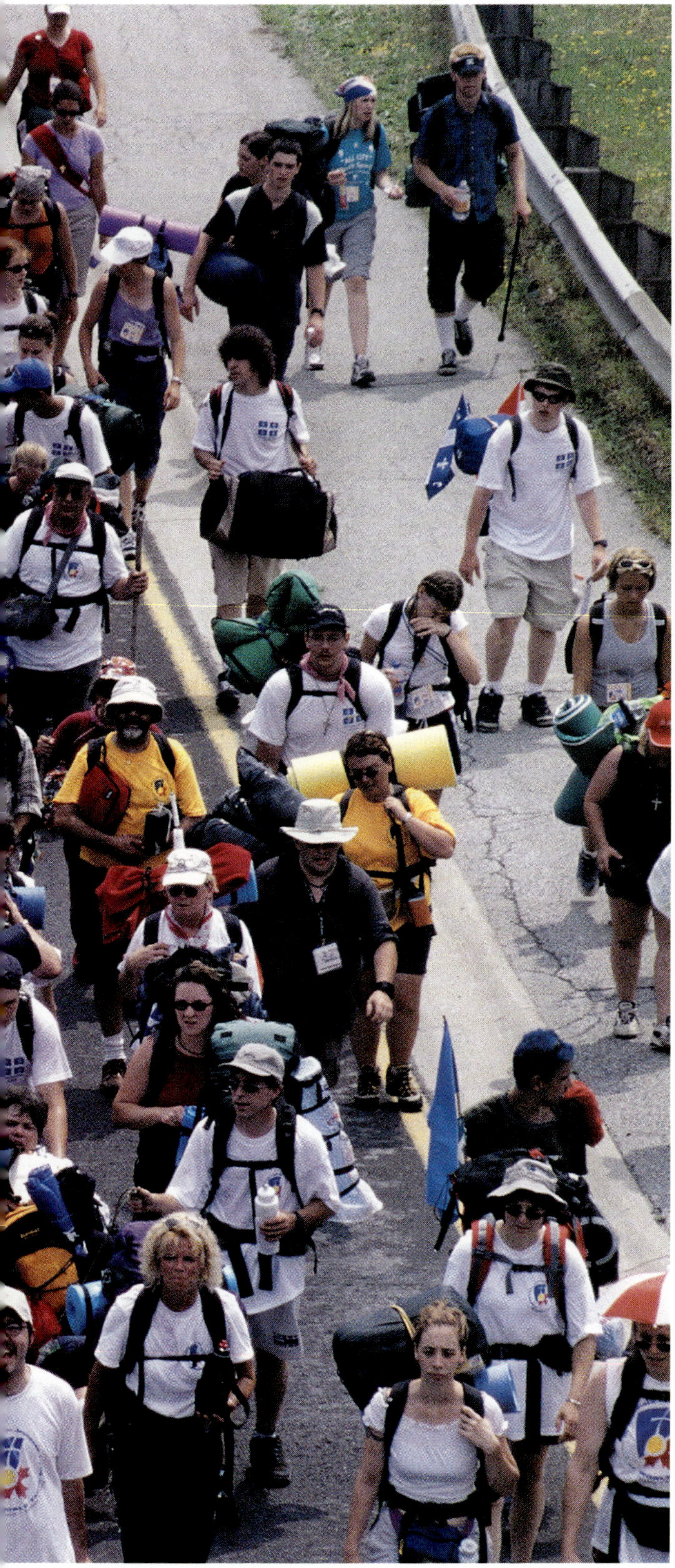

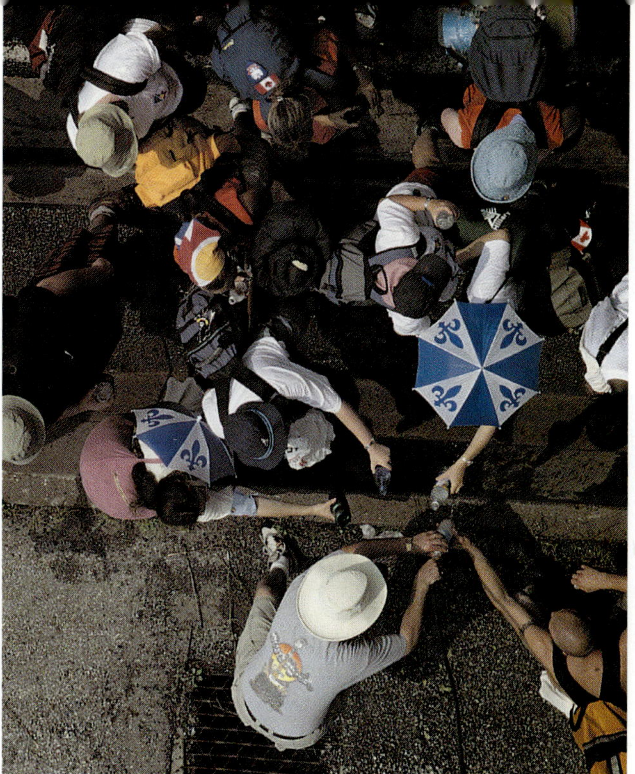

"Follow me" (JOHN 1:43).

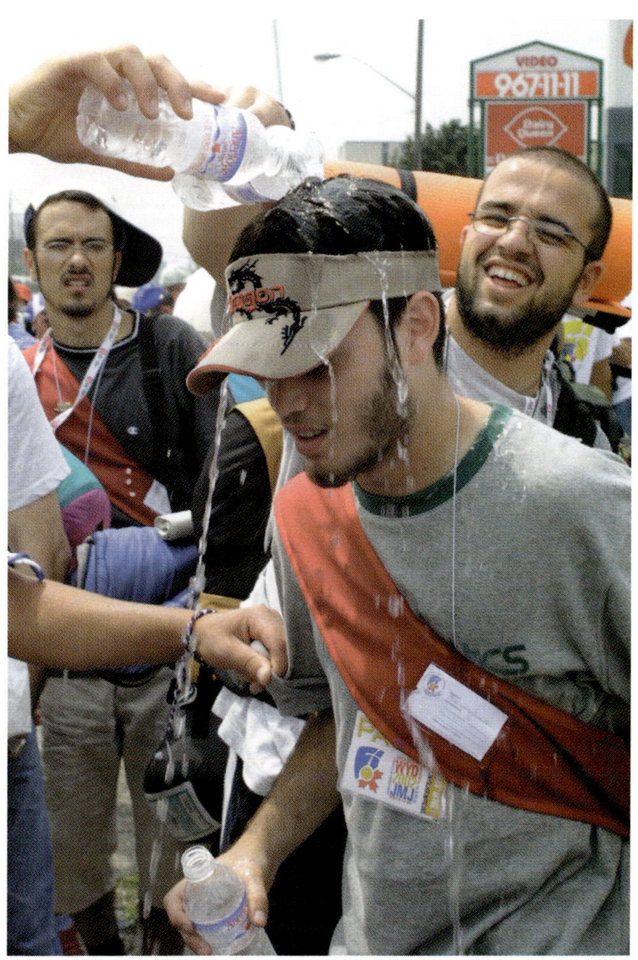

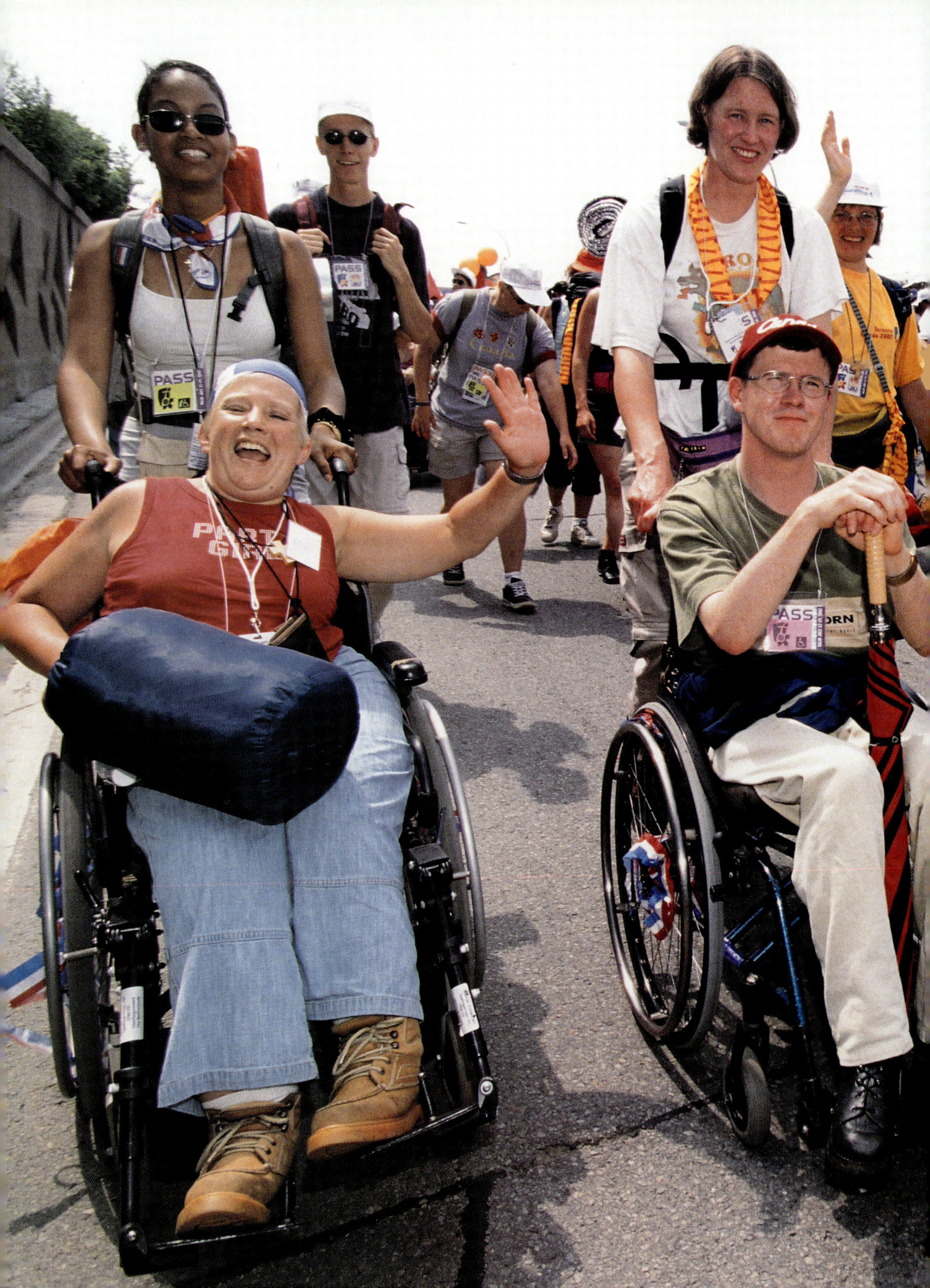

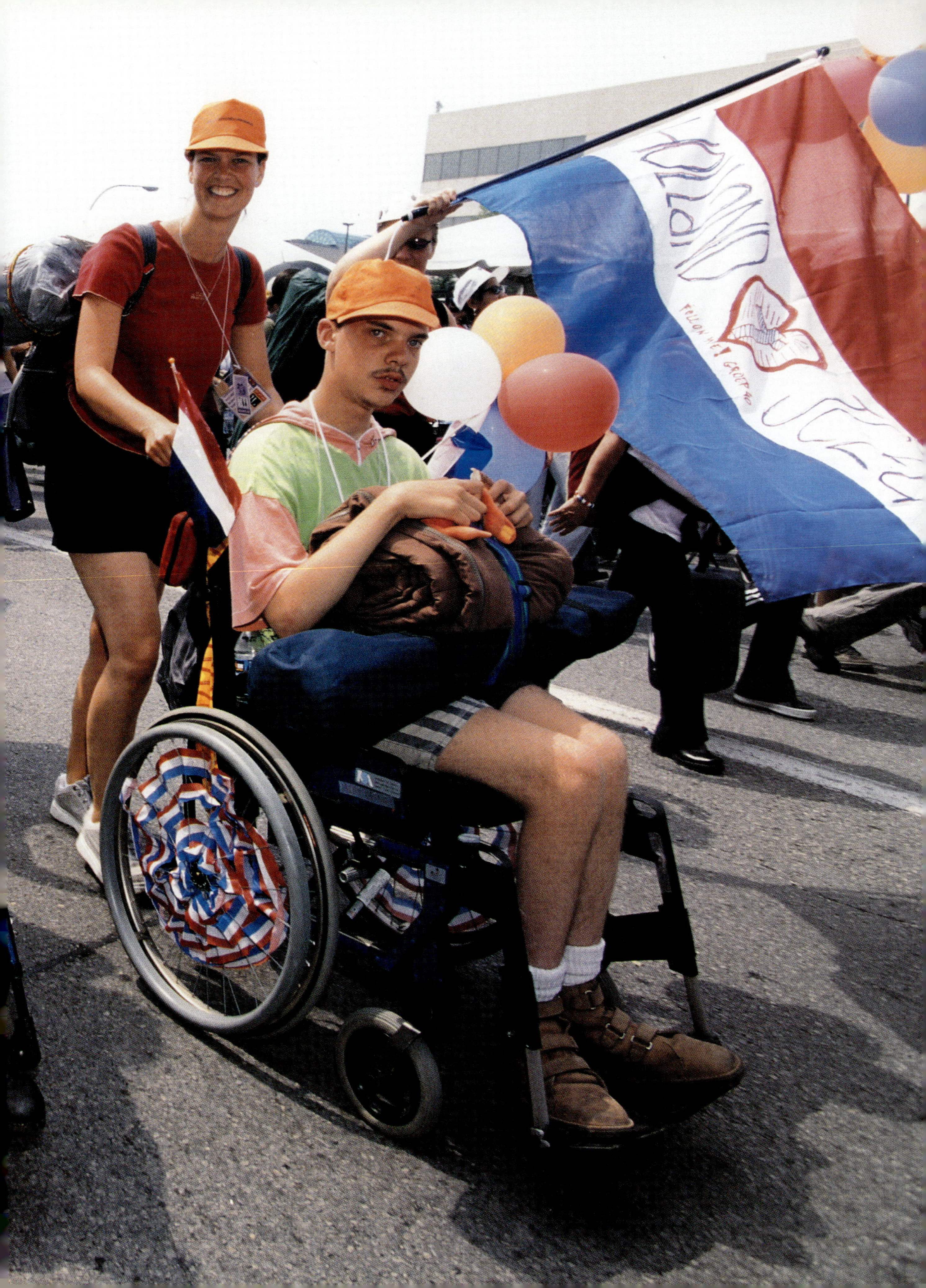
HOLLAND
veel het groep te

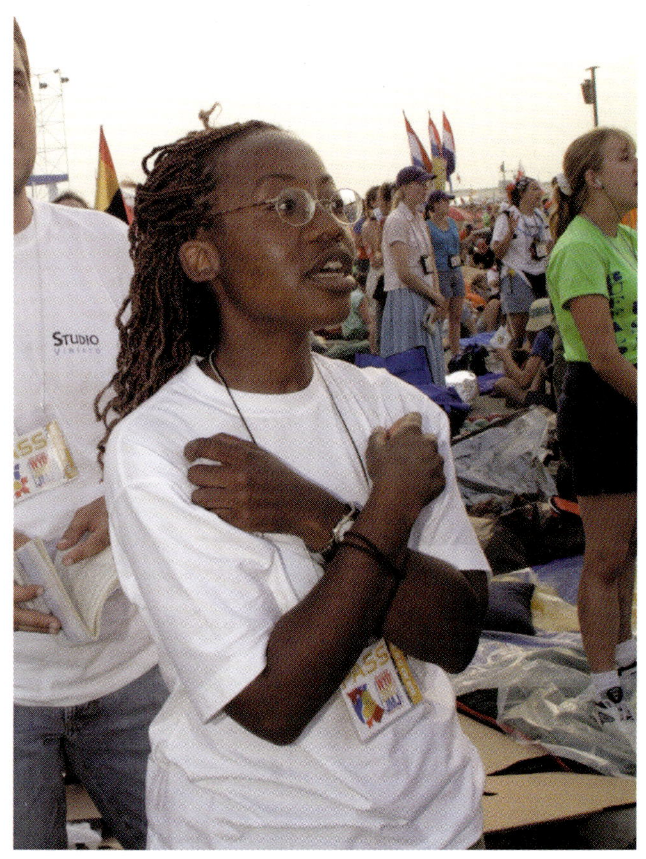

*A new generation
of builders
is needed. Moved not
by fear or violence
but by the urgency
of genuine love, they must
learn to build, brick by brick,
the city of God within
the city of man.*

JOHN PAUL II

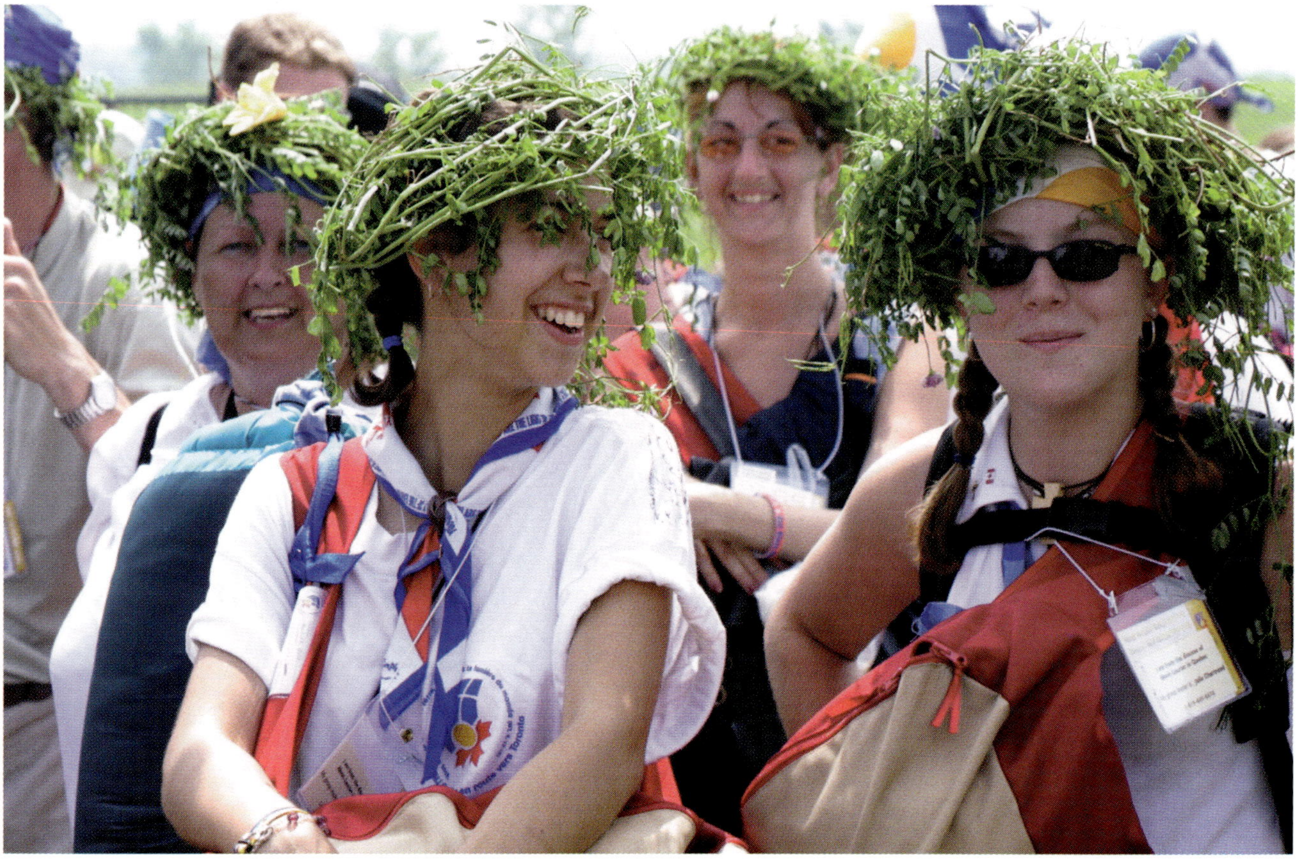

The future is in your hearts and in your hands

On July 27, an army of young people carried sleeping bags, backpacks, flags and other World Youth Day paraphernalia through scorching heat for the long walk from Exhibition Place to Downsview Lands for an evening vigil with Pope John Paul II.

They sang, chanted, waved flags and formed a multicultural community of believers on the move as they made their way to the site of a former Canadian military base in northwest Toronto. They shared a common goal: to secure a position as close to the stage as possible.

The pontiff arrived by helicopter and then wound his way by popemobile through an estimated crowd of 600,000 as a procession of bishops and cardinals and busloads of VIPs took their seats in front of the massive stage. The Litany of the Saints concluded as the pope ended his drive through the ever-swelling crowd.

Just before sunset, the Liturgy of Solemn Vespers began with these dramatic words: "As the fading sun dies away we gather with lighted candles in a hopeful act of defiance against the darkness."

Liturgical dancing, singing, scripture readings and prayers preceded the pope's homily, during which loud cheers from his youthful audience forced him frequently to pause. He asked them, "On what foundations must we build the new historical era that is emerging from the great transformations of the twentieth century?" Moments later, he added, "Christ alone is the cornerstone on which it is possible to solidly build one's existence."

Among those with the pontiff on the giant Downsview stage were the Liturgy Group, which was made up of two people from each of the 78 conferences of bishops worldwide, almost 700 young people from countries that had hosted previous World Youth Day gatherings, cantors, musicians, Eastern Rite Catholics and aboriginal peoples from around the world.

The solemn ceremony, based on the salt and light theme of World Youth Day 2002, included hymns, personal testimonies, meditations, psalms and canticle prayers. One of the most striking sights during this prayerful event was the lighting by the pilgrims of the vigil candles they had received in their red and beige knapsacks when they first arrived in Toronto. As night fell, the Downsview Lands site was illuminated by the flickering of hundreds of thousands of candles.

At the end of the vigil, in a symbolic gesture, the pope gave pieces of salt to 12 young people representing all WYD pilgrims. He explained how they, and all Christians, must work to become the salt of the earth. He then gave his final blessing.

The vigil, which was broadcast live across Canada, concluded with the singing of the World Youth Day theme song, "Light of the World." The pope then returned by helicopter to his temporary residence in the motherhouse of the Sisters of St. Joseph as the throng of pilgrims bade him farewell until the next morning, when he would preside at the closing mass of WYD 2002.

Many of the tens of thousands of young people, exhausted by the walking pilgrimage early in the day and the evening's vigil, broke open their sleeping bags or huddled under structures improvised from cardboard boxes to rest for the closing mass. Others were happy to stay awake, listening to the pop music that boomed from the loudspeakers or chatting with friends into the early hours of the morning.

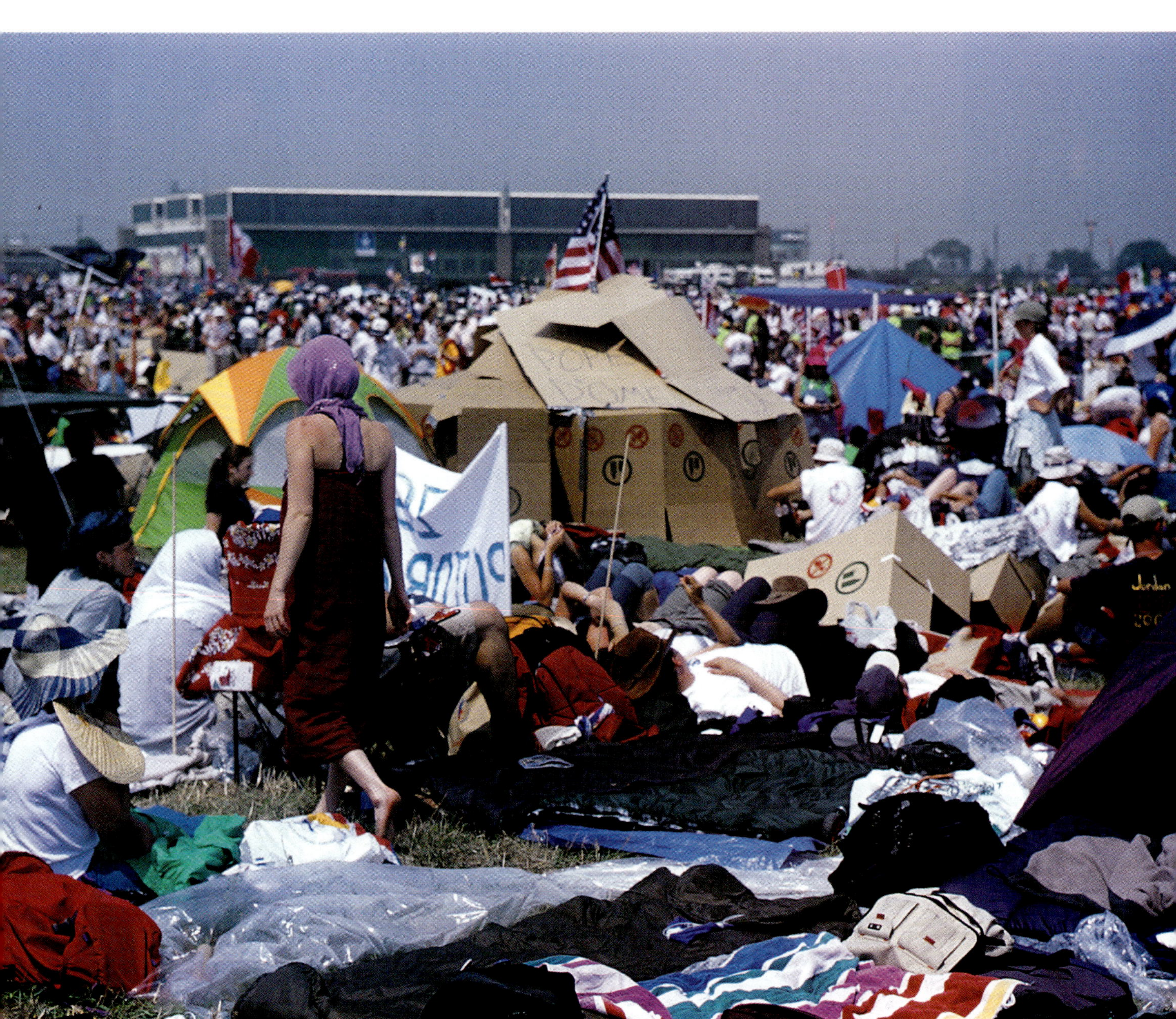

> *Allow me, dear young people, to consign this hope
> of mine to you: you must be those "builders"!
> You are the men and women of tomorrow.
> The future is in your hearts and in your hands...*

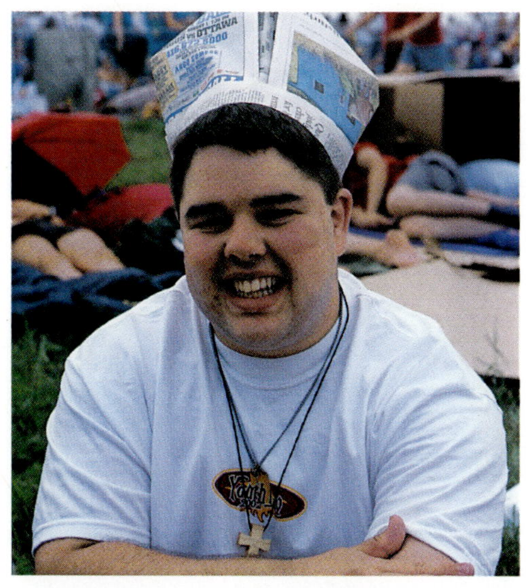
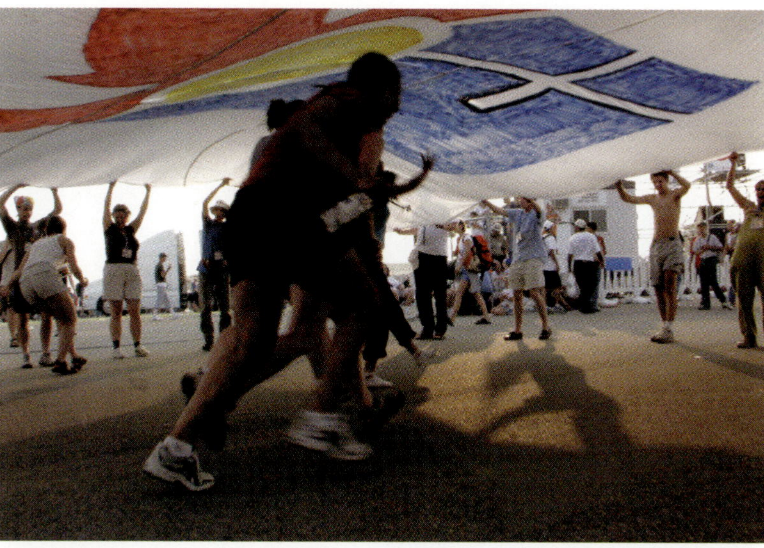
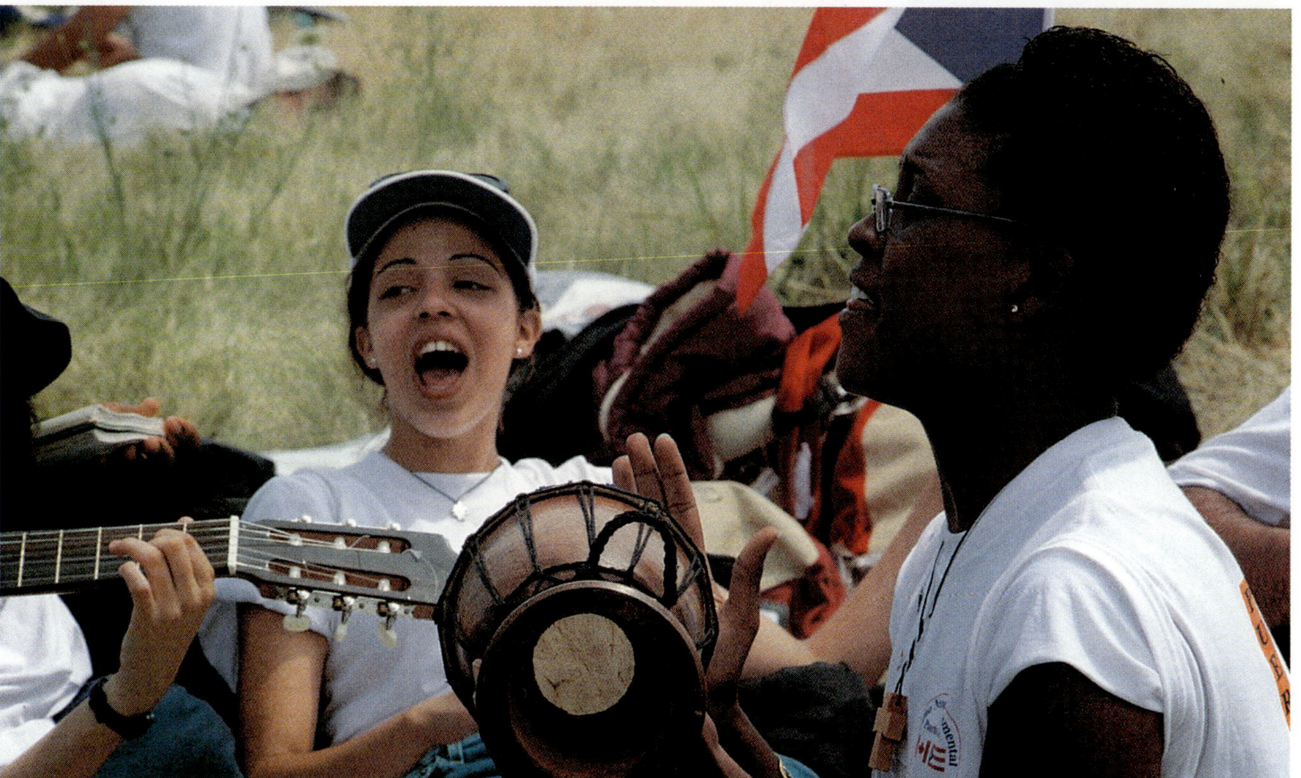
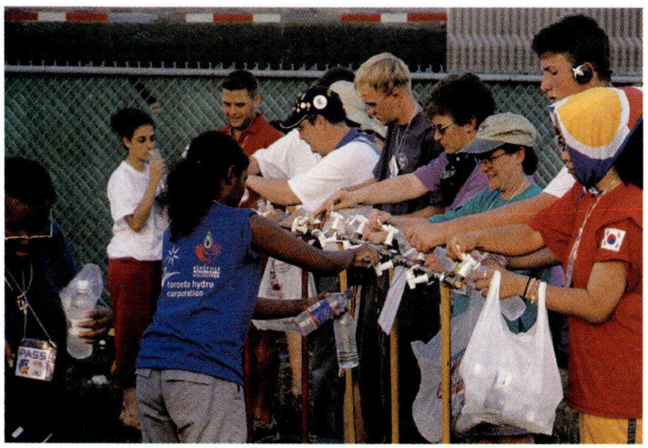
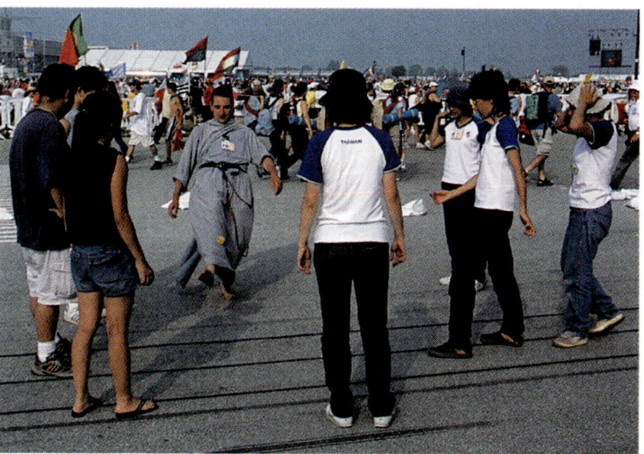

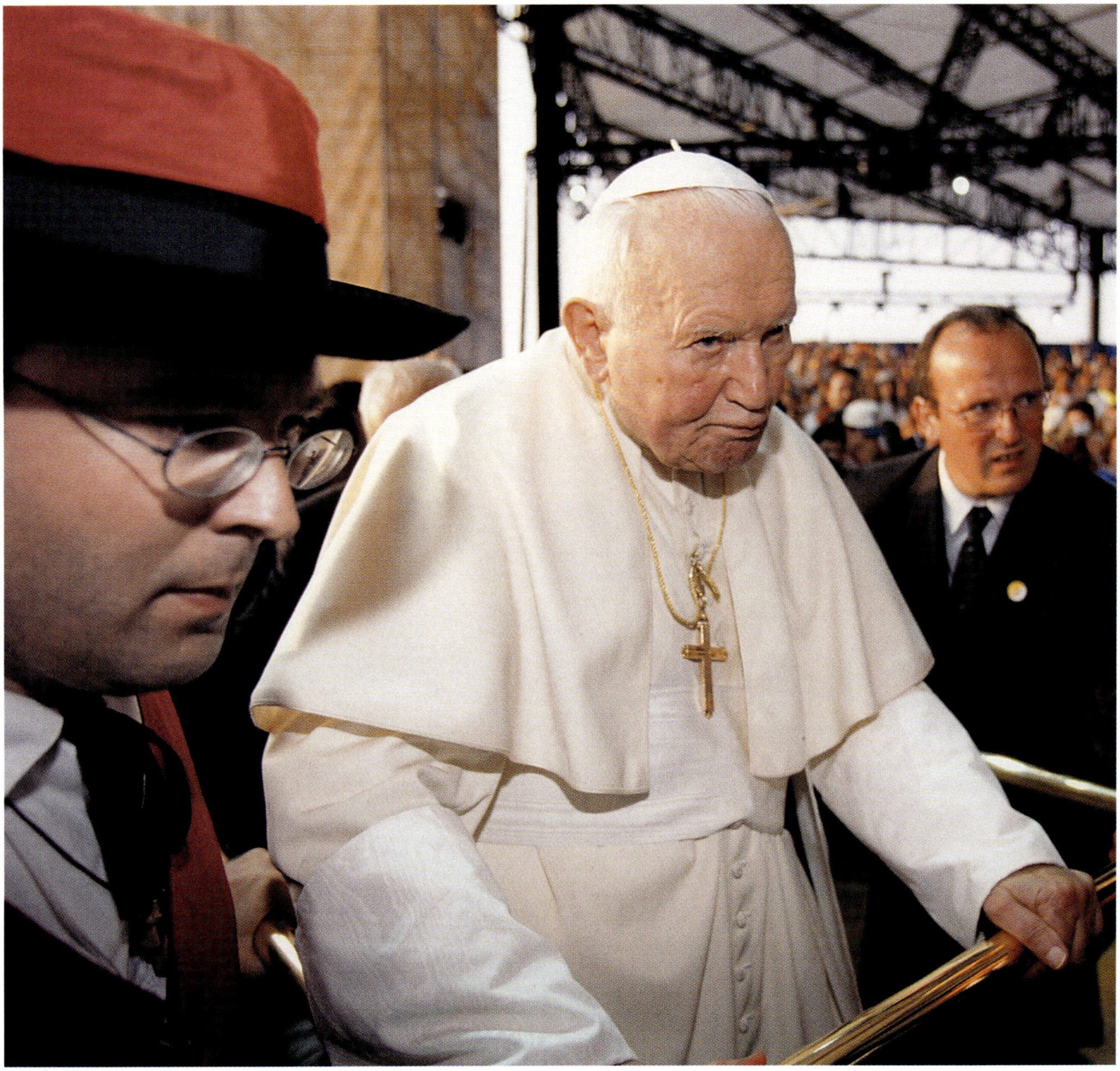

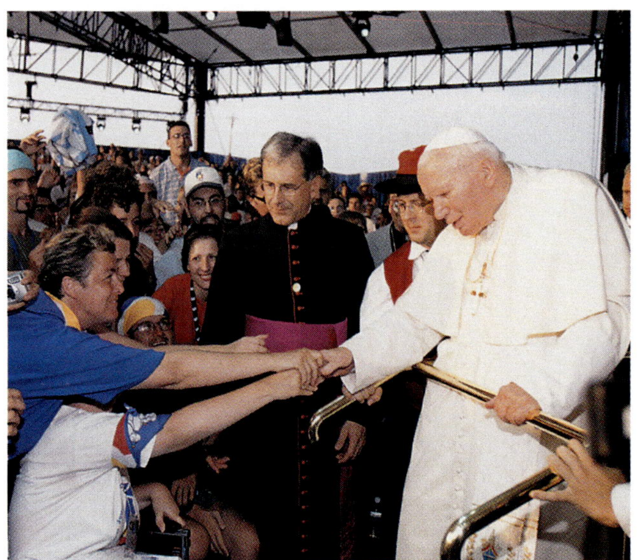

... God is entrusting to you the task, at once difficult and uplifting, of working with him in the building of the civilization of love.

John Paul II

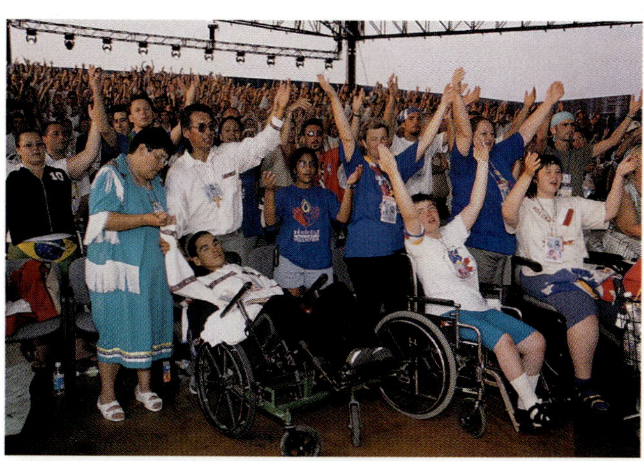

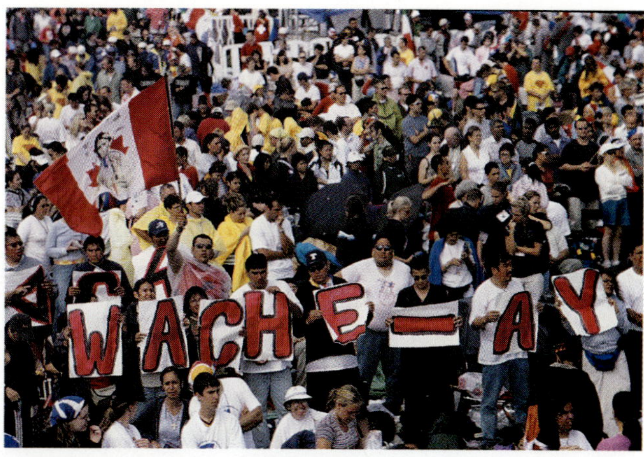

WACHE=AY

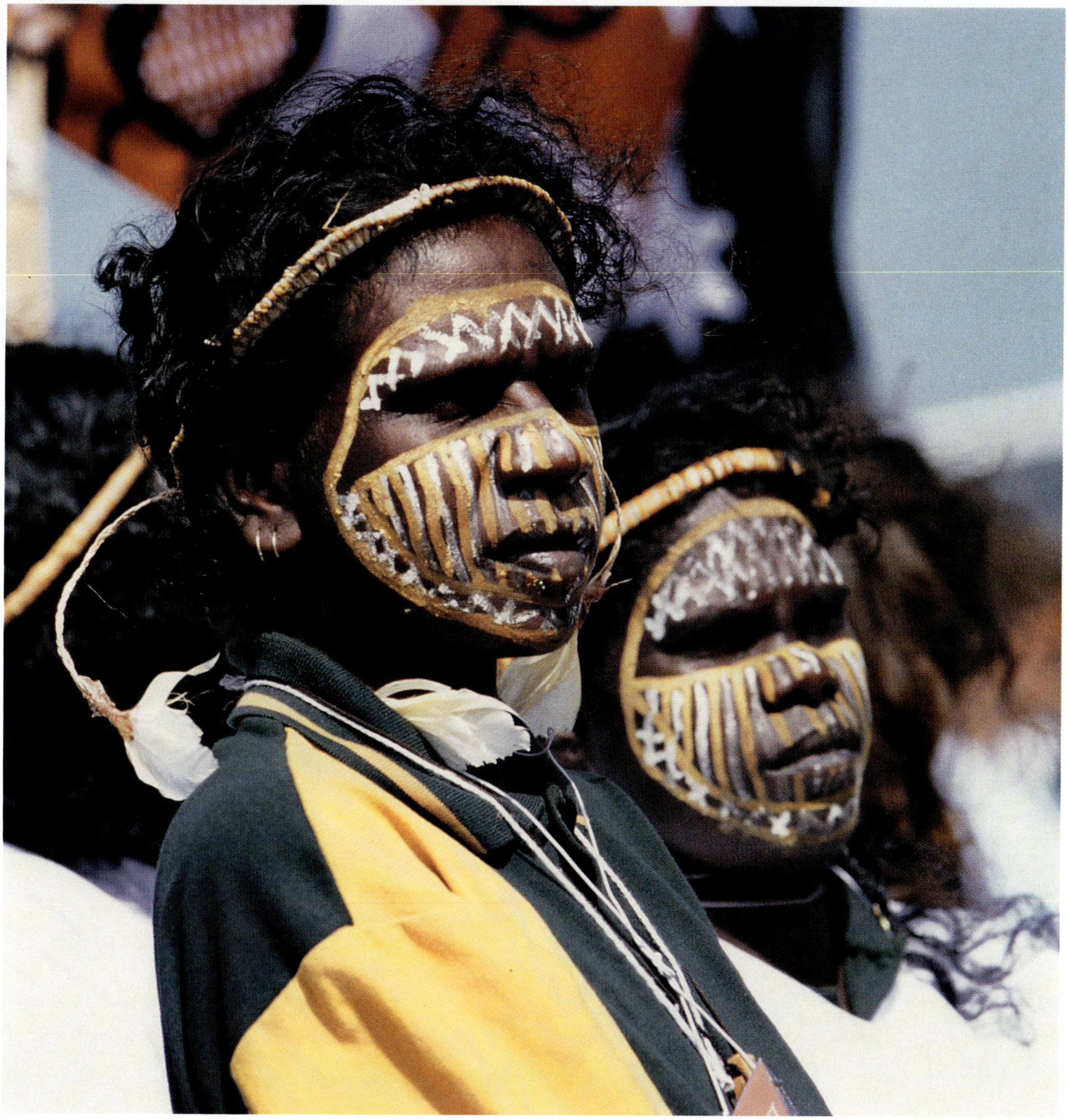

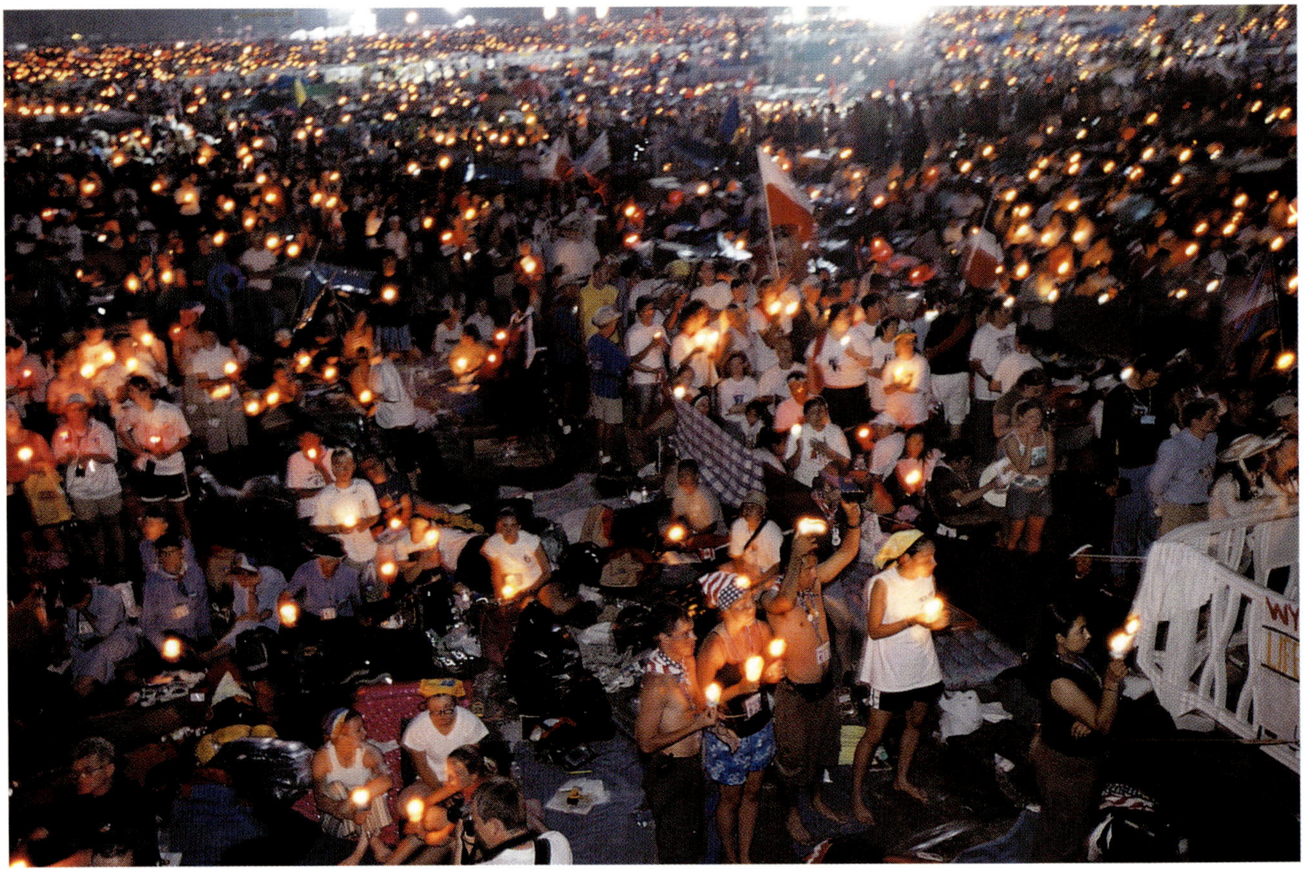

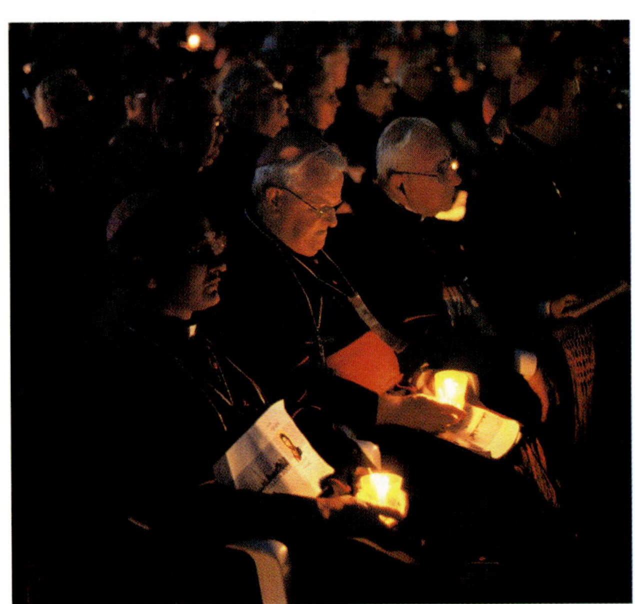

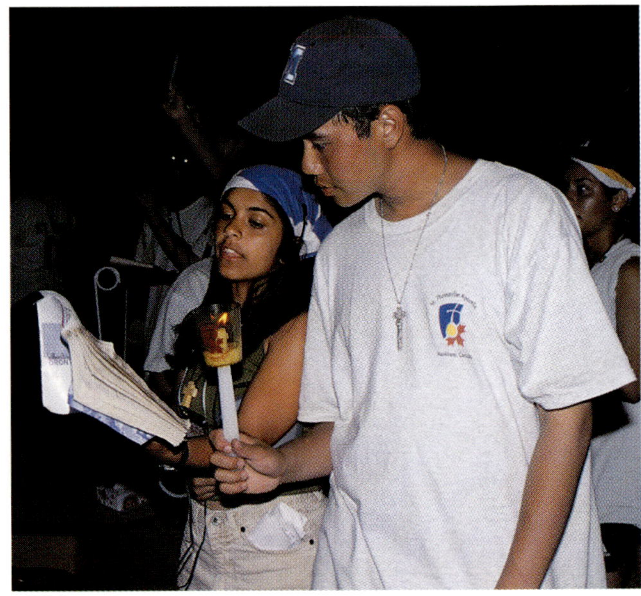

Dear young people, let yourselves be taken over by the light of Christ, and spread that light wherever you are.

John Paul II

I say to you this evening: let the light of Christ shine in your lives! Do not wait until you are older in order to set out on the path of holiness! Holiness is always youthful, just as eternal is the youthfulness of God.

JOHN PAUL II

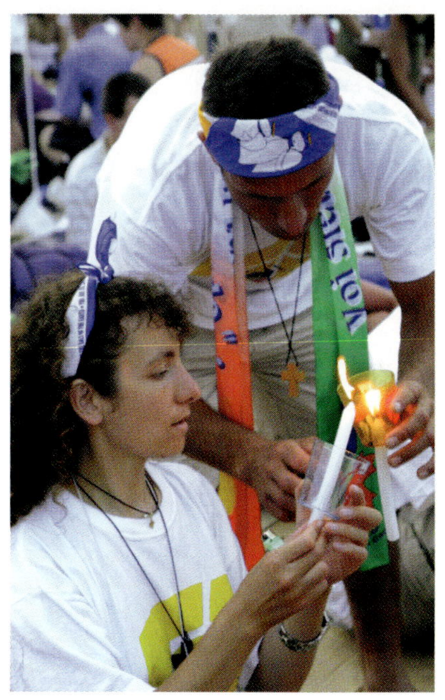

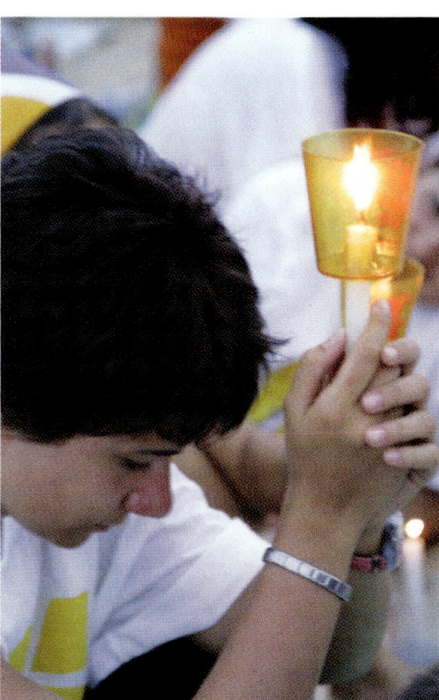

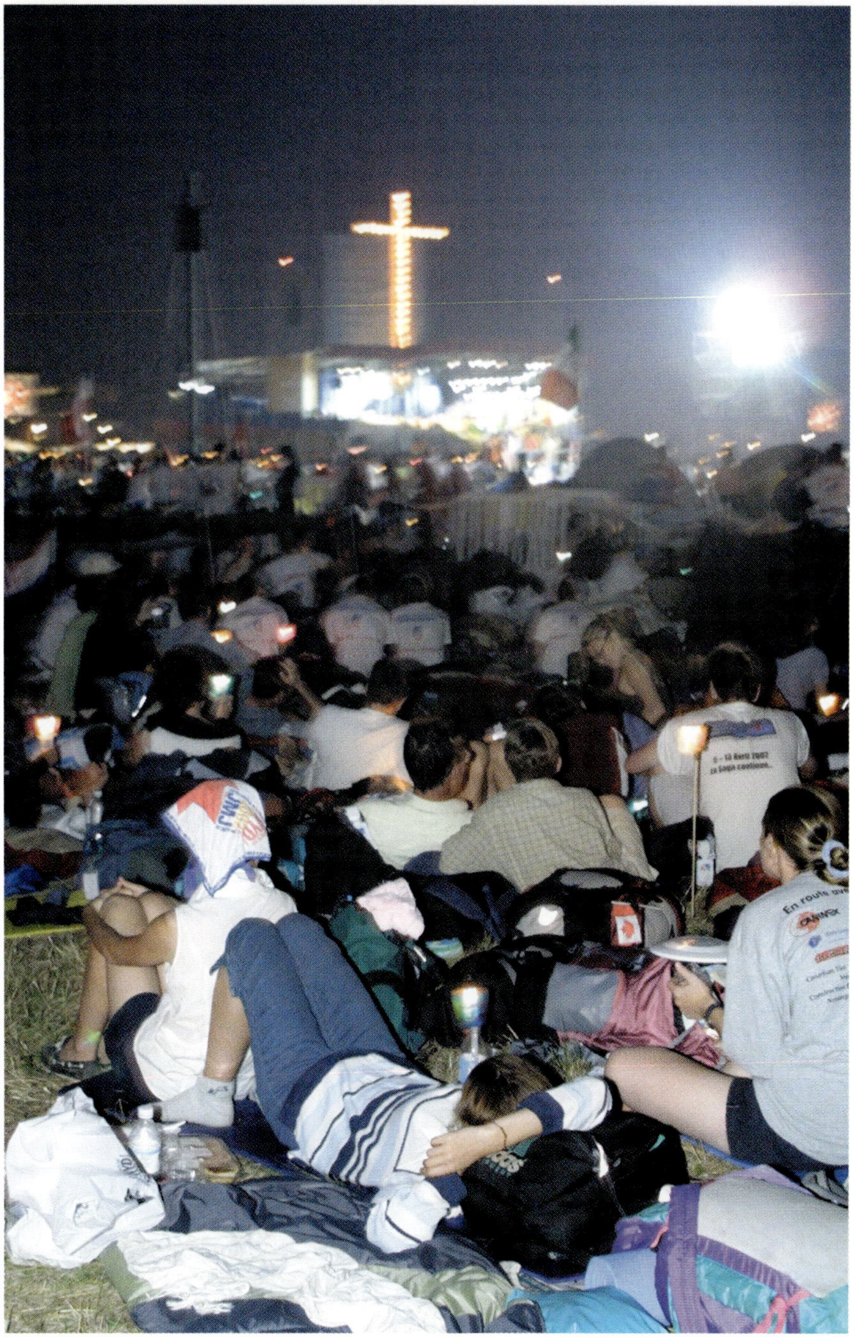

You are our father and our grandfather

All day long pilgrims stream through Toronto. From every point on the compass they converge on Downsview Lands. In an extension of the previous evening's Way of the Cross, the pilgrims walk towards the "fifteenth station" to meet the One for whom it is unnecessary to "search among the dead." Like all pilgrims everywhere, they beg their tired feet and sore legs to get them to their destination, to their heart's desire. Friends and travelling companions meet others along the way. By day's end they number in the hundreds of thousands. Together they arrive at the park thirsty, famished and exhausted. Together they pitch their tents for the night, enthusiastic, smiling and peaceful. A scene from Exodus!

Their lanterns twinkle starlike on that starless night, creating a personal firmament for the weary pilgrims. The scene is so intimate, so cosy, so full of expectation. And then it's as if an old friend has dropped in for a visit. The family is finally together, as if seated by the fireside, to talk, to listen, to tell stories, to laugh and to sing.

"You are our father and our grandfather," exclaims Rémy Perras who was invited to speak on behalf of the youth present. The immense crowd expresses its deep affection for their Holy Father with prolonged and robust applause. John Paul II, accepting gladly this paternal mission, passes on his spiritual legacy: "Allow me to consign this hope of mine to you: you must be the builders! ... God is entrusting to you the task, at once difficult and uplifting, of working with him in the building of the civilization of love."

Minutes later he adds: "Let the light of Christ shine in your lives." On that vigil night, the young people's best friend sees in their illuminated faces the fulfilment of his most fervent wish.

"Light of the world! Salt of the earth!
Be for the world the face of love!
Be for the earth the reflection of his light!"

*That is the most beautiful and precious gift
that you can give to the Church and the world.
You know that the pope is with you,
with his prayer and fond blessing.*

John Paul II

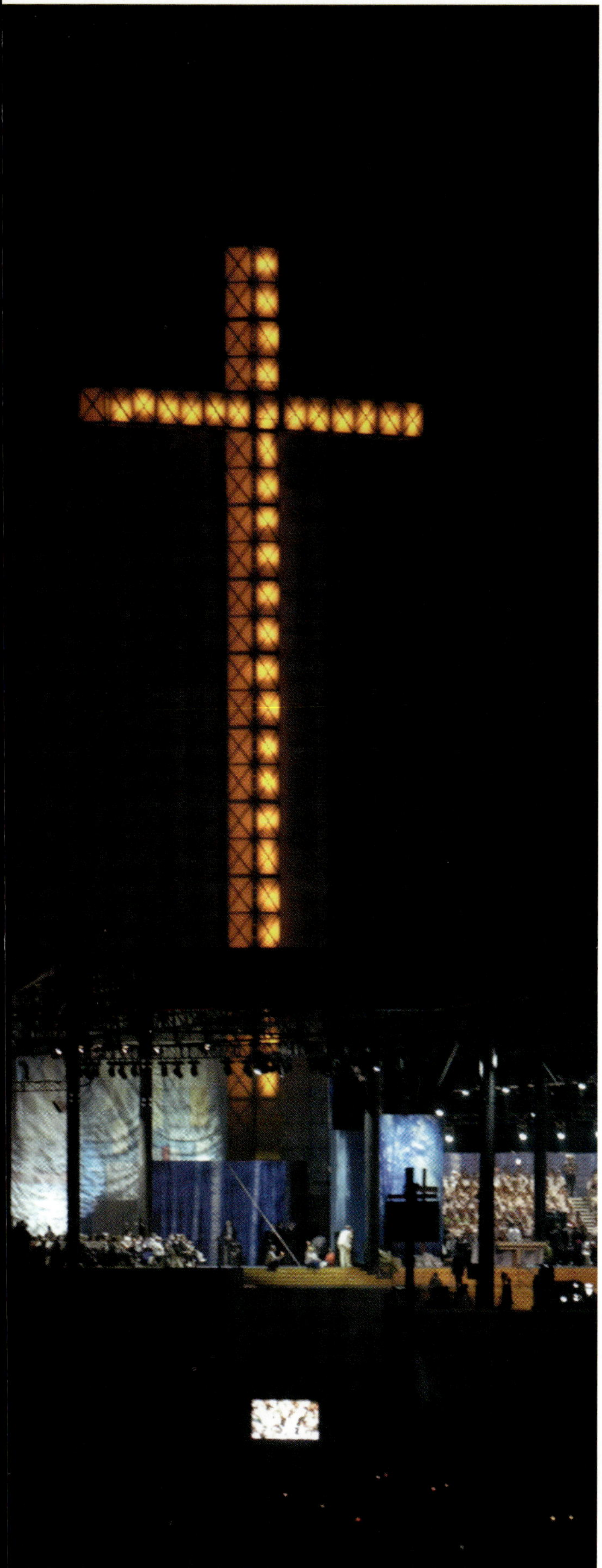

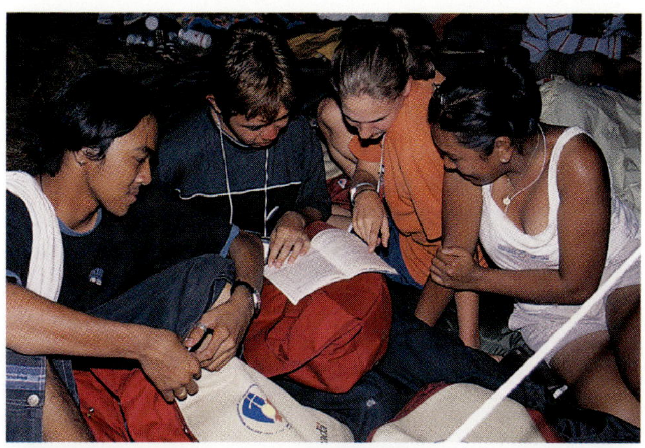

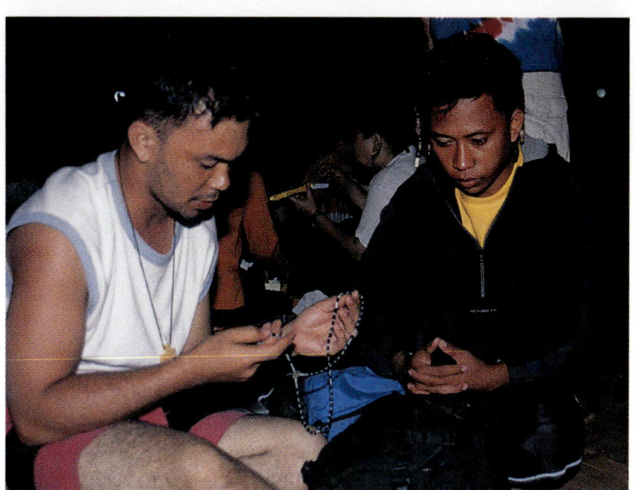

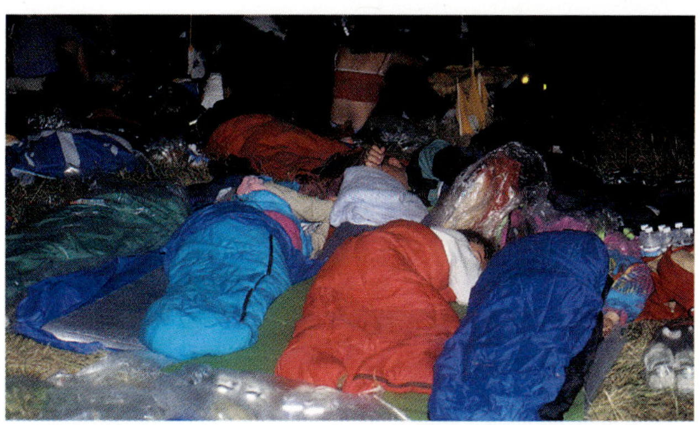

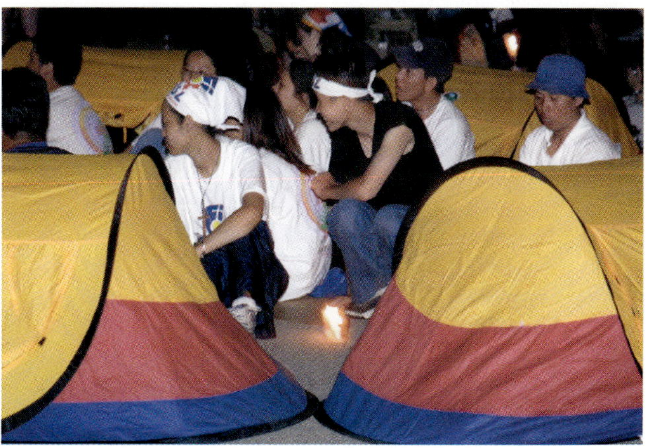

Closing Eucharistic Celebration

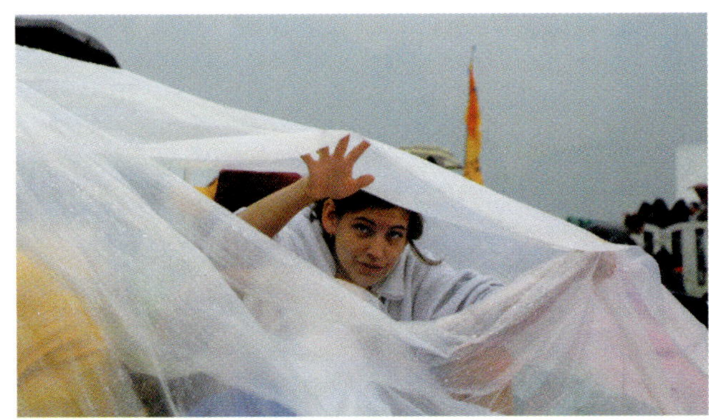 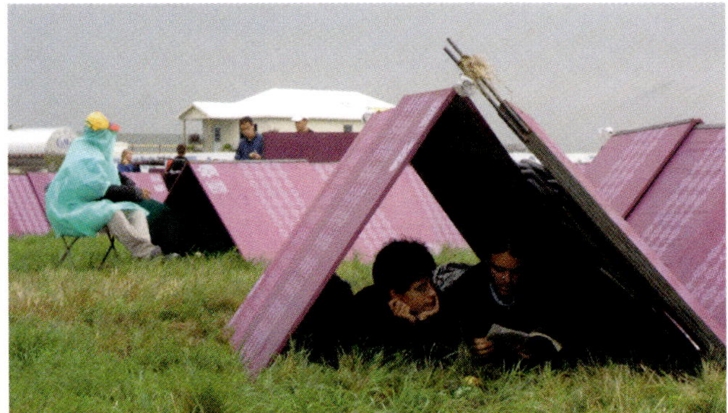

Listen to the voice of Jesus in the depths of your hearts!
His words tell you who you are as Christians.
They tell you what you must do to remain in his love.

JOHN PAUL II

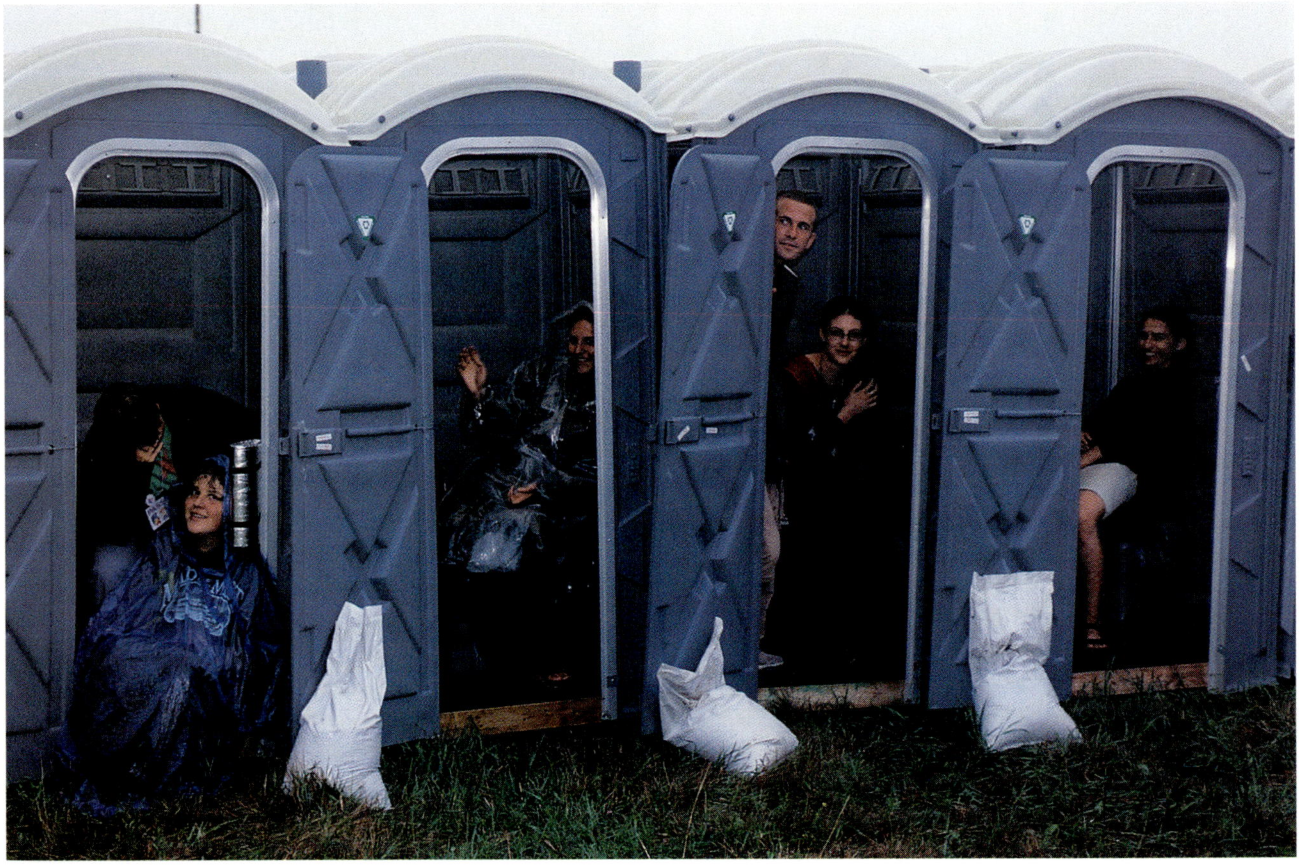

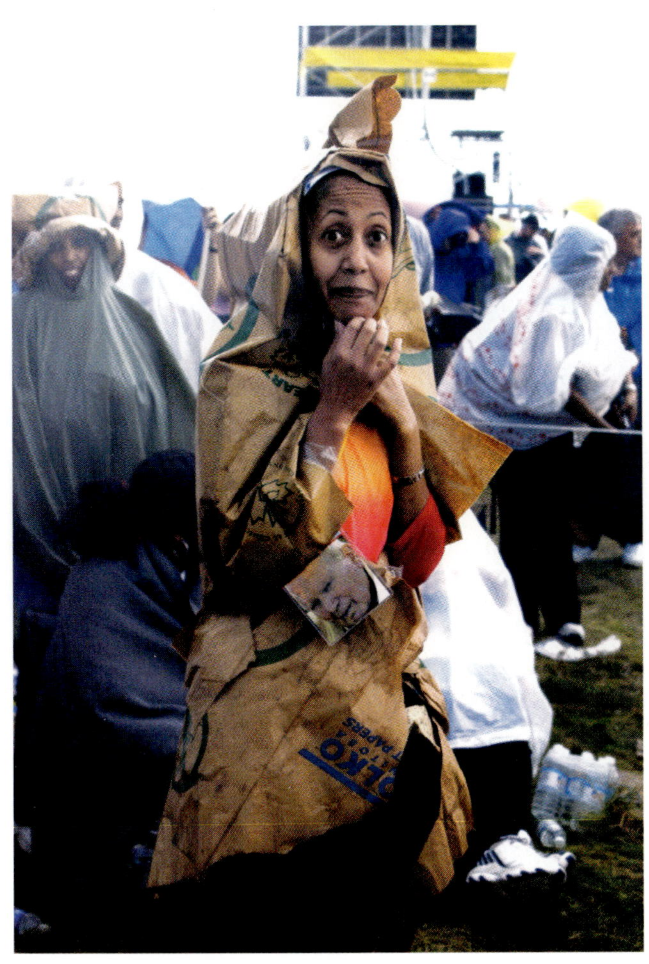

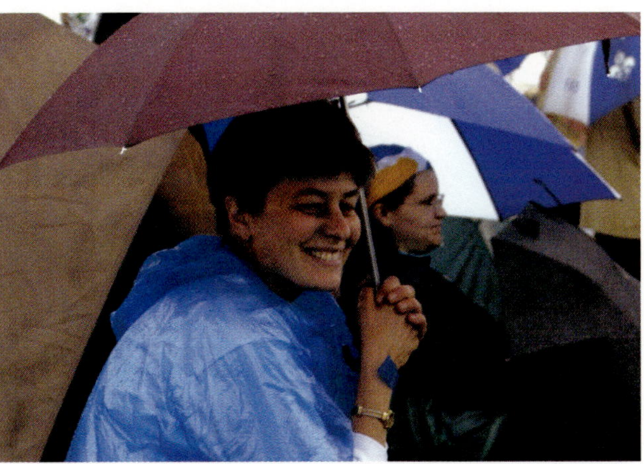

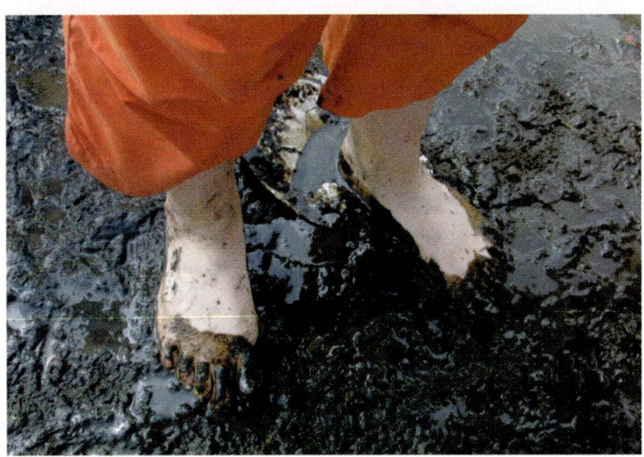

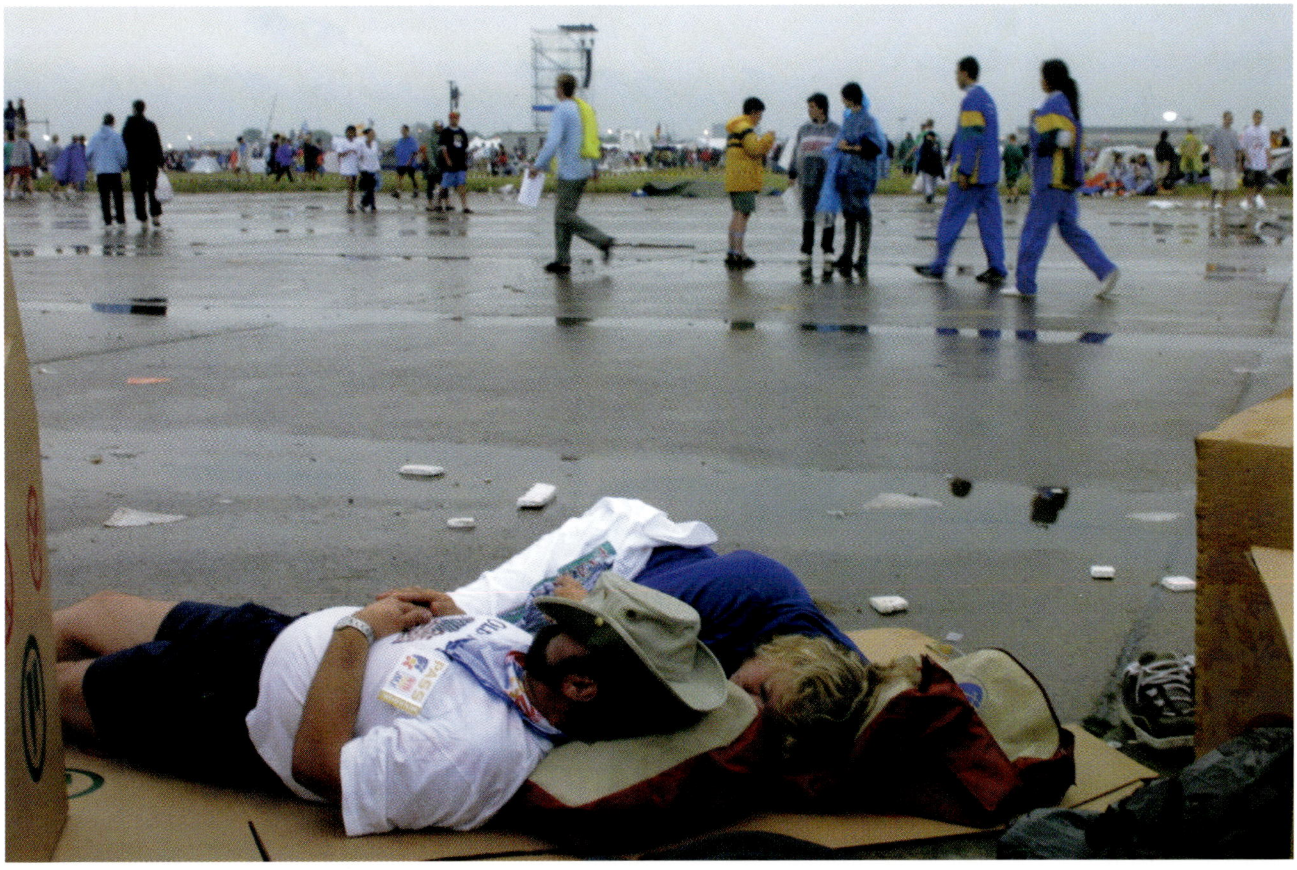

You too are called to be transformed

A torrential downpour failed to dampen the spirits of those who had spent the night in the humid air of Downsview Lands to take part with Pope John Paul II in the closing mass of World Youth Day 2002.

Those who managed to sleep during the overnight vigil on the grounds of the former air base were jolted awake by thunder and a drenching rain that forced them to seek cover under sleeping bags, cardboard boxes and any other materials they could find. By the time the mass was about to begin, the crowd has swelled to over 800,000 pilgrims and those who had joined them.

Pope John Paul II arrived onstage to the music of Handel's Hallelujah Chorus, followed by an aboriginal honour song and greetings to the pontiff from Cardinal Aloysius Ambrozic, Archbishop of Toronto.

"Be the salt of the earth, be the light of the world," the pope encouraged the assembled youth in his opening remarks. "Do not be afraid to follow Christ on the royal road of the Cross!"

As the mass progressed, the clouds dispersed and the sun once again shone on World Youth Day 2002.

In his homily, which was interrupted by cheering and applause, the Holy Father observed, "Even a tiny flame lifts the heavy lid of night. How much more light will you make, all together, if you bond as one in the communion of the Church? ... If you love Jesus, love the Church."

"You are young and the pope is old," he said to his listeners, only to have them playfully interject with chants of "The pope is young!"

Cardinal James Francis Stafford introduced the Creed for the Profession of Faith and the pope recited it with the congregation responding. The Holy Father then presided over the preparation of communion and presented the consecrated hosts to the eucharistic ministers for general distribution to the largest gathering of its kind in Canadian history.

During the Angelus, three young people brought the Eastern Rite World Youth Day 2002 icon, *The Adoration of the Magi*, on stage for the pontiff to see. The image of the three magi was chosen because they, like the young people at WYD 2002, travelled from distant lands to find God.

Before giving his solemn blessing at the end of the mass, the pope asked the pilgrims to put on the small wooden crosses they had received in their pilgrim knapsacks. He then once again commissioned the pilgrims to go out into the world to be the salt of the earth and the light of the world.

Pope John Paul II departed Downsview waving to the sea of World Youth Day pilgrims, who for the last time chanted "JP2, we love you!" as their eyes filled with tears.

The harm done by some priests and religious to the young and vulnerable fills us all with a deep sense of sadness and shame. But think of the vast majority of dedicated and generous priests and religious whose only wish is to serve and do good! There are many priests, seminarians and consecrated persons here today; be close to them and support them!

JOHN PAUL II

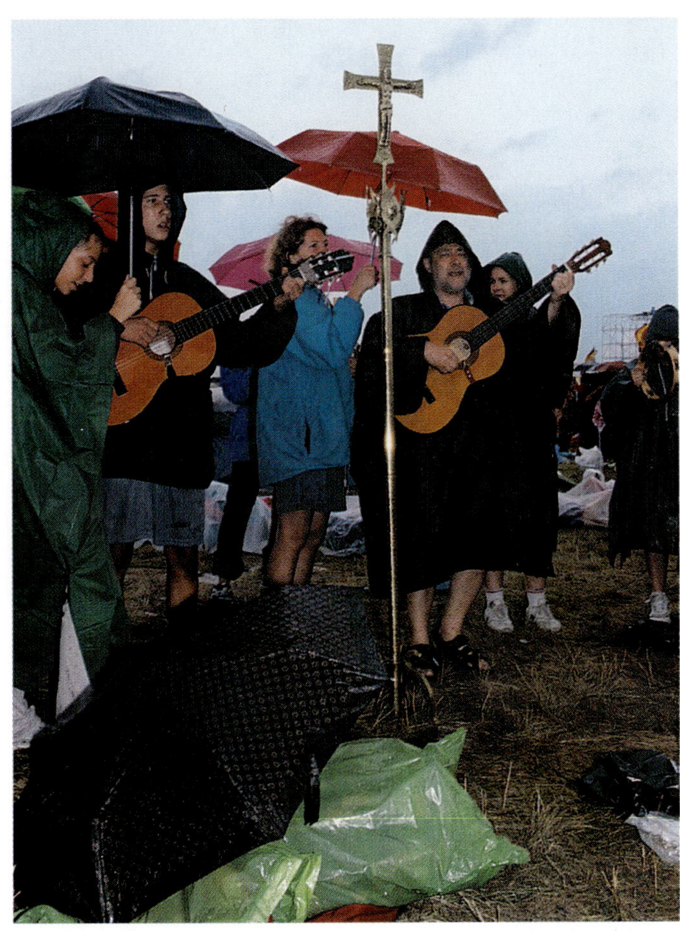

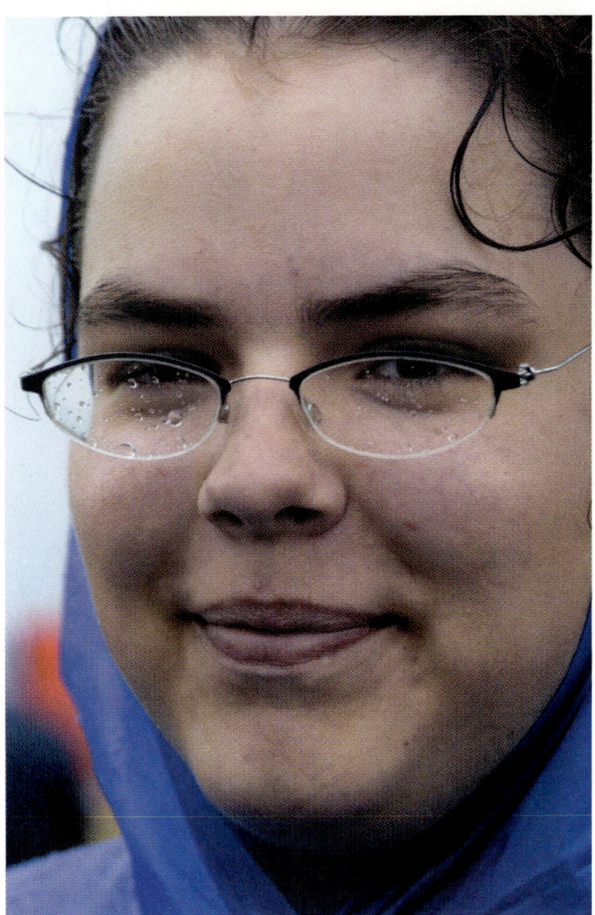

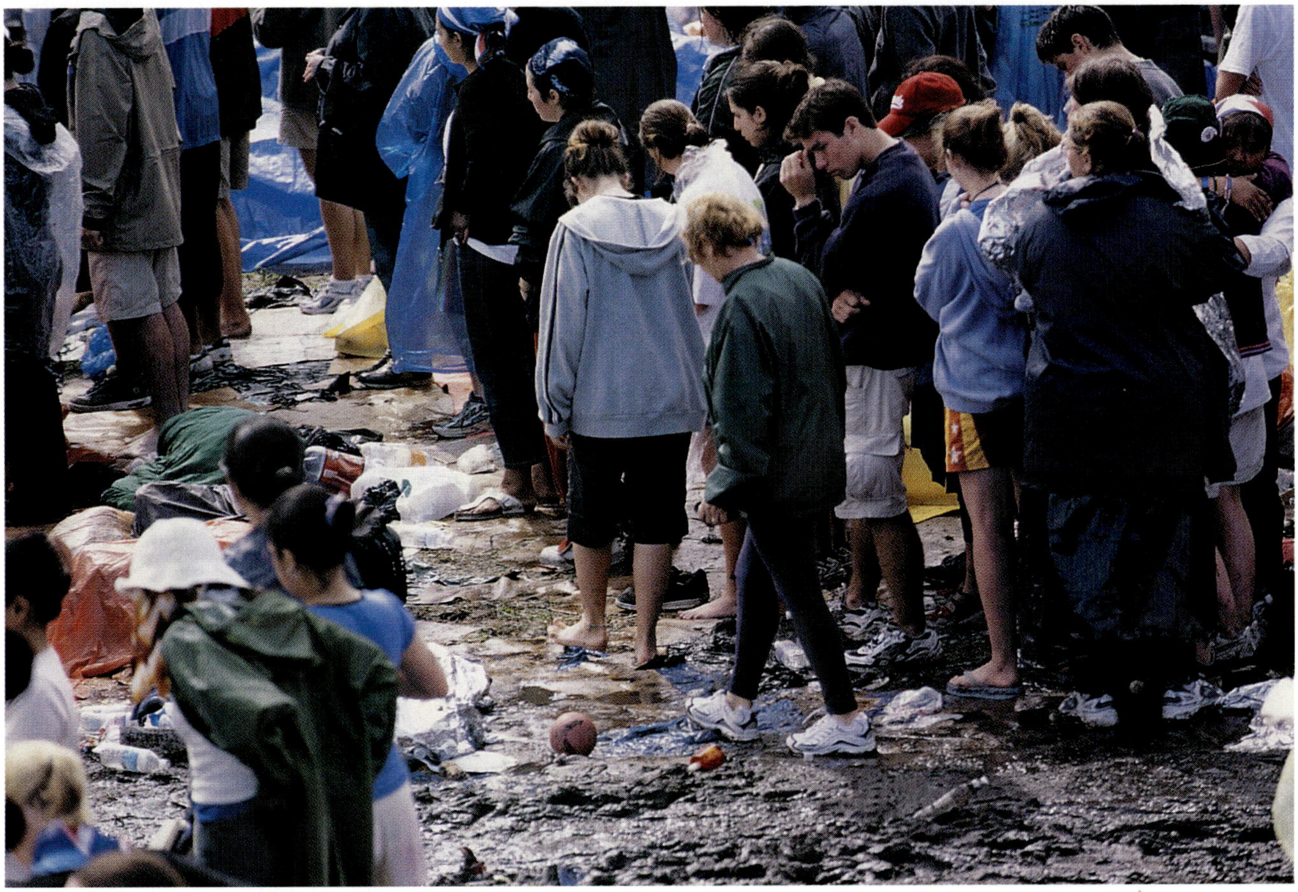

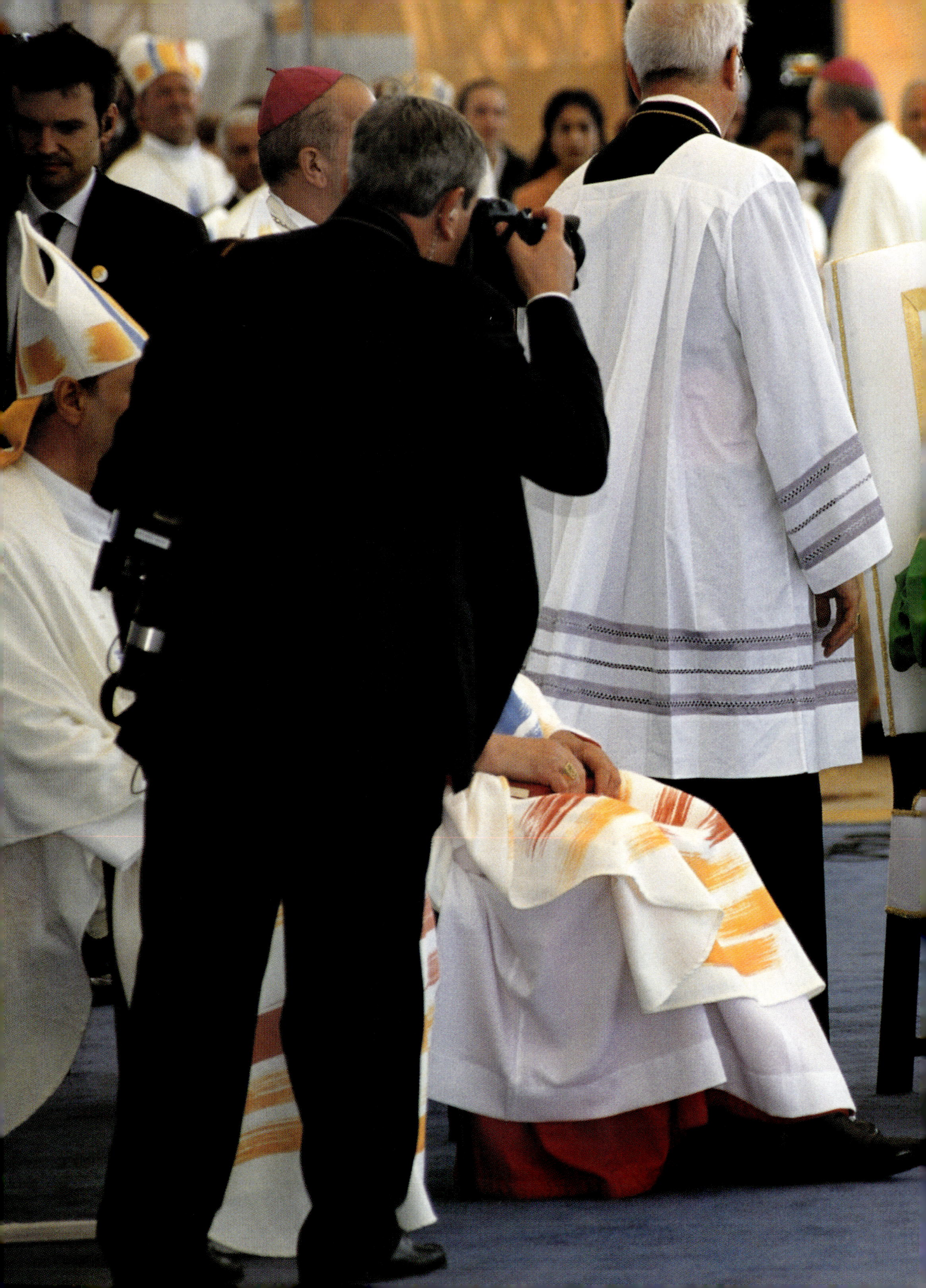

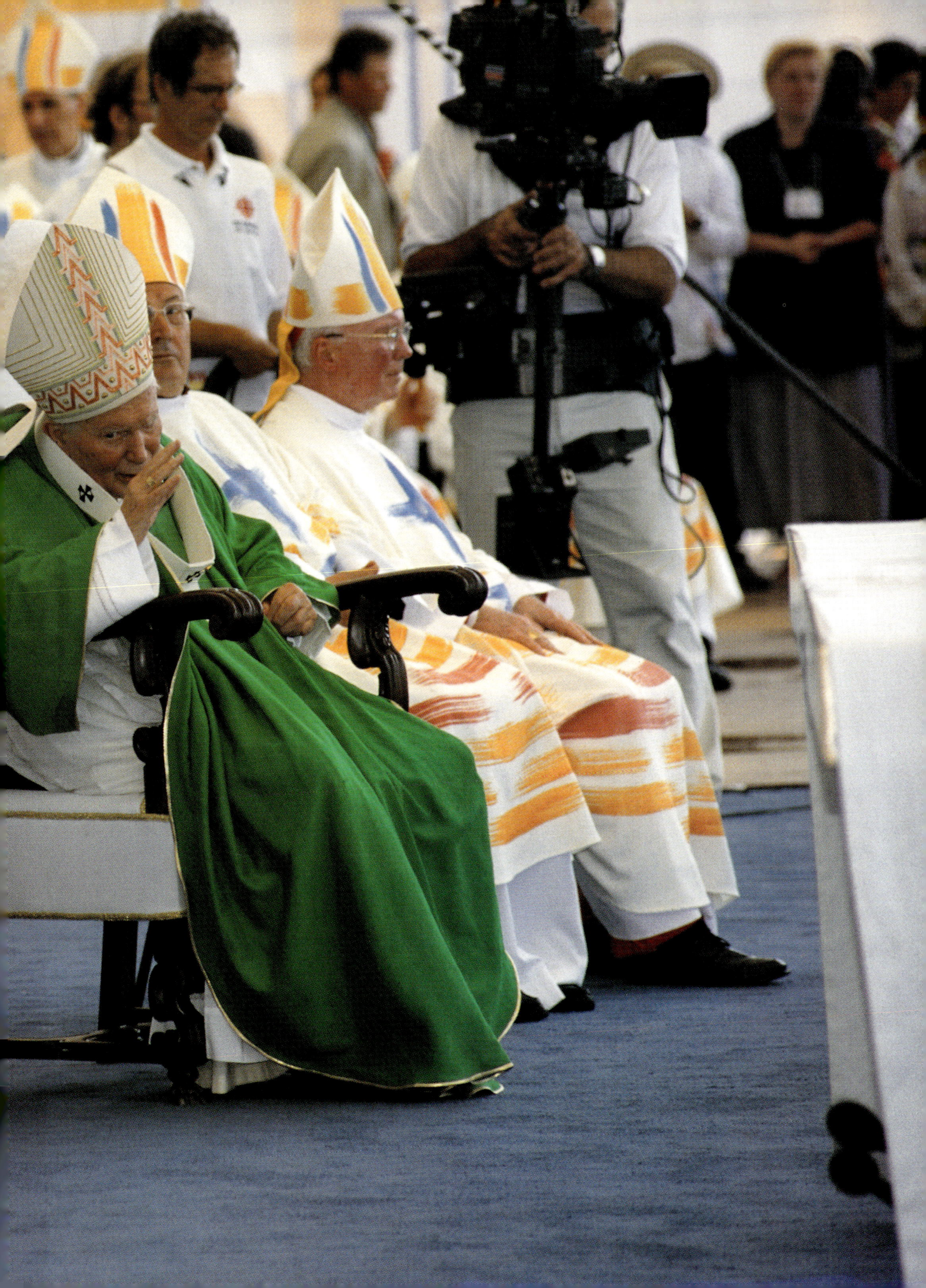

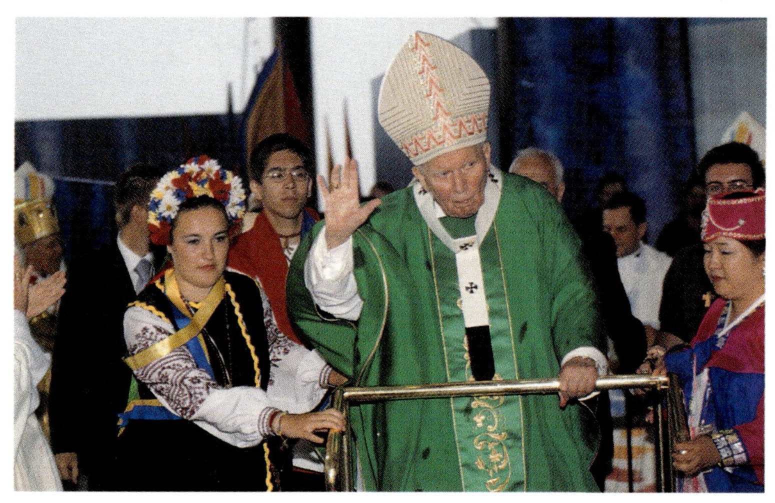

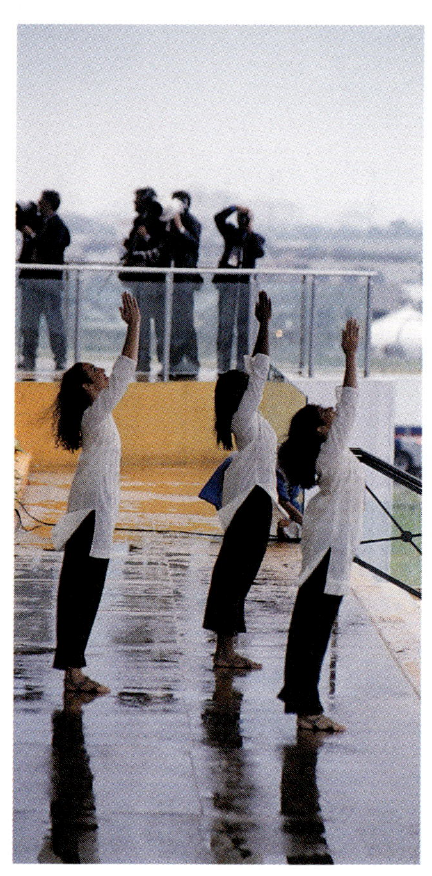

At difficult moments in the Church's life, the pursuit of holiness becomes even more urgent. And holiness is not a question of age; it is a matter of living in the Holy Spirit.

JOHN PAUL II

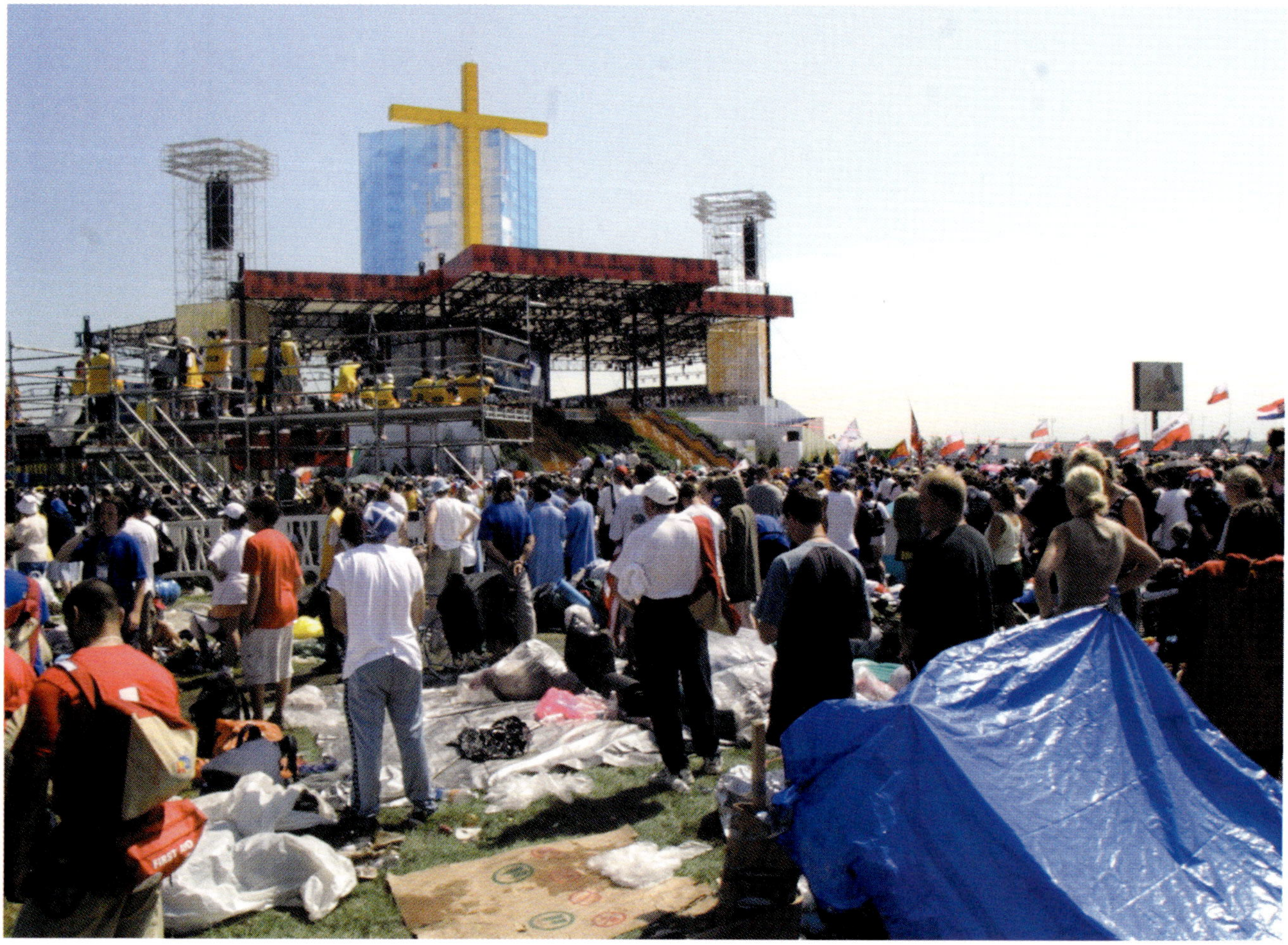

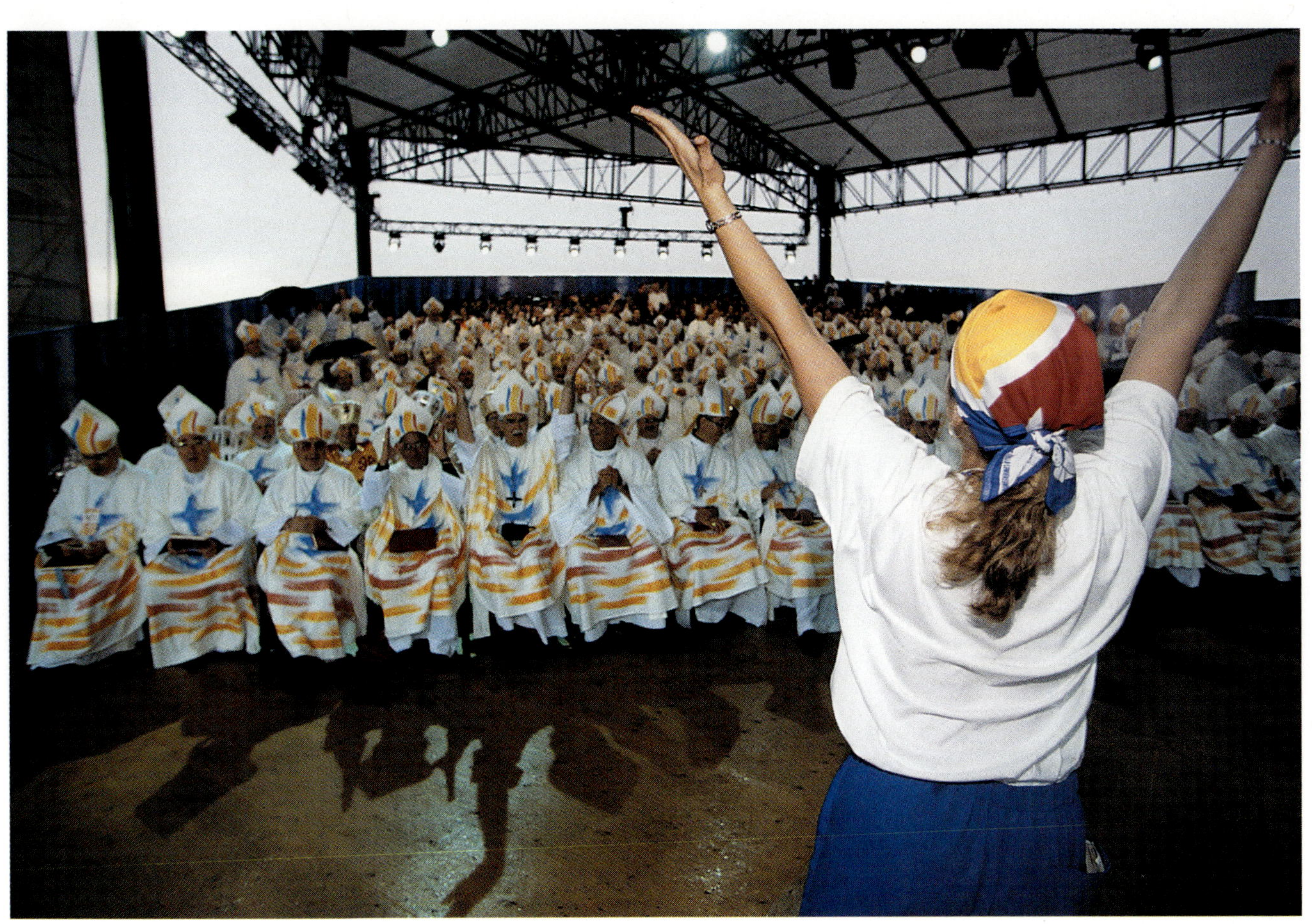

*The world you are inheriting is a world
which desperately needs a new sense of
brotherhood and human solidarity.
It is a world which needs to be touched
and healed by the beauty and richness of God's love.
It needs witnesses to that love.
It needs you—to be the salt of the earth
and the light of the world.*

JOHN PAUL II

O Lord Jesus Christ, keep these young people in your love.
Let them hear your voice and believe what you say,
for you alone have the words of life.

JOHN PAUL II

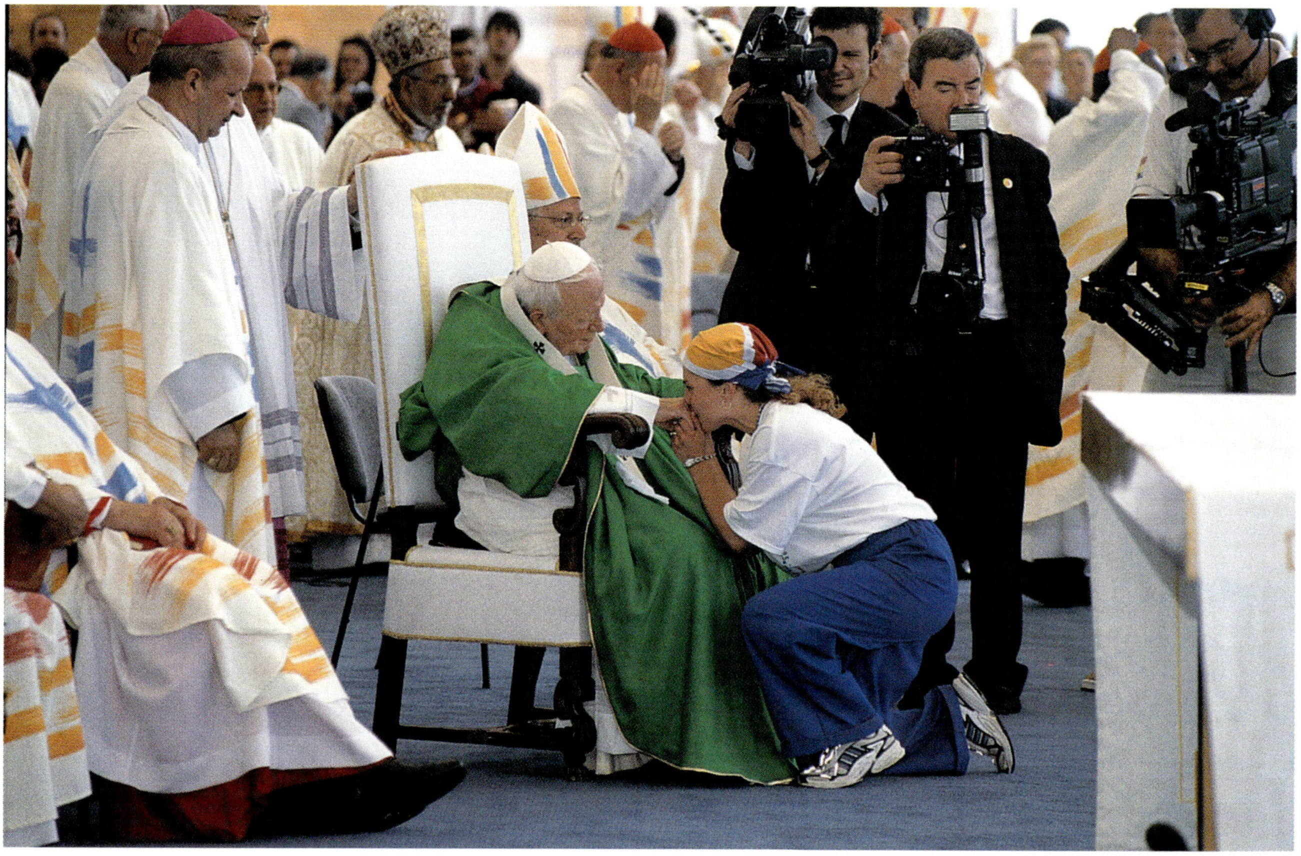

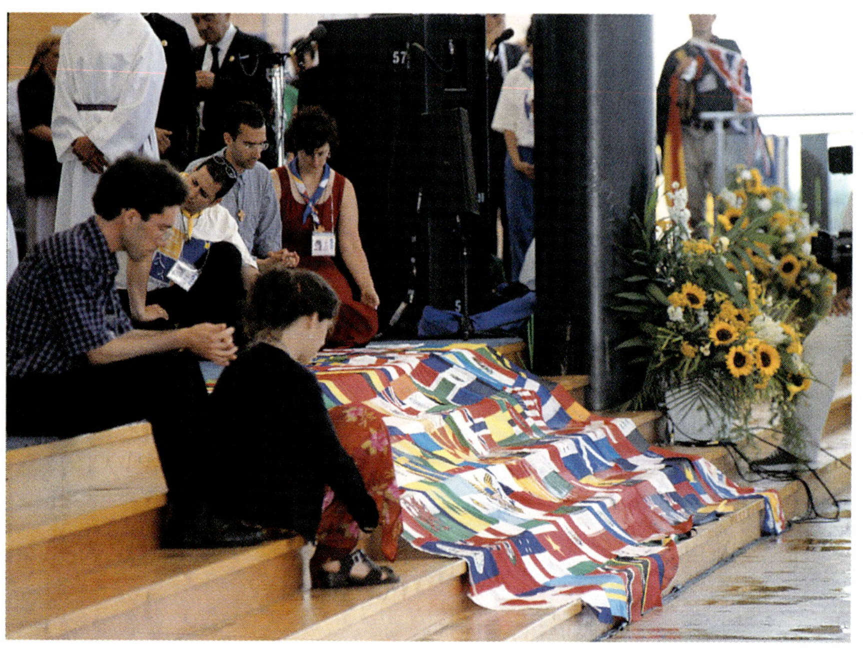

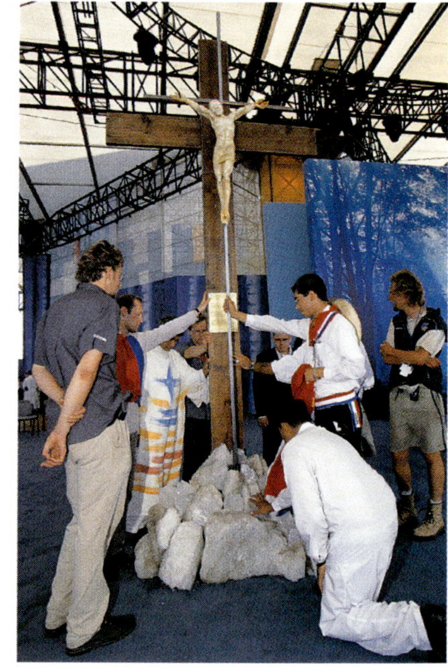

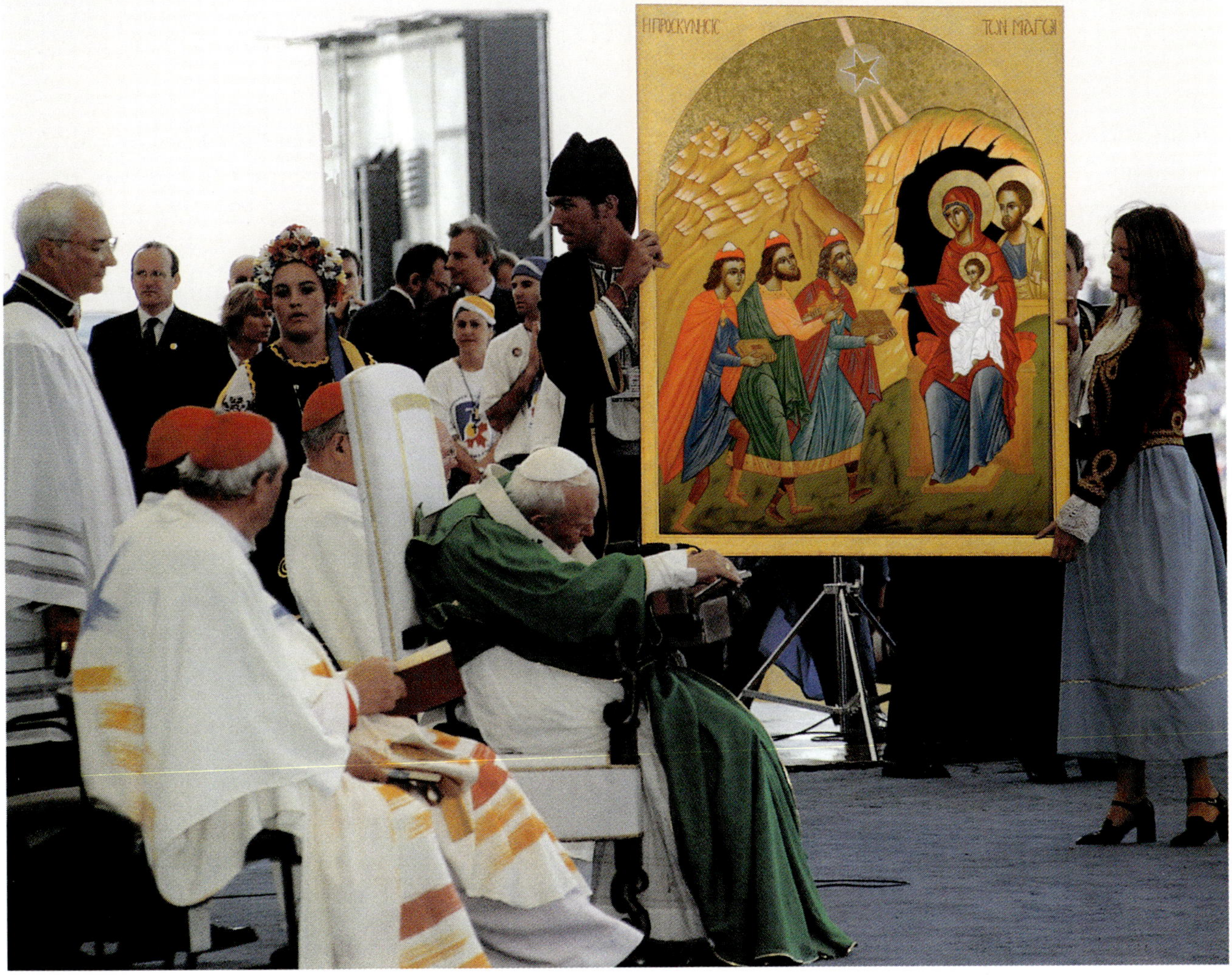

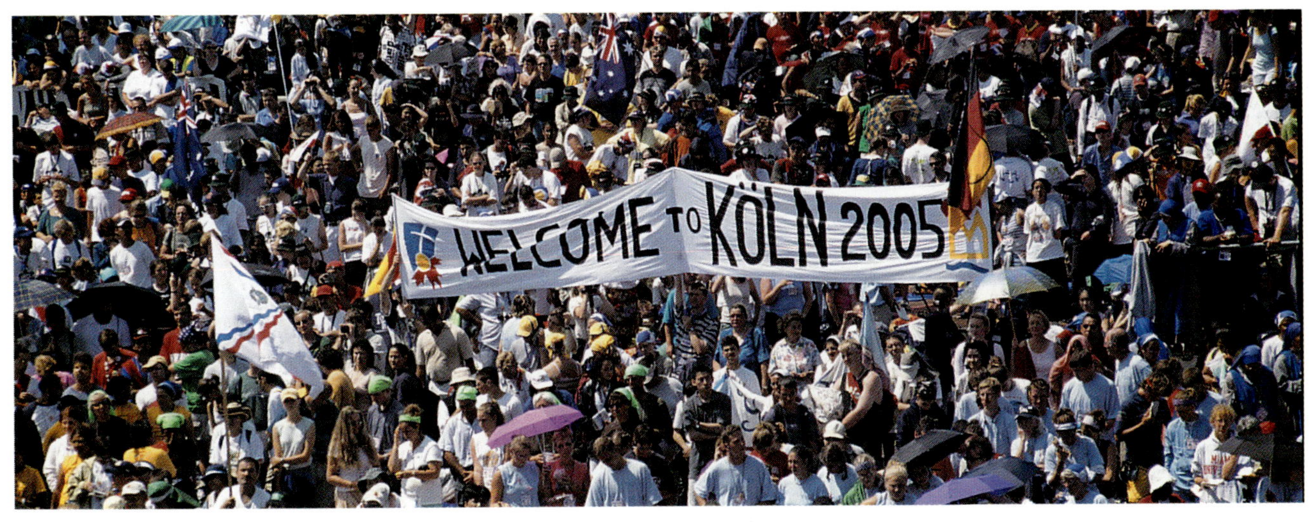

I wish formally to announce that the next World Youth Day will take place in 2005 in Cologne, Germany.

JOHN PAUL II

The water of life

"Rain is the water of life, the water of baptism." With these words, John Paul II begins the mass, as if to acknowledge the courage of these hundreds of thousands of "sentinels of the dawn" yanked from their sleep by a violent thunderstorm. And the liturgy, with no place in its script for bad weather, opens with the sprinkling of holy water!

Yesterday, the pilgrims had lit their lamps as night fell. Following Jesus' advice, they had prayed, then slept but lightly, for fear of being caught off guard by the weather. The storm arrived under cover of darkness, but they had their lanterns at the ready.

Despite the driving rain, another 200,000 people have joined the chilled, waterlogged souls who camped out all night. Nothing can dash the hopes of this assembly, not even their obvious physical discomfort. Nothing can stop them. They are in this together; they will pray with the pope, no matter the obstacles. Already the crowd is responding in a literal way to the call that the pope will later issue in his homily: "With your faith, hope and love, with your intelligence, courage and perseverance, you have to humanize the world we live in... 'loose the bonds of injustice... share your bread with the hungry... remove the pointing of the finger, the speaking of evil... Then your light shall rise in the darkness' " (Isaiah 58:6-10).

Then, just as the Holy Father is about to proclaim Matthew's gospel, the very gospel in which Jesus tells his closest followers, "You are the light of the world," the wind chases away the clouds. "We have sun," exclaims a thoroughly delighted pope, as he reminds his listeners, "Saint Paul tells us that Jesus leads us from darkness into light."

The explanation is appreciated but unnecessary. The pilgrims already grasp the message.

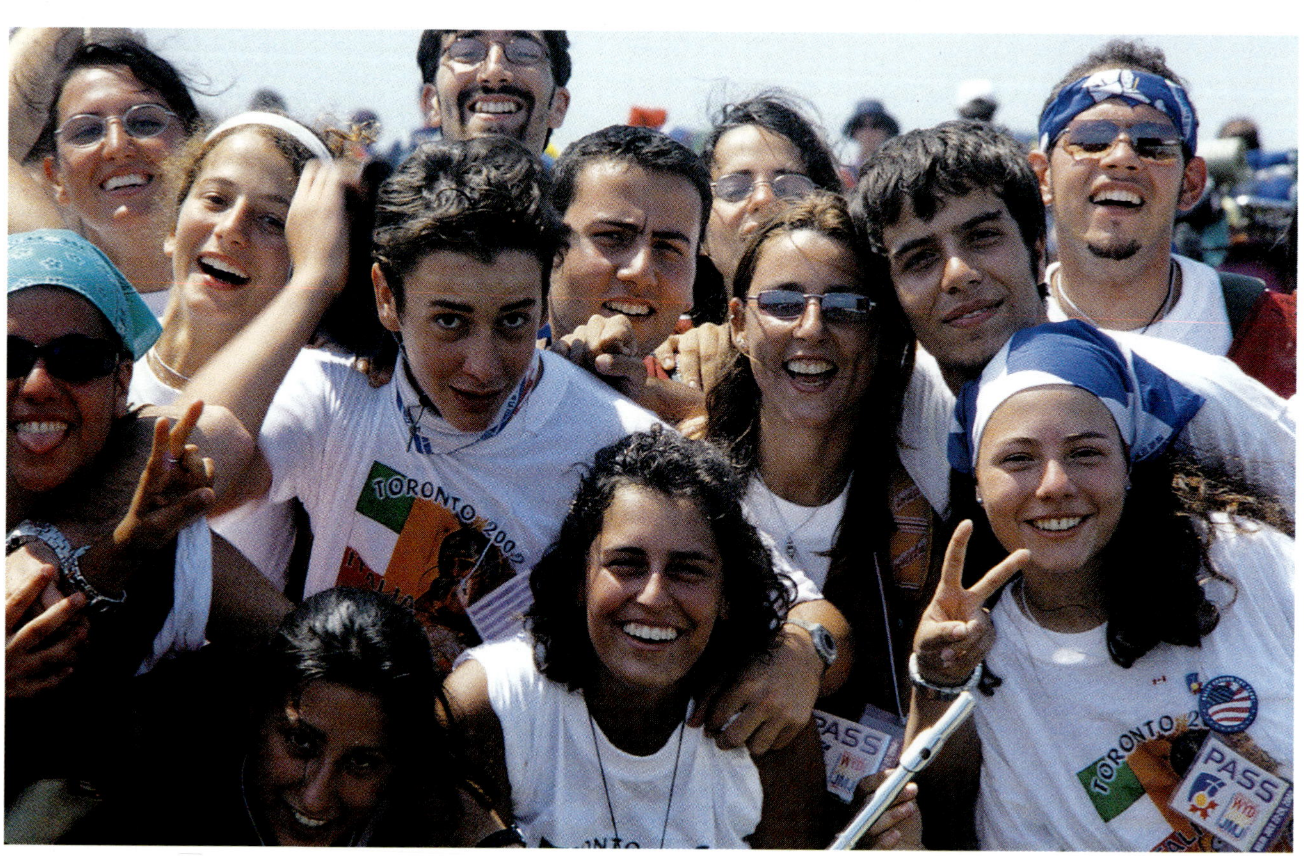

*Teach them how to profess their faith,
bestow their love, and impart their
hope to others ...*

*Make them convincing witnesses to
your Gospel in a world so much in need
of your saving grace ...*

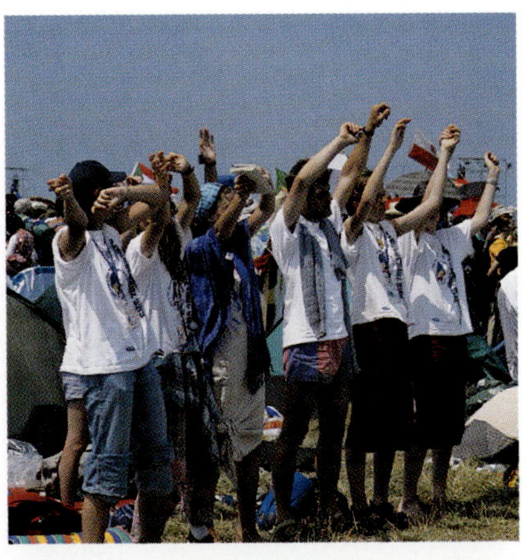

*Make them the new people
of the Beatitudes, that they may be
the salt of the earth and the light
of the world at the beginning of
the Third Christian Millennium!*

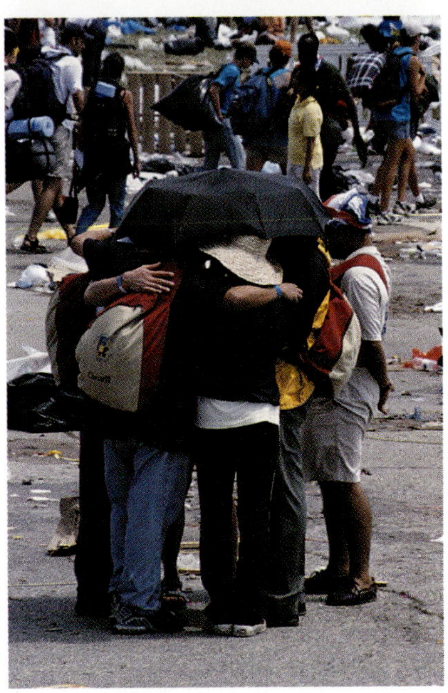

*Mary, Mother of the Church,
protect and guide these young men
and women of the twenty-first century.
Keep us all close to
your maternal heart.*

JOHN PAUL II

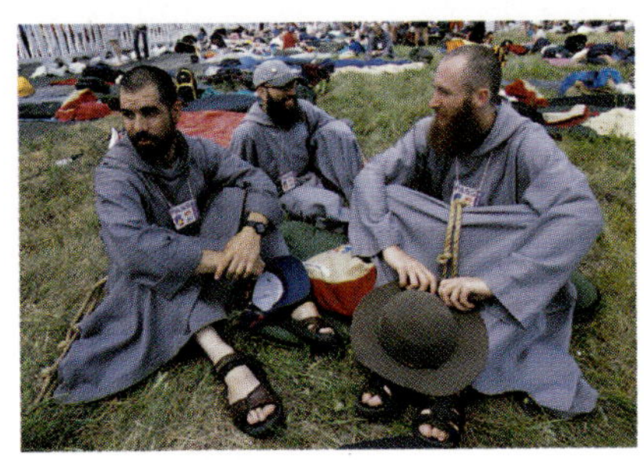

As We Prepare to Return Home

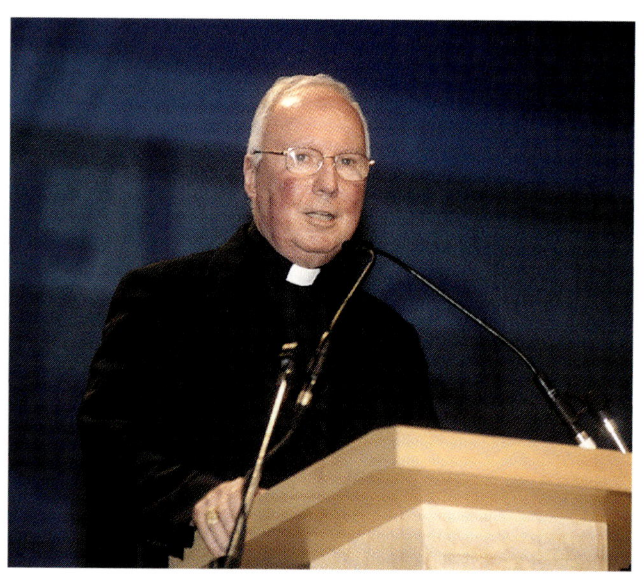

Holy Father, you have been a model of spiritual paternity over these last few days. This is why we thank you for inviting us to be pilgrims with you. Thank you for conveying to us your teachings through the exercise of your petrine ministry. The clergy and the young laypeople have learned that being a priest means going all the way up and all the way down a steep staircase; its narrow steps introduce us to the heavenly realities that you, Most Holy Father, have allowed us to glimpse. On behalf of the young people gathered here in Toronto, I thank you, Holy Father.

CARDINAL JAMES FRANCIS STAFFORD

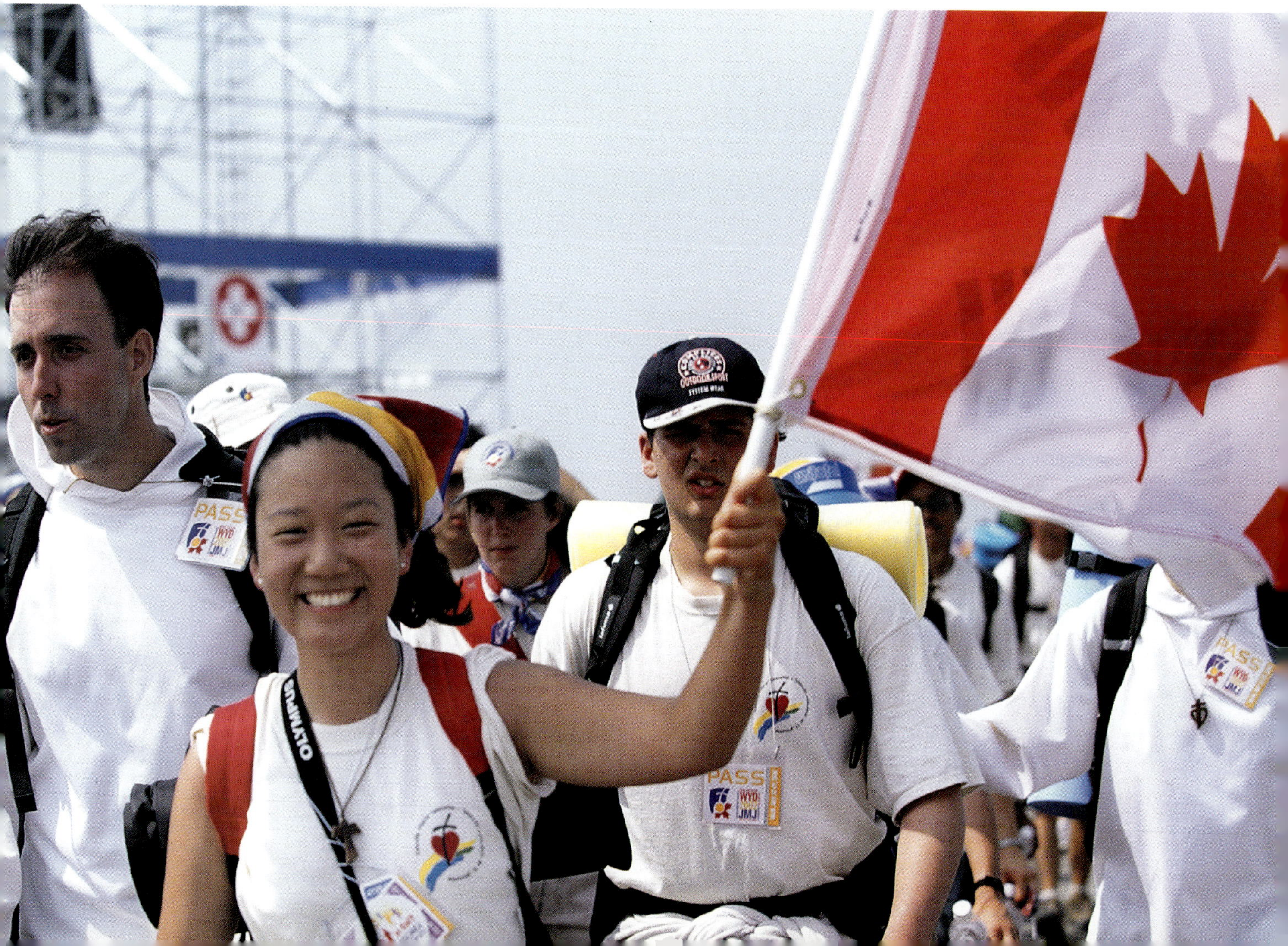

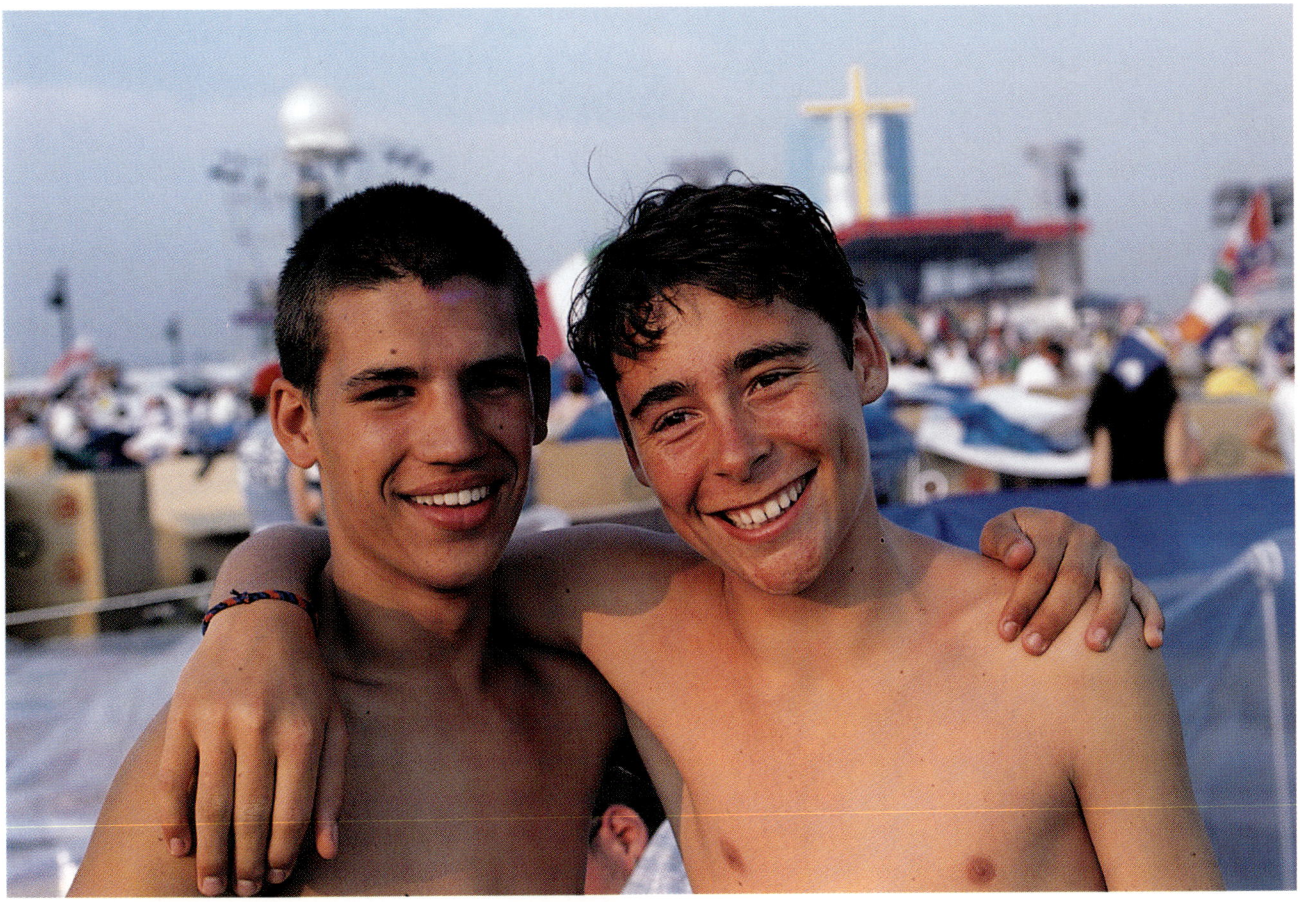

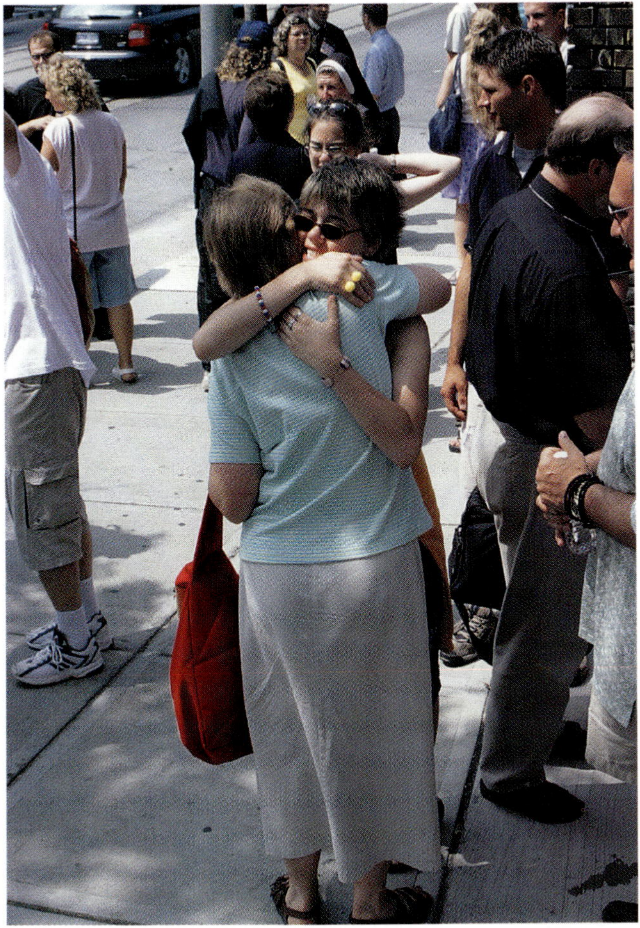

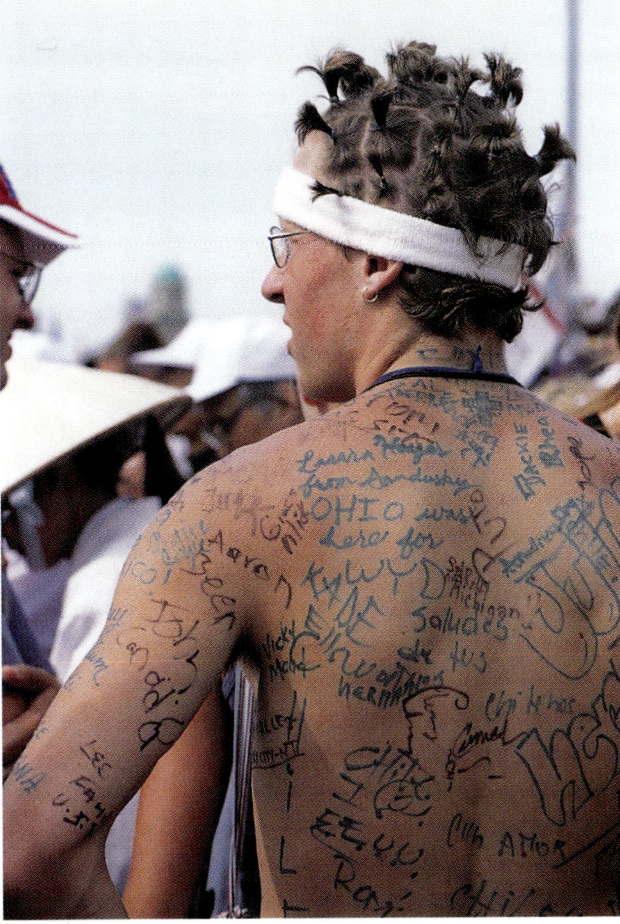

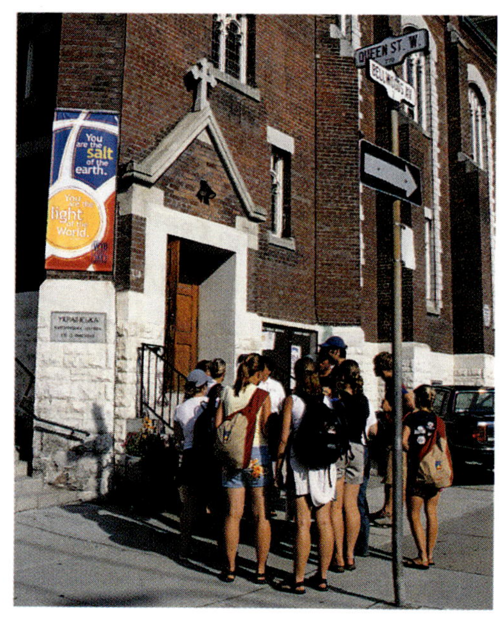

My heartfelt greetings goes to the other Christian Churches and communities represented here, as well as the followers of other religious traditions. My wish for all of you who are here is that the commitments you have made during these days of faith and celebration will bring forth abundant fruits of dedication and witness.

JOHN PAUL II

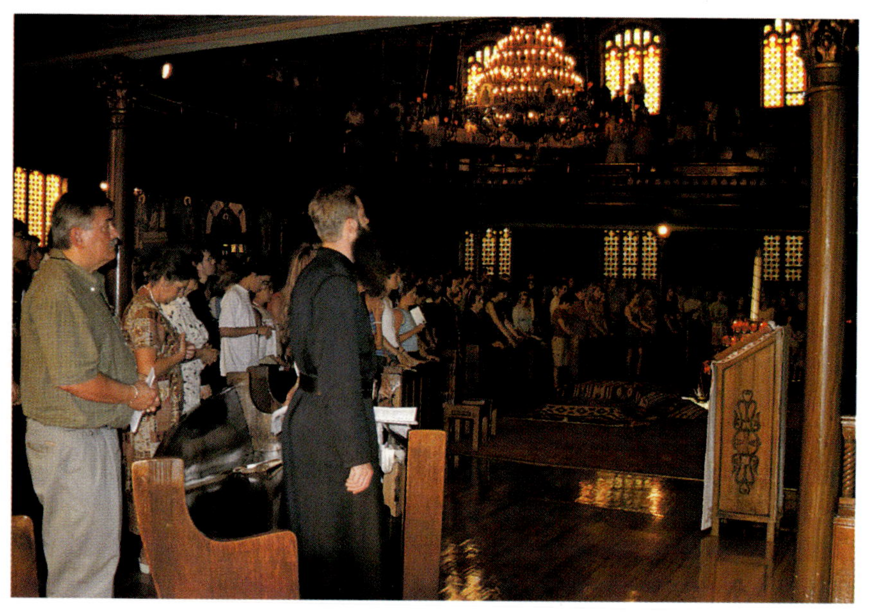

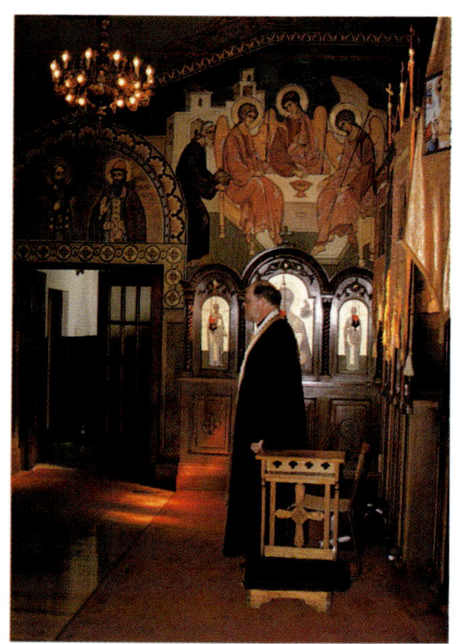

As we prepare to return home, I say, in the words of Saint Augustine: "We have been happy together in the light we have shared. We have really enjoyed being together. We have really rejoiced. But as we leave one another, let us not leave him."

JOHN PAUL II

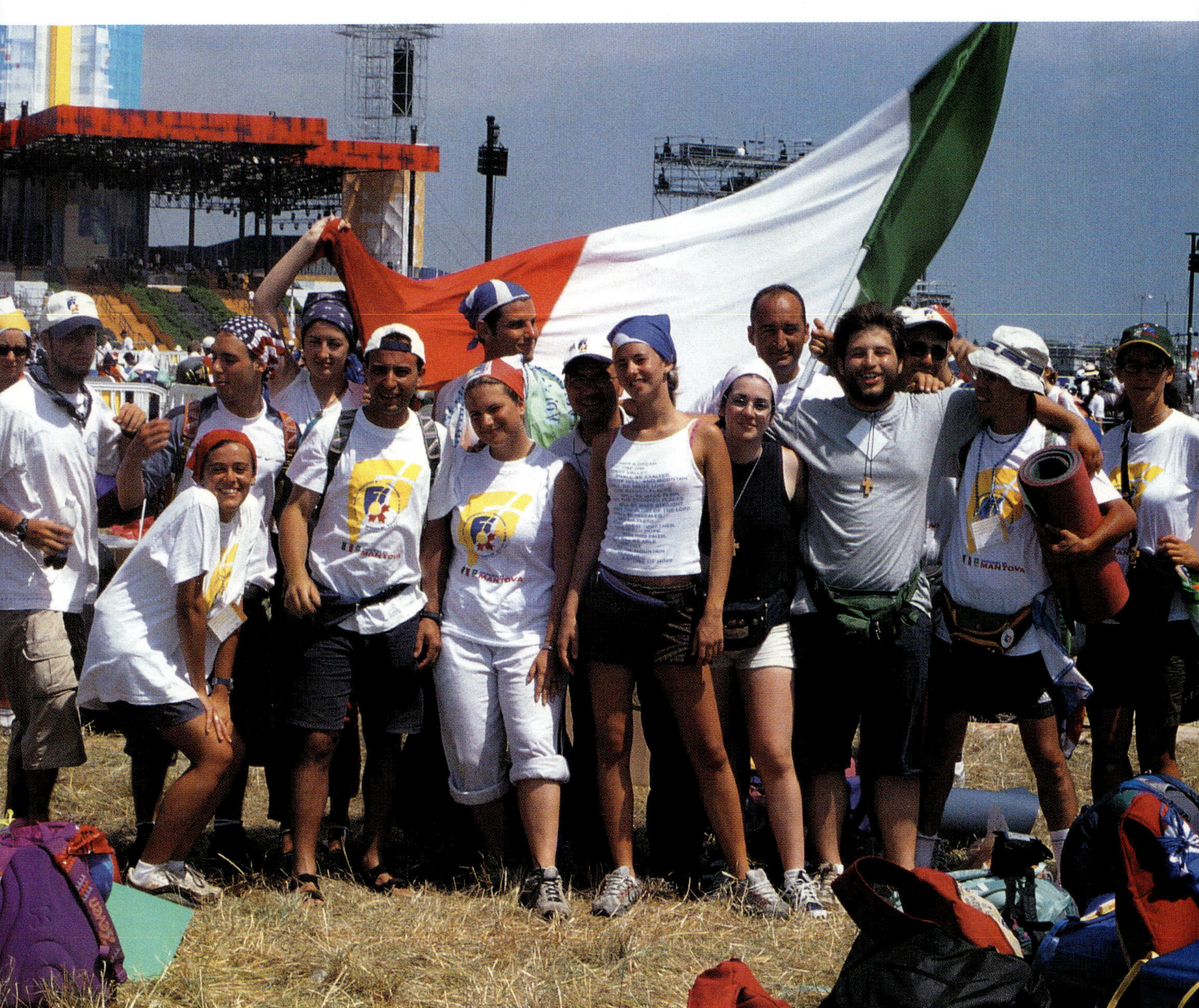

May you always treasure the memory of Toronto!

JOHN PAUL II

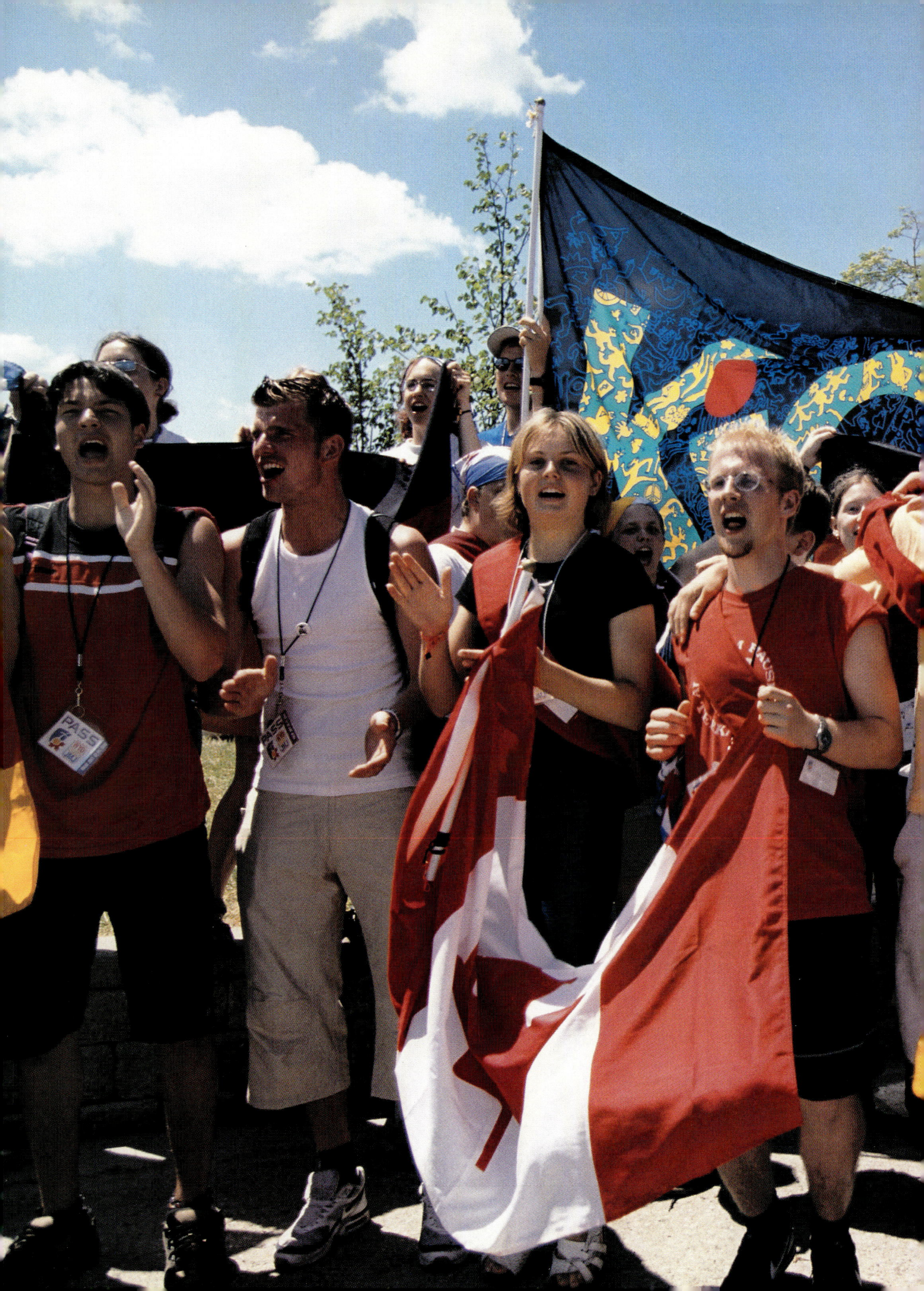

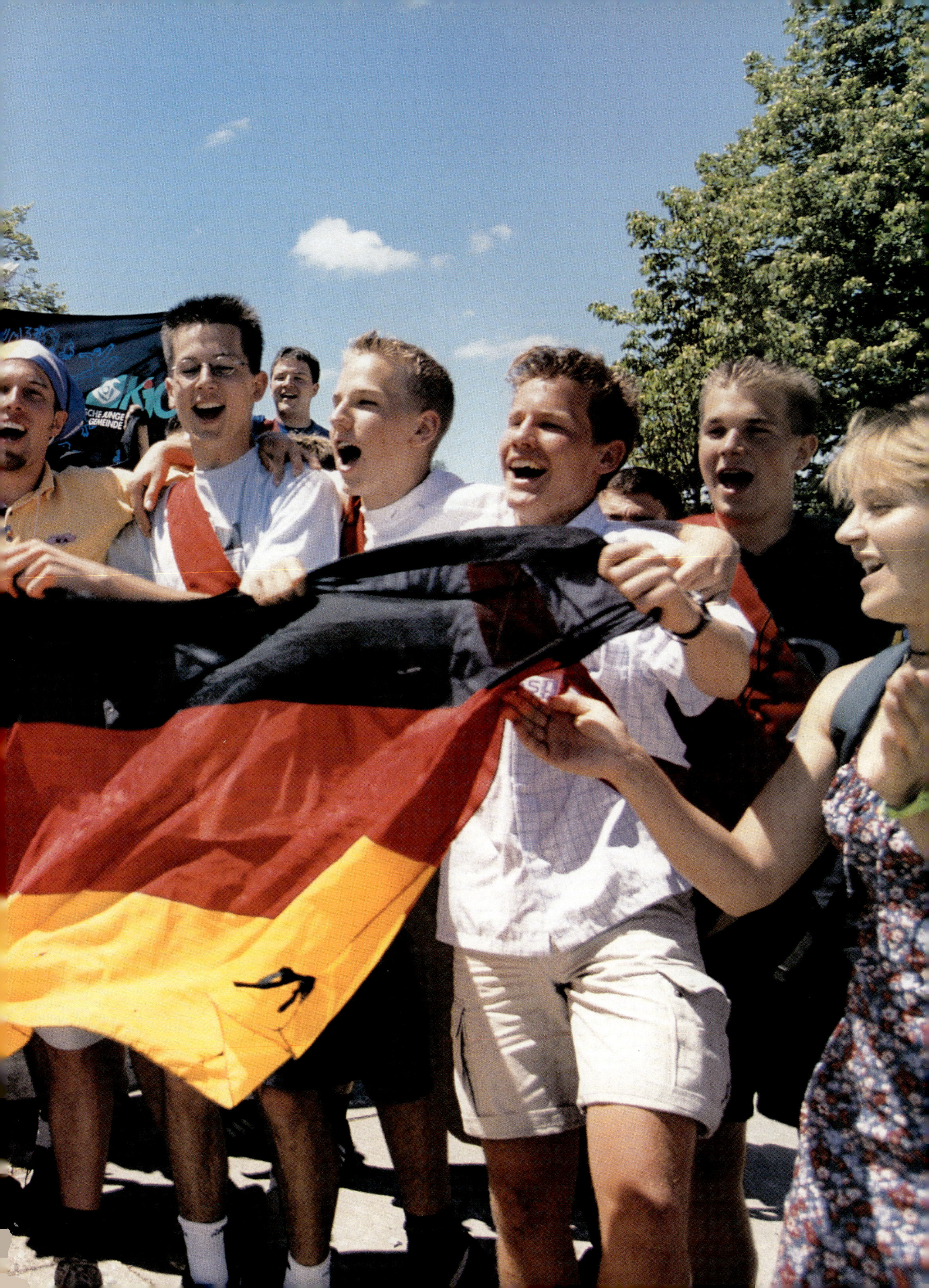

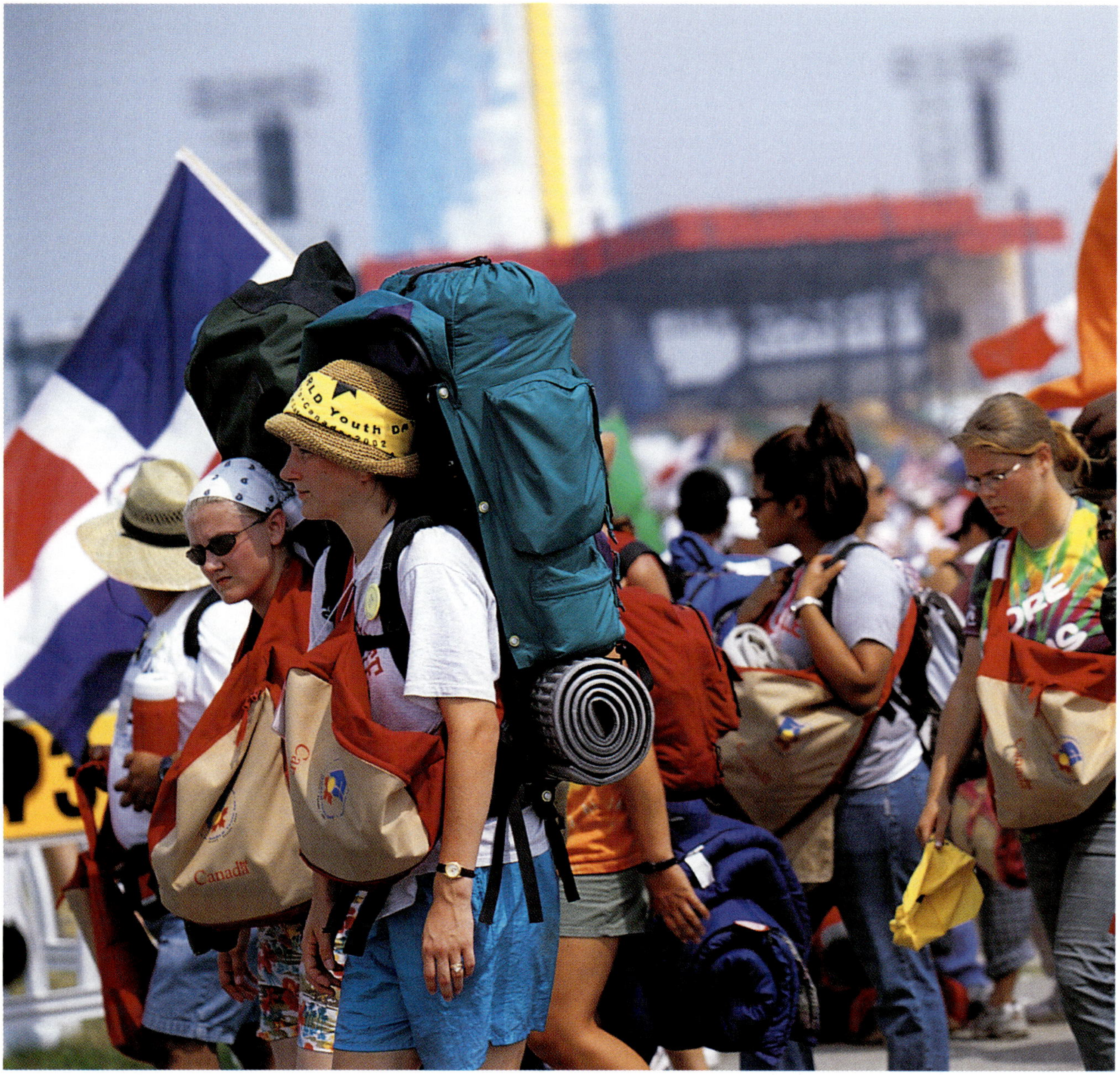

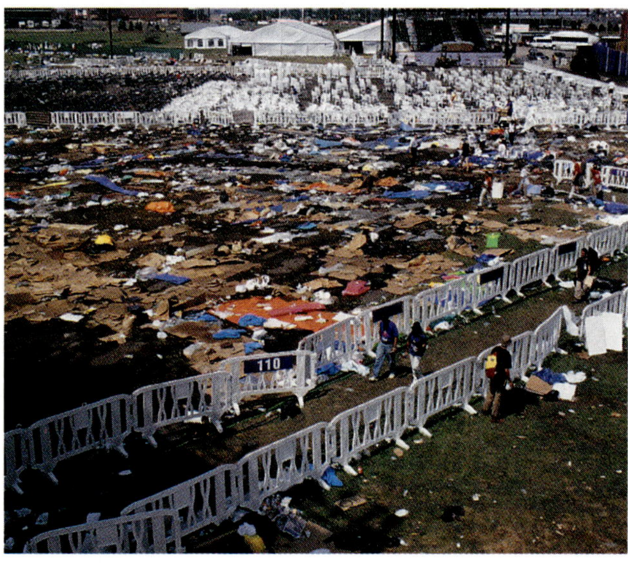

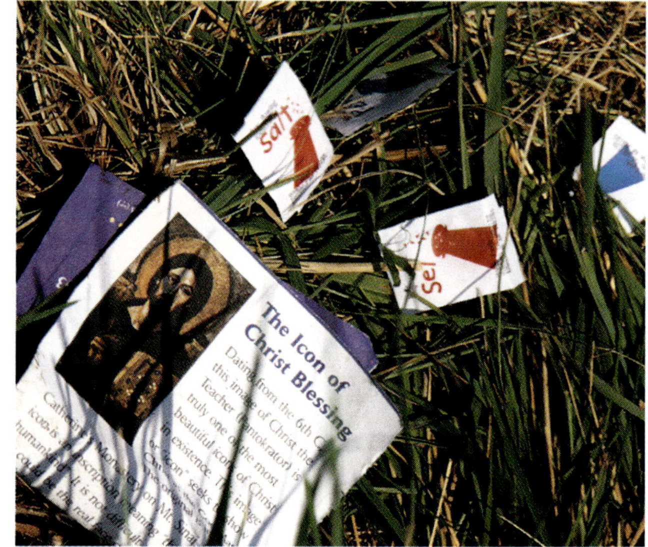
Salt
Sel
The Icon of
Christ Blessing

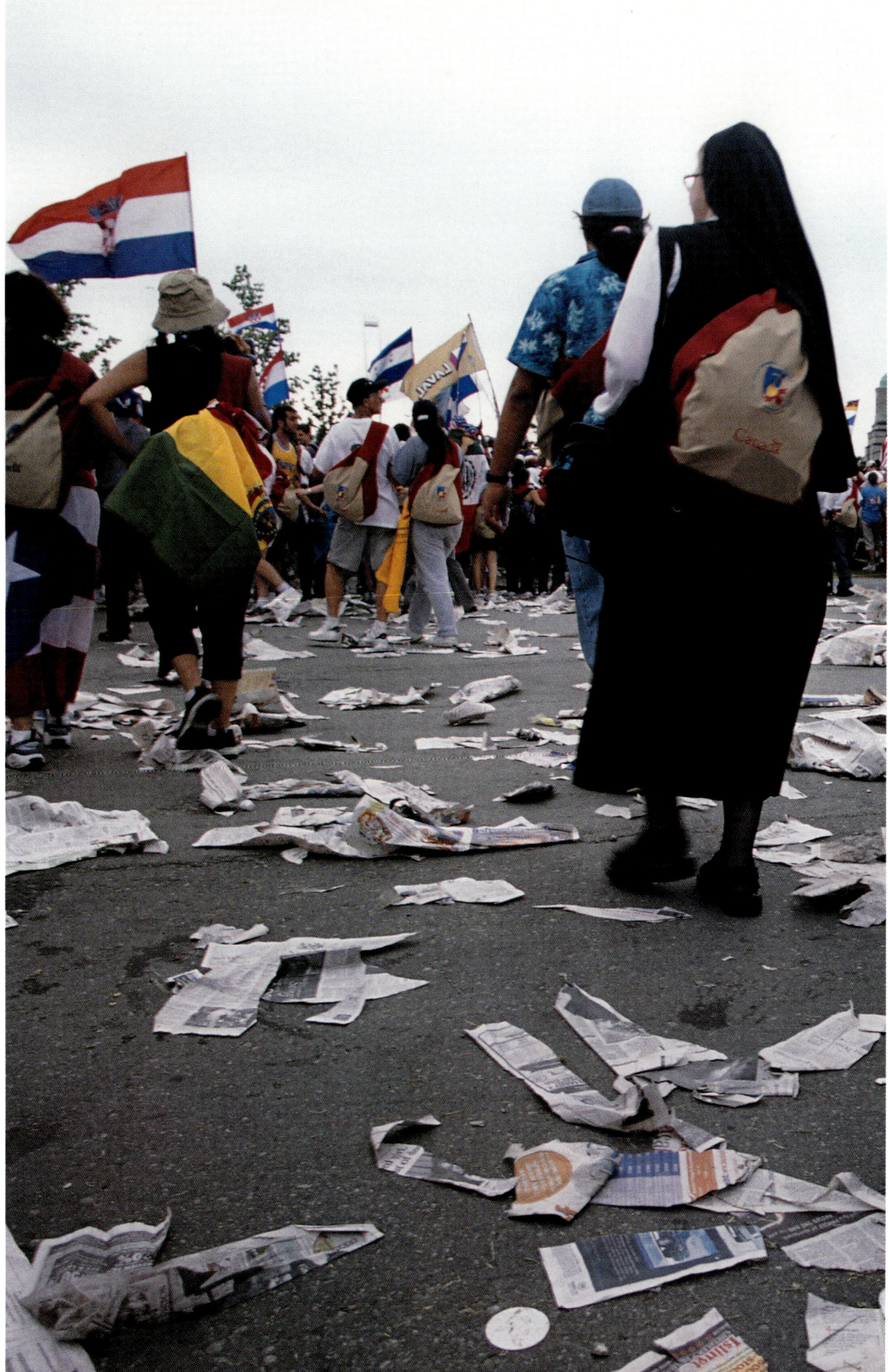

What WYD means to me...

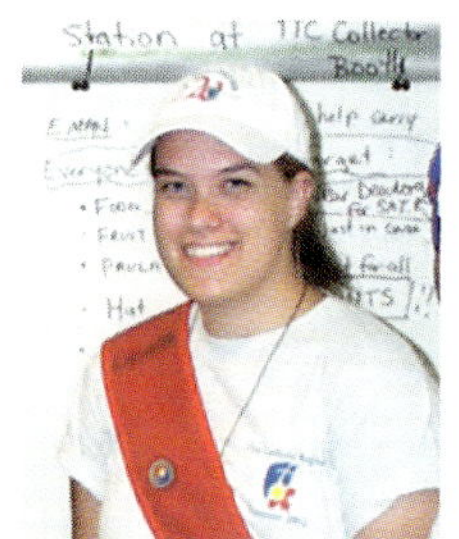

JAMES WIELGOSZ

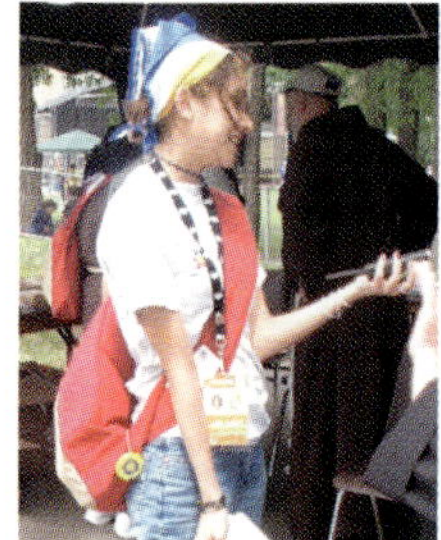

CHANTAL SWITALSKY

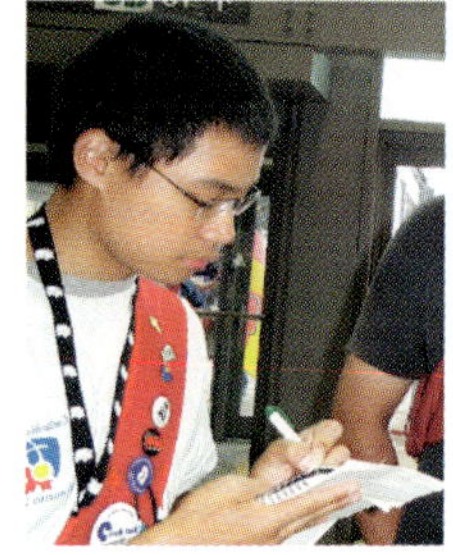

SANDRA VALENZUELA

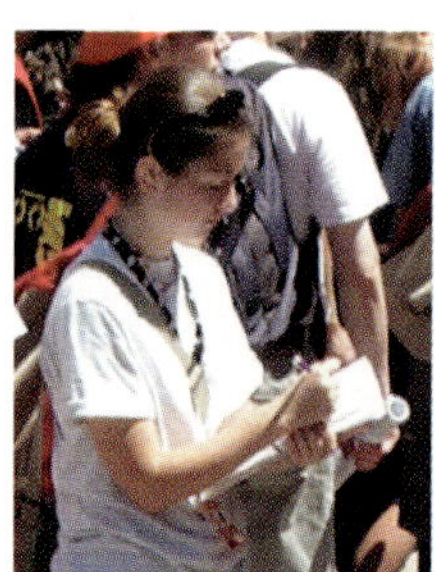

IMMANUEL
LANZADERAS

JAMES WIELGOSZ, age 19
During World Youth Day 2002, Toronto underwent what can only be described as a miraculous transformation, turning a normally cold city into a bustling community brimming with joy and excitement.

CHANTAL SWITALSKY, age 20
Attending the Papal Mass made me realize that shyness has no place alongside my Catholic faith, as it may have had in the past. My faith is now something to be sung for all to hear, something I share with hundreds of thousands of youth around the world.

SANDRA VALENZUELA, age 19
A sense of kindness and friendliness seemed to be floating in the air. Seeing the Pope was completely overwhelming. Knowing that I went to a Mass celebrated by Pope John Paul II and that I survived heat, rain, and cold to be there gave me a sense of happiness.

I'm proud to say that I was at Downsview Park with hundreds of thousands of other people and was touched by the event.

IMMANUEL LANZADERAS, age 19
Suddenly it was OK to be Catholic. I was surrounded by other young people of faith, not of labels or judgments. These people came here to meet God, and the Pope came to join them. World Youth Day reminded me about two things: that it's more than OK to go to Mass and think about the priesthood, and that I've got a Polish grandfather who loves me. Now I'm not just living for an event, I'm living always to be that warm Catholic Canadian, one of many, who welcomed the world.

MICHALINA RATAJCZAK, age 19
It was an experience outside of time. Unsophisticated songs praising God, sung by pilgrims on the streets of Toronto, made its citizens' inner critics shrivel and die, at least for a little while. At the centre of this hubbub and exultation, a sweet old man, proclaiming that he believes in and loves youth. He happens to be the Vicar of Christ. Pope John Paul II epitomized strength in the face of frailty, faith in the face of physical degeneration. I suspect that is why he is the star of World Youth Day, even when his age made him bereft of his earlier energy.

The most powerful man in the Church was battling with his human elements, as each one of us must do in life. Just as Jesus was human and divine, just as the Church is a combination of the sinful and the sublime, the Pope struggles with a degenerative disease while being a beacon of holiness for youth.

MICHALINA
RATAJCZAK

SUSAN FOHR, age 23
I will not soon forget what I witnessed in Toronto, but it is not enough to remember merely the sights and the sounds. I hope to hold onto the joy of the

"

event and the message that yes, young people can make a difference. Now the challenge is to take that joy into the wider world and to be salt and light in the places that need it most.

PAULINA RATAJCZAK, age 22

Why do we love the Pope so much? Because of his gentleness, genius, understanding, compassion, vitality, vigour, perseverance. Because of his courage to stand behind his religion and defend it and not change with the times. Because he hears young people. Because he trusts us! Unflinchingly, he tells us the truth and the reasons behind Catholicism, knowing that we seek the same truth. And he knows we are up to the challenge to follow Jesus with all our hearts. He believes in us.

LORRAINE J. RODRIGUES, age 23

My faith was strengthened through being part of the community of pilgrims and witnessing their enthusiasm and love for Jesus Christ at catechesis, concerts, the Way of the Cross, Vigil and Papal Mass. I have a renewed sense of the importance of my faith and I have learned how I can be a better Roman Catholic—things that range from being more involved in community service to self-respect and respect for differences in others. I have been truly blessed to have seen and heard the Pope and to have experienced what World Youth Day is all about.

CHRISTL DABU, age 22

What I saw in the Pope, in many of the pilgrims and in people in Toronto reflected the message of World Youth Day—that everyone needs to accept the trials of being a Christian and not be afraid to live out their love for Christ. Still, I will never forget being part of the 800,000 people who gathered for the final Mass in unity, strength and love, making a little sacrifice of comfort in order to answer Christ's call to be "the light of the world."

EMANUEL PIRES, age 22

We arrived at Strawberry Island at around 1:00 p.m. We were taken to the Pope's cabin and met him on the porch. As we lined up to greet him, some of us were saying to one another how we wanted to just run up and hug him, to tell him how much he meant to us. At that point, the Pope smiled and waved to us. Suddenly I felt calm.

We were introduced to his Holiness one at a time. When it was my turn, I began to feel nervous again. I kissed his ring and looked up. He acknowledged me and said "Toronto" while nodding his head and giving an incredible smile.

As we were being seated for lunch in the dining hall, I saw that I would be two seats from the Pope. I wanted to pinch myself—I couldn't believe it.

We were in awe being there with him. When it was my turn to chat with him, I said, "My name is Emanuel. I'm from the Archdiocese of Toronto, and I am an architecture student at the University of Toronto. One day I'd like to design a church for you."

The invitation to meet the Pope came at a time when my faith in myself was wavering. I wasn't sure if all the work I was doing in my parish, at the Toronto Archdiocesan Office of Catholic Youth and at *The Catholic Register* was making a

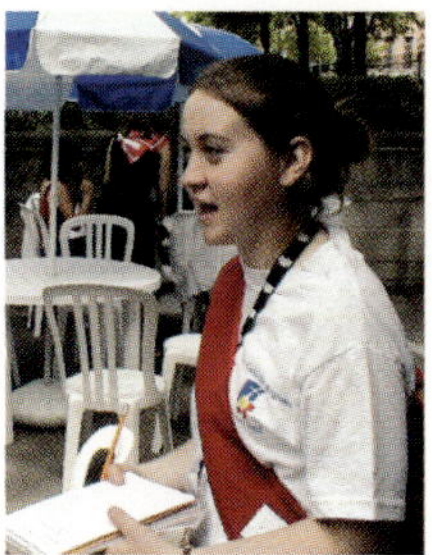

SUSAN FOHR

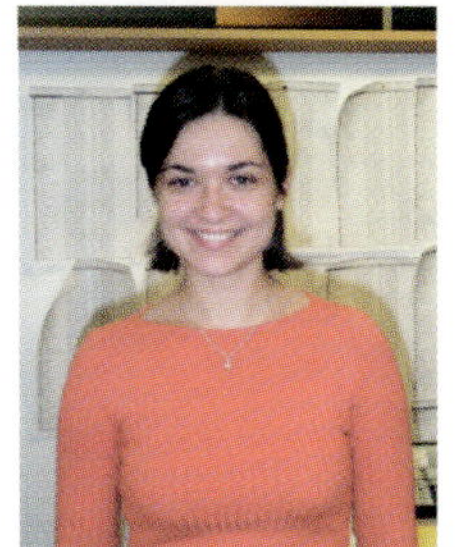

PAULINA RATAJCZAK

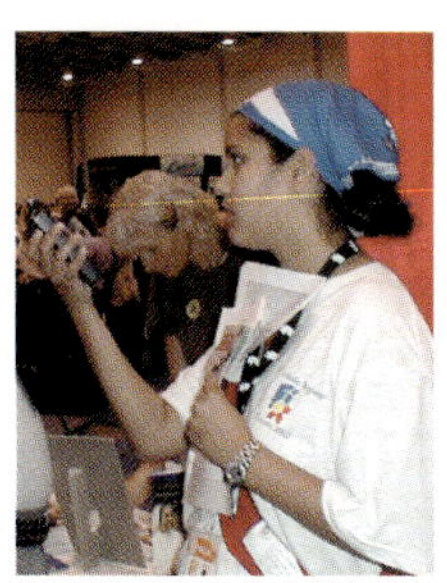

LORRAINE J.
RODRIGUES

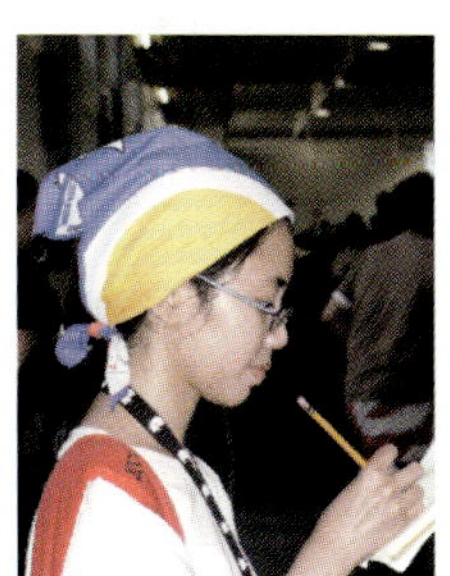

CHRISTL DABU

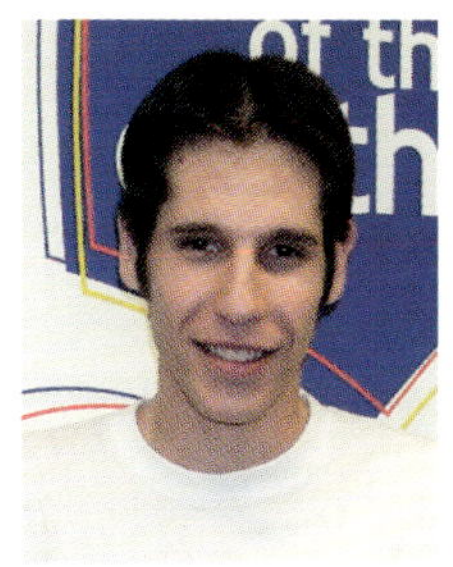

EMANUEL PIRES

difference. But sitting with those 14 pilgrims from around the world and the Pope, all that changed. Being there affirmed my faith and the importance of WYD to the young Catholics of the world. For me, those 13 other pilgrims were beacons of hope—the hope that will take away our fears and be a light in the darkness. Fourteen pilgrims from around the world and the Pope: it was a symbol of what WYD is all about. Viva il Papa!

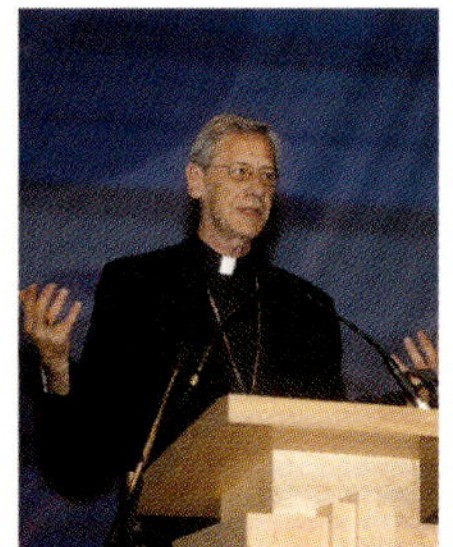

Bishop Jacques Berthelet

BISHOP JACQUES BERTHELET, C.S.V.
President of the Canadian Conference of Catholic Bishops

The Bishops of Canada now invite Catholics in every diocese from coast to coast to coast to join them in taking to heart the Pope's message in his welcome at the Mass at Downsview, when he said: "You, young people, are the vitality and strength of the Church throughout the world. Young people are not just the future of the Church, they are very present in the Church of today."

The faithful of Canada must now welcome these young pilgrims home with open hearts, open minds, and open spirits. We look forward to their new fervour, their enthusiasm, and their dreams as we build the Church of Jesus Christ, responding to the Pope's challenge of the new millennium to "set out into the deep."

Invite them to share their World Youth Day experience. Listen to them. Love them. Allow the winds of youth to blow through our communities and our hearts. Let us all be "salt of the earth and light of the world."

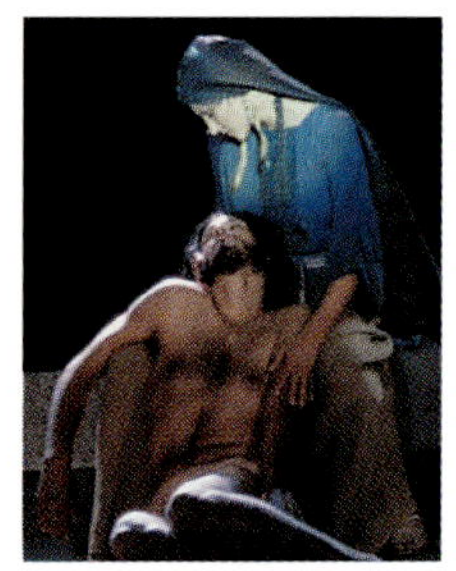

Ursula Fiedorczuk

URSULA FIEDORCZUK, age 19
During the performance of the Way of The Cross, at the fourth station, when I went on to the stage, I saw a crowd that far exceeded my expectations. But soon I forgot about everything. I felt that I *was* Mary, that it wasn't just acting. I heard the audience's reactions—some people wept, somebody yelled: "I love you, Mary." I was deeply moved. At the twelfth station, when the Cross was erected, I burst into tears.

It was all for him—the Holy Father. At the end, we all began to cry, we felt so happy. At the last station, we received an extraordinary reward. Father Rosica announced a great surprise for us—the Holy Father wanted us to be at the airport for his departure!

I don't know how to describe it all. It was very special to be so close to the Holy Father. I couldn't take pictures, because my face was streaming with tears. He looked fantastic, a lot younger and livelier than on TV. He is so full of life and energy, and he has these magnetic eyes.

It is God who wanted all that to happen this way. Maybe it's not a coincidence that my middle name is Mary. This will definitely be the most important event in my life.

This work is about the parable of the sower.
It's our job to sow the seeds lavishly.

FR. THOMAS ROSICA, C.S.B., CEO of World Youth Day 2002

Acknowledgements

Novalis wishes to thank all those who made this publication possible, especially Fr. Thomas Rosica, C.S.B., and the superb staff at the World Youth Day 2002 office; His Eminence Cardinal Aloysius Ambrozic and the staff at the Toronto archdiocesan offices; Joe Sinasac and the Youth Speak News team at *The Catholic Register*; Zbigniew Bełz, Margaret P. Bonikowska and the photographers at *Gazeta*; Dan Iannuzzi and the staff at *Corriere Canadese* and *Correo Canadiense*; the Bayard team from *La Croix* and *Pélerin* from Paris; Peggy Wittman of WP Wittman Limited; John L. Allen and *The Word from Rome*; Benjamin Koo and the staff of Book Art Inc.; Charles Chiu and the staff of Colourgenics Photo and Digital Imaging Inc.; Greg Radwan of the St. Stanislaus-St. Casimir's Polish Parishes Credit Union Ltd.

Photo Credits

Care has been taken to trace ownership of copyright material contained in this book. The publisher will gladly receive any information that will enable them to rectify any reference or credit in subsequent printings.

Legend: t=top, b=bottom, l=left, r=right, c=centre

1: Ian Crysler. 6,8-9: Bill Wittman. 10: CP/AP/ Pier Paolo Cito. 11: (both) Joseph Sinasac/*The Catholic Register*. 12: Bill Wittman. 13: World Youth Day 2002 Office. 14: Bill Wittman. 15: (tl) Ramon Gonzalez/*Western Catholic Reporter*; (tr) World Youth Day 2002 Office; (bl) Renato Gandia/*Western Catholic Reporter*; (br) Phyllis Pitre/Diocese of Charlottetown. 16-17: Bill Wittman. 18: André Leduc. 19: (tl,tr,bl) Bill Wittman; (br) Ian Crysler. 20: Steve Martin/Diocese of London. 21: (t) Art Babych; (b) Diocese of Montreal. 22-23: Bill Wittman. 24,25: Maria Delia Zamora. 26: (t) Fortunato Aglialoro; (b) Diocese of Montreal. 27: (b) Ian Crysler. 28,29: Ian Crysler. 30: (l) Dick Hemingway; (br) Bill Wittman. 31: (t) Ian Crysler; (bl) Maria Delia Zamora; (br) *Corriere Canadese*/Gregory Varona. 32-33,34: Bill Wittman. 35,36,37: Maria Delia Zamora. 38: (tl,bl) Maria Delia Zamora; (cl) Bill Wittman. 38-39: Maria Delia Zamora. 41: Bill Wittman. 42: (l) Ian Crysler. 43: (tl,b) Dick Hemingway; (tr) Ian Crysler. 44-45: Ian Crysler. 46: (l) Dick Hemingway; (c,r) Ian Crysler. 47: (t) Ian Crysler; (b) Maria Zamora. 48-49: Catherine Bauknight. 49: (t) Bill Wittman. 50: Bill Wittman. 51: Maria Delia Zamora. 52: (l) Maria Delia Zamora; (r) Dick Hemingway. 53: Ian Crysler. 54-55: André Leduc. 56-57: Ian Crysler. 58-59: Maria Delia Zamora. 60: (bl,c) Catherine Bauknight; (r) Dick Hemingway. 61: Dick Hemingway. 62: Ian Crysler. 63: (tl) *Corriere Canadese*/ Gregory Varona; (tr) Catherine Bauknight; (b) Dick Hemingway. 64: Maria Delia Zamora. 65: (l) Dick Hemingway; (r) Bill Wittman. 66: (t) Ian Crysler; (b) Bill Wittman. 67: (t) Bill Wittman; (b) Maria Delia Zamora. 68: (t) Michael Swan/*The Catholic Register*; (b) Maria Delia Zamora. 69: Maria Delia Zamora. 70-71: Catherine Bauknight. 72-73: Ian Crysler. 74: (tl) Ian Crysler; (b) Maria Delia Zamora. 75: (tl) Stephen Foster; (tr) Ian Crysler; (br) Maria Delia Zamora. 76: (t) *Gazeta*/Tadeusz Wójciak; (c) *Gazeta*/Tadeusz Wójciak; (b) *Gazeta*/Tadeusz Wójciak. 77: (tl,tr) Ian Crysler, (b) Dick Hemingway. 78: (tl,tc) Maria Delia Zamora; (tr) Catherine Bauknight; (b) André Leduc. 79: (tl) Colin McConnell; (all others) Dick Hemingway. 80: (tl) Catherine Bauknight; (all others) *Gazeta*/Zbigniew Bełz. 82: (t, br) Catherine Bauknight; (bl) *Gazeta*/Zbigniew Bełz. 83: (t) Catherine Bauknight; (bl) *Gazeta*/Tadeusz Wójciak; (br) *Gazeta*/Zbigniew Bełz. 84: Ian Crysler. 85: (tl) Bill Wittman; (tr) Ian Crysler; (cr) Maria Delia Zamora. 86: (br) Maria Delia Zamora; (all others) Ian Crysler. 87: (bl) Maria Delia Zamora; (br) Ian Crysler. 88: Ian Crysler. 89: (tl,tr) Ian Crysler; (b) Dick Hemingway. 90-91: Bill Wittman. 93: André Leduc. 94: (t) Ian Crysler; (b) Catherine Bauknight. 95: Ian Crysler. 96-97: Catherine Bauknight. 98: (t) Bill Wittman; (b) Catherine Bauknight. 99: Dick Hemingway. 100-101: André Leduc. 102: Bill Wittman. 103: (t) Maria Delia Zamora; (b) Catherine Bauknight. 104: (tl) Maria Delia Zamora; (tr,b) Catherine Bauknight. 105: (t) Catherine Bauknight; (b) Dick Hemingway. 106-107: Dick Hemingway. 108: Maria Delia Zamora. 109: (l) Dick Hemingway; (tr) Catherine Bauknight; (br) Maria Delia Zamora. 110-111: Catherine Bauknight. 112: Ian Crysler. 113: (t) André Leduc; (b) Ian Crysler. 114-115: André Leduc. 117: (t,br) André Leduc; (bl) Ian Crysler. 118: (tl) Maria Delia Zamora; (tr,b) André Leduc. 120-121: André Leduc. 122-123: Dick Hemingway. 123: (tr) Dick Hemingway; (br) Rebecca Stevenson. 124-125: Bill Wittman. 126: Rebecca Stevenson. 128: Dick Hemingway. 129: (tl) Ian Crysler; (tr) *Corriere Canadese*/Gregory Varona; (c, bl) André Leduc; (br) Dick Hemingway. 130: Bill Wittman. 131: (tl) Bill Wittman; (tr,b) Catherine Bauknight. 132: (t) Catherine Bauknight; (bl) Dick Hemingway; (br) Maria Delia Zamora. 133: Rebecca Stevenson. 135: (l) Ian Crysler; (r,top two) Maria Delia Zamora; (r,second from bottom) Bill Wittman; (br) Rebecca Stevenson. 136: (tl,tr) Rebecca Stevenson; (b) Ian Crysler. 137: (tl) Michael Swan/*The Catholic Register*; (cr,b) Rebecca Stevenson. 139: (tl) Ian Crysler; (tr) Rebecca Stevenson; (b) Catherine Bauknight. 140-141: Bill Wittman. 142: (tl,tr) Bill Wittman; (b) Catherine Bauknight. 143,144,145: Bill Wittman. 146: André Leduc. 147: (tr,tc) Dick Hemingway; (br) Catherine Bauknight. 148: (b) Catherine Bauknight. 149: (t) Ian Crysler; (bl, br) Maria Delia Zamora. 150: Maria Delia Zamora. 151: André Leduc. 152-153: Bill Wittman. 154: (t) Maria Delia Zamora; (bl,br) André Leduc. 155: Dick Hemingway. 156-157: Youth Speak News team/*The Catholic Register*. 158: (tl,cl,bl) Youth Speak News team/*The Catholic Register*; (r) Bill Wittman. 159: Bill Wittman. 160: World Youth Day 2002 Office.

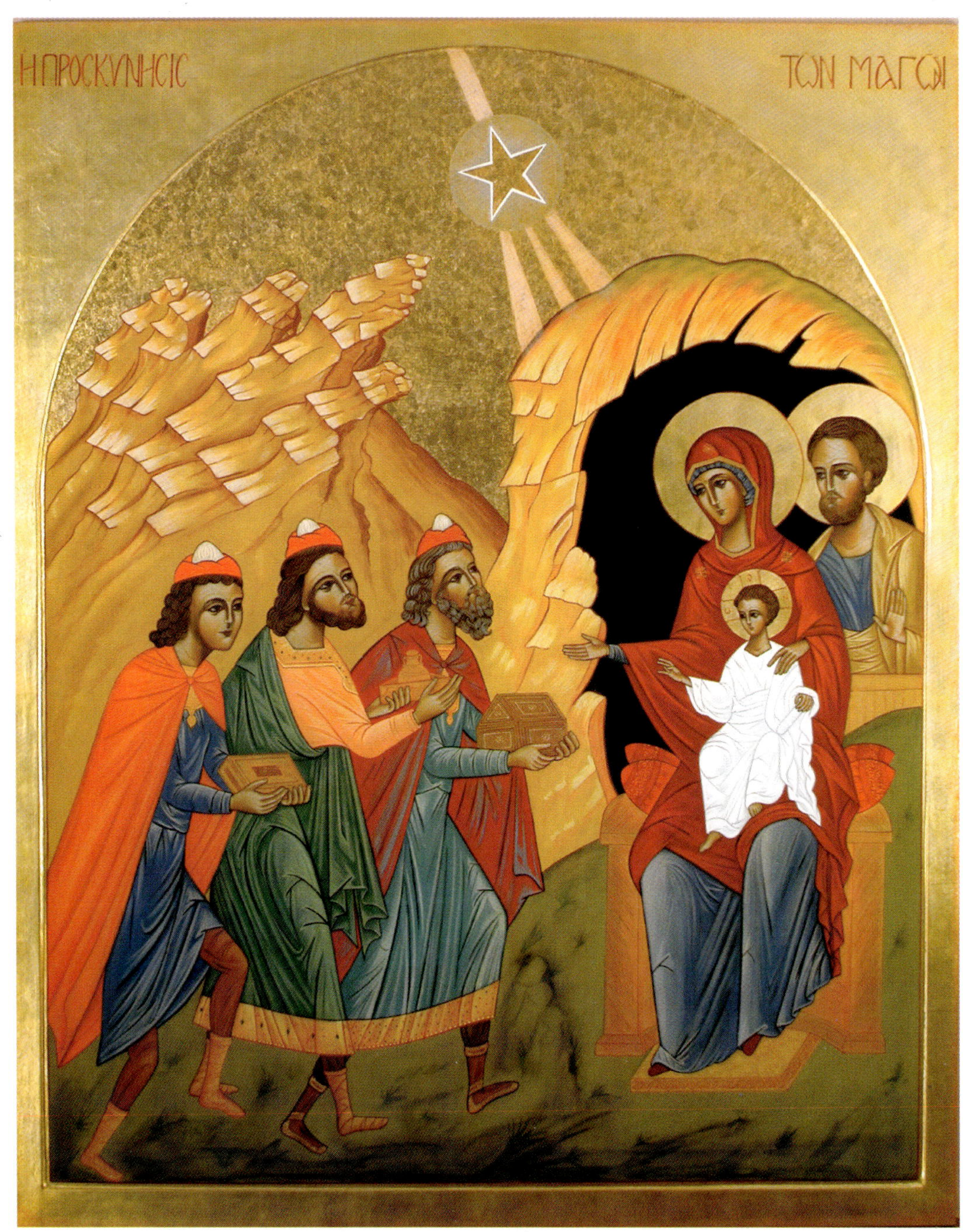

World Youth Day Icon 2002
The Adoration of the Magi

Since Apostolic times, in both the East and West, the holy icons of the Church have been venerated and defended by Orthodox-Catholic Christians as divinely inspired "windows into heaven," making visible the unseen realms of the spiritual world. As a form of sacred art, icons make an encounter with God possible through the sacred persons and events portrayed.

This icon was commissioned for WYD 2002. It was painted by Sr. Marie Paule, a Cloistered Benedictine Sister of Calvary in the Holy Land. The icon depicts the Magi, the wise men, coming to encounter the Christ child. Much the same, WYD pilgrims are the present-day Magi who have come to Toronto for an encounter with Jesus Christ and St. Peter's successor, Pope John Paul II.